MICROSOFT® WORKS

FOR THE APPLE® MACINTOSH®

SECOND EDITION

MICROSOFT₍ WORKS

FOR THE APPLE₍ MACINTOSH₍

SECOND EDITION

CHARLES RUBIN

PUBLISHED BY
Microsoft Press
A Division of Microsoft Corporation
16011 NE 36th Way, Box 97017, Redmond, Washington 98073-9717

Library of Congress Cataloging in Publication Data
Rubin, Charles, 1953–
Microsoft Works on the Apple Macintosh / Charles Rubin. — 2nd ed.
        p.   cm.
Includes index.
1. Macintosh (Computer)—Programming.   2. Microsoft Works (Computer
program)   I. Title.
QA76.8.M3R83   1989   89-3203   005.36'9 — dc19   CIP
ISBN 1-55615-202-7

Printed and bound in the United States of America.

1 2 3 4 5 6 7 8 9   MLML   3 2 1 0 9

Distributed to the book trade in the
United States by Harper & Row.

Distributed to the book trade in
Canada by General Publishing Company, Ltd.

Distributed to the book trade outside the
United States and Canada by Penguin Books Ltd.

Penguin Books Ltd., Harmondsworth, Middlesex, England
Penguin Books Australia Ltd., Ringwood, Victoria, Australia
Penguin Books N.Z. Ltd., 182–190 Wairau Road, Auckland 10, New Zealand

British Cataloging in Publication Data available

Adobe Illustrator™ is a trademark of Adobe Systems, Incorporated. PageMaker® is
a registered trademark of Aldus Corporation. Apple®, AppleTalk®, HyperCard®,
ImageWriter®, LaserWriter®, Mac®, and Macintosh® are registered trademarks
and FDHD™, Finder™, and MultiFinder™ are trademarks of Apple Computer,
Incorporated. MacDraw®, MacPaint®, and MacWrite® are registered trademarks
and Claris™ is a trademark of Claris Corporation. CompuServe® is a registered
trademark of CompuServe, Incorporated. Dow Jones News/Retrieval® is a registered
trademark of Dow Jones and Company, Incorporated. Hayes® is a registered
trademark of Hayes Microcomputer Products, Incorporated. IBM® is a registered
trademark of International Business Machines Corporation. Helvetica® is a
registered trademark of Linotype Company. VisiCalc® is a registered trademark of
Lotus Development Corporation. MCI MAIL® is a registered service mark of MCI
Communications Corporation. Microsoft® and Multiplan® are registered
trademarks of Microsoft Corporation. Spellswell™ is a trademark of Working
Software, Incorporated.

Project Editor: Ron Lamb   Technical Editor: Mark Dodge

Contents

	Introduction		*vii*
Chapter	1	Microsoft Works in Perspective	1
Chapter	2	Using the Word Processor	21
Chapter	3	Using the Draw Tool	49
Chapter	4	Word-Processing Projects	83
Chapter	5	Using the Spreadsheet	137
Chapter	6	Spreadsheet Projects	183
Chapter	7	Using the Database	237
Chapter	8	Database Projects	267
Chapter	9	Using the Communications Application	317
Chapter	10	Using Works as a System	347
	Appendix		*399*
	Index		*405*

Introduction

This book is for people who want to make the most of Microsoft Works on the Apple Macintosh. You're probably using Works and a Macintosh because you want to get down to work as quickly and easily as possible. The Mac, with its graphic interface, and Works, with its collection of four major productivity programs, is about the simplest combination you could have chosen.

What Works Offers

Works combines four major productivity applications—a word processor, a spreadsheet with business graphics, a database, and a communications application—in one program. Version 2.0 of Works offers some major enhancements over version 1.0:

- A spelling checker for the word processor.

- A feature that lets you attach notes to cells and a larger cell matrix in the spreadsheet.

- Sophisticated drawing capabilities in both the spreadsheet and word processor.

- A macro capability in all four applications.

Since it was originally released in 1986, Microsoft Works has consistently been one of the 10 best-selling productivity programs for the Mac. A lot of Mac owners have found that they can become more productive by using one program that combines the basic tools they need. Even if you use Microsoft Word, Microsoft Excel, PageMaker, or other programs to handle specific tasks for which you need a level of performance that Works doesn't provide, you'll probably still use Works to handle less complex jobs because it's so fast and simple. But if you're like many Mac owners, Works is all the productivity software you'll ever need.

The Works package comes with a good manual, a written tutorial, and (in version 2.0) a HyperCard tour that shows off Works' basic capabilities. This book is not a substitute for these materials; rather, it augments them by showing you how to use Works to handle typical business and personal tasks. After all, knowing what a hammer is and how to drive a nail doesn't mean you know how to build a house. Figuratively speaking, the documentation supplied with the Works program shows you what the hammer is and how to use it; this book shows you how to build houses.

Working at Al's Videorama

Throughout this book, we'll tackle the business and personal computing tasks of Al Chroma, the fictional owner of Al's Videorama. We'll assume that Al is a retired motion picture projectionist who has opened his own videotape rental store in a California city. We'll use Works and the Mac to help Al organize his business records, prepare custom sales materials, analyze his profits, and perform other common business tasks. We'll also help Al with some personal computing projects.

As we help Al with each activity, you'll see step-by-step descriptions of how Works handles the job. Reading these descriptions will show you how to use Works' various features to their best advantage in a detailed, real-life context, and it will give you ideas about how to apply Works' power in your own life.

What You Need to Begin

If you're using version 2.0 of Works, you'll need at least a Mac 512KE with either two 800 KB disk drives or one 800 KB disk drive and a hard disk. If you're using version 1.0 or 1.1 of Works, you'll need, at a minimum, a Macintosh 512K with at least one 400 KB or 800 KB disk drive, although I strongly recommend two drives. (I also strongly recommend that you upgrade to 2.0.)

Although some of the material in this book covers the basic operation of the Works tools, the focus is on using Works to solve problems. Therefore, the instructions in this book assume that you've spent enough time with Works to know how to start the program, open and close files, manipulate windows, and generally move from one Works tool to another. The instructions also assume that you know enough about the Mac to use the mouse, Clipboard, Finder, and other interface tools, such as menus and dialog boxes.

How This Book is Organized

This book focuses on version 2.0 of Works. The examples and explanations are based on version 2.0 of the program, although most of the data-handling projects can be performed just as well with an earlier version of the program. Where a project or explanation differs markedly between version 2.0 and earlier versions, the difference will be explained. In addition, I'll point out tips for using various program features as we go along. These tips are identified as such and are set off from the main text.

We'll begin our orientation to Microsoft Works in Chapter 1 with a description of Works features that are common to all of its applications. In Chapters 2 through 9, we'll get into the specific features of each Works tool—the word processor, the spreadsheet, the database, and the communications tool, in that order. Chapters 2, 3, 5, 7, and 9 explain the features of each tool and how to get the most out of them. (Although the Draw tool isn't treated as a separate application in Works—it doesn't use a separate document type or menus—it is sophisticated enough to merit its own chapter, Chapter 3.) Each chapter that details a tool's features is divided into several sections:

- An introduction, giving a general description of the tool and how it is used.

- A quick tour of the tool's menus, covering each command and how it is used.

- A series of specific tips on how to make the most of the tool's capabilities.

- A collection of general operating tips for the tool.

- A list of the tool's specifications, including its maximum file size, maximum width of printed documents, and so on.

In Chapters 4, 6, and 8, we'll see how the tools discussed in the immediately preceding chapter can solve problems at Al's Videorama. The projects in these chapters show you most or all of Work's word-processing, spreadsheet, and database-management features at work in a real-world scenario. (The real-world applications for the drawing tools are included in the chapters on the word-processor and the spreadsheet, and the applications for the communications tool are included in Chapter 9.)

In Chapter 10, we'll consolidate what we've learned about each Works tool, using the program to combine data from various documents and to move data between Works and other programs. After discussing the basics of data interchange, we'll use this capability to handle additional tasks for Al Chroma.

Works has a lot of power all by itself, but there are other hardware and software products that will expand its capabilities. The Appendix, which follows Chapter 10, presents some Works enhancement products. It explains the general features of these products and offers advice about how to choose them.

Getting Down to Business

Making a computer and software work for you isn't simply a matter of plunking down your money, plugging in a machine, and pushing a button or two. It's an educational journey in which you acquire basic knowledge and build on that knowledge through experience. During this journey, there will certainly be times when you won't understand something and you'll wonder if you'll ever learn it at all; but there will also be times when you'll have the thrill of conquering a problem and will wonder how you ever got along without a computer.

The Macintosh and Microsoft Works are far simpler to learn and use than most other computer tools you could have chosen, but when something can make as much of a difference in your life as the Mac and Works, it's only natural that the change won't happen overnight. If you look at this change as a journey and you don't try to learn too much at once, you'll find it a journey well worth taking. Turn to Chapter 1 and let's take the first steps.

Chapter 1

Microsoft Works in Perspective

In this chapter, we'll look at the two general features that make Works and the Macintosh such a useful team: the Mac's simple user interface and Works' integration of four major applications in one package.

What's a User Interface?

An interface is the control panel of a computer—the means of communication between human and machine. Before the Macintosh came along, user interfaces for personal computers were cryptic: Typically, you saw a blank screen with a blinking rectangle (the cursor) on it, and the computer waited for you to type in the proper command before it would do something. It was up to you, the user, to remember or look up the dozens or even hundreds of different commands needed to use such a computer.

Instead of presenting you with a blank screen and waiting for you to type some complex command, the Macintosh uses graphics and words to show you the various things you can do at any time. All you have to do is choose the operation you want to perform.

Along with being easier to learn and use, the Mac's interface also helps take the anxiety out of computing. With a traditional computer, you may be afraid of typing the wrong command inadvertently. If you don't understand something on the Mac, you can pull down a menu to see a list of commands. If you're about to do something irreversible, the

Mac warns you. The Mac supplies you with the information you need to work it as you need that information, so you can concentrate on getting your work done.

This simple Macintosh interface is available whenever you run a program or application. (Different computer programs, such as word-processing programs, spreadsheet programs, and so on, are often called applications, because they each apply the computer differently. They tell the computer to work with information differently. A spreadsheet program usually tells the Mac to treat the character 5 as a specific numeric value that can be calculated, for example, while a word-processing program tells the Mac to treat it as a text symbol like any other letter or number.) Whatever type of program you run on a Mac, the interface—the way you tell the Mac to do things—always remains the same.

What is Integrated Software?

What makes Works different from other programs on the Mac is that it combines, or integrates, four different applications (or tools) into one program. Other programs let you work with only one type of data (for example, words or numbers, but not words and numbers); Works lets you work with four different types of data. Works contains a word-processing program for working with text, a spreadsheet program for working with numbers, a database program for working with groups of facts, and a communications program for transmitting data between your Mac and other computers. (In addition, there's a "fifth" tool, the Draw tool, that works only with the word processor and spreadsheet. Although Chapter 3 details the features of the Draw tool, Works really has only four applications.)

Now, you could use four separate programs to work with data in different ways, but it's much easier to have all four applications integrated into one package. Here's why:

Integrated software is easier to learn

If you used four different programs to work with data, you would have to learn four different sets of commands. With Works, many of the commands are the same in every application, so you learn them only once.

Integrated software is easier and faster to use

With four different programs, you may have to change program disks each time you want to do something different. Works combines all four applications on one disk, so you don't have to change disks when you want to work with data in a different way.

Integrated software lets you transfer data more easily

Many times, you'll want to move data from one application into another application. You might want to copy some spreadsheet figures into a word-processor report, for example. If you were running two different programs, you would have to switch disks and perhaps even convert the data from one program's format to the other program's format. Different programs store and represent data in different ways. A spreadsheet stores numbers in rows and columns, but a word processor usually keeps text in sentences and paragraphs. With Works, you can copy data between programs directly; you don't need to switch disks or convert the data format.

Because it is an integrated software package, Works makes it easier to convert data to different formats. The four integrated applications on the Works disk allow you to take the number 7 from the spreadsheet and quickly convert it to a text 7 in the word processor. You can also convert a series of spreadsheet numbers easily to sections of a pie chart with the Works chart feature. And you can take a customer record from the database file and move it into the spreadsheet for additional calculations.

As we'll see later in this book, being able to move data around in this way also means you can reuse data. If you've already entered inventory data into the spreadsheet, you can convert that data to a database file and then manipulate the data in different ways without typing the same data into the computer again. After you store the information in one format, you can convert it to different formats, rather than retyping it in different formats over and over again.

The Mac's interface and Works' integration are a more transparent computing system than you can find almost anywhere. Because they're easy to use and because they let you work with data in a variety of ways with a minimum of hassle, they let you focus on doing your work, rather than on manipulating a program to get the work done.

Now, let's look at some specific features that are present in all four Works applications.

Features Common to All Four Works Applications

Works makes computing transparent by unifying the commands for the four different programs as much as possible, and by making it simple to move data from one program to another, or even between Works and outside programs.

The opening screen

When you start Works, the program's opening screen appears. You can speed up creating and opening files by double-clicking: Double-click on one of the four application icons to create a new document for that application, or double-click on a file name in the list box to open that file.

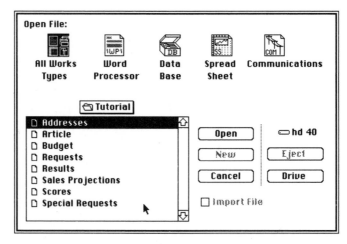

This screen lets you create new documents or open existing documents for any of the four Works applications. The four applications are represented by icons. You select an icon to indicate the type of document you want to open or create, and then you point to and click on either the New or Open button.

If you are opening a file from a disk, the list of files that appears on this screen will contain only those files for the application you have selected. If you click on the Word Processor icon, for example, the list of available files will contain only word-processor files.

If you want to show all the Works files on a disk, you can choose the All Works Types icon.

Works shows you only the Works files on a disk. If you have Multiplan files, MacWrite files, or MacPaint files on a disk, Works doesn't show you the names of these files because you can't open them.

You see non-Works files on a disk only when you use the Import File feature. (Microsoft Works, like many programs, creates files in its own special format. When you convert files in other formats for use with Works, you are importing them, and when you convert Works files to other formats for use with other programs, you are exporting them.) You can import files from certain other programs into Works by clicking the Import File box on the main program screen. If you click the Import File box, you'll see the names of files you can import into a Works application along with files created in Works.

Notice that the name of the disk containing the files you are viewing also appears, above the Eject button. The type of icon beside the name tells you the type of disk: a floppy disk or hard disk. If you want to look at the files on a disk in a different disk drive, you click the Drive button. If you want to eject the current disk and insert another disk, you click the Eject button.

So, instead of presenting you with a blank screen, Works starts off by showing you a lot of things you need in order to use it in an economical and intuitive way. It's economical because it conveys a lot of information about how to use the program with only a few icons and labels. It's intuitive because you can point to things you want to do, and pointing is one of the most natural human ways of expressing what you want.

The menus

Along with icons, buttons, and a list of files, there are also four menu titles (including the Apple icon) in the menu bar at the top of the opening screen. Each Works application has its own menus, but the four menus shown on the opening screen are common to every Works application.

The Apple menu contains a set of desk accessories you can use as you work. These desk accessories are a standard feature in every Macintosh program and may include an alarm clock, a calculator, the Note Pad, the Scrapbook, an accessory that lets you select the type of printer you're working with, and others. The one accessory that is unique to Works is the first one on the menu, About MS-Works. When you choose this accessory, you see a box that contains the copyright and other information about the program.

TIP: If you're working under MultiFinder and you find yourself running short of memory, you can increase the amount of memory set aside for Works so that you can work with larger documents (or more documents at once), provided you have sufficient memory in your computer. To do this, you must reset the Application Memory Size for Works in the Finder:

☐ Close any open files, and then quit Works. (You can't change the Application Memory Size while an application is running under MultiFinder.)

☐ If necessary, display the Finder screen under MultiFinder.

☐ Select the Works program icon.

☐ Choose the Get Info command from the File menu, or press Command-I.

The Get Info dialog box will appear, like this:

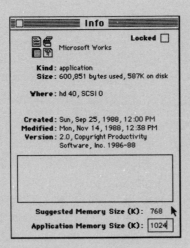

☐ Double-click in the Application Memory Size box in the lower-right corner of the Get Info box, and enter a larger memory size.

Version 2.0 of Works has a default Application Memory Size of 768 KB. If you run short of memory as you work and you have enough available memory, try increasing this to 1024 KB by typing *1024* in the Application Memory Size box. If you are running Multifinder on a Mac Plus with 1 megabyte of memory, you will see the following dialog box when you start Works:

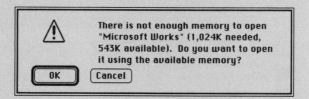

If you have not changed the application memory size to 1024 KB, the dialog box still will appear, but it will read ... *768K needed, 538K available....* Using Apple system software version 6.0.2 and assuming you have no other programs loaded in Multifinder, 538 KB is the amount of remaining available memory after you've loaded the System and Multifinder. This doesn't mean that you can't run Works; it simply means that changing the application memory size isn't going to help if you don't have enough memory. Try using the Set Startup command in the Finder's Special menu. Click the Finder option in the Set Startup dialog box (with Multifinder as the current selection), and then click OK. Then choose Restart from the same menu. This will give you 816 KB to work with. If you still run into memory problems, consider either dividing your work into smaller pieces or investing in a memory upgrade.

Version 1.1 of Works has a default Application Memory Size of 352 KB. Try increasing this to 512 KB by typing *512* in the Application Memory Size box.

☐ Click the close box for the Get Info window, and restart Works.

Microsoft® Works 2.0

© 1986, 1987, 1988 by

Productivity Software, Inc.

Powerful integrated Word Processing, Spreadsheet, Database,
Communications, Charting & Drawing program for improving
personal productivity.

Spelling Checker portion © 1986, 1987, 1988 by Working Software, Inc.
Macro Portions © 1986 by H.C.W. Anderson.   Boston Fonts © 1986 by C. E. Maurer.

Additional Dictionaries available by writing:
Working Software, Inc.
Box 1844,
Santa Cruz, CA 95061

Approximately 99% of Memory Free
Name: Mark Dodge   Organization: MS Press

The most useful aspect of this screen is that it tells you, at the bottom, the amount of memory you currently have available in your Macintosh. The amount of available memory diminishes as you create larger and larger files with Works and keep them open on the desktop. If you're working with large files, you might want to check the About MS-Works accessory periodically to be sure you have enough memory to continue working.

The File, Edit, and Window Menus

Most of the commands on the File, Edit, and Window menus are common to every Works application. The File menu offers the typical Open, Close, Save, Save As, Print, and Quit commands, like other Mac programs. Notice that some of these and several other commands are followed by an ellipsis (...). The ellipsis after a command name means choosing that command produces a dialog box (where you must make further choices before the command is executed), rather than executing the command right away.

Along with these standard File menu commands, Works adds commands and features of its own. First, notice that the Open, Close, Save, Print, and Quit commands have keyboard alternatives.

One File menu command that's new in Works version 2.0 is the Close All command. This command closes all the files on the desktop—that is, all the files you currently have open in Works. Works gives you the option of making the Close All command act as if it were a Save All command, using the check box at the bottom of the dialog box:

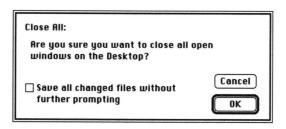

When you click on the check box labeled *Save all changed files without further prompting* and carry out the Close All command, Works will, without interruption, save any edits you have made and will simply close any open files that remain unchanged. However, if there are edited, open files with the name Untitled, Works will prompt you for a name. If you choose not to click the check box, Works will prompt you with the following dialog box for each open file on the desktop (Letter to Lou, in this example):

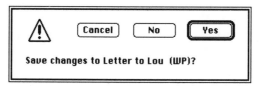

The Delete command lets you delete a file from a disk without having to return to the Finder to do so. When you choose Delete, a dialog box appears, displaying a list of files in the current folder and on the current disk drive. You can select files in other folders by double-clicking on the name of the folder in the list box or select files on other disks by clicking on the Drive button. Move the mouse pointer to the small box just above the list box and hold the mouse button down. If you are inside a folder, you will see the name of the disk it is on, and any additional folder levels in between.

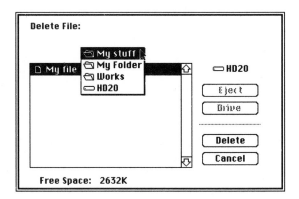

You select a file to delete either by double-clicking the file's name or by selecting it and clicking the Delete button. You can't delete a file that is currently open on the desktop.

Another new File menu command in version 2.0, Make Works Desktop, lets you make a Works desktop file that will start Works and load a group of documents. The desktop file appears in the Finder as a document file called Works Desktop. (It's called Resume Works in versions 1.0 and 1.1 of the program, and is created for you by Works when you quit the program with files open on the desktop.)

To create a desktop file, you simply quit Works while you have one or more documents open on the desktop. To load Works and the documents you had open when the desktop file was created, select and open the Works Desktop (or Resume Works) file, or double-click on it in the Finder. The Works program will load along with all the documents you previously had open (with their window sizes and positions as they were when you last saved).

Although Works on its own creates a desktop file if you quit the program with documents open, the Make Works Desktop command in version 2.0 lets you create a desktop file without quitting Works. You simply choose the Make Works Desktop command and either accept the default

TIP: Double-clicking is a quick way to open, create, or delete files in Works dialog boxes. To create a new file in the New or Open dialog box, simply double-click on the icon for the tool representing the type of document you want to create. To open or delete a file, double-click its name in the Open or Delete dialog box.

name for the desktop file (Works Desktop) or type a new one. You then click the Save button. The desktop file will contain instructions to load Works and all the documents you had open at the time you chose Make Works Desktop. If you start Works by double-clicking on this desktop file, you'll be returned to the place where you were working.

Another new feature in Works 2.0 is a change in the dialog box that appears when you choose the Print command. The Print dialog box now contains a Print Preview check box. When you click on this check box and then click the OK button to print the document, the document is displayed on the screen, rather than sent to the printer, like this:

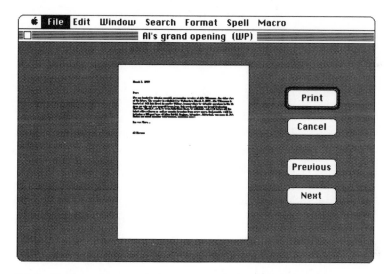

This display shows miniature versions of the formatted pages in your document, including text, graphics, margins and headers, one page at a time. The first page shown is the first page in your document, unless you've specified that a different range of pages be printed in the From and To boxes in the Print dialog box. In that case, the first page in the range you have specified is shown first. To display different pages in the document, click the Next or Previous buttons. (The Previous button will display only up to four previously displayed preview pages—less if you're short on memory.)

If you like what you see and want to print, click the Print button, or press the Return key. To close the Print Preview window and return to your document, click either the Cancel button or the close box.

TIP: If you have several projects, each of which uses a specific group of documents, you can save a lot of document-loading time by using the Make Works Desktop command in version 2.0 to create a different desktop file for each project. Simply open the files associated with that project, choose the Make Works Desktop command, give the desktop file a descriptive name that associates it with that project, and click the Save button. Repeat the process for each project's desktop file.

Like any other file, the Works Desktop (or Resume Works) file can be renamed in the Finder, so you can rename a desktop file after quitting Works.

NOTE: If you don't rename the Works Desktop or Resume Works file, be aware that the file will be overwritten by a new desktop file each time you quit Works with documents open.

The standard Print Preview display shows a document in a reduced size, so it's difficult to read text or look at graphics closely. But it's easy to examine the contents of a page more thoroughly. When you move the mouse pointer to any place on the page that is shown, the pointer changes to a magnifying-glass icon. To view part of a document close-up, place the magnifying-glass icon over the part you want to see, and then click the mouse button. The display will zoom in to that part of the document, and you'll be able to see text or graphics even larger than they were on your original document screen. After you go into zoom mode, the mouse pointer changes to a hand icon, and you can move the document around to view different parts of it on the screen by holding down the mouse button and dragging the page.

One especially nice aspect of Works' Print Preview feature is that after you click the check box in the Print dialog box to select the preview, Works displays a preview of any subsequent document you print, unless you again click in the Print Preview check box, quit Works, or shut down your Mac.

The Print Window command prints the currently active window. It doesn't print the entire file in that window, only the text or graphics that are shown on the screen. Print Window is the command you use to make hard copies of spreadsheet graphs.

The Eject Page command advances the paper in an ImageWriter printer to the top of the next sheet. You use this command primarily when you want to start printing again on a new sheet of paper after you've used the Print Window command. If you're using a Mac 512, 512E, Plus, or SE, Print Window uses no more than half a sheet of standard-sized paper to print a window, and it stops the printer in the middle of the page after it's finished. So, you could print two windows on one piece of paper. But if you want to print only one window on a page, you can choose the Eject Page command. The Eject Page command doesn't work with any printer you access over an AppleTalk network, such as a LaserWriter.

The only other Works-specific command on the File menu is Print Merge, which is discussed in Chapter 2.

The Edit menu controls cutting and pasting of information between an application and the Clipboard with the Cut, Copy, and Paste commands. We'll learn more about the Clipboard later in this chapter, after we learn about some Works-specific commands on the Edit menu.

The Undo command cancels the last editing action you made in Works, whether it was a formatting change, a line you drew with the Draw tool, or text you deleted. Undo is the handiest way to remove unwanted lines from a drawing in Works 1.0 or 1.1 or to recover text you accidentally deleted.

The Clear command deletes selected text in the word processor or communications application, deletes the contents of the selected cell(s) in the spreadsheet or the selected field(s) in the database, and deletes a selected picture in the word processor.

The Select All command does exactly that—it selects an entire document—all text and drawings in the word processor, all filled or empty cells and drawings in the spreadsheet, all records in the database, and all text in a communications window. This command is handy when you want to copy an entire document to the Clipboard or when you want to apply a format (line spacing, for example) to a whole document.

NOTE: You cannot use the Select All command when the Draw tool is on.

The Edit menu may also contain additional commands that are specific to the application you're working with. See the chapter on using a specific application for descriptions of these commands.

The Window menu lets you control what you see on the screen. (This menu is identical in every Works application, so it will be discussed only in this chapter.) Normally, documents appear in a full-sized window. You can make a window smaller or larger by dragging the size box in its lower-right corner. In Works 1.0 and 1.1, the Window menu's Full Window command lets you change a window you've made smaller with the size box back to a full-size window. When you have a full window displayed, this command changes to Small Window. Choosing Small Window returns the active window to the size it was before you chose the Full Window command.

In Works 2.0, the Full Window/Small Window command has been eliminated from the Window menu, because you can toggle between a full window and a smaller window by clicking the zoom box in the upper-right corner of the window. The zoom box is now a standard feature of the Mac interface.

Other commands on the Window menu let you view the contents of the Clipboard (Show Clipboard), access on-line instructions about how to use Works (Help), and display different documents that are open on the desktop (the names of all open files are listed at the bottom of the menu). The list of open documents tells you how large each file is and which Works application was used to create it.

The Macro Menu

The fifth menu common to all Works 2.0 applications, the Macro menu, lets you create and use macros to speed up repetitive operations. The Works macro function lets you record a series of keystrokes and mouse commands and store them under one keystroke combination so that you can play them back later. You play back a macro by holding down the Option key along with the key under which you have stored it. The Microsoft Works manual contains a full description of the macro feature in Chapter 2, "Common Tasks Command Reference," but because this is such a powerful productivity-enhancing feature, we'll go into it in some detail.

The Macro menu contains commands for turning macros on and off, for playing back macros you have stored, for recording new macros, and for opening and saving macro files. The Macro menu commands are dimmed (not available) unless you have a document open on the Works Desktop. To record a macro:

☐ Open or create a new document and then select the Macros On command from the Macro menu.

❑ Choose the Start Recording command from the Macros menu. A dialog box appears, asking you to type a key that will be used in the future to play back the Macro, like this:

Start Recording:
Key   Description of new macro

[Record]
❑ Record pauses
[Cancel]

You can use any key on the keyboard to activate a macro except Shift, Option, Command, Caps Lock, E, I, N, U, ~, Delete (Backspace), +, =, −, ' (open single quote), and _ (underline).

Note that this dialog box contains a check box you can click if you want to record not only the macro operation itself, but also the pauses you make between parts of the operation.

❑ Press the Tab key and type a short description for the macro.

❑ Click the Record button, or press the Return key.

❑ Type the text or numbers or select the menu commands you want to store under the macro.

❑ Choose the Stop Recording command from the Macro menu. A second dialog box will appear, like this:

*** Currently recording ***   [Stop]
❑ Record previous delay   [Continue]
❑ Record future delays   [Cancel]

This dialog box contains buttons to stop recording, continue recording, and cancel recording. The dialog box also contains check boxes you can click to record the previous delay and to record future delays. The Record Previous Delay check box records only the delay that occurred immediately before you chose the Stop Recording command. The Record Future Delays check box lets you record all pauses you make in recording the macro from that point on, if you continue recording.

❑ Click the Stop button, or press the Return key.

When you have finished recording your macro, you might want to save it for future use. Choose Save Macro File from the Macro menu. A Save dialog box appears, asking you to name the macro file where you want to save the Macro. Microsoft Works always suggests the name Microsoft Works (keys), but you can change the name or select a different folder or disk where you want to save the file. This feature lets you create different macro files for different purposes. To work with a particular macro file, you open it with the Open Macro File command. If you already have a macro file open and you don't want to save the current macro in it, you can use the Save Macro File As command on the Macro menu. Otherwise, you can add the macro to the currently open

---

TIP: Here are a couple of pointers about using the Macros menu:

- You can't start or stop macros while a dialog box or Works message is displayed on the screen.

- You can use the keyboard to issue some of the Macro menu commands.

These are the key combinations and the commands they execute:

Key Combination	Command/Action
Option-+(plus)	Start Recording
Option--(minus)	Stop Recording
Option-Delete	Playback And
Command-.(period)	Stop a macro in progress

- Because the Option key is one of the keys you press to invoke macros, you can't type any special characters created with the Option key (such as bullets, which you create by pressing Option-8) while the Macro feature is turned on. If you try to use the Option key to invoke a special character key with macros on, Works will warn you with a beep. (That is, of course, unless you've defined a macro for that key or you're typing an Option-key shortcut to issue a Macro menu command.) To create special characters using the Option key, be sure the macro function is off.

---

file with the Save Macro File command. You can have only one macro file open on the desktop at a time. Once you save the macro file, you'll be returned to your document.

As we'll see in upcoming chapters, the Works macro function can make a wide variety of repetitive tasks easier and faster to perform, from creating a custom letterhead to formatting a budget worksheet, all at the touch of a key.

By using five common menus, then, Works lets you understand how to do many filing, printing, and editing tasks in every one of its applications without learning four different sets of commands.

The Works desktop

Works uses a desktop metaphor to make computing as transparent and flexible as possible. Having files in memory is like having a group of paper documents on top of a desk. You can have several different paper documents on a desk at a time, and you might move from one document to another as you go through your day. If you want to move information from one document to another, you cut and paste it with scissors and tape. When you are using Works, you can open up to 14 different documents at a time and then select one or the other to work with by choosing it from the Window menu. You can also move data between documents easily. The Works desktop is really your Mac's memory. You have as much room on the desktop for files as your Mac's available memory allows.

The Clipboard

Along with several files, the desktop also makes use of the Clipboard, which is a document supported by almost all Mac software, where you can put data you want to move from one place to another. Using the Edit menu's Cut or Copy command, for example, you can cut or copy data from any Works document and put it on the Clipboard. Using the Paste command from the Edit menu, you can move data from the Clipboard into another document or from one place to another place in the same document. (You can move graphics created with the Draw tool only between the spreadsheet and the word processor, because these two applications are the only ones in Works that support drawings made with the Draw tool.)

The Clipboard is the main Macintosh feature that lets you use data from one application in a different application. With the Works desktop's multiple-file capability and the Clipboard, you have a powerful environment for working with data the way you want. If you want to move some spreadsheet data into a word-processor document, you can choose the spreadsheet document from the Window menu, copy the data to the Clipboard, choose the word-processor document from the Window menu, and paste the data from the Clipboard into the document. This process, which might require swapping disks, restarting programs, and perhaps even converting data formats if you were using two different programs, is fast and easy with Works.

File compatibility—importing and exporting

The final feature that makes Works a powerful computing tool is its ability to share files easily with other programs. When you create Works files, they're stored in a data format unique to Works, and you can't share them directly with other programs. But Works lets you use files created by other programs and lets other programs use files that were created by Works.

Works can import and export files in three different formats. The first is text, or ASCII format, which is the industry standard for data interchange. Text files are simply strings of characters, without any formatting information in them, and most personal computer programs can create or use text files. The Works word processor, spreadsheet, and database can all import and export their data as text files. The spreadsheet can export its data either with numeric values only, or with both numeric values and formulas. (The formulas will transfer as text, however, not as working formulas.) The database exports text files with individual records separated by carriage returns, and with individual fields separated by tabs. Another text file export option is the Works communications tool: When you send a Works word-processor file via the communications tool and you use the Send Text command, Works converts the file being sent from the Works word-processor format to a text file.

The second format is called SYLK (for SYmbolic LinK), which was created by Microsoft Corporation to facilitate data interchange among its own programs. The SYLK format lets you transfer spreadsheet files between Microsoft Multiplan, Excel, and Works with all the formatting and formulas from the original file intact, unless the destination program (such as Works) doesn't support some formulas created by the originating program (like Excel). If the destination program doesn't support it, Works will translate compatible formulas and convert incompatible formulas to text. Many Microsoft programs, whether for the Mac, the Apple II series, or the IBM PC and its compatibles, use the SYLK data-interchange format. (Some restrictions apply to these transfers. See Chapter 10 for more information.)

The third data-interchange format supported by Works is RTF (for Rich Text Format). This is a word-processing file format supported by Microsoft Word on both the Apple Macintosh and the IBM PC, and by many other Mac and PC-DOS (or MS-DOS) programs. RTF retains all formatting information in a word-processor file. Assuming you can move the file from an MS-DOS disk to a Mac disk, you can import many MS-DOS word-processing files with their formatting intact.

Finally, a growing number of Mac programs directly support file imports, exports, or both from Works because it is such a widely used program. Microsoft Word version 3.0 or later, for example, can load and convert Works files. As to exporting files, Microsoft Word, Acta, and MacWrite are among the programs that can create formatted files Works can load and convert to its own format.

So by using Works' file import, export, and conversion features, you can make use of almost any kind of data from any source you can imagine. Works becomes a simple, fast tool that allows you to combine data from different sources, convert data to different formats, and use four different tools to work with it flexibly.

Putting Works to Work

As you've seen so far, Microsoft Works and the Mac are a simple, flexible, and relatively transparent personal-computing team. In the chapters that follow, you'll see how you can put this power to good use.

Chapter 2

Using the Word Processor

Word processing is the most popular personal computer application because nearly everyone needs to put a few words down on paper from time to time, and most people who've used typewriters find it fairly easy to make the conceptual transition to a word-processing program. In both cases, you type at a keyboard, and what you type appears in front of you. But a word processor has an important advantage over a typewriter: You can store what you've typed and change it later.

In this chapter, we'll look at the advantages of word processing on a Macintosh in general (and with Works in particular). After that, we'll explore each of the menus that are available in the Works word processor. Finally, we'll cover some basic tips that can help make the word processor a more effective writing tool.

Word Processing on the Mac

The Macintosh is ideally suited for word processing because its light gray screen and black letters look a lot like the output from a typewriter. But there are a number of other Mac-related advantages for those who work with words.

What you see is what you get

When you put words on a Macintosh screen, they appear exactly as they will appear on paper. The margins, line spacing, indentions, and justification you apply to your text will show up faithfully on the screen, so you don't have to guess at how your finished document will look. (Letter spacing or word spacing may differ if you're printing to a LaserWriter or other laser printer. If you use a font, such as Works' default Boston font, that isn't built into your laser printer, your display may not match your printout.) While these particular format settings are common to every word-processing program, the Macintosh allows you to set them more easily — you can point to markings on a ruler to set margins, and you can select a portion of a document if you want to use a different format in just one place.

You get more formatting options

With other computers, you are at the mercy of your printer when it comes to selecting the type font, size, and style that will be printed on paper. Every Macintosh word processor offers a variety of type fonts, and you can embellish them by using a range of type styles and sizes.

You can include drawings or graphs in a document

Thanks to the Macintosh Clipboard, you can easily move drawings created with MacPaint, MacDraw, or other programs into word-processor documents. Instead of trying to describe a new building or the design of a new product, you can show it right in your letter or report.

These features are hallmarks of word processing on the Mac, regardless of the word-processing program you are using. Microsoft Works adds several important items to the list. To familiarize you with these features, let's look at the commands Works offers.

A Quick Tour of Works' Word-Processor Menus

As you do in every Mac application, you access Works commands primarily via pull-down menus in the menu bar at the top of the screen. (You can also issue many Works commands directly from the keyboard by pressing the Command key in combination with a letter key. Keyboard commands are explained in detail later in this chapter, but every menu command that has a keyboard equivalent shows that equivalent next to the command name on the menu.)

Each Works application has a different set of pull-down menus, but, as mentioned in Chapter 1, five menus are substantially the same in every application. (In Works versions prior to 2.0, there are four common menus because the Macro feature is not supported.) In this chapter, we'll look at the word processor-specific commands on these common menus first, and then we'll look at the menus that are unique to the word processor. (The Window menu, which is the same in every Works application, is discussed in Chapter 1.)

Note that Works versions 1.0 and 1.1 have two different word-processor menus: Font and Style. In Works 2.0, the Font and Style options have been added to the Format menu, and two other menus, Spell and Macros, have been added to the menu bar.

The File menu

The Open and Save As commands on the File menu work in slightly different ways in different Works applications. When you're working in the word processor, the list of files displayed when you first use the Open command contains only word-processor files. Text files and files from other Works applications or other programs are not shown. But the word processor can import text files created by other Works applications or by other programs. To see text files in the Open dialog box, click the Import File check box beneath the Cancel button. With the Import File box checked, you can select and open text files in the word processor.

The Save As dialog box has options for saving word-processor files in four different formats. When you save a document by using Save As, and you give the document the name of a file already in the same folder, Works will ask if you want to replace the existing file. Click the No button or press the Return key if you would prefer to rename your file and preserve the existing one.

- The default option (the Normal option button) saves a document as a standard Works word-processor file, which you can open only by using the word processor. When you use Save As to save a standard document, the name of the document on the desktop (shown in the title bar at the top of the window) changes to match the name you've just given the newly saved file.

- The Export option button saves a document as a standard text file, which you can load by using many other programs (or other Works applications, as we'll see in Chapter 10.) When you save a document as text (or as Rich Text—discussed later in this chapter), the file is saved on disk with the name you give it, but the name of the document you have open on the desktop remains unchanged.

- When you click the Export option button, the Export As Rich Text Format check box becomes active. If you click this box, Works will save the file as text, but it will include formatting information as well. Many Macintosh and MS-DOS programs can read both text and formatting information from Rich Text Format (RTF) files.

- The Stationery option button saves a document with the name you give it, but leaves the name of the document you have open unchanged on the desktop. The Stationery option lets you store a document in a file that you can easily re-use. When you open a document that was saved by using the Stationery option, the document opens as an untitled document (instead of with the name you used to save it). If you create a letterhead format and save it using the Stationery option with the name Letterhead, for example, that file will open as an untitled document whenever you open it.

The only command on the File menu specific to the word processor is the Print Merge command. This command appears in every Works application, but it is active only in the word processor.

The Print Merge command tells Works that you want to print a form letter or some other type of word-processor document that will contain data merged from a database file. When printing a form letter, you must use Print Merge (rather than Print) so that Works knows it must pull data from a database file. If you use the Print command instead, Works will print one copy of the document containing the merged file and either the field names or the field data from the first record in the database file, depending on whether Show Field Data or Show Field Names is active on the Edit menu. (See the discussion of Prepare To Merge later in this chapter.)

The Edit menu

The word processor's Edit menu contains four commands (other than the Clipboard and Undo commands that are common to every Works application).

The Select Picture command, which appears only in version 1.0 and 1.1 of Works, selects graphics in a word-processor document, whether they're drawings you've made with Works' Draw tool or pictures you've copied into a Works document from another program by using the Clipboard. Works 2.0 doesn't have this command because you can select any picture in Works 2.0 simply by clicking on it while using the Draw tool. In version 1.0 and 1.1, you use the Select Picture command to select pictures in a document one at a time, in the order in which you made them. If there are two drawings side by side, for example, choosing Select Picture once highlights the first drawing, choosing Select Picture again highlights the second drawing, and choosing Select Picture a third time highlights the first drawing again. We'll explore this option more in Chapter 3.

The Draw On command (which changes to Draw Off after you've selected it), lets you draw directly in word-processor documents. In versions 1.0 and 1.1 of Works, you can draw only lines and boxes in three line thicknesses. In Works 2.0, you have far more drawing options, as described in Chapter 3. Works 2.0 also lets you use the Draw On command to enhance spreadsheet documents.

Anything you draw with this tool in the word processor is treated as a picture by Works, and pictures are independent of text. For example, if you draw a box around some text and then select the box and move it, only the box will move—the text will stay where it is. (To move text, you employ conventional techniques, such as the Cut and Paste commands, the Spacebar, the Delete key, and the Tab key.)

To change a picture in Works 1.0 or 1.1:

□ Choose the Undo command immediately after you've drawn the picture.

Or:

□ Select the picture by using the Select Picture command, choose the Clear command to delete it, and then re-draw the picture or the part of the picture you've selected.

In Works 2.0, you can change pictures much more easily, as we'll see in Chapter 3.

The Prepare to Merge command is available only in the word processor. You use this command when selecting database files and specific fields within those files to merge into a word-processor document.

When you select a field to merge, a box (called a merge box) appears at the insertion point displaying the database file name and the field name. A pair of merge boxes in the salutation of a letter might look like this:

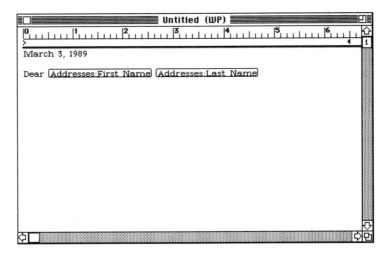

The actual length of a merge box will depend on the length of the database file and field names. Merge boxes appear at the location of the insertion point when you choose the Prepare to Merge command. Once a merge box is displayed in a word-processor document, you can delete it, move it, or copy it just as you would ordinary text.

When you merge database fields into a word-processor file by using the Prepare To Merge command, Works ordinarily shows the data from the database files in the merge boxes. To see the names of the database files and data fields, use the Show Field Names command. When you choose the Show Field Names command, it changes on the Edit menu to Show Field Data, which will display the contents of each field in the merge boxes. The Show Field Data/Show Field Names command also determines which type of data will appear in a single-copy printout of the word-processor file made by using the Print command. If you use the Print command, Works will print one copy of essentially what appears onscreen; using the Print Merge command will give you multiple printouts, each with its own merged data.

The Multiple Labels command, which is new in Works 2.0, lets you print data from more than one database record on a single word-processor page. After you merge at least one database field into a word-processor document, you can choose the Multiple Labels command to paste the same field or fields in a column next to the original fields. This option lets you create two-across or three-across labels with Works, as we'll see in Chapter 4. Normally, if you use the same field more than once in a single document, the same data will be repeated. When the Multiple Labels command is active (a check appears next to the command on the menu), each copied field in the same document will include data from the next record in the database.

The Search menu

The Search menu is unique to the word processor. It lets you find text (the Find command), find text and replace it with text you supply (Replace), and jump to a particular page number (Go To Page #). All of these commands have keyboard alternatives.

You use the Find command to locate one occurrence of text at a time. The dialog box that appears when you select Find contains an entry box (called Find What) that lets you enter the string of characters you want to locate. It contains check boxes that tell Works to match only whole words with your search string, to match uppercase and lowercase letters exactly as in your typed example, or both. One new feature in Works 2.0 is the addition of two buttons, which let you enter Tab or Return characters in the search-string box so that you can find these characters as well as text characters.

The Replace command works the same as the Find command, except that it contains an extra entry box (called Replace With) where you enter the string of text with which you want to replace the searched-for string. To change "Age" to "Ape", for example, you would type *Age* in the Find What box, and then type *Ape* in the Replace With box. As in the Find dialog box, you can choose to match whole words, check for uppercase and lowercase letters, and search for or replace with Tab and Return characters. The Replace dialog box also contains three buttons that do not appear in the Find dialog box. The Replace button executes your replacement on the current selection only. The Replace All button replaces all occurrences of the searched-for string. The Replace, Then Find button replaces the current selection and then moves to the next occurrence without replacing it. This is handy if you want to verify each replacement without having to click both the Replace and Find Next buttons each time.

The Find and Replace commands search the entire document, from the current position of the insertion point forward, no matter where the insertion point is at the time. So, if you're working in the middle of a document, the Search and Change functions will search to the end of the document and then start again at the beginning until they return to your original position.

The Go To Page # command helps you move to a specific page quickly. Works displays page numbers in the right scroll box, but you can also use this command to determine which page you're on. When you choose the Go To Page # command, the page-number window in the dialog box that appears always shows the current page number. To move to a different page, enter a new number, click the OK button, and Works will jump to that page.

The Format menu

The Format menu is a hierarchical menu. In a standard Mac menu, the commands are arranged in one column from top to bottom. A menu with a particularly long list of commands might stretch down the entire screen and might even have a scroll arrow at the bottom, indicating that you can drag the mouse pointer below the bottom of the screen to reveal more commands on the list. A hierarchical menu lets a program display far more commands without forcing users to scroll down below the bottom of the screen to reveal them.

Hierarchical-menu commands are indicated by an arrow to the right of the command name. When you select a hierarchical-menu command, a sub-menu of commands pertaining to the original command appears to the right or left of the menu, depending on your system and installed fonts. (If you have installed a font with a long name, the sub-menu may appear to the left on a Mac Plus or SE.)

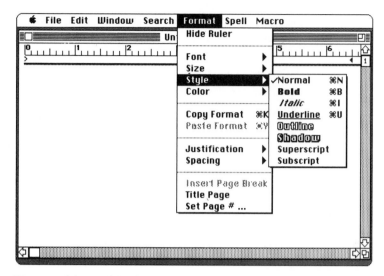

To use a hierarchical-menu command, you point to the command, hold down the mouse button to reveal the command's sub-menu, and continue to hold down the button as you move the pointer to select a command from the sub-menu. When you've highlighted the command you want, release the mouse button and both menus will disappear.

The Format menu in Works 2.0 includes several hierarchical commands. With this one menu, you can control all of Works' format options except page headers and footers (which you control with the Page Setup command on the File menu).

The Works word processor, spreadsheet, and database each contain Format menus, but the menu is quite different in each tool. The word processor's Format menu begins with the Hide Ruler command. This command hides the ruler that normally appears at the top of a document window. Hiding the ruler gives you one or two more lines of space in which to display text. If you want to adjust paragraph indents, insert tabs, or set first-line indents, however, the ruler must be showing. The Hide Ruler command changes to Show Ruler when the ruler is hidden.

The next four commands — Font, Size, Style, and Color — are hierarchical commands. Selecting the Font command reveals the Font sub-menu, which shows the fonts currently available in your System file. The System file on the Works Startup Disk comes with Geneva, Boston, Monaco, and Chicago fonts, but you can add more fonts to the System file using Apple's Font/DA Mover program (described in the Macintosh documentation).

The Size command reveals a sub-menu showing the sizes available for the currently-selected font, like this:

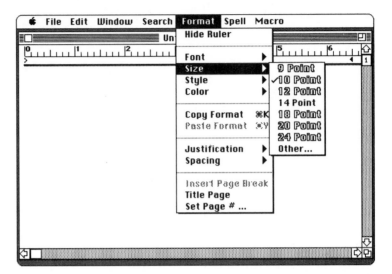

You can tell which sizes are available for the currently-selected font, because their sizes are shown in outline type. Font sizes shown in bold type are not available. You can select sizes that aren't available if you like, but your Mac will have to create them by approximation, and they won't look as good as sizes you actually have installed in your System file.

You'll also notice an Other command at the bottom of the Size sub-menu. If you have installed larger font sizes, such as 36-point or 48-point type that aren't normally shown on the Size menu, you can specify that size in the dialog box that appears when you choose the Other command. You can also specify intermediate sizes, such as 15-point, but again, your Mac will have to approximate them, and they won't look as good as sizes you actually have installed in your System.

If you're printing on an ImageWriter, it's a good idea to install double-sized fonts for the font sizes you normally use so that the quality of printing is better. When you choose the Best quality option in the Print command's dialog box, your Mac uses a reduced version of the font that is twice as large as the one specified in the document to produce the highest quality text. If you want to print Geneva 12 in Best quality, your Mac will use a reduced version of Geneva 24 to print it. If the double-size font isn't available when you want to print in Best quality, your Mac makes do with what it has, but the result isn't as good.

The Style command has its own sub-menu, which lets you select Normal, Bold, Italic, Underline, Outline, Shadow, Superscript, or Subscript styles for your text. The Normal, Bold, Italic, and Underline commands have the keyboard equivalents Command-N, Command-B, Command-I, and Command-U, respectively.

Next is the Color menu, which lets you apply one of eight colors to text or graphics in word-processor documents. If you're using a Mac 512, a Mac Plus, a Mac SE, or a monochrome display on a Mac II, you won't be able to see the color changes unless you select white, which will make text invisible on the Mac's white screen. When you're working with the Draw tool, you can choose to color either the black dots or the white dots that make up a picture. (See Chapter 3.)

The next two commands on the word processor's Format menu let you copy the format of one paragraph and paste it into other paragraphs. Rather than forcing you to insert extra rulers when you want to change formats, (as with MacWrite and some other programs), Works uses only one ruler and lets you format each paragraph as you go. Works assumes that you want the same format as the previous paragraph unless you change it. The settings on the ruler show the line length and indent settings of the currently selected paragraph. The Copy Format command can copy indent, justification, tab stop, and line spacing information from one paragraph, and the Paste Format command will apply the copied format to other paragraphs. Note that these two commands have keyboard equivalents for faster copying and pasting.

Justification and Spacing, the next two commands on the Format menu, are hierarchical commands. Choosing the Justification command reveals a menu with commands for left, center, right, or justified text. The sub-menu that pops out when you select the Spacing command lets you choose single, one and one-half, or double line spacing for text, as well as six-line-per-inch spacing. The six-line-per-inch spacing is useful if you're printing on a business form.

The last three commands on the Format menu control page breaks, page number printing, and page numbering. Works inserts page breaks according to the page-length option you set in the Page Setup dialog box. The Set Page Break command lets you insert a manual page break anywhere you choose, for example, so that you can be sure Works starts a new page at the beginning of a new section of a document. To set a page break:

☐ Move the insertion point one line below the place where you want the page break to appear, and choose the Set Page Break command.

The Remove Page Break command replaces the Set Page Break command, but only when the insertion point is on the line directly below a manually inserted page break. If so, the Remove Page Break command will remove the break. You can also remove a manual page break simply by backspacing over it.

The Title Page command tells Works not to print a page header or footer on the first page of a document. When you define a header or footer on the Page Setup menu, Works normally prints it on every page of a document. But you can have the header or footer start printing on the second page of the document if you choose the Title Page command. This command has a check mark next to it when it is selected. Choosing Title Page does not affect the numbering of a document, however. When a header containing a page number prints on the second page of a document, for example, it will still print *Page 2.*

If, for some reason, you want your document to begin with a page number other than 1, you can set a new first-page number with the Set Page # command. Simply select the command, type in a number from 0 to 2,000, and then press the Return key. The new page numbers will appear in headers or footers if you have inserted formatting commands for them, and the numbers in the right-hand scroll box of the document window will adjust according to the first page number you set.

The Spell menu

One of the big improvements in Works 2.0 is the inclusion of a built-in spelling-checker function. The spelling checker works only in the word processor. It is essentially a Works-specific version of the award-winning Spellswell program, and it has a number of features that will help you make every document letter-perfect:

■ It uses a 60,000-word main dictionary and any number of auxiliary dictionaries. You can buy auxiliary dictionaries from other vendors, or you can create one on your own.

- There's also a homonym dictionary and homonym-checking option that spots usage errors, such as using "to" when you mean "two" or "too."

- You can add new words to your own, custom dictionary as you go, and you can have the spelling checker remember unique words only for the current document, if you like.

- The program displays misspelled words in context, as well as in a dictionary window that you can use to select alternate spellings. You can move the dictionary window around the screen to see other parts of your document.

- The program will suggest alternatives to misspelled words, or you can type a word in the program's dialog box and it will suggest the correct spelling.

- When you replace a misspelled word with a correct one, the spelling checker inserts the new word in the document with the same style, size, and font as the original word.

- You can scroll through the dictionary to look up the spelling of a word.

- When you add words to a dictionary, you can easily add up to 16 variants of the word with different suffixes.

- You can select options so that the program checks to see that the first word after every period is capitalized and that proper nouns are capitalized. (It's even smart enough to suggest capitalized replacements for words that should be capitalized.)

- Two other options tell the program to ignore combinations of letters and numbers, or hyphens in words, so that it doesn't stop you dozens of times when checking technical material.

- Another option tells the program to watch for double-word errors, such as "the the," which are difficult to catch in proofreading.

- Another option tells the program to check for two spaces after every period.

- When the spell check is done, the program tells you how many words are in the document, and how many incorrect ones were found.

> **TIP:** The spelling checker in Works is about the most sophisticated one around, but it's no substitute for the human eye. You should always use the spelling checker on a document before you make the final printout, but you should also proofread the document yourself to be sure there are no mistakes the spelling checker didn't catch.

The Spell menu has only three commands. The Correct Spelling command instructs Works to check the spelling of the current document or the currently selected portion of a document. You can check everything from one word to an entire document. When you use the Correct Spelling command with a word or group of selected words, Works checks spelling on the selected words only. If you select part of a word, Works will check the entire selected word. If the insertion point is flashing, indicating no selection, Works will check the entire document.

The first time you use the spelling checker, you'll be asked to specify the location of the main dictionary, called MsWorksDict, and (if you have the homonym-checking option checked) the location of the homonym dictionary, called MsWorksHymn. If no misspelled words are found, the next thing you see is a dialog box telling you the number of words in the document, like this:

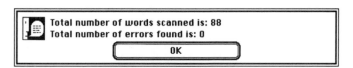

If the program finds a word it doesn't know, it highlights the word in context and then displays the dictionary window, which shows you the word along with a suggested correction in the dictionary list, like this:

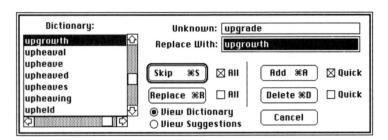

The dictionary window contains buttons that you can click to skip over the word in question, replace the word with the suggested alternate (or another alternate you type in or find in the dictionary), add the word to the current dictionary, or delete a word from the current dictionary. You can also scroll through the list of words, or you can have the program suggest alternate spellings for the word.

If you click the All check box next to the Skip or Replace buttons, the spelling checker will skip or replace all occurrences of the word throughout the document; if the All box is not checked, the program will stop at each occurrence of the word.

The Add and Delete buttons also have check boxes next to them, labeled Quick. If these boxes are checked, you will add or delete only the currently displayed version of the word in question. If the Quick boxes aren't checked, the spelling checker will display a list of different versions of the word in a box like this:

```
╔══════════════ Adding word to Dictionary ══════════════╗

   ☒ breakup                    ☐ Must Capitalize

   ┌─────────────────────┐     ┌─────────────────────┐
   │ ☐ breakups          │     │ ☐ breakupal         │
   │ ☐ breakupes         │     │ ☐ breakupless       │
   │ ☐ breakuped         │     │ ☐ breakupness       │
   │ ☐ breakupd          │     │ ☐ breakuplike       │
   │ ☐ breakuping        │     │ ☐ breakupment       │
   │ ☐ breakuper         │     │ ☐ breakupable       │
   │ ☐ breakupest        │     │ ☐ breakupible       │
   │ ☐ breakuply         │     │ ☐ breakupally       │
   │ ☐ breakup's         │     │ ☐ breakupous        │
   └─────────────────────┘     └─────────────────────┘

      ( Add Word Now )              (   Cancel   )
```

This box lets you add or delete not only the specific version of the word that the program found, but also any plural, adjectival, adverbial, and other forms of the word at the same time. The form of the word that was found is checked in this dialog box, but you can add other forms of the word at the same time simply by clicking in the boxes next to them.

The spelling checker only uses one spelling dictionary at a time. It automatically loads its main dictionary (after you've told the program where the dictionary is located the first time you use it), unless you tell the program to use an alternate dictionary by using the Dictionary command on the Spelling menu.

The other two commands on the Spell menu are Options, which lets you set program options such as capitalization after periods or checking homonyms, and Dictionary, which lets you check spelling with another dictionary from your disk. We'll see the spelling checker in action in Chapter 4.

The Macro menu

As discussed in Chapter 1, the Macro menu is common to all Works 2.0 applications, and it works the same way in each of them. We'll see how to put macros to use in the word processor in Chapter 4.

Making the Most of the Word Processor

With its built-in spelling checker, macro feature, and enhanced drawing tools, version 2.0 of the Works word processor now has most of the features most people want, and it's still easy to use. In fact, the Works word processor retains several features that have made it one of the best on the market for simply getting things done quickly. On the other hand, there are some tasks that you can't do with the word processor. Here are some tips for making the most of what the word processor has.

Keep Works running at top speed

When you create a document with Microsoft Word, later versions of Mac-Write, FullWrite professional, or other programs, you store most of the document on disk, rather than in your Mac's memory. This disk-storage feature is called virtual memory. Thanks to virtual memory, a document can usually be as large as the amount of disk space you have available. (This isn't true of FullWrite because of its memory management scheme.) But you have to trade unlimited file size for performance: When you scroll to a part of the file that isn't currently in memory, the program must find that portion on the disk and load it, and you have to wait while that happens.

Works, on the other hand, stores documents entirely in memory. This means that you can scroll to any place in the document and get there immediately. And, thanks to its memory-resident files, Works lets you enter, edit, search for, or replace text, or change document formatting as quickly as any other program you'll find.

The problem with memory-resident files is that they can be only as large as the amount of available memory permits. If you're using Works on a Mac with one megabyte of random-access memory (RAM), a word-processor document can be from 180 to 240 pages, depending on the formatting options and graphics it contains. (Macs with more memory can accommodate proportionally larger documents.) Works doesn't tell you exactly how much memory you have available at any time, but you can find out the percentage of available memory by selecting the About MS Works command from the Apple menu. The percentage is shown at the bottom of the program's copyright screen.

The Works desktop is divided up among any documents you have open, so although you might be able to create one document 220 pages long, you can't have two such documents on the desktop. Also, the Clipboard's memory space is shared with the desktop, so if you are using nearly all your desktop space for open documents, you won't be able to copy as much to the Clipboard as you would if the desktop were less cluttered.

If you're like most users, you'll probably never run out of memory with Works, because you don't work with large files. But there are a couple of ways to resolve memory problems. First, if you have several large documents open on the desktop, close one or more of them to make room for an especially large document you want to work on, particularly if the document contains several graphics. (Graphics use a lot of memory.) Second, if you're using MultiFinder, you can limit memory problems by setting a large Application Memory Size in the Works Get Info dialog box. See Chapter 1 for details.

Aside from limiting the maximum size of documents you can create, the only other problem with Works' memory-resident files is that the program slows down as documents become larger. You won't notice the problem if you never work with documents larger than 30 pages or so, but if you work with longer documents than that, Works' scrolling, inserting, and formatting performance will be slow, and it will get slower as your documents grow. Fortunately, you can avoid performance problems almost entirely with a few simple techniques.

First, most long documents can be divided into logical sections, such as chapters. If you create a separate word-processor document for each chapter or other document division, you'll avoid the large single documents that cause problems.

Even when you break up long documents into sections, you may end up with documents of 40 KB or 50 KB that slow Works down. But Works' speed with individual documents is determined not only by the amount of text, but by the number of fonts, styles, and graphics you have in a document. Large fonts or graphics, in particular, slow down the word processor's scrolling and text-entry functions.

To keep the word processor running at full speed, follow these steps in creating a document:

☐ First, enter and edit all the text in the document using one font and style.

☐ Second, check the spelling of the text.

☐ Third, apply font and style formatting to the document.

☐ Fourth, create any drawings or column layouts you want to add.

This procedure will not only maintain the word processor's speed when it is needed most, but it will also keep you focused on one task at a time as you work.

Use the desktop to manage multiple files

Most Mac word processors now let you have more than one file open at a time. Works lets you have up to 14 documents open on the desktop at once. Because it's an integrated set of applications, Works lets you have word processor, spreadsheet, database, and communications documents open at the same time on the desktop. You can use the Window menu to quickly switch between open documents, cutting and pasting data between windows easily with the Clipboard. (We'll see this feature in action later in this book.)

As you work throughout the day, leave documents open on the desktop unless you know you won't need them again. That way, you can easily return to a document by using the Window menu whenever you need to work on it. Some documents you might always want to have open include Stationery documents for letters, reports, or memos, or lists of tasks. Use the Make Works Desktop command (in version 2.0) to create a Works desktop file, which will load documents you want to have available every time you start work. The Resume Works file (in versions 1.0 and 1.1) serves the same purpose (without a corresponding menu command) by remembering all the files you had open on the desktop the last time you quit Works. When you begin your next work session, simply double-click on the Works Desktop (or Resume Works) file to start Works and load all of your desired documents.

Use the Merge feature to create custom database formats

The Print Merge command on the Edit menu lets you transfer information from a database file to a word-processor document. With ordinary database reports, you are limited to printing individual records on individual lines, and you can use only one font and font size for the entire report. But if you transfer database information to a word-processor document with the Print Merge command, you can arrange the merged data for invoices, personnel forms, or other documents in any way you want on a page, and you can apply different fonts and font sizes to different bits of merged database information. We'll see how this works in Chapter 8.

Use the Draw tool for emphasis

Even if you're not artistic, you can use the Draw tool to emphasize certain parts of a document. Use it to put headings inside boxes, for example, or to circle certain phrases you want readers to pay special attention to. The layout options in the Draw tool also let you break text into multiple columns or paste in graphics from other sources to illustrate your points. It's easy to forget you have built-in drawing features, because you're probably accustomed to working without them; but after you begin experimenting with the Draw tool, you'll find yourself thinking about how to visually enhance your text in every document.

Simplify formatting with Copy Format and macros

Works doesn't have a style-sheet feature, which lets you quickly define the look of a document, but you can accomplish some of the same results with the Copy Format command and the macro feature. If you change the format of one paragraph and then want to apply that format to several other paragraphs, use the Copy Format command:

☐ Copy the paragraph's format with the Copy Format command (Command-K)

☐ Select the paragraphs you want to format in the same way

☐ Choose the Paste Format command (Command-Y) to apply that format to the selected paragraphs.

If you know you'll want to use some document or paragraph formats frequently, you can create macros that apply those formats at the touch of a key. Just record the formatting commands as you apply them the first time, and then you can play them back to use the same format the next time. Keep in mind that actions requiring selection of specific text or graphics within a document are usually not appropriate macro actions. Macros use screen coordinates to record placement of the mouse pointer or cursor. This works fine for selecting menu commands using the mouse because the location of the menus on the screen does no change unless you change applications. But if the portion of the document that is on the screen when the macro is played back does not match the screen that was active when the macro was originally recorded, placement of the pointer or any text selection within the document is likely to be different than was originally intended.

Combine headers and footers to maximize page information

Headers and footers are strings of information, such as document name, page number, and so on, that appear on every document page. Headers appear at the top of the page, and footers appear at the bottom. Most Mac word processors let you create headers or footers that can contain several lines of text, or even graphics. Works limits you to one line for each header or footer, which you create by typing text in the Header or Footer boxes in the Page Setup dialog box. If you have a lot of information that you want to appear on each document page, put text in both the Header and Footer boxes to divide the information. For example, you might put the document name and page number in the header, and the date, author, and project name in the footer. This gives you two lines' worth of space, instead of one.

Along with header or footer text, you can enter special header or footer formatting commands to print document names, dates, or page numbers, as well as to align the text. Here's a list of the header or footer formatting commands:

Command	Formatting action
&L	Left justify text that follows
&C	Center text that follows
&R	Right justify text that follows
&P	Print the page number in the header
&D	Print the current date in the header
&T	Print the current time in the header
&F	Print the name of the document in the header
&B	Print the text that follows in boldface
&I	Print the text that follows in italics
&&	Print an ampersand (&) in the header

You can combine as many of these commands as you like, as long as the total text of the header or footer (including the special characters) doesn't exceed 99 characters. If you want to center a header that says, "This is the header," and include the current date and page number, for example, you could type:

&CThis is the header - &D - Page &P

The special characters tell Works to center the following information (the &C command), print the current date (the &D command), and print the page number (the &P command). All other characters will appear exactly as typed, including dashes, spaces, and any other information you want to include.

Using the Page Setup dialog box, you can also choose the font, font size, and color of the header or footer text. When the Page Setup dialog box is visible, the Format command in the menu bar is black, and the other commands are gray. You can use the Format menu as usual to choose your header and footer formats, but you don't see the changes in the Page Setup dialog box. The font, size, and color are Chicago 12, black onscreen, but your formatting choices will appear when you print. If you don't change any formats, Works assumes you want to use the same font format as is used in the document itself.

Use headers or footers to chain document files

Unlike some other word processors, Works doesn't have a file-chaining feature that lets you print several documents as if they were one. You can work around this limitation manually by creating identical headers or footers in each document that you want to chain, and by using the Set Page # command to be sure the page numbers are continuous from one document to the next. Here's the procedure with two documents we'll call Text1 and Text2:

☐ Create a header or footer for Text1, including the &P command to insert a page number.

☐ Scroll to the end of Text1, and be sure the document ends either at the end of a section, or at the end of a page. Text2 will begin printing at the top of a new page, so either it must be the beginning of a new section in the document (where starting a new page would be expected) or it must continue from the bottom of the previous page (in which case Text1 might need to end in the middle of a sentence at the end of the previous page, with Text2 picking up where Text1 left off).

☐ Make a note of the ending page number in Text1. It's in the scroll box in the right-hand scroll bar when the page displayed is the last page in the document. (Note: The page number doesn't change in the scroll bar until the page break between pages is above the top of the screen, so be sure the page break that separates the last document page has scrolled up beyond the top of the screen.)

☐ Open Text2, and enter exactly the same header information, including the page numbering command.

☐ Choose the Set Page # command from the Format menu, and enter the page number that follows the last page number in Text1.

☐ Be sure the Title Page command is not checked on Text2. Otherwise, the first page of Text2 won't contain a page number.

☐ Print both documents; they will be numbered continuously.

Create a separate document for front matter

When you number a document using the &P command in a header or footer, page numbering of the document usually begins on the first page of the document. You can choose the Title Page command from the Format menu to suppress page numbering on the first page of the document, if you like. (This system is common with reports, letters, and other business documents.) The Title Page command doesn't change the page numbering sequence—documents are still numbered from 1 on up, unless you change the beginning page number with the Set Page # command—but it doesn't print a *1* on page 1.

The Title Page command is useful when you don't want page numbers on the first page. But what if you have several pages of front matter that you don't want numbered? Suppose you have a title page, a copyright page, and a table of contents, and you don't want any of these numbered? Works can't suppress page-number printing on any page except the first document page (unless you don't number pages at all), so the only option is to print the title page, copyright page, and table of contents as a separate document with no page numbering.

Use multiple windows to see different parts of the same document

High-powered word processors such as Microsoft Word and WordPerfect let you see two different views of the same document, either by opening multiple windows on the same file or by splitting the screen window in half. Works doesn't have these features, but with a little creative file management and screen layout, you can approximate it. Normally, the purpose of viewing different parts of the same document at once is to look at one part while you edit another. This suits our work-around solution perfectly.

- ☐ Open an existing document. (We'll again call it Text1.)

- ☐ Open a new word-processor document (Untitled).

- ☐ Return to Text1 using the Window menu, and use the Select All command to select all the text.

- ☐ Copy the text to the Clipboard (command-C).

- ☐ Display the untitled document, and paste the Text1 text into it (command-V).

- ☐ Resize the Text1 window so that it occupies the upper half of your screen.

- ☐ Resize the untitled document so that it occupies the lower half of your screen.

- ☐ Scroll the untitled document to display the portion you want to look at.

- ☐ Make your changes in Text1.

Using this method, you can easily move back and forth between two different areas of the same document. But remember, the untitled document is only a temporary view: Be sure to make all your editing changes in the original document, and then close the untitled document without saving the changes when you're finished.

Basic Word-Processor Tips

Presented in the following section of this chapter are four general tips that apply to working with any Works tool or any other program. Some of these are mentioned earlier in this chapter, and some will be mentioned again later in this book. All can help you with your work if you use them.

Enter and edit text first, format last

A cardinal rule of working with any word-processing or spreadsheet program is: Wait until you've finished creating your document before you format it. Works has a lot of powerful formatting options you can use to dress up your documents, but most of them require you to move one of your hands from the keyboard to the mouse, pull down a menu, select an option, and sometimes specify a value. It's very disruptive trying to do all of that while you're in the middle of typing or editing text. You can get so distracted by format options that you lose the flow of the text. This is especially important when you're first entering text and you're trying to put words in a logical order, but it's also true when you're reading over text you've already entered. It's impossible to judge the flow of a letter if you're constantly interrupting that flow by fiddling with the Format, Font, and Style menus.

Along with disrupting your creative mood, formatting a document before you're satisfied with its contents can also be a plain old waste of time. You may not be able to judge how you want a document to look until you know exactly which words it will contain. This is especially true with documents that have complex formats, such as business forms, flyers, or lengthy reports. Nine times out of ten, you'll end up adjusting the format of a document just before you print it, so why not wait and make all your formatting choices then?

Another argument for the "Edit first, format later" method is that it lets you work faster. It's fine to want a document to be double-spaced, but if you apply double spacing when you're still editing the text, you'll have to scroll twice as many times to see the same amount of text. For the same reason (as mentioned in a tip earlier in this chapter), it's best to wait until you've finished entering text before you add drawings to a document. Drawings take up lots of space on the screen and in your Mac's memory, and make scrolling that much slower.

Use the keyboard as much as possible

Using the keyboard, rather than the mouse, is a matter of efficiency. Being able to point to commands with the mouse is convenient when you're just learning, but word processing is primarily a matter of typing at the keyboard. The less your hands leave the keyboard, the more efficient your word processing will be. Apple added a set of cursor-movement keys to the keyboards of the Mac Plus and later Mac models for exactly this reason. So, if you have a newer Mac keyboard, you can use the cursor keys to move through a document.

No matter what type of keyboard you have, however, you can use the Go To Page # command by pressing Command-G on the keyboard and then entering the number of the page where you want to go.

Naturally, there are some editing and formatting tasks that are faster with the mouse, such as selecting odd amounts of text, but if you set yourself the goal of sticking to the keyboard as much as possible, you'll find your data-entry and editing speed improving dramatically.

Along with selecting text and moving around in a document, the keyboard can be used to issue 26 different word-processor commands. These commands are listed in the table in Figure 2-1. For help in remembering them, you might want to make a copy of the list and tape it to the front of your Mac for quick reference.

Action	*Command*	*Menu*	*Keyboard equivalent*
Open a file	Open	File	Command-O
Close a file	Close	File	Command-W
Save a file	Save	File	Command-S
Print a file	Print	File	Command-P
Quit Works	Quit	File	Command-Q
Undo a command	Undo	Edit	Command-Z
Cut text	Cut	Edit	Command-X
Copy text	Copy	Edit	Command-C
Paste text	Paste	Edit	Command-V
Turn Draw tool on or off	Draw On/ Draw Off	Edit	Command-J
Prepare document for Print Merge	Prepare To Merge	Edit	Command-M
Get Help	Help	Window	Command-?
Find text	Find	Search	Command-F
Replace text	Replace	Search	Command-R
Go to a page	Go To Page #	Search	Command-G

Figure 2-1. *(continued)*
Works offers keyboard equivalents for 26 word-processor commands.

Figure 2-1. *continued*

Action	Command	Menu	Keyboard equivalent
Copy a format	Copy Format	Format	Command-K
Paste a format	Paste Format	Format	Command-Y
Start recording a macro	Start Recording	Macro	Option-+ (plus)
Stop recording a macro	Stop Recording	Macro	Option-– (hyphen)
Play back a macro	Playback and	Macro	Option-Delete
Stop a macro in progress			Command-. (period)
Normal text style	Normal Text	Format	Command-N
Boldface text	Bold	Format	Command-B
Italic text	Italic	Format	Command-I
Underlined text	Underline	Format	Command-U
Activate last window listed on Window menu			Command-, (comma)

As you'll notice, most of these commands are mnemonic — that is, the letter key assignment helps you remember the command that the key combination carries out. To help yourself remember the letter key for the Cut and Paste commands, think of cutting as crossing out, or X-ing, text, and think of pasting as inserting text, which typographers and proofreaders specify by a caret (^) symbol.

It isn't hard to remember these commands, and once you begin using them regularly, you'll get things done much more quickly.

Store custom formats for common documents

The word processor uses certain default formats for every new document, as indicated in the specifications section at the end of this chapter. These defaults are fine if you always use standard paper and want 1-inch margins all around your documents, but they're not so fine if you don't. If you want settings other than these defaults, you can either change them every time you format a new document, or you can create a stationery document with the custom formats you prefer and then store it as a template for your future work.

Suppose, for example, that you normally work with U.S. legal-size paper (8 ½ by 14 inches), and you want a 2-inch bottom margin. To store and reuse this custom format:

- ☐ Open a new document.

- ☐ Choose the Page Setup command from the File menu.

- ☐ Change the Bottom Margin setting to 2 inches.

- ☐ Change the Paper option to US Legal.

- ☐ Save these changes by clicking the OK box or by pressing the Return or Enter key.

- ☐ Choose the Save As command from the File menu, click the option to save the document as stationery, and save the document with a name, such as Legal Format, that helps you remember that this file contains your formatting preferences.

This Stationery file will now be available whenever you want to begin a new file with this format. Because you saved it as a stationery file, you can open it as a new, untitled document.

Recycle text when possible

Just as you can make a dummy document containing custom formats, you can also save sections of actual text you use repeatedly. If you're a lawyer, for example, you might enter a number of boilerplate legal paragraphs into a file named Boilerplate, and then copy the relevant paragraphs as needed into new documents. You may have to make some minor changes in the boilerplate paragraphs to suit each specific document, but that will be much faster than retyping entire paragraphs from scratch each time.

If you're a salesperson, you could save your monthly sales report and then recycle parts of it each successive month. You would simply load the old report, make the changes to update it, and then save the changed document under a different name with the Save As command. This would leave your original report intact and store a copy of the new one as well.

The ability to store and recycle text is probably the major advantage of using a word processor over using a typewriter, and it can save you hours of extra work. The two examples just mentioned are only the beginning. You could recycle invitations, letters, babysitting notes, invoices, progress reports — anything you have to write more than once that contains roughly the same text as something you did before.

Word-Processor Specifications

Here are some specifications you might want to refer to as you use the word processor.

Maximum file size: Approximately 180–240 pages with 1 MB of RAM (maximum document size increases proportionally in Macs with more than 1 MB of RAM).

Maximum paper height: 273 inches.

Maximum paper width: 15 inches.

Minimum paper height: 1 inch.

Minimum paper width: 1 inch.

Default paper size: US Letter (8½ by 11 inches).

Default top, bottom, left, and right margins: 1 inch.

Default line length: 6½ inches.

Default tab settings: Every ½ inch.

Default font: 10-point Boston.

Maximum length of search/replace strings: 80 characters.

Maximum length of headers or footers: 99 characters.

Range of numbered pages in a document: 1–2,000.

Maximum number of merged fields from a database: 780 (Maximum of 13 database files on the desktop with the word-processor document, merging all 60 possible fields from each database file.)

Chapter 3

Using the Draw Tool

Microsoft Works' word processor was the first word processor with a built-in drawing tool. In versions 1.0 and 1.1 of the program, you could draw lines, ovals, or boxes. Using these simple shapes, you could put boxes around text, create organizational charts, or make simple floor plans. The Draw tool in Works version 2.0 is a completely new program module that has most of the features of stand-alone drawing programs such as MacDraw. With the new Draw tool, you can: create additional shapes; fill shapes or draw lines in a variety of patterns and colors; arrange text in columns; and draw freehand shapes and 90-degree arcs. But before we get into the specifics of Works' new Draw tool, let's see how a drawing program differs from other graphics programs.

Drawing on the Macintosh

Any program that lets you draw on a computer screen has the same basic features, whether it's a painting program for artists, a drawing program, or a computer-aided design (CAD) program for architects and engineers. All have a set of tools for creating lines or shapes, a way to position or resize the objects you create on the screen, and a way to alter or erase; most also have a way to insert text. Objects are composed of lines (either straight lines or the outlines of shapes) on a contrasting background (the normal screen color), as well as line and fill patterns you can use to visually distinguish the shapes or lines you draw.

On personal computers, graphics programs fall into two general categories: drawing programs (CAD programs are special-purpose drawing programs) and painting programs. The Works Draw tool uses the same basic technology as MacDraw, Adobe Illustrator, and other drawing programs. A drawing program differs from a painting program such as MacPaint in the way the program creates, stores, and prints images.

Any object on a computer screen—a text character, a line, or a shape—is really only a pattern of pixels, which are individual dots of light that are either on or off. On a monochrome Macintosh screen, any pixel can be either white (on) or black (off). On a Macintosh II color monitor, any pixel can be one of four or eight colors, depending on whether you're using a standard video card or an extended video card and whether you have enough memory (displaying eight colors requires more than 1 MB of RAM).

In a text-based program such as a word processor or database, the program turns on certain patterns of pixels to represent characters as you type them. With a painting program, you can turn any pixel on or off as you like—the program doesn't keep track of whether you've created a specific shape; it only keeps track of whether you've turned pixels on or off. If you create a circle, for example, the program notes that you've turned on some pixels in an area of the screen. If you want to change the shape of the circle, you must use tools that work with pixels—tools such as a pencil (which lets you turn individual pixels on and off); a spray can (which turns on groups of pixels in a pattern of varying intensities, depending on how much you spray); or an eraser (which lets you wipe out all or part of a drawing by turning the pixels in its path white).

A drawing program, on the other hand, treats anything you draw as a specific object. An object is defined by vectors, which are the ends and intermediate points of the lines making up the object. When you draw a line, the program notes the locations of the pixels where you begin and end the line. It then turns the pixels in between black to create a line. After you've drawn a line, the program recognizes that line as a specific object, rather than simply a series of pixels. You can alter the shape or size of the line simply by dragging one of its end points to a new location. If a rectangle isn't big enough, you can simply drag the side outward to make it bigger. Also, because a drawing program creates and locates objects by plotting specific points on the screen, you can easily reposition objects along an invisible grid so that they line up exactly with one another. You can also make objects a specific size when creating or resizing by aligning them with an invisible grid.

With a drawing program, you can group objects together so that changing the location or fill pattern of one object in the group changes the locations and fill patterns of all the objects in the group. With a painting program, you would have to erase an image's fill pattern pixel-by-pixel to apply a different pattern. But a drawing program lets you simply select the object and choose a different fill pattern, replacing the original. You can alter the thickness of borders or lines just as easily.

Drawing programs also work in multiple layers. You can draw one object and place it on top of another object. Rather than wiping out the first object (as in a painting program), the overlapping object merely hides the one behind it. Finally, you can draw objects on top of text or place text on top of objects with the Draw tool in Works. We'll see how these techniques come in handy in Chapter 4.

Drawing with Works

The Draw tool in Works versions 1.0 and 1.1 creates black lines and outline shapes made with three different line thicknesses, and it works only in the word processor. The Draw tool in Works version 2.0 is active in both the spreadsheet and the word processor, and it lets you fill shapes or draw lines using different patterns or colors. You can create arcs and freehand lines as well as shapes, and you can enter text and treat it as an object, moving it or shaping it with the tools on the Tools palette. The balance of this chapter applies to the Draw tool in Works 2.0.

To use the Draw tool in Works version 2.0, you must be working in either a word processor or spreadsheet document. You activate the Draw tool by choosing the Draw On command from the Edit menu, or pressing Command-J. (This command is called Draw in versions 1.0 and 1.1, and there is no keyboard command for it.) Although previous versions of Works simply display a dialog box in which you select the type of object you want to draw (line, oval, rounded square, or square) before returning you to the document, version 2.0 adds several new menu items and two Draw-specific menus to the document you're working in, along with a palette of tools that stays on the screen as you work. (You can drag the palette around so that it doesn't cover up parts of the screen where you're drawing.) The Draw tool in Works 1.0 and 1.1 doesn't alter the word processor's menus or their commands. In all versions of the program, however, you work with the Draw tool in a separate mode, and you must turn the Draw tool off to return to regular document editing.

After you activate the Works Draw tool, any text or spreadsheet data you've typed on the screen remains exactly where it was. Any objects you draw appear wherever you place the cursor, whether that's on top of existing text, above, beside, or below it. In effect, the Draw tool's screen is a layer on top of any existing text; when you move, edit, or resize drawn objects, the text beneath them doesn't change.

Drawing objects

In versions 1.0 and 1.1 of Works, the only types of objects you can draw are lines and boxes. If you want to add text to a drawing, you must exit the Draw tool (by choosing Draw Off from the Edit menu) and then type text in the word processor. In Works 2.0, you can type text directly in the drawing layer. The program treats such text in the same way it treats any other object you create in the drawing layer—the Draw text appears on top of text you entered in the document's word-processing mode, and you can alter it only by using the Draw tool's commands.

To make a drawn object in Works 2.0, you begin by selecting the Draw On command from the Edit menu or by typing Command-J. The Tools palette appears:

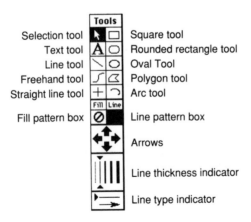

Selection tool	Square tool
Text tool	Rounded rectangle tool
Line tool	Oval Tool
Freehand tool	Polygon tool
Straight line tool	Arc tool
Fill pattern box	Line pattern box
	Arrows
	Line thickness indicator
	Line type indicator

When the Tools palette appears, the selection tool (or pointer) is selected. You use the items on the palette to perform the following functions:

- The selection tool selects an object you've already created.

- The text tool creates text or text objects.

- The line tool makes straight lines at any angle.

- The freehand tool works like a pencil in drawing a line.

- The straight-line tool makes straight horizontal or vertical lines only.

- The fill-pattern box shows the pattern you've selected from the Fill Pattern menu.

- The arrows move a selected object up, down, left, or right one pixel at a time when you click the mouse on the corresponding arrow.

- The line-thickness indicator shows the thickness of lines or borders currently selected.

- The line-type indicator shows whether you've chosen plain lines or lines with an arrow at the end. The arrowhead appears at the end of the line or at the point where you release the mouse button. (Arcs or freehand lines cannot have arrows.)

- The rectangle tool creates squares and rectangles.

- The rounded-rectangle tool makes squares and rectangles with rounded corners.

- The oval tool creates ovals and circles.

- The polygon tool makes multi-sided shapes consisting of straight lines.

- The arc tool draws 90-degree arcs.

- The line-pattern box shows the currently selected fill pattern for lines and borders. The dotted line indicates no line; the line you draw will be invisible on the screen and will not appear when you print.

To draw a graphic object, you select the shape, line thickness, and line type you want from the Tools palette and then move the cursor to the place on the screen where you want to begin drawing. Then, you hold down the mouse button and drag the mouse. As you move the mouse, the line or shape extends outward from the original cursor position.

Once you release the mouse button, the shape or line you've drawn is selected. You can tell it's selected, because its vector points, or selection handles (the small boxes in corners and at midpoints of lines that make up objects), are showing:

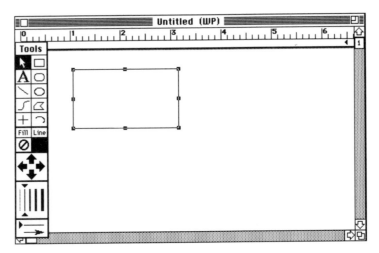

You'll notice that after you draw an object, the Tools palette returns you to the selection tool, which is the default.

> **TIP:** To draw several objects with the same tool without selecting that tool from the Tools palette each time, hold down the Command key while drawing the additional objects.

Moving objects

You can move selected objects one pixel at a time using the arrows in the Tools palette. You can also move an object by selecting it, placing the pointer on its border (rather than or one of its selection handles), and dragging it with the mouse.

> **TIP:** To move an object along a perfectly straight horizontal, vertical, or 45-degree diagonal line:
>
> ☐ Select the object with the selection tool.
>
> ☐ Hold down the mouse button.
>
> ☐ Hold down the Shift key and drag the object.

Selecting and deleting objects

You can select one or more objects by choosing the selection tool, holding down the mouse button, dragging a selection box around the object or group of objects that you want to select and then releasing the mouse button—everything inside the selection box will be selected. To deselect any single object or group of objects, click away from it, either on another part of the screen or on the Tools palette. If you select a group of objects with the selection box and then find you have selected more objects than you want, hold down the Shift key and click on the objects you want to de-select; their selection handles will disappear. Conversely, if you hold down the Shift key and click on unselected objects, they will be added to the selected group.

You can always select an object by clicking on its border, but if an object is filled with a pattern (or is a text object), you can select the object by clicking anywhere on either its fill pattern or its border. Whenever an object is selected, you can change its fill or line pattern by using the Fill Pattern and Line Pattern menus, and you can move, copy, cut, delete, or resize the object.

When you're working with a complex group of objects that are close to each other, you might want to select some of the objects by dragging a selection rectangle around them without including other objects that are also inside the selection rectangle. You can always shift-click on selected objects to de-select them, but you can also freeze objects in advance so that you don't select them when you drag a rectangle around them. To freeze an object:

☐ Select the object or group of objects.

☐ Hold down the F key.

□ Select the object or objects again. Their handles will disappear and they will be frozen.

□ Drag the selection rectangle around them again. The objects you froze won't be selected.

To reactivate the frozen object or objects, hold down the F key and click on the object or group. The handles will reappear, indicating that the object or group has been ''thawed.''

To delete an object forever:

□ Select it and press the Delete key, press the Backspace key, or choose the Clear command from the Edit menu.

To delete and object and put it on the Clipboard:

□ Select it and choose the Cut command from the Edit menu, or press Command-X.

> **TIP:** To erase part of an object, draw a second object on top of the portion of the original object you want to erase, fill the overlapping object with the white fill pattern, and select white for the line pattern. The part of the original object that you covered with the second, white object will appear invisible.

Resizing objects

You use the handles, which appear when you select an object, to resize the object. The handles appear only at the end of lines or arcs, but they appear at the corners of selected rectangles as well as at the midpoints between those corners of squares, rectangles, circles, or ovals. Here's how to use the various handles to resize various objects.

To resize a line or an arc:

□ Select it and then drag one of its ends.

> **TIP:** To increase an arc's angle to greater than 90 degrees, drag one of its handles. You can extend an arc to a full 360-degree oval or circle this way.

To resize a square, oval, or circle:

☐ Select it, and then drag one of its handles.

To resize a polygon, arc, or freehand shape:

☐ Select the object.

☐ Choose the Group Picture command from the Format menu.

☐ Drag either a corner handle (to resize in all dimensions) or a mid-point handle (to resize only one dimension).

Using this technique with a 90-degree arc changes the shape of the arc, rather than increasing its angle beyond 90 degrees. Every arc you draw is initially 90 degrees.

To reshape a polygon or freehand shape:

☐ Select it.

☐ Drag the handle you want to reshape.

To resize in two dimensions at once, drag a handle at one of the object's corners. To enlarge only one dimension of an object (a rectangle's length, for example), drag the midpoint handle on the side you want to move in or out.

The best way to become familiar with these techniques is to try them out. You'll quickly see that making, editing, and resizing shapes in Works is a simple process. We'll take on some projects using drawn shapes in Chapter 4.

Making text objects

Text objects are areas of the drawing layer that contain text, rather than lines or shapes. A text object stands by itself in a document—that is, it is not linked to other areas of text in the word-processor document. (See the section titled ''Columns and Linked Columns'' later in this chapter for an exception to this rule.) Each text object you create can contain up to 32 KB of text. The number of text objects in a document is limited only by the amount of memory you have available.

To create a text object:

☐ Click the text tool in the Tools palette.

☐ Place the cursor where you want the text to begin.

☐ Click the mouse button. A one-line text box three inches wide will appear:

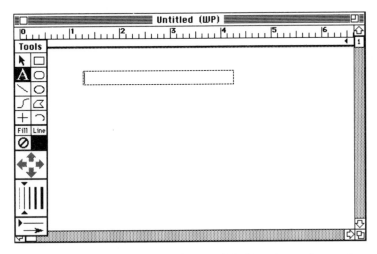

After you complete this procedure, a blinking insertion point appears at the left edge of the text box, and you can begin typing. Works always creates this standard text box if you simply click anywhere in the work area of the screen when the text tool is selected. To create a larger text object, hold down the mouse button and drag until the outline is the size you want, and then begin typing.

Whatever the size of the text object you create, Works will wrap the text you enter to fit within the left and right edges of the object's outline on the screen. If you type more lines of text than the outline's original depth can accommodate, the text will extend below the bottom of the text box you drew.

You can select, move, or resize a text object, but there's a difference between selecting the text object and the text itself. To select a text object, which is the box that contains the text, use the selection tool. Selection handles will appear around the border of the object, exactly as they do around shapes. To select the text within a text object, use the text tool and drag the cursor across the text you want to select.

To resize or move a text object, select it with the selection tool and drag one of its handles. To resize the text in a text object, select it with the text tool and then change its size by using the Size command on the Format menu. In fact, to change the font, size, style, color, or justification of text, you must first select it with the text tool.

If you had a lot of patience, you could move or resize text areas by creating them in the word processor (with Draw off) and positioning them using the margin and indent settings. But creating text objects and simply dragging them around is much simpler and more appropriate for many tasks.

Columns and linked columns

So far in this chapter, you've seen how you can create text objects and place them precisely on the screen. But the Draw tool offers even more text formatting power. Along with simple text objects, you can create linked columns in which text flows from one column to another.

A text column is slightly different from a text box because it has a specific number and link designation. These designations let Works keep track of where the text goes when you link columns. In any one Works document, you are limited to 32 KB of text in one column or a total of 32 KB of text in several linked columns.

To create a text column:

☐ Choose the text tool from the Tools palette.

☐ Place the insertion point where you want the upper-left corner of the column to be.

☐ Hold down the Option key, press the mouse button, and drag to create the column size you want. (Holding down the Option key tells Works you are creating a text column, rather than a text box.)

After you release the mouse button to fix the size of the column, the column outline appears on the screen, as it does with a text box. In addition, however, Works displays a header at the top of the column, showing the column number and linked column number.

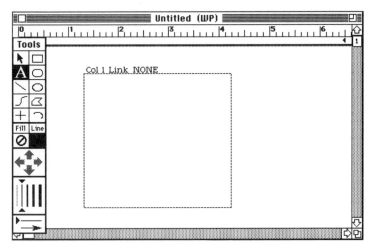

Columns are always numbered in the order you create them, and newly created columns have no link established. These two factors are the reason the header for the first column you create in a document looks like the one just shown.

> **TIP:** You can convert any existing text box into a column. Hold down the Option key while selecting the text box with the selection tool.

You can select and edit a column header exactly as you can select and edit any other text. So although the headers start out with column numbers, you can change them to more descriptive names. You might change the *Col 1* designation in a newsletter to *Lead Story*, for example. The only limitation on editing a column header is that you must keep the same format—*Col ColumnName Link LinkName*, followed by a carriage return—as the default header. You can use uppercase or lowercase letters in a column header. To rename a column *Lead Story*, for example:

☐ Choose the text tool from the Tools palette.

☐ Click on the column to select it.

☐ Select the column number in the header text.

☐ Type *Lead Story*, and the new header will replace the old header.

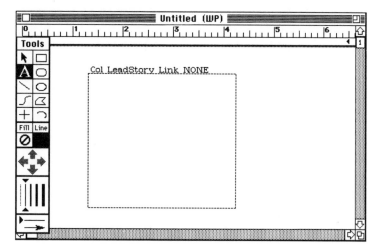

To link two or more columns:

☐ Create the columns as just described.

☐ Choose the selection tool, and hold down the Option key while clicking on the columns in the order in which you want them to be linked.

If you want text to flow from column 1 to column 2, for example, hold down the Option key and click in column 1, then in column 2. The column 1 header will change to show the new link with column 2. You can link columns in any order, whether they're on the same document page or not, and you can change the linking order any time.

To change the linking order of columns:

☐ Hold down the Option key and click in the columns in the new order you want.

Or:

☐ Select the header in each linked column, and change the link number or name to the new order you want.

When you change the linking order of columns, Works displays error messages about existing links. Be sure that the last column linked in the new order doesn't remain linked to a previous column. If your original link order was 1,2,3, for example, and you change it to 3,2,1, the link designation on Column 1 will still be Column 2. Be sure to edit the column header so that the Column 1 link says *None.*

TIP: To avoid getting error messages entirely when changing the linking order of columns, change the links in reverse order, from the last column in the new linking order to the first. To change links 1,2,3 to 3,2,1, for example, you would change the link in column 1 to NONE, then change the link in column 2 from 3 to 1, and finally, change the link in column 3 from NONE to 2.

After you create a column, choose the text tool to enter text in it, or paste text in from the Clipboard.

When you first enter or copy text from the Clipboard into a column that is linked to another column, the text fills up the first column and then extends below the column box—it won't immediately flow from the first column to the second. You must de-select the first text column by clicking anywhere outside its box to have the text distribute itself properly from the first linked column to the next.

New word-processor documents have a default style—the 10-point Boston font—and text boxes and columns in the Draw tool have the same default style whether you are using the Draw tool from the spreadsheet or the word processor. You can change the style by selecting the text column or box and then choosing new text attributes from the Format menu. The following are some simple rules to remember about text styles in the Draw tool:

- When you enter text in a text box or column, the text takes on the style of that text object.

- When you paste text from the Clipboard into a text box or column, the text retains the style it had when you first placed it on the Clipboard.

- You can force text pasted from the Clipboard to take on the style of the text box or column into which you are pasting it by holding down the Option key when you choose the Paste command using the Format menu only (not the Command-V key combination).

TIP: Use the right tool for the job: Use the word processor's superior text-handling features to create and edit large amounts of text, and then create text objects in the Draw tool to design layouts. You can enter large amounts of text in the word processor more quickly, and then use the word processor's spelling checker to make sure your work is letter-perfect. It's best to reserve the text feature in the Draw tool for designing columns, and for entering short bits of text such as headlines. The Draw tool has different memory limits for text, depending on whether you create a simple text box (using the text tool only) or a column (by holding down the Option key), as shown in the following table:

Type of object/column	Memory limit
Text objects only	32 KB each, but as many objects as available memory permits
Individual text columns	32 KB per document
Linked text columns	32 KB total for all linked columns in one document

Spreading text

The final advantage to treating text like an object is that it lets you flow (or spread) text along an arc or diagonal line, rather than simply displaying it on a straight line. Expensive drawing programs let you flow text along a line of any shape; Works 2.0 can spread text only along a diagonal line or an arc.

To spread text:

☐ Make a text box and enter the text you want to spread.

☐ Copy the text to the Clipboard using the Cut command. If you want the original text box to remain in the document along with the spread text version, use the Copy command.

☐ Create the line or arc along which you want to spread the text. The line or arc will remain selected when you finish drawing it.

☐ With the line or arc selected, choose the Spread Text command from the Format menu. The text you copied to the Clipboard will be distributed along the line or arc.

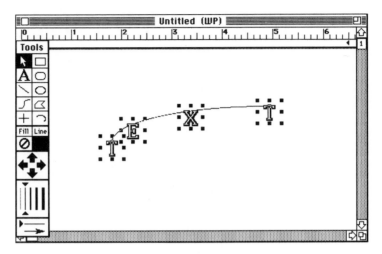

To remove the selection handles click in another part of the screen. Notice that the text is spaced so that it runs the length of the arc. You can change the size, font, style, pattern, or color of each individual letter by selecting it and using the commands on the Format menu. You might also want to select the line or arc you used and delete it.

TIP: If you want to change the spacing between letters or move all of the text together after you spread text, you can treat the entire string as one object by following these steps:

☐ Choose the selection tool from the Tools palette.

☐ Select the first letter in the group.

☐ Hold down the Shift key and select all the other letters, one at a time.

☐ Choose the Group Picture command from the Format menu. After you do this, handles appear around the entire group, and the handles on individual letters disappear.

☐ Drag a handle to resize the entire group, or point to the area inside the handles, hold down the mouse button, and drag to move the whole group.

You can return to working on individual letters by choosing the Ungroup Picture command from the Format menu and selecting any specific letter. The Spread Text command can help you create a lot of interesting visual effects.

A Quick Tour of the Draw Tool's Menus

As mentioned earlier in this chapter, the Draw tool in Works versions 1.0 and 1.1 doesn't alter the word processor's menus or menu commands in any way. In version 2.0, the word processor menus undergo some changes.

The Apple, File, Edit, and Window menus

The Apple, File, Edit, and Window menus remain exactly the same as in the word processor or spreadsheet. (See Chapters 1, 2, and 5 for descriptions of these menus and their commands.)

The Format menu

In Works version 2.0, the Format menu carries most of the Draw-specific functions. It contains exactly the same commands, whether you're using the Draw tool in the word processor or the spreadsheet. The Format menu is divided into two areas, with formatting commands at the top and Draw tool functions below.

The formatting commands Justification, Font, Size, and Style are the same as they are in the word processor's Format menu. Each of these is a hierarchical command that reveals a sub-menu of more specific commands, as you can tell by the arrow to the right of these command names.

The last two formatting commands, Color–Black Dots and Color–White Dots, are the keys to making color drawings in Works using a color Mac with a color monitor. Whenever you use a fill or line pattern with an object, the Draw tool turns on a specific arrangement of pixels to create that pattern. If you fill a square with a solid black pattern, for example, the Draw tool turns all the pixels inside that square black. If you select the white pattern, Works turns all the pixels inside the square white. The other patterns, however, are combinations of black and white pixels.

The Color–Black Dots and Color–White Dots commands let you choose different colors for the white and black pixels used to make up a pattern. Each of these two hierarchical commands reveals a sub-menu containing eight color options: Black, White, Red, Green, Blue, Cyan (light blue), Magenta, and Yellow. By choosing combinations of these colors, you can create lines or filled objects that look like yet another color to the eye using regular patterns of pixels like gray fill patterns, or you can create two-color patterns using irregular patterns of pixels like brick or checkerboard.

- To make a line or object all one color, select the line or object and then choose the same color from both the Color–Black Dots and Color–White Dots menus.

- To blend two menu colors to make a third, choose a fill or line pattern with evenly-distributed dots (rather than one that looks like parallel lines, bricks, shingles, or other items) and then select one Black Dots color and a different White Dots color. Because the pixels are so regularly arranged and so close together in these patterns, the two different colors will seem blended to the eye, exactly as the black and white dots in these patterns create various shades of gray. Depending on the density of dots in the pattern you select, for example, red dots and white dots will create shades of pink.

- To create color patterns, choose line and fill patterns that don't have regularly distributed black and white pixels (bricks or shingles, for example), and then select one color for black dots and a different color for white dots.

If you're blending colors or creating two-color patterns, you'll have to experiment with different color combinations to find ones that look exactly right.

TIP: You can preview mixed colors on the Line Pattern or Fill Pattern menus before applying them to actual objects, as long as you're using a color Mac and a color monitor, by following these steps:

- Choose the black dot and white dot colors you want from the Format menu.

- Hold down the Shift key, and pull down either the Line Pattern or Fill Pattern menu. All the patterns will be displayed with the colors you selected.

It's best not to change the colors of patterns when you're using a monochrome monitor because you might cause the pattern to disappear from the screen. Choosing a dark color for the white dots in a pattern, for example, might cause the whole pattern to look black. You could, however, switch the black dots to white and the white dots to black to produce reverse images of patterns. Also, patterns with dot colors other than black and white will print as solid black on the ImageWriter and LaserWriter IISC (although color patterns will print in shades of gray on a LaserWriter Plus, LaserWriter IINT, or other PostScript-based printer).

The lower half of the Format menu contains commands for manipulating or displaying objects in other ways. The Group Picture command assembles several individual objects into a group so that you can move, resize, or change the fill or line pattern of every object in the group simultaneously. You assemble a group of objects by holding down the Shift key and clicking on all the objects to be placed in the group (or drawing a selection rectangle around the objects) and then choosing the Group Picture command or typing Command-G. The Ungroup Picture command breaks up a group you've established this way and makes each member of the group a separate object again. You can also ungroup a picture by typing Command-U.

The Grid Setting and Grid On commands control an invisible grid you can use to precisely align objects in the Draw tool. If you want to place objects along the same horizontal or vertical line, you can turn on an invisible grid. When the grid is on, everything you draw (including circles, polygons, and freehand lines) lines up with (or "snaps to") the nearest horizontal and vertical line intersection. You'll also notice that when the grid is on and you move an object, the object jumps from one grid point to another rather than moving freely.

The Grid Setting command lets you adjust the coarseness or fineness of the grid in inches $\frac{1}{2}$ to $\frac{1}{36}$ inch) or centimeters (1 to $\frac{1}{14}$ centimeter). The Grid On command turns on the grid. The grid remains invisible whether it's on or off, however. You can tell the grid is on because the Grid On command has a check beside it on the Format menu.

The Bring To Front and Send To Back commands let you choose which of several overlapping objects is on top. When you draw objects that partially or completely overlap each other, the Draw tool keeps each object in its own invisible layer. Whichever object you drew last is the one on top—the one that is completely visible. The Bring To Front and Send

To Back commands let you shuffle a pile of overlapping objects so that you can see one that was formerly hidden.

To see an object that is partially hidden underneath another:

☐ Select the partially hidden object with the selection tool.

☐ Choose the Bring To Front command, or type Command-F.

To see an object that is completely hidden underneath another:

☐ Select the topmost object with the selection tool.

☐ Choose the Send To Back command, or type Command-B.

The Show Column Boxes command controls whether you see column outlines in the Draw tool. When you create a column (by selecting the text tool, holding down the Option key, and dragging the mouse), the outline of the column appears as you draw. Normally, the outline remains visible at all times. But when you choose the Show Column Boxes command, the outline is visible only when the column is selected. (The column header is never visible unless the column is selected.) A check mark appears next to the Show Column Boxes command in the Format menu to show that it has been selected.

The last command on the Draw tool's Format menu is Spread Text. Use this command to paste text onto the path of a diagonal line or arc. The Spread Text command is available only when you have created text in the Draw tool and copied it or cut it to the Clipboard and you have selected either a straight line or an arc on the screen. Otherwise, the Spread Text command is dimmed on the Format menu. You can't spread text along a freehand line, a circle, a square, or a polygon.

The Fill Pattern and Line Pattern menus

The Fill Pattern and Line Pattern menus contain a selection of patterns you can use to add some visual variety to the objects you draw. Both menus contain the same selection of 39 patterns, including one that indicates no pattern at all (which creates a transparent fill or line pattern). The pattern you currently have selected shows up under the Fill or Line box in the Tools palette. Whenever you use the Draw tool with a new document, the fill pattern is set to none (indicated by a slashed circle), and the line pattern is set to black.

There's a difference between the no pattern and white pattern setting on each of these menus. With the no pattern setting, an object is drawn as an outline only, and is transparent in the middle; a white-filled object looks the same, but its inside actually contains a color. You can see the difference when you place both types of object over another object:

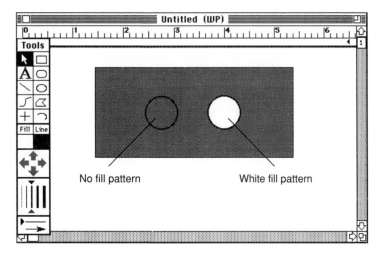

The circle on the left was made with the no-fill option, so you can see through it to the gray pattern in the box underneath it; the circle on the right was filled with white and covers up the gray pattern under it.

Another difference between white-filled and transparent objects is the way in which you can select them. You can select an object filled with the white pattern (or any other except the no-fill pattern, for that matter) by clicking anywhere in its filled area or on its border. To select a transparent object, click on its border. (Clicking inside a transparent object has no effect because the Draw tool considers the object empty.)

As you might guess, the Fill Pattern menu selections apply to areas inside objects created with the oval tool, the rectangle tool, and the polygon tool; the Line Pattern menu selections change the pattern of any drawn line, including freehand lines and curves, as well as the borders of circles, ovals, rectangles, squares, and polygons.

Fill and line patterns can apply only to a particular object or to any object you draw, depending on when you choose the pattern. If you choose a pattern when no objects are selected, that pattern appears in the fill or line box on the Tools palette, and it will affect any subsequent drawing. If you choose a pattern when an object on the screen is selected, the pattern will replace the existing pattern in that object only, and the patterns shown in the fill and line boxes on the Tools palette will remain unchanged.

The Macro menu

The Macro menu contains the same commands in every Works tool, and the macro feature works the same way in each of them. Macros can make reproducing some types of objects or column layouts in the Draw tool much easier. The one major restriction with the Draw tool is that you can't use a macro to draw a freehand object because macros record only

TIP: Despite all the Draw tool's strengths, it has one limitation that needs to be mentioned because it affects your ability to work with large graphics: You can't scroll past the bottom of the Draw tool's screen when working in the word processor.

In any stand-alone drawing program, the screen is a window onto a much larger layout area, and this window scrolls both horizontally and vertically when you draw an object that's bigger than the visible window. When you're drawing an object in the Works word processor, you can scroll horizontally, but you can scroll vertically only one screen beyond the end of your text. So, when you draw in a document that contains *no* text, your drawing can be only one screen tall.

The one-screen vertical limit is a problem with large shapes, but it's particularly annoying when you want to design a full-page layout. You begin creating the column box, only to find that you can't make the column any taller than the screen window, which is less than half a page. Fortunately, there's a solution to this. To create columns or objects taller than the screen window, simply make the document longer by inserting carriage returns to increase its size. To make a full-page, blank document:

the points at which you click and release the mouse button, not the points in between. We'll look at some Draw tool macros in Chapter 4.

Making the Most of the Draw Tool

The Draw tool in Works 2.0 is an improvement over the limited lines and boxes earlier versions of Works were able to produce. It doesn't have the features of a stand-alone drawing program, but the Draw tool in Works 2.0 was expressly intended to complement the word-processor's text-handling strengths and the spreadsheet's number-crunching features. In reviewing the Draw tool's power, we'll see that its strengths come from its close integration with the word processor and spreadsheet, and its weaknesses appear most clearly when it is measured for its sheer drawing or page-layout prowess.

□ Press the Return key repeatedly in the word processor until the first automatic page break—a solid line—appears on the screen. Your document will then be a full page long, but it will still be blank because it contains only invisible carriage returns.

□ Scroll to the top of the document, and then choose Draw On from the Edit menu to activate the Draw tool.

□ Create the column or shape you want. The screen window now scrolls down beyond the end of the document. The line containing the last carriage return you entered now is at the beginning of a new screenful of available drawing area. In other words, you can draw a graphic that's only one screen longer than the word-processor document.

If you'll be doing a lot of large drawings, you can create a blank, one-page word-processor document consisting entirely of carriage returns and then save it with a name such as Drawing Paper, using the Stationery option under the Save As command on the File menu. After that, you can open a new, untitled document that's a full page long whenever you want to draw.

You can create layouts

Any drawing program lets you place objects on a page, but no stand-alone drawing program has Works' column feature. Using the column feature, you can design custom text layouts for newsletters, flyers, flow charts, overhead slides, and dozens of other projects that require precise control over the placement of text in various blocks on a page. The text tool in Works combines the wordwrap, text styling, and editing features of the word processor with the Draw tool's ease of creating and placing objects. The column-linking feature makes it particularly easy to design layouts in which text begins on one page and jumps to another. You can use any of several techniques to make the most of the column feature, particularly with complex layouts.

First, divide the layout, drawings, and text into separate documents. Making a complex layout from start to finish involves designing the layout, creating any graphics you want to add, and writing and editing the text that goes into the layout. You can build a complex layout more efficiently if you focus on one of these activities at a time.

Start with the graphics:

☐ Open a new word-processor document, choose the Draw On command, and create the graphics you want to use in your layout. After you create the graphics, you'll have a good idea how much space they take up, and you'll be able to plan your layout accordingly.

☐ Save this word-processor document using the name Newsletter Graphics or some other descriptive name.

Now plan and create the layout itself:

☐ Sketch a rough layout on paper. Note the size of the columns you want to create, the top and bottom margins, the gutters between columns, and the approximate location and size of any graphics or headlines.

☐ Open a new word-processor document and insert enough carriage returns to extend the size of the draw layer to one full page (or use a piece of Drawing Paper stationery you have already created).

TIP: Works' speed is a function of how much memory you have available: When you have lots of free memory, Works is fast; but when you near the limit of available memory, Works slows down. A full page of complex graphics uses a lot of memory, and (depending on the amount of memory you have available) you might find that it takes a long time for the computer to re-draw the screen each time you make a change or scroll to a different part of the drawing. A one-megabyte Macintosh has ample memory to run the Draw tool fairly quickly, but if you're running under MultiFinder and you have enough memory available, be sure you re-set the Application Memory Size to 1024 KB. (See the MultiFinder User's Manual for the procedure.) The default memory size for Works under MultiFinder is 768 KB, and that's not enough to use the Draw tool effectively.

☐ Draw the columns and text objects in roughly the places you want them to appear on the screen. Use the ruler at the top of the window to gauge the spacing between columns and leave blank areas for the graphics you want to add. Remember that the document's margins are set with the Page Setup command. The ruler at the top of the screen shows merely the width of lines in the document; you have to add any left and right margins to the line width, according to the size of paper you're using. Thus, if you want a newsletter with ½-inch left and right margins, the total width of the lines in your layout can be no more than 7½ inches (assuming you're using paper 8½ inches wide). In a standard two-column layout, you could use two 3½-inch columns with a ½-inch gutter between them.

TIP: If you're creating several identical columns—two columns the same height across a page, for example—it's faster and more accurate to create the first column, copy it, move the selection tool to the general area in which you want the copy to appear, and then paste the copy there.

TIP: If you want the columns to be a certain distance apart, to line up with each other, or both, use Works' precise alignment keys, as follows:

☐ Choose the Grid Setting command from the Format menu, and click on the button representing the size of the grid you want to set. (If you want the columns to be half an inch apart, for example, choose the ½ or ¼ inch setting.) DO NOT TURN THE GRID ON.

☐ Select the second column you drew.

☐ Hold down the V key for vertical alignment (tops lined up, for example); the H key for horizontal alignment (spacing between columns, for example); or the B key for both horizontal and vertical alignment at the same time.

☐ Drag the second column until part of it is on top of the first column, and then move the second column away from the first column until it is roughly aligned with the first column.

☐ Release the mouse button. The second column will snap into line with the first column at the distance you set in the Grid Setting dialog box.

If you turn the grid on, the grid will be relative to the entire document rather than relative to the objects you are working with, existing objects will not snap to it, and the precise alignment won't work. When you use the precise alignment keys with the grid off, however, Works creates an invisible grid that is precisely aligned with edges of the object you drag to, and then it aligns with that first object any objects you select and move while holding down the V, H, or B keys.

☐ Align the columns with one another.

☐ Finally, link the columns in the order in which you would like text to flow.

Your layout is now finished. If you are laying out more than one page, you can change the procedure, depending on whether you want to have linked columns of text flowing from one page to another. If each page is self-contained, use a separate document for each page's layout, and save them as Layout 1, Layout 2, and so on. If you want text to flow from page to page, extend the length of the document for as many pages as you need by inserting carriage returns, watching as page breaks appear, and by watching the numbers in the right-hand scroll box change.

If you'll be re-using the layout in the future, use Works' Stationery option so that you can open this layout as an untitled document whenever you produce a new newsletter.

Next create and edit your text:

☐ Start a new word-processor document, enter the newsletter text, exclusive of headlines. Now you're ready to use the other word-processor tools to shape it up before you place it in the layout:

☐ Use the spelling checker to check for typos;

☐ Format paragraph indents, spacing, and the font, size, and style of the text; and

☐ Save the text as Newsletter Text or something else descriptive.

Finally, put it all together:

☐ Open the document containing the graphic or activate its window, select the graphic, copy it to the Clipboard, and paste it into position in the layout document.

☐ In the layout document, select the graphic and resize it to fit properly between the columns and text boxes. Use the Tools palette to touch up the graphic, if necessary. (Repeat this step and the previous one for each graphic on the layout page.)

☐ Open or activate the text document, select the portion of text that you want to flow into the first column or group of linked columns, and copy it to the Clipboard.

☐ Activate the layout document, and paste the text into the target column.

□ De-select the target column to allow the text to flow from column to column. Repeat this step and the two previous steps until all the text has been pasted into the layout.

□ Use the text tool in the layout document to edit the copy so that it fits properly in the columns.

□ Add any headlines and subheads you need.

You probably won't follow this process exactly the same way each time you create a layout using text and graphics, but these steps provide a good idea of how things will happen in general. As you gain experience with Works, you may well discover better ways of working or find that a different order of operations suits you better.

For now, let's move on to other ways to make the most of the Draw tool's capabilities.

Create a graphics library document or add on a graphics library

A graphics library lets you store individual shapes or drawings and then select one of them easily when you want to re-use it. Architecturally oriented programs, for example, come with their own libraries of common design symbols, including furnishings, electrical symbols, and the like. You can simulate a library feature in either of two ways, depending on how much you use pre-drawn graphics:

- If you use pre-drawn graphics only occasionally, create one word-processor document and copy the drawings you want to re-use into it. Save the file as Standard Graphics or some other descriptive phrase, and then simply open it and copy the graphics from it as you need them. If you have only one or two standard graphics, you can also use the Scrapbook desk accessory on the Apple menu as a place to store them.

- If you use lots of pre-drawn graphics, get a program called SmartScrap, which is a Scrapbook desk accessory that lets you create and access multiple Scrapbook files. A SmartScrap file can also display its contents visually, and you can move directly to the page containing a particular drawing, rather than having to turn the pages in order (as you do in Apple's standard Scrapbook). Finally, you can use SmartScrap's companion desk accessory, The Clipper (included in the same package), to select only a portion of a stored graphic to paste into a drawing, rather than having to select the entire page, as you do in Apple's Scrapbook.

View an entire page with Page Preview

To see an entire page in reduced size, use the Page Preview feature of Works' Print command:

- ☐ Choose the Print command from the File menu, or press Command-P.
- ☐ Click the Print Preview option box so that an X appears in it.
- ☐ Click the OK button or press Return. A reduced, full-page layout appears on your screen.

The Print Preview option remains checked until you specifically un-check it by clicking on it, so you can turn it on once and then get quick, subsequent previews of your document by pressing Command-P (Print) and Return (OK).

Magnify parts of your screen with CloseView

To magnify your screen so that you can see or work on small parts of a drawing more clearly, use the CloseView utility supplied with Apple System Software Version 6.0 or later. CloseView is a program that installs as an icon in the Control Panel and lets you change the magnification of the screen anywhere from two to sixteen times its normal size. It is fully described in the Macintosh Utilities User's Guide supplied with System 6.0 and later.

Re-use page layouts

Thanks to the text-column feature in the Draw tool, you can create handsome page layouts for flyers, newsletters, reports, and other documents. This feature gives Works some of the power of dedicated page-layout programs such as Aldus PageMaker. You can simulate another PageMaker feature—master pages—as well, saving elements that are common to all even-numbered or odd-numbered pages in a document—borders, headers, and so on. Simply save each layout that you create.

TIP: To re-use a layout:

□ Create the layout you want for the first page of a document, select that page, and copy it to a new file.

□ Name the new file First Page Layout or something similar, and save it by using the Stationery option of the Save As command. With the layout saved as stationery, you can open it as an untitled document when you want to use it.

□ As you create other page layouts that you want to re-use, save each page as a separate Stationery file.

□ When you want to make a new document by using previously saved layout files, open a new word-processor document, insert enough carriage returns to make the document as many pages long as you want it to be, and then copy in the individual page layouts from the Stationery files as you need them.

Master pages in page-layout programs let you use different headers on even-numbered and odd-numbered pages of a document. Although Works documents can have only one header throughout, you can add a header to a set of page layouts created with the Draw tool by turning the Draw tool off and then creating the header using the Page Setup dialog box in the word processor. You can't access the Page Setup dialog box when the Draw tool is active.

Aligning objects on the screen

Although Works doesn't have a vertical ruler or a crossbar cursor, features that most stand-alone drawing programs offer to help align objects accurately, it does have some built-in features you can use to align objects precisely with one another or to create objects of an exact size.

To align objects precisely with the edges of the document:

□ Choose the Grid Settings command from the Format menu, and click the grid size you want.

□ Choose the Grid On command from the Format menu.

□ Select the type of object you want to draw from the Tools palette, and then move the insertion point to the place where you want the object to begin. As you move the cursor, it will "snap to" the nearest grid point, according to the size of grid you have selected.

□ Draw the object. As you draw, the object's edges will "snap to" the grid point nearest to the position of the insertion point.

Using this technique, you can line up several objects along a horizontal or vertical line and make them all exactly the same size.

Sometimes, you might begin drawing without the grid on and then want to align one or more objects with an object you've already drawn. To do this:

□ Select the objects you want to align with the original object.

□ Hold down the V key (for vertical alignment only), the H key (for horizontal alignment only), or the B key (for both vertical and horizontal alignment) and drag the object close to where you want it aligned with the original object. When the object is approximately where you want it, release the key, and then release the mouse button.

The alignment keys also let you draw lines exactly in the middle of other objects. If you are creating an organizational chart, for example, you might want to draw connecting lines from the middle of each rectangle in the chart.

To draw a line extending from the middle of a rectangle:

□ Select the straight-line tool.

□ Hold down the B key.

□ Move the cursor to a place close to the mid-point of the rectangle's top line.

□ Draw the line.

□ Release the B key.

□ Release the mouse button.

The line will extend from the exact middle of the top of the rectangle.

You can also use the Draw tool's grid feature to make rectangles, squares, or circles a certain size. If you set the grid at ½ inch and turn the grid on, for example, you can draw a rectangle, square, or circle that is any multiple of ½ inch by dragging it close to that size and letting it snap to the grid. You can also re-scale objects drawn to the grid by selecting them and resizing them to a smaller or larger grid point.

Using the keyboard

Works' pull-down menus and Tools palette make the Draw tool easy to learn for those new to the program. But as you gain expertise, you'll find that using keyboard shortcuts helps you get your work done more quickly. Figure 3-1 contains a list of the keyboard shortcuts that apply to the Draw tool.

DRAW TOOL KEYBOARD COMMANDS

Action	Command	Menu	Keyboard Equivalent
Open a file	Open	File	Command-O
Close a file	Close	File	Command-W
Save a file	Save	File	Command-S
Print a file	Print	File	Command-P
Quit Works	Quit	File	Command-Q
Undo a command	Undo	Edit	Command-Z
Cut a selected object	Cut	Edit	Command-X
Copy a selected object	Copy	Edit	Command-C
Paste a selected object	Paste	Edit	Command-V
Turn Draw on or off	Draw On/Draw Off	Edit	Command-J
Turn on the Help screen	Help	Window	Command-?
Group pictures	Group Picture	Format	Command-G
Ungroup pictures	Ungroup Picture	Format	Command-U
Bring an object to the front	Bring To Front	Format	Command-F

Figure 3-1. *(continued)*
Keyboard commands for the Draw tool.

Figure 3-1. *continued*

DRAW TOOL KEYBOARD COMMANDS

Action	Command	Menu	Keyboard Equivalent
Send an object to the back	Send To Back	Format	Command-B
Start macro recording	Start Recording	Macro	Option-+ (plus)
Stop macro recording	Stop Recording	Macro	Option-- (hyphen)
Play back a macro	Playback and	Macro	Option-Delete
Stop a macro in progress			Command-. (period)
Display the last document on the Window menu			Command-, (comma)
Continue using the same tool			Command
Select multiple objects			Shift-click, or draw selection box
De-select one or more objects in a group			Shift-click
View color patterns on the Line or Fill Pattern menus			Shift-pull menu
Restrict movement to horizontal, vertical, or diagonal			Shift-drag
Align an object horizontally with another			H-drag
Align an object vertically with another			V-drag

(continued)

Figure 3-1. *continued*

DRAW TOOL KEYBOARD COMMANDS

Action	Command	Menu	Keyboard Equivalent
Align an object vertically and horizontally with another			B-drag
Freeze object so that it can't be selected			F-click

These tips and techniques will help you as you use the Draw tool. As you gain experience, you'll discover other ways to create the drawing effects you want.

Draw Tool Specifications

The following are some specifications you might want to refer to as you use the Draw tool.

Maximum file size: Limited by memory, the document size (as indicated by the number of carriage returns), and the number of objects, columns, and fill patterns.

Maximum number of layered objects: Limited by memory.

Maximum size of text object: 32 KB.

Maximum number of text objects per document: Limited by memory.

Maximum size of text columns per document: 32 KB total text in any one column or in all linked columns.

Maximum paper height: 273 inches (with the Custom Size Paper option in the Page Setup dialog box).

Maximum paper width: 15 inches (with the Horizontal option checked in the Page Setup dialog box).

Minimum paper height: 1 inch.

Minimum paper width: 1 inch.

Default page size: 1 screen.

Default font: 10-point Boston.

Chapter 4

Word-Processing Projects

In this chapter, we'll use the Works word processor to help Al Chroma, the owner of Al's Videorama, the video rental store of the future, with some word-processing projects in his business and personal life. Al, a retired film projectionist, wants to apply state-of-the-art retailing techniques to his new business enterprise, so he has purchased a Mac SE, LaserWriter IINT, and Microsoft Works from his local Apple dealer. We'll help Al create a letterhead for the store's stationery, a personal letter to a relative, a sales flyer, an organizational chart, a form letter, and a set of mailing labels.

A Letterhead

Al realizes that stationery is a high priority for a new business. So, although he could have opted for a drab, ordinary-looking letterhead available from a catalog at an instant print shop, he wants to design his own letterhead to reflect the Videorama's unique identity. We can help him by creating a custom logo with Works' Draw tool and then saving the letterhead as stationery so that he can use it to create new files whenever he wants.

Creating a logo

We'll start by creating the logo and address line that go at the top of the letterhead page. Since there is very little text involved in the business name and address, we'll use the Draw tool's text function so we can position the text accurately in relation to the logo we'll create. Figure 4-1 shows the finished logo as printed on Al's new LaserWriter.

Figure 4-1.
LaserWriter printout of Al's Videorama logo.

Al has decided to use a drawing of a television as the main feature of the logo for his business. The name, address, and telephone number of his business will be inside the borders of the television screen. So let's start by typing the text of the name, address, and phone number using the Draw tool's text function.

- □ Open a new word-processor document.

- □ Turn on the Draw tool by pressing Command-J.

- □ Select the text tool and click in the blank document. (Don't worry about the position of the text at this point.)

- □ Type *Al's Videorama* and then press the Return key.

- □ Type the address shown in Figure 4-1 and then press the Return key.

- □ Type the telephone number shown in Figure 4-1.

You now have three lines of text displayed in the Draw tool's default font (Boston 10). We'll want the name of the store to be larger than the address, and we want to use a font other than Boston because Boston 10 isn't a LaserWriter font. We'll change the font and size using the Format menu.

- □ Hold down the mouse button and drag the insertion point across the store name to select it. Then change the font to Helvetica by choosing Helvetica from the Font sub-menu on the Format menu. The font changes, and the text is still selected.

- □ Choose 24 Point from the Size sub-menu to make the text bigger.

- □ Make the text boldface by choosing Bold from the Style sub-menu.

- □ Make the text italic by choosing Italic from the Style sub-menu.

On the Macintosh screen, this text looks blocky (unless we have 24-point Helvetica installed in the System file), but it will look smooth when we print it on the LaserWriter because Helvetica is a resident LaserWriter font. Now that the name of the store is larger, we'll fix the rest of the letterhead text.

- □ Select the address and phone number, and change them to Helvetica bold, using the same techniques just described. Change the size to 12 points.

- □ With the address text still selected, choose the Center option from the Justification sub-menu so that the address and phone number are centered below the store name.

To make the text look like the text in Figure 4-1, we need to add a horizontal line separating the store name from the address. First, we'll make some extra room for the dividing line, and then we'll draw the line.

- □ Using the text tool, click after the *a* at the end of *Videorama* to place the insertion point there, and then press the Return key to add a line between the name and the address.

- □ Select the vertical/horizontal line tool (the cross) from the Tools palette. Because the store's name is so large, let's choose the second line thickness (the third choice from the left in the line width box—the first choice is an "invisible" line).

- □ Drag a line between the store name and the address, from one edge of the store name to the other.

The finished text and dividing line now look like this:

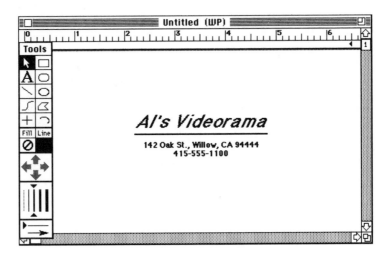

Now we're ready to draw the television logo around this text object. Refer to the finished logo in Figure 4-1 as we draw the various parts of the picture.

- □ Choose the rounded-rectangle tool from the Tools palette.

- □ Select the white fill pattern for the rectangle from the Fill Pattern menu.

- □ Place the crosshair cursor immediately beyond the upper-left corner of the text you've created, hold down the mouse button, and drag the mouse past the lower-right corner of the text. An outline of the box appears as you drag, and you can position the box so that it is approximately centered around the text.

- □ Release the mouse button when the rectangle is the right size.

Because you selected a white fill pattern, the rectangle now covers up the store name and address. To make the name and address visible, select the white rectangle by clicking on it with the selection tool, and then choose Send To Back from the Format menu or press Command-B. Choosing Send To Back moves the rectangle in back of the text.

This rectangle will represent the screen of the logo's television. Now, it's time to draw the cabinet of the television.

- □ Choose the rounded-rectangle tool again, but select a light-gray fill pattern for it from the Fill Pattern menu.

❑ Place the crosshair cursor about ¼ inch outside the upper-left corner of the screen rectangle, hold the mouse button down, and drag the rectangle until it is about ½ inch to the left and ¼ inch below the white rectangle's lower-right corner.

❑ Release the mouse button. Again, the new, gray rectangle is covering the white rectangle and text. So choose the Send to Back command from the Format menu to make everything appear. Now you can see why we chose a white fill pattern for the screen rectangle: If we had used a no-fill pattern, the rectangle would have been transparent, instead of white, and it would have allowed the television-cabinet rectangle's gray fill pattern to show through.

Finally, we'll draw two smaller, rounded rectangles to represent the areas for the television knobs and the speaker.

TIP: If you don't initially draw the screen and television cabinet rectangles of the logo so that they're symmetrical with one another and the text, you can always select them and drag them into position. When an object (like the screen rectangle) is almost the same size as another object it contains (like the text object containing the store name and address), you might find it difficult to select the outer object. In this case, you might keep trying to click on the edge of the screen rectangle, but end up selecting the text object every time instead. When two objects are almost the same size, you can freeze one of them so that you can't select it, and then select the other one easily.

❑ Select the logo text object, hold down the F key, and click on the text object again. The selection handles disappear, which means this object is frozen and can't be selected.

❑ Select and align the screen rectangles as necessary. You can now select it without fear of selecting the text object instead.

❑ To unfreeze the text object, hold down the F key and click on the text object again.

☐ Choose the rounded-rectangle tool and then choose a white fill pattern. Draw the controls area to the right of the television's screen, as in Figure 4-1.

☐ Select the rounded-rectangle tool again, using a horizontal line-fill pattern, and draw the smaller speaker area below the controls area, as in Figure 4-1.

The last parts of the logo are the two television knobs inside the controls area. We'll use circles to represent these.

☐ Choose the oval tool from the Tools palette, and then choose a black fill pattern.

☐ Place the crosshair cursor approximately where the top knob's upper-left edge should be, hold down the Shift key and the mouse button, and drag down and to the left to create a small circle. By holding down the Shift key when you draw a shape using the oval tool, you create a perfect circle. Repeat this process for the lower knob, or simply copy the first knob, and paste.

You might have to try drawing the knobs several times to get them right. If you make a mistake, simply choose the Undo command immediately after drawing, or select a circle and press the Delete key or press Command-X to cut the circle from the drawing.

TIP: To align the two small rectangles representing the controls area and speaker area:

☐ Choose the Grid Setting command from the Format menu, and set the grid to a small increment, such as $\frac{1}{18}$ inch.

☐ Select the speaker rectangle, and then click on the controls area rectangle to select it instead.

☐ With the controls area rectangle selected, hold down the B key and drag the rectangle so that it's approximately in line with the speaker rectangle.

☐ Release the mouse button, and then release the B key. The upper rectangle aligns with the lower one.

Selecting and resizing such small circles would be difficult, as would selecting and dragging them. So you can use the precise-alignment keys.

- ☐ Turn on Apple's CloseView utility to see the results of your actions more clearly.

- ☐ Draw one circle where you want it.

- ☐ Copy the circle to the Clipboard.

- ☐ Paste the copy below the original circle.

- ☐ Select the upper knob, and then select the lower circle.

- ☐ Hold down the B key, and drag the lower circle over the upper circle and roughly into position. Release the mouse button. The lower circle will snap into alignment with the upper one.

The only task remaining in creating the letterhead is to position the logo properly on the page. Al has decided he wants the left edge of the logo to be one inch from the left edge of the paper and the top to be one inch below the top edge of the paper. Al plans to use one-inch top, bottom, left, and right margins in his page setup, so we want to place the logo at the upper-left corner of the document.

- ☐ Point to the word *Tools* in the Tools palette, hold down the mouse button, and drag the palette out of the way so that the upper-left corner of the screen is clear.

- ☐ Be sure the selection tool is active. Then point to the area immediately beyond the upper-left edge of the television drawing, hold down the mouse button, and drag a selection rectangle around the entire television logo. Everything inside the rectangle will be selected.

(If the text object inside the rectangle isn't selected, it's because the ends of the box extend left or right beyond the edges of the selection rectangle. Either use the selection tool to select the text object and make it narrower, or make the selection rectangle you draw wider to include the wider text object.)

- ☐ Drag the logo to the upper-left corner of the screen.

Now our logo is finished, and it's time to save the file so that Al can use it in the future. This basic exercise with the Draw tool shows you some of the tool's strengths and offers some tips for using the tool. It's easy to draw filled shapes and lines, for example, but it's hard to draw very small shapes, select them, and move them. (Because they're so small, you often end up dragging a resizing handle instead of moving the object you're pointing to.) If you want to create logos or other art that can't easily be done with the Draw tool, remember that you can use clip art or another graphics program and import the graphic to the draw layer of a Works word-processor document by means of the Clipboard.

Saving the letterhead as stationery

We'll save the finished letterhead to disk as Al's Letterhead, and we'll use the Stationery option so that it will open as an untitled document each time Al uses it to write a letter.

☐ Select the Save As command from the File menu.

☐ Type the new file name, *Al's Letterhead*, into the space in the dialog box.

☐ Click the Stationery option button below the Save and Cancel buttons to save the document as Stationery.

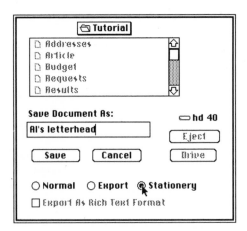

☐ Check the drive indicator to be sure the file will be saved to the proper disk. If you want to save the file to a different disk, click the Drive button to change drives, or click the Eject button and insert a different disk.

☐ Click the Save button to save the file to the current disk.

New files don't have names until you save them. If you use the Save command with an untitled file, Works will display the Save As dialog box, giving you a chance to name the file and select the save option you want. If you want to determine which drive is the current one and have Works warn you if you're about to overwrite an existing file, use the Save As command. Save As produces the dialog box we saw when we used Save, letting you type a different name for your file or change drives before saving.

A Personal Letter

The next day, Al wants to dash off a note to his cousin Lou, explaining about the new store.

Entering the text of the letter

Let's assume Al has just started up Works for the day, and he wants to use his new letterhead.

☐ With Works' opening screen displayed, double-click on the Al's Letterhead file shown in the list box. If the letterhead file is not on the list, change to the correct folder, click the Drive button to look on another disk, or insert the disk on which it is stored.

☐ When the letterhead is displayed, press the Return key a few times to move the insertion point until it is a line or two below the logo.

☐ Choose the Helvetica font from the Font sub-menu (on the Format menu), with 12-point type from the Size sub-menu. Enter the text shown in Figure 4-2. (Don't enter the numbered legend under the drawing yet—we'll get to it later.)

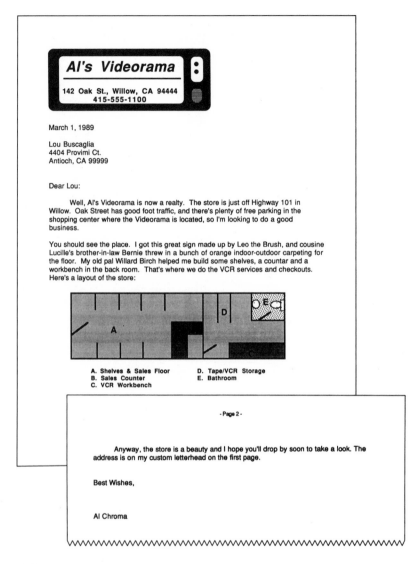

Figure 4-2.
Laser printout of a letter to Al's cousin Lou.

After we've entered the basic text, we'll indent the paragraphs and run the spelling checker. First, indent the first line of the top paragraph.

☐ Place the insertion point anywhere within the first paragraph.

- Point to the bottom of the left indent marker (the black triangle at the left side of the ruler) and press the mouse button. (If the ruler isn't displayed at the top of your document, choose Show Ruler from the Format menu.)

- Drag the first-line indent marker (the square dot) out of the left indent marker until it is below the ½-inch mark on the ruler, and release the mouse button. The first line of the paragraph will be indented ½ inch. (You must point to the bottom of the indent marker to drag the first line indent marker. If you point to the top, you'll drag the indent marker itself, and everything except the first line of the paragraph will be indented.)

We could repeat these steps to indent the first line of the lower paragraph, but it's easier to copy this paragraph's format onto the paragraph below.

- Be sure the insertion point is still within the top paragraph.

- Press Command-K (or choose the Copy Format command from the Format menu).

- Select the last two paragraphs by dragging the mouse over them. (Selecting any part of a paragraph will suffice to apply formats to it.)

- Press Command-Y (or choose Paste Format from the Format menu). The first line of these two paragraphs will now be indented, as well.

We want the closing line and Al's name to be flush left, so we'll leave their formats alone.

Correcting the spelling

To be sure the text is perfect before we use the Draw tool to add the store layout the letter mentions, we'll use the Spell menu to check the document.

- Choose Correct Spelling from the Spell menu.

Works will search for the dictionary file (called MsWorksDict) in the Microsoft Works folder and in the System Folder on your disk. If the dictionary is in a folder with another name, the spelling program will display a dialog box and ask you to locate and open the dictionary file. If Works finds the dictionary file, it will check the document against the dictionary immediately.

☐ In our example, Works won't recognize some of the words in our document because they aren't in the dictionary and will display the Dictionary dialog box, like this:

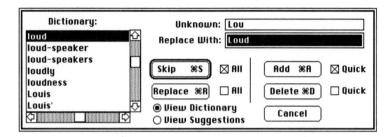

On a Mac Plus or a Mac SE, the Dictionary dialog box covers almost half the screen. You can drag the dialog box around the screen to reveal text that it has covered, if necessary. The first word displayed in the Unknown box is *Lou*, a proper name. Because Al isn't sure how many letters he'll be writing to Lou, we'll skip over this word instead of adding it to the dictionary.

☐ Click the Skip box, press Command-S, or press Return to skip the word.

In fact, the next two words, *Buscaglia* and *Provimi*, also are proper names not known to the dictionary, and Al wants to skip all of them.

☐ Press Return as *Buscaglia* and *Provimi* are displayed in the Unknown box.

The next unknown word is *Ct*, an abbreviation for Court. (Works doesn't include periods at the ends of abbreviations when it displays an unknown word.)

☐ Add *Ct* to the dictionary by pressing Command-A. (You can also click the Add button.)

We'll also add the next two words, *Al's* and *Videorama*, to the dictionary because Al will use these a lot. The next unknown word is *cousine*.

Al has misspelled the word *cousin*, but Works has guessed that the correct spelling is *cousin's*, and has displayed this word in the Replace With box. We know that Al meant to write *cousin*. To fix this spelling error, enter the proper spelling in the Replace With box before clicking the Replace button. There are three options for doing this.

- Edit *cousin's* by deleting the *'s* from the end. Click at the end of the word in the Replace With box and press the Backspace key twice to delete the *'s*.

Or:

- Retype the entire correct spelling in the Replace With box.

Or:

- Scroll the dictionary list (clicking the Up arrow in the scroll bar) to find the correct spelling and then select the word. Works will place the selected word in the Replace With box.

When the correct spelling is in the Replace With box, click the Replace button or press Command-R to replace the spelling in the document.

The next two words, *Lucille's* and *Bernie*, are proper names, so we'll skip those. After that, Works stops on the word *carpeting*. A glance at the Dictionary list tells us that while the dictionary contains the word *carpet*, it doesn't contain *carpeting*. (You have to scroll up the list of words to see *carpet*.) We'll add this word, because we know this is a proper spelling.

Of the remaining words, *Willard* is a proper name, so skip over it; *countar* is misspelled, so scroll the dictionary list to find the right spelling and then select it to put it in the Replace With box. *VCR*, *checkouts*, *Al*, and *Chroma* are proper names or words we'll add to the dictionary.

> **TIP:** Unless you know you want to add several suffix variations of a word to the dictionary when you check documents, click the Quick option box next to the Add and Delete buttons so that Works will add only the word in the Unknown box to its dictionary, rather than displaying a list of optional suffix variations for you to decide whether to add.

Works has now checked the entire document, and asks us if we want it to remember which words were skipped when we check this document in the future.

☐ Click the Yes button so that only new mistakes we introduce in future edits will be questioned during spelling checks of this document. (If you tell Works not to remember skipped words and you haven't added those words to the dictionary, it will question those words each time you check the document's spelling.)

After we tell Works to remember the skipped words in this document, the spelling function shows how many words are in the document, and how many words were unknown to the dictionary.

☐ Click the OK button to return to document editing.

Now we've finished correcting errors in the document—or have we? One remaining mistake in this document points out the limitations of all spelling programs, including the one in Works: The spelling checker won't tell you if a word contained in its dictionary is misused. Although you can set the Works homonym dictionary to check for misused homonyms (to, too, and two, for example), Works can't check for other proper words in the wrong places.

In the first sentence of the letter, Al has used the word *realty* when he actually means *reality*. Because *realty* is a perfectly good word, the spelling checker didn't catch it. That's why it pays to proofread documents yourself, even after you've run the spelling checker. Because we're back in the document-editing window now, we can simply fix this error ourselves.

Drawing a floor plan

As you can see by the text of the letter, Al wants to include a simple floor plan of the store for his cousin Lou. This is another good time to use the Draw tool. According to the text of the letter, though, the layout should appear after the second paragraph of text. To make room for it, we'll add some carriage returns to create blank drawing space.

☐ Click to the right of *store:* in the last line of the second paragraph to move the insertion point there.

☐ Press Return until the page-break indicator appears.

The amount of space between the bottom of the last paragraph and the bottom of the first page should be plenty for our drawing. Let's begin by creating the outer walls of the store.

□ Activate the Draw tool by pressing Command-J.

□ Select the rectangle tool from the Tools palette.

□ Move the cursor a half an inch to the right of the text margin, and about a quarter inch below the last line of text. Hold down the mouse button, and drag the mouse until the rectangle is about 2 inches high and its right edge is about an inch to the left of the right text margin (under the 5½-inch mark on the ruler). The document now looks something like this:

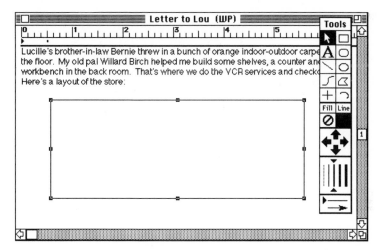

Remember, you can adjust the size or position of this rectangle or any object you draw in Works by selecting it and dragging its border to move it, or by dragging one of its handles to resize it.

Before we draw the interior walls and fixtures in the store, we'll embellish the entire store space a little.

□ Select the rectangle by clicking on its border.

□ Choose the next heaviest line width from the line-width box on the Tools palette.

□ Choose a light-gray fill pattern from the Fill Pattern menu.

Now, let's draw some walls, shelves, and other fixtures.

☐ Choose the straight-line tool (the crosshair).

☐ Choose the same line thickness used for the walls (if it isn't already selected).

☐ Place the cursor about 2 inches from the right edge of the rectangle, and draw a straight, vertical line from the top of the rectangle to the bottom. To make the ends of this line meet exactly with the horizontal wall lines, place the horizontal bar of the crosshair cursor directly on top of the wall line (it turns white when the cursor is on it), both before you press the mouse button to start drawing the vertical line and before you release the mouse button when you finish. The layout now looks like this:

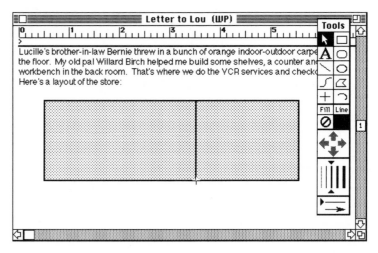

Note how the crosshair cursor has turned white because it's on top of the horizontal wall line.

Now we'll draw a few lines to indicate shelves for videotapes, a filled rectangle to represent the check-out counter, and a rectangle with a slightly different fill pattern to indicate the bathroom in the back part of the store. Remember, any new lines or rectangles you draw will appear on top of the original outer-walls rectangle. To draw a filled rectangle, like the one for the store counter, set the fill pattern after choosing the rectangle tool, but before actually drawing the object.

Finally, we'll use the text tool to add some numbers and a legend so that Al's cousin Lou will know exactly what the drawing contains. The finished drawing looks like this:

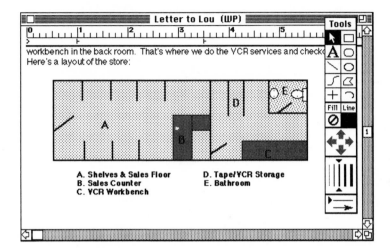

The text inside the drawing was added with the Draw tool; the legend below the drawing was typed in the word processor itself. Adding text in the Draw layer is easy.

- ☐ Click on the text tool in the Tools palette.

- ☐ Choose the no-fill pattern from the Fill Pattern menu.

- ☐ Choose 14-point Geneva bold from the Format menu.

- ☐ Click the pointer in the middle of the floor between the shelves in the front area of the store, and type *A*.

- ☐ Click the pointer on the sales counter and type *B*.

- ☐ Repeat this process for areas C, D, and E, as shown in the previous illustration.

Because we're using Geneva text, it won't appear quite as smooth on the screen as it will when it's printed on Al's LaserWriter. Don't worry about how each character looks, but if the text doesn't fall exactly where you want it in the drawing, move it.

- ☐ Choose the selection tool from the Tools palette and click on the text box you want to move. Handles appear on the text box.

- Grab a handle at one end of the box and drag to shrink the box so that it's a little bigger than the letter the box contains. (Remember, Works always creates a text box about 3 inches long, no matter how much text you type.)

- Point to the middle of the text box and drag it to where you want it.

- Click anywhere away from the text box to hide its handles and to see the new position of the letter clearly.

The handles for narrowing the text box containing the letters at the right side of the drawing will be off the screen to the right, but you can scroll the document to the right by clicking in the bottom scroll box to reveal these handles. Then you can drag them to the left, toward the letter they contain.

To add the text for the legend, return to the word processor and place the labels in two columns under the drawing. If your store layout drawing is too tall, you might not have enough room on the page to type three lines of legend text. (You'll see the page break line at the bottom of the screen.) Rather than printing the legend on another page, resize the drawing to make it a little shorter, or move it up toward the bottom of the second paragraph.

- Choose the selection tool from the Tools palette.

- Drag a selection rectangle around the entire store-layout drawing.

- Point to the middle of the drawing, hold down the mouse button, and drag the drawing up.

Or:

- Point to the middle handle on the bottom border of the outer rectangle and drag up to make the drawing shorter. (You'll have to reposition the drawn elements in the lower half of the drawing, as well.)

There are five legend items, so we'll put the A, B, and C items in the first column, and the D and E items in the second.

- Click in the left margin directly under the drawing, and press Return to move down a space.

- ☐ Choose 12-point Helvetica bold type from the Format menu.
- ☐ Click in the Ruler at the 1-inch and 3½-inch marks to set two tabs.
- ☐ Press the Tab key and type *A. Shelves & Sales Floor.*
- ☐ Press the Tab key again and type *D. Tape/VCR Storage.*
- ☐ Press Return and then Tab, and type *B. Sales Counter.*
- ☐ Press Tab and type *E. Bathroom.*
- ☐ Press Return and then Tab, and type *C. VCR Workbench.*

The floor plan is done. Check to be sure there aren't any extra carriage returns at the top of the second page of the letter before going on: The text of the third paragraph (beginning *Anyway, the store is a beauty*) should be directly under the page-break marker.

Numbering pages and printing

Before Al prints the letter, he wants to add a page number to the second page of the letter.

- ☐ Turn off the Draw tool by pressing Command-J.
- ☐ Choose the Page Setup command from the File menu.
- ☐ Click in the Header box and type *&C- Page &P -.*
- ☐ Format the header while the Page Setup dialog box is still active. Using the Format menu, choose 9-point Helvetica type.

This header command will center the page number (the &C command) and insert the text - *Page 2 -.* The &P command tells Works to print the current page number. (For a complete list of header and footer formatting and page numbering commands, see "Making the Most of the Word Processor" in Chapter 2 of this book or check your Microsoft Works User's Guide.)

At this point, Al's header command will print a page number on both the first and second pages of the letter. A page number on the first page would mar the impact of his letterhead, so Al wants the number to print only on page 2. This calls for the Title Page command, which suppresses a page number on the first page of a document.

- ☐ Choose the Title Page command from the Format menu. The command is checked when it's active.

To see how the letter looks before he actually prints it, Al can use the Print Preview feature in the Print dialog box.

☐ Choose the Print command from the File menu.

☐ Click on the Print Preview box in the lower-left corner.

☐ Press the Return key, or click the OK button. A reduced version of the first page of the letter will appear on the screen, like this:

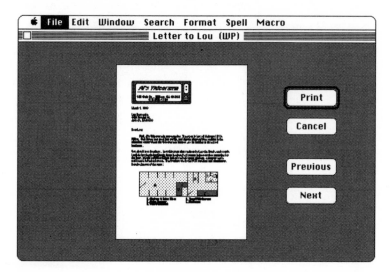

To see the second page, click the Next button. You can also print directly from this screen by clicking the Print button, or cancel the operation and return to the document by clicking the Cancel button.

A Sales Flyer

As part of his promotional effort, Al will print handbills announcing the Videorama's grand opening and distribute them in supermarket parking lots. Because we already have that nice letterhead in a disk file, we can use it as the basic form for the flyer and then build on it. Let's load the letterhead file and then get to work.

☐ Load the file, Al's Letterhead.

This stationery file will open as an untitled document. The basic letterhead is fine for written correspondence, but a flyer being handed out to shoppers headed to or from their cars needs to be more of a grabber. We'll jazz up the format a little with the Draw tool.

Let's assume we've designed the basic layout of the flyer on paper, and we're ready to create the appropriate text boxes, fill patterns, and other effects with the Draw tool. The finished flyer is shown in Figure 4-3.

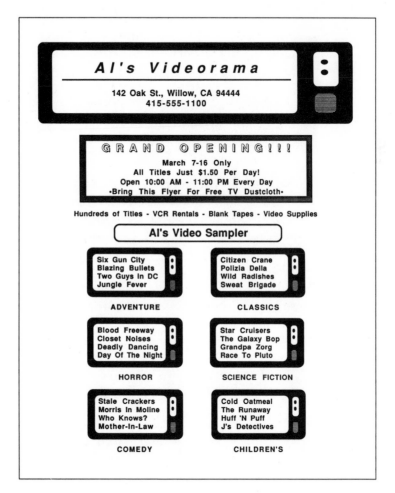

Figure 4-3.
Sales flyer.

As you can see, this flyer contains several distinct blocks of text, each of which is formatted in a different way. The Draw tool's text boxes are ideal for such a layout.

Creating a blank draw page

We want to use the same store logo we designed for Al's letterhead, so we'll start with a new page of letterhead stationery. But we need to use the whole page with the Draw tool, and that means inserting a number of carriage returns in this document until the first page break is shown. Because it's likely that we'll often need a full page of carriage returns to use as blank Draw tool letterhead, we'll save this page of carriage returns as a stationery document we can re-use.

- ☐ Open the Al's Letterhead document.

- ☐ Insert carriage returns until the first page break appears and the insertion point is below the page break.

- ☐ Save the document with the name, Draw Page w/Logo, and click the Stationery option before saving it.

Now we can load a new, untitled drawing page any time and not have to worry about inserting carriage returns. If we don't want to use the logo, we can simply select it and delete it, or we can create another stationery page containing only carriage returns without the logo.

Centering the logo

With our page ready to go, we first want to move and enlarge the store logo so that it occupies most of the width of the page and is centered, rather than flush with the left margin, as it is now.

The first step is to decide how wide we want the printing on the page to be. Because this is a flyer, we'll want more space for text and graphics than we would in a normal letter. Let's set the document margins at $\frac{1}{2}$ inch all around, rather than the normal 1 inch.

- ☐ Choose Page Setup from the File menu.

- ☐ Double-click in the Left Margin box to select it, and type .5.

- ☐ Press the Tab key to move to and select the Top Margin box, and type .5.

- ☐ Press the Tab key again to move to the Right Margin box, and type .5 again.

❑ Press the Tab key once more to move to the Bottom Margin box and type *.5* again.

❑ Press the Return key or click the OK button to save these changes to the page setup and return to the document.

With only ½ inch on the left and right of the page used by margins, our lines can be 7½ inches long (assuming we're using regular, 8½ by 11 paper). Even though we won't be typing text in the word processor, it's a good idea to drag the right indent marker to the 7½-inch mark on the ruler so that we can use it as a positioning guide as we draw the layout.

With a longer line length established, we can stretch the logo to fill the extra space.

❑ Turn on the Draw tool by selecting it from the Edit menu or by pressing Command-J.

❑ Drag a selection rectangle around the entire logo. (Because the logo is positioned against the top of the document, the easiest way to select the logo is to point to the lower-left corner, press the mouse button, and drag to immediately past the right edge of the logo and up to the top of the screen, to surround the logo.)

At this point, the entire logo is selected, and you can drag the handle in the middle of its right side out to the 7½-inch mark on the ruler. If the text box containing the name and address doesn't stretch with the graphics, it's because you didn't select it (the text box was too wide to be selected with the selection rectangle you drew, as described earlier). To select the text box as well:

❑ Select Undo from the Edit menu, or press Command-Z, if you have already stretched part of the logo.

❑ Repeat the previous step, selecting the entire logo. If the text is still not selected, hold down the Shift key (to maintain the selected graphics and expand the selection) and click on the name *Al's Videorama* to select the text block. Now, both the logo graphics and text box are selected, as you can see by the selection handles that appear on them.

After you drag the logo's handle to the right to stretch it, however, you'll see that while the text is centered on the screen in the logo, the text still is sized to fit the smaller screen of the letterhead logo:

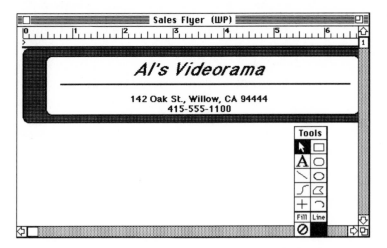

The easiest way to stretch this text to fill the entire screen is to insert spaces between the store name letters and use a different font size for the address and phone number.

- □ Click on the text tool in the Tools palette, and then select the text name, *Al's Videorama.*

- □ Change the type style to Normal by using the Format menu. (We're changing the style of this text because it's easier to place the insertion point between regular letters than italic letters.)

- □ Move the insertion point between the *A* and the *l* in *Al's*, and insert a space. Repeat this for every pair of letters in the name, and leave three spaces (instead of one) between *Al's* and *Videorama.*

- □ Select the entire name again, and change the style back to italic.

For the address, we'll simply enlarge the type from 12-point to 14-point Helvetica.

- □ Select the address and telephone number with the text tool.

❑ Choose 14 Point from the Format menu's Size sub-menu.

The rest of the flyer is a series of text boxes, some of which have filled rectangles, rounded rectangles, or television logos around them.

Text in graphic boxes

The box containing the grand opening information is one filled rectangle.

❑ Select the rectangle tool from the Tools palette.

❑ Choose a gray fill pattern from the Fill Pattern menu.

❑ Choose the black line pattern from the Line Pattern menu.

❑ Choose a medium line thickness from the Line Thickness box.

❑ Drag a rectangle about 5½ inches long and about 1½ inches tall under the Videorama logo, as shown in Figure 4-3. The box should start approximately below the 1-inch mark on the ruler and end at about the 6½-inch mark. (You can always resize or move the rectangle to get it in the right spot.)

Now, we'll add the text inside the rectangle.

❑ Select the text tool and, holding down the mouse button, drag a box that fits snugly inside the borders of the rectangle you just drew.

❑ Type *GRAND OPENING!!!*, adding a space between each letter and three spaces between *GRAND* and *OPENING*.

❑ Press Return, and type the text of the second line, as shown in Figure 4-3.

❑ Type the text of the third and fourth lines.

❑ With the text tool still selected, drag the pointer across the first line of text to select it.

❑ Choose Helvetica from the Font sub-menu, 18 Point from the Size sub-menu, Bold and Shadow from the Style sub-menu, and Center from the Justification sub-menu.

❑ Select the second two lines of text, and choose Bold from the Style sub-menu and Center from the Justification sub-menu.

◻ Click the selection tool in the Tools Palette to see how the letters look. The text box appears as a white box on top of the shaded fill of the larger rectangle, as in Figure 4-3. The text is centered inside the text box. Select the text box itself with the selection tool and then resize the box to make it align more evenly with the edges of the filled rectangle.

Now that you've finished this text box, you should have no trouble with the other elements of this flyer. The line of text below the grand opening box is simply a text box containing 12-point Helvetica bold type. You'll have to draw a wider text box than the 3-inch box Works creates for you when you choose the text tool. After you enter the text and format it, you may have to select the text box with the selection tool and drag it so that it's centered under the grand opening box.

The box that contains the text *Al's Video Sampler* uses 18-point Helvetica bold, centered, with a rounded rectangle around it. Be sure to use the no-fill pattern when you create the rounded rectangle; otherwise, use the white fill pattern and then send the box to the back so that the text inside it is in front. Again, when you complete the box and text, you can select and drag them to center them on the flyer.

Creating and formatting the text inside the television screens

The last parts of the flyer are the six television screens containing featured video titles in each of six categories. These elements present a bit more of a challenge because they must be aligned with each other and centered on the flyer. We've already drawn a nice television for Al's letterhead, so we'll copy that one, resize it, change the text it contains, and then make five additional copies of the modified graphic to finish the flyer.

◻ Open the stationery document Al's Letterhead.

◻ Turn on the Draw tool.

◻ Drag a selection rectangle around the logo. (It doesn't matter whether the text of the logo is selected because we won't be using this text anyway.)

◻ Press Command-C or choose Copy from the Edit menu to copy the logo to the Clipboard.

◻ Choose the Sales Flyer document from the Window menu to activate it. The Draw tool is still on.

□ Scroll to the blank area below the box that says *Al's Video Sampler,* and click the selection pointer. (This tells Works where to paste the copy from the Clipboard.)

□ Press Command-V or choose Paste from the Edit menu. The copy of the logo appears:

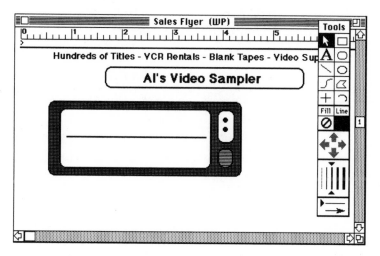

Now we need to resize this logo to the proper shape and prepare the drawing of the screen to hold the text of movie titles.

□ Drag a selection rectangle around the logo.

□ Drag the handle in the lower-right corner of the logo up and to the left so that the television shrinks to about 2¼ inches wide and about 1¼ inches tall.

You'll notice in the previous illustration that the logo still contains the dividing line that separates the name of the store from its address and phone number. We want to get rid of this line, but we can't select it—even by using the F key technique described in the letterhead exercise—because trying to do so invariably selects the entire drawing of the screen, not simply the line. Instead, we'll replace the drawing of the screen with a new, blank one.

□ Click on the drawing of the screen to select it.

□ Press the Delete key, press Command-X, or choose Cut from the Edit menu.

- □ Choose the rounded-rectangle tool, select the white fill pattern on the Fill Pattern menu, and drag to create a new rectangle over the filled rectangle.

Finally, we need to fill this new, blank drawing of a screen with video titles.

- □ Choose the text tool and drag to create a text box that fits just inside the screen border.
- □ Choose 12-point Helvetica bold from the Format menu.
- □ Type the adventure video titles shown in Figure 4-3. (Type each movie name and press Return.)
- □ Choose the selection tool from the Tools palette. Select the text box and drag it to center the titles on the screen, if necessary.

Finally, we'll add the title of the video category beneath this television graphic.

- □ Choose the text tool, and click beneath the television graphic. This action creates a one-line by 3-inch text box.
- □ Choose 12-point Helvetica bold, centered, from the Format menu.
- □ Type *ADVENTURE*.
- □ Select the text box by using the selection tool and center it about ¼ inch below the television graphic.

Let's use this graphic as a template for the five other television screens.

- □ Drag a selection rectangle around the television and the text box containing the category name.
- □ Press Command-G or choose Group Picture from the Format menu. Grouping the pictures makes it much easier to select and position the objects.
- □ Press Command-C or choose Copy from the Edit menu.
- □ Click the pointer about 1 inch below and 2 inches to the side of the completed ADVENTURE logo.
- □ Press Command-V or choose Paste from the Edit menu.

Repeat the last two steps four more times, until you have six copies of the smaller television logo, as in Figure 4-3. Be sure to click well away from other copies as you paste them into the document so that each copy of the logo is by itself—it'll be easier to select and move them that way.

Aligning objects with each other

The rest of this exercise amounts to moving the six television logos into line with each other and with the rest of the document, as well as replacing the text in each of the five new logo copies so that they represent the other video categories shown in Figure 4-3. We'll line up the logos first. We'll use Works' Print Preview feature frequently to be sure our flyer is arranged the way we want it as we complete it.

By "eyeballing" the logos, we'll line up the first category logo under the text that begins *Hundreds of Titles* (see Figure 4-3) and then use the alignment keys to arrange the five other logos in line with it.

- □ Select the original adventure screen and category name.

- □ Drag it until the television's left edge is ¼ inch inside the left margin of the *Hundreds of Titles* line. (The television's left edge should line up with the 1⅛-inch mark on the ruler at the top of the screen.)

- □ Press Command-P or choose Print from the File menu.

- □ Click the Print Preview box.

- □ Press Return or click the OK button to see how the flyer will look when printed out. If the first logo isn't aligned properly, return to the document and fix it. (Click the Cancel button on the Print Preview screen to return to the document.)

- □ Choose the Grid Settings command on the Format menu and click the ⅛-inch setting button. DON'T TURN THE GRID ON.

- □ Select the first television logo by clicking on it.

- □ Click on the second television logo and title, hold down the B key, point to the center of the logo, and drag the entire selection until the television's bottom edge is roughly on the same horizontal line as the first television's, and its left edge is roughly under the 4-inch mark on the ruler.

□ Release the mouse button and then the B key. The first logo copy will align vertically and horizontally with the adventure logo.

□ Print the flyer, using the Print Preview command, to see how the alignment looks and to adjust it if necessary.

Now, we'll align the second two logos.

□ Select the first television logo again.

□ Select the third logo, hold down the B key, and drag the logo until it is about ¼ inch below the category name, *ADVENTURE*, in the left-hand logo on the first line.

□ Release the mouse button and then the B key.

□ Align the third and fourth logos.

□ Align the fifth logo with the left-hand logo in the second row.

□ Align the sixth logo with the fifth logo.

As you work, use Print Preview to be sure elements are lining up right. Another trick to double-check your alignment is to use the straight-line tool to draw two long lines—one horizontal, one vertical. Position these lines by clicking on them and dragging them in place relative to the logo you are using as your guide. Using this procedure, you can see how the others are lining up. Delete the guide lines when you complete the drawing.

Editing text boxes

All that remains is to replace the text on the logo copies so that they match the flyer in Figure 4-3.

□ Select the second logo and press Option-Command-U, or choose Ungroup Picture from the Format menu.

□ Use the text tool to select the text on the television screen in the second logo and type in the names in the classics category.

□ Use the text tool to select the category name *ADVENTURE* under the second logo and type *CLASSICS.*

□ Repeat the last three steps for the other four logos.

Be sure to check the spelling of all the words in the flyer manually. Because this text was created with the Draw tool, we can't use the spelling checker on it. When the flyer is finished, check it on the Print Preview screen to be sure everything looks good.

Because we're using the Helvetica font (which is a LaserWriter font) and Al has a LaserWriter, the flyer should print almost exactly as it appears on the screen. If some of the graphics or text don't print out exactly where you want them, adjust these elements individually in the document by selecting them and moving or resizing them. And don't forget: Save the finished document as Sales Flyer.

An Organizational Chart

After Al hires his employees, he wants to make an organizational chart showing where everyone fits in the Videorama hierarchy. This is another graphic-intensive document in which we can use the Draw tool to do everything.

All the boxes in this chart are rounded rectangles with medium black borders and no fill pattern. The text inside them is entered with the text tool. The finished chart is shown in Figure 4-4.

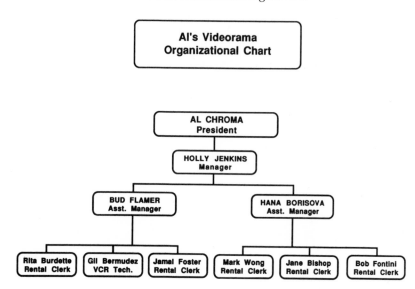

Figure 4-4.
An organizational chart for Al's Videorama.

As you can see, we've used the sideways printing option from the Page Setup dialog box to print the chart sideways on paper so that we have the room we need for the boxes on the chart. It's a good idea to make a stationery document for drawing in this sideways orientation, so let's make one.

☐ Open a new word-processor document.

☐ Choose Page Setup from the File menu.

☐ Click the sideways icon under Orientation.

☐ Set ½-inch top, bottom, left, and right margins.

☐ Press Return or click the OK button to return to the document.

☐ Drag the right-indent marker on the ruler until it is under the 10-inch mark.

☐ Press Return as many times as is necessary to make the first page break appear and the insertion point appear below it.

☐ Save the document as Wide Draw Page and click the Stationery button to save it as stationery.

Now, we can begin drawing the chart on the copy of this blank draw document that is still on the screen.

Drawing and copying boxes

All the boxes in the chart are created with the same tool, but we won't use the rounded-rectangle tool to put every box on the screen.

☐ Turn Draw on, and choose the rounded-rectangle tool with a medium line thickness (the third option from the left in the line thickness box on the Tools palette) and no fill pattern.

We want the boxes to be centered on the screen. Because Works' Justification options work only with text, we'll have to "eyeball" the position of the upper boxes and then line up the lower boxes with them to create a symmetrical chart. We know that we now have a document that's 10 inches wide, so let's draw a title box 4 inches wide, a box for Al's name about 3 inches wide, and manager and assistant manager boxes 2 inches wide. These measurements will leave 1 inch of space between boxes.

☐ Place the cursor under the 3-inch mark on the ruler, about ½ inch down from the top of the page, and drag a rectangle that's about 1 inch tall so that its left edge is lined up under the 7-inch mark on the ruler.

□ Hold down the Command key (to continue working with the same tool) and, starting ½ inch below the bottom of the title box, draw a second box 3 inches wide and ½ inch tall between the 3½-inch and 6½-inch marks on the ruler.

□ Hold down the Command key again and draw a third box for the store manager ½ inch below Al's box and running between the 2-inch and 4-inch marks on the ruler.

Instead of drawing the two assistant manager's boxes from scratch, we'll duplicate the manager's box and then use the alignment keys to place the two assistant managers' boxes on the same horizontal plane.

□ Select the manager's box (the 2-inch box you just drew).

□ Press Command-C or choose Copy from the Edit menu to copy it to the Clipboard.

□ Choose the selection tool from the Tools palette and click below and to the left of the box you just copied.

□ Press Command-V or choose Paste from the Edit menu. The duplicate box appears.

□ Click again, this time to the right of the duplicate box you just pasted in, and press Command-V again to paste another box.

We've placed the title, president, and manager boxes in line with each other, but now we need to align the two assistant managers' boxes with each other.

□ Choose the ¼-inch setting in the Grid Settings dialog box. (The Grid Settings command is on the Format menu.) DON'T TURN THE GRID ON.

□ Select the assistant-manager box that's on the left and drag it so that it is about ½ inch below the manager box and its left edge is roughly under the 2-inch mark on the ruler.

□ Select the assistant-manager box that's on the right, hold down the H key (for Horizontal alignment), and drag the box so that it's between the 6-inch and 8-inch marks on the ruler, and roughly on the same horizontal plane as the box to its left.

□ Release the H key and then the mouse button. The box should "snap to" the same horizontal line as the other assistant-manager box.

We'll use the same method of drawing one box and duplicating it to create the six sales-clerk boxes. There's already a copy of the assistant-manager box on the Clipboard, so let's duplicate it in the row below those two boxes.

☐ Click the selection tool in the area below the assistant-manager box that's on the left and press Command-V. A duplicate of the box appears.

As you can see from the completed chart in Figure 4-4, the sales clerk boxes are narrower, only about 1½ inches wide. We'll resize and place this first box, and then duplicate it five times.

☐ Select the box you just pasted into the document (the first sales clerk box).

☐ Drag the handle in the middle of its right border toward the center of the rectangle, until the box is about 1½ inches wide.

☐ Drag the box until it is about ½ inch below the row of assistant-manager boxes and about ¼ inch from the left margin of the document.

☐ Copy the box to the Clipboard.

☐ Click the pointer to the right of the box and paste in a duplicate.

☐ Repeat the last step four more times as you paste in boxes across the bottom row of the chart.

Now, you have all the boxes you'll need in the chart, but they're probably not aligned and spaced properly. We'll use the alignment keys.

☐ Choose ¼ inch from the Grid Settings box on the Format menu. DON'T TURN THE GRID ON.

☐ Select the box at the left edge of the document.

☐ Select the second box from the left, hold down the B key, and drag the box until it is approximately ¼ inch from and on the same horizontal plane as the box on the left.

☐ Release the B key and then the mouse button. The box snaps into alignment.

☐ Select the two aligned boxes by dragging a selection rectangle around them or Shift-clicking.

☐ Select the third box, hold down the B key, and drag the box roughly into position with the two selected boxes: ¼ inch to the right and on the same horizontal plane.

☐ Continue this process until all six boxes line up.

This is a good time to save this document. Save it as Organizational Chart before you continue. It's also a good time to check the overall layout and spacing of the chart with the Print Preview command.

☐ Choose Print from the File menu or press Command-P.

☐ Click the Print Preview option in the Print dialog box.

☐ Press Return or click the OK button. The layout appears on the screen.

If you've followed these instructions, the boxes are centered on the page and aligned with each other. But there's a lot of extra blank space at the bottom of the page, so the chart looks squished up against the top of the page. Let's fix that.

☐ Click the Cancel button in the Print Preview window.

☐ Drag a selection rectangle around all the boxes on the chart, except the title box at the top.

☐ Point to the border of any box and drag the group of boxes down about ¾ inch. Be sure you drag straight down, rather than moving the group of boxes to the left or right. (You must point to the border of a box to drag; otherwise you'll de-select the boxes.)

Now, there's room to make the title box even deeper, so select it and drag the handle in the middle of its lower border down about ¼ inch.

> **TIP:** You can be sure to drag any object or text object along a perfectly straight line by holding down the Shift key as you drag. Simply select the object, press the Shift key, hold down the mouse button, and drag the object where you want it. The movement will be constrained to horizontal, vertical, or 45-degree diagonal lines.

Drawing the lines

The next step is to draw the connecting lines that indicate the specific chain of command. Again, we can use the precise alignment keys to be sure the lines connect to the middle of each box.

First, we'll draw the horizontal lines. As you can see in Figure 4-4, we need horizontal lines above the two assistant-manager boxes, and above each of two groups of three sales-clerk boxes.

◻ Select the straight-line tool.

◻ Place the vertical part of the cross cursor as close to the middle of the assistant-manager box on the left as you can and the horizontal crossbar on the cursor about ¼ inch above the border of the box.

◻ Draw a line to the right, stopping when the vertical bar in the crosshair is in the middle of the top line of the assistant-manager box on the right.

◻ Repeat this process for each of the two groups of three sales-clerk boxes, as in Figure 4-4.

Now for the vertical lines.

◻ Select the straight-line tool again and place the center of the crossbar cursor near the middle of Al's box.

◻ Hold down the B key, press the mouse button, and drag the line down until the crossbar on the cursor overlaps the top part of the border of the manager box.

◻ Release the B key and then the mouse button. The line appears. (Because we held down the B key before drawing the line from Al's box, the line came out of the box exactly in the middle, as long as we were within the distance indicated in the Grid Setting dialog box.)

◻ Repeat the last three steps for the line connecting the manager box with the horizontal line linking the assistant-manager boxes.

Now, we'll connect the ends of the line linking the two assistant-manager boxes with each manager box.

- □ Select the straight-line tool again.
- □ Place the crosshair cursor so that its center is directly on top of the left end of the horizontal connecting line.
- □ Drag a line straight down until the crossbar in the cursor overlaps the top of the assistant-manager box.
- □ Repeat this process for the other assistant-manager box.

By now, you get the idea of how to connect lines with boxes. Let's move on to the text.

Entering the text

We'll enter each name and title as a text box. We'll draw a text box inside each graphic box and then center the text inside it.

- □ Scroll the document so that the title box is visible.
- □ Choose the text tool from the palette.
- □ Click in the center of the title box.
- □ Select 18-point Helvetica bold, with center justification from the Format menu.
- □ Type *Al's Videorama*, press Return, and type *Organizational Chart*.
- □ Drag the text box to center it, if necessary.

The rest of the boxes contain text in 12-point Helvetica bold. If, as you create each text box and enter the text, you find that the text isn't perfectly centered between the top and bottom of the box that contains it, you can select the text with the selection tool and move it up or down. By leaving the justification of each text box on center, Works will center the text in each text box for you. If you draw each text box like a graphic box using the text tool, by clicking dragging the text tool cursor so that the dotted borders of the text box line up with the inner sides of the graphic box's border, the text will already be centered in the graphic box, as you type.

Recording a style macro

One problem with a chart like this is that Works always defaults to 12-point Boston text with a plain style each time you create a new text box, forcing you to change the font and style options to Helvetica bold. (There are eleven text boxes in this chart.) You can speed up this process with Works' macro feature.

Setting a type font and style to Helvetica bold requires choosing two commands from two menus.

☐ Choose Macros On from the Macro menu.

☐ Choose Start Recording from the Macro menu, or press Option-+ (the plus key next to the Delete or Backspace key on the top row of the keyboard, not the keypad plus).

A dialog box appears, asking you to enter the letter key you want to use to activate the macro, and a brief description of the macro.

☐ Enter *H* (for Helvetica), and the description, *Helvetica bold*.

☐ Press Return or click the Record button to start recording the macro.

☐ Pull down the Format menu and choose Helvetica from the Font sub-menu. (If you don't have Helvetica, use a font other than the one you're currently using.)

☐ Choose Bold from the Style sub-menu.

☐ Choose Stop Recording from the Macro menu, or type Option-– (hyphen, not the keypad minus sign).

☐ Press Return or click the Stop button to turn off macro recording.

When you choose Macros Off from the Macro menu, you are asked if you want to save the changes to the macro file. Be sure you do save the changes. With this macro recorded, you will be able to set the font and style of any text, in boxes, columns, or in the word processor to Helvetica bold whenever you press Option-H with macros turned on.

You can, of course, store all your macros for all applications in one file—the default Microsoft Works (keys) macro file. If you have only a few macros, this approach is probably the easiest. But if you develop a large macro inventory, it can be helpful to separate your macros into smaller groups with specific functions. The Works macro feature lets you create and store as many macro files as you want, each of which can contain several macro key definitions for different purposes. You can use the Save Macro File As command on the Macro menu to save macro sets that are specifically for use with the Draw tool, for example, and then use separate macro files in the word processor, spreadsheet, or database. You can even have separate macro files for specific documents or projects. Simply open the macro file you want to use when you start working.

Two other Draw tool operations you might want to automate with macros are:

- Selecting the Print Preview option in the Print dialog box and then clicking the OK button to display a document on the screen.

- Setting all the margins in the Page Setup dialog box to 0, or any size other than the default so that you have more room to work.

You'll probably think of other repetitive tasks you can automate with the macro feature. However, you can't automate the process of turning macros on and off, or the processes of starting, continuing, or stopping macro recording.

Solving chart problems

The organizational chart in this exercise was designed to fit the box and page sizes we set, but circumstances aren't always so neat in real life. If you design an organizational chart of your own, you might find that you have more positions than are shown in this chart or that the names or titles are too long to fit inside the boxes. There are a couple of remedies to these problems.

If your organization has more positions than are shown on this chart, either you can create more boxes at the same level by staggering them in two rows, or you can make the boxes smaller so that they all fit in one row. A staggered row of boxes at the same organizational level might look like this:

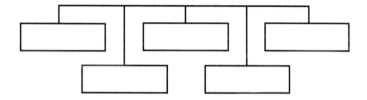

By alternating the boxes at two different levels, you can fit almost twice the number of boxes in the same horizontal space.

You can also make the boxes smaller to fit more in a line and then make the text smaller in each box so that it will fit inside the smaller boxes. There are two other tricks you can use to put more people on a one-page organizational chart: Make the chart vertical or reduce the size of the chart when you print.

A vertical organizational chart is best for organizational structures that have lots of people at each level, but few levels. Here are the Al's Videorama chart boxes laid out vertically:

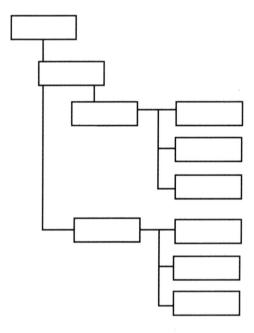

Because the name and title boxes are stacked, rather than side by side, you get more room for more boxes at the same level.

Finally, if you're using a LaserWriter, you can always reduce the size of your chart during printing. The LaserWriter's Page Setup dialog box has a Reduce or Enlarge option that is normally set at 100%, which means to print the document at full size. But you can print your chart at 90%, 80%, or another smaller size so that it will fit on one piece of paper. (If you're printing on an ImageWriter, you can use the 50% Reduction option.) To see how a print reduction will look before printing, use the Print Preview option to view the reduced document on the screen.

A Form Letter

In addition to distributing flyers in parking lots, Al wants to do some direct-mail advertising. So, he has acquired a mailing list from the Couch Potato Society of America (a group of devoted television viewers), and he wants to send each local member a letter announcing a special pre-opening preview at the Videorama. This is a great application for the form-letter capability in the Works word processor. Any version of Works can handle this project because all versions have the merge function.

To create a form letter, Al must make two files: a word-processor file containing the text of his message, and a database file containing the names and addresses of the people to whom he'll send the letter. Let's assume Al has created the database file and saved it with the name Potatoes. For our purposes, we'll use the Addresses sample file from the Tutorial folder on the Works Program disk. (See Chapters 7 and 8 for information about making and using database files.)

Entering the text, checking the spelling, and saving

The form is a simple, one-paragraph note written in 12-point Helvetica. Instead of using the Al's Letterhead file, Al will print the letter on blank paper and have it printed onto his letterhead by a local printer, so we can begin typing the sales letter on a new word-processor document. The finished letter text is shown in Figure 4-5.

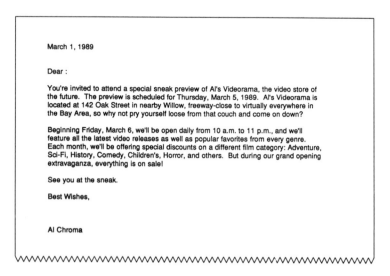

March 1, 1989

Dear :

You're invited to attend a special sneak preview of Al's Videorama, the video store of the future. The preview is scheduled for Thursday, March 5, 1989. Al's Videorama is located at 142 Oak Street in nearby Willow, freeway-close to virtually everywhere in the Bay Area, so why not pry yourself loose from that couch and come on down?

Beginning Friday, March 6, we'll be open daily from 10 a.m. to 11 p.m., and we'll feature all the latest video releases as well as popular favorites from every genre. Each month, we'll be offering special discounts on a different film category: Adventure, Sci-Fi, History, Comedy, Children's, Horror, and others. But during our grand opening extravaganza, everything is on sale!

See you at the sneak.

Best Wishes,

Al Chroma

Figure 4-5.
A sales letter for Al's Videorama.

Notice the blank space between the date and the greeting, and the blank space between *Dear* and the colon in the greeting line. These spaces will hold data merged into this form letter from the database.

After you enter the text of the letter, run the spelling checker by choosing Correct Spelling from the Spell menu. If you type this letter accurately, there will be no actual misspelled words in the document. Nevertheless, the spelling program will identify several suspect words. Here's a list of the words the speller will question, along with explanations of why the word was questioned and which action you should take:

Questioned Word	Explanation	Action
Al's	Proper name variant not in dictionary	Add
Videorama	Proper name not in dictionary	Add
freeway	Not in dictionary	Skip
a.m.	Period after *m* should have two spaces	Skip
to	First word of sentence (after a.m.) should be capitalized	Skip
p.m.	Capitalized in dictionary	Skip
Sci	Not in dictionary	Skip
Fi	Not in dictionary	Skip
Al	Proper name, not in dictionary	Add
Chroma	Proper name, not in dictionary	Add

If you've been doing these exercises in order, you'll notice that the dictionary didn't mark *Al's*, *Videorama*, *Al*, and *Chroma* as misspelled. That's because we added these names to the dictionary when we were checking Al's letter to his cousin Lou. If you haven't done the exercises in order, you should add these words to the dictionary so that the spelling checker doesn't question them any more.

The period after the *m*, in *a.m. to* is questioned because the spelling checker assumes that a period always ends a sentence. It flags this occurrence because there's only one space after the period, and the speller expects two spaces after the end of a sentence. The *p.m.* usage is questioned because the dictionary finds P.M. with capitals only. We'll skip over these "errors" for now, because they're not really errors; but you can change the spelling checker so that it doesn't flag usages with one space after a period by un-checking the check box on the Options screen, which is displayed when you choose Options from the Spell menu.

Finally, the words *Sci* and *Fi* are legitimate abbreviations of science fiction in Al's business, so we'll skip over these. (We won't add them to the dictionary, because someday Al might make a mistake and type *Fi* when he means *Fin*, for example, and we'd want the speller to let us know about it.)

This example should give you some idea when you should skip words and when you should add words to the dictionary. It should also give an indication how the spelling checker decides whether to question words and usage. With the text entered and corrected, we'll save the letter on disk as Sales Letter.

☐ Choose the Save As command from the File menu.

☐ Type the new file name, Sales Letter, in the entry line.

☐ Click the Save button in the dialog box to save the file with this new name onto the current disk.

Preparing the document for merge printing

The merging of database data takes place when we print the document, but we first have to set up the document to receive merged data.

☐ Load the Addresses sample file on the Program Disk onto the desktop. When you load the file, it becomes the active window. You still want to work with the sales-letter file, though.

☐ Choose the Sales Letter file from the Window menu to make it the active window.

Each letter will have a name, address, and greeting made up of merged data from the database file. To set up Works so that it will merge data, we must indicate where in the letter the data goes, and specify which database fields are to be merged at which locations.

☐ Move the insertion point to the first place in the letter (the first line of the address block, which is the blank line directly above *Dear*). In this location, we want to merge the name of the addressee.

□ Choose the Prepare to Merge command from the Edit menu (or press Command-M). The following dialog box appears:

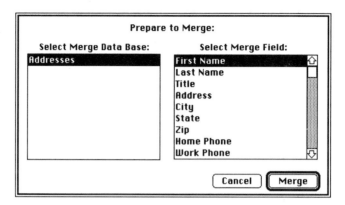

The dialog box shows all the database files currently on the desktop in its left-hand window. Normally, the uppermost file name in the file window is highlighted for us, and the fields in that file are shown in the right-hand window. The Addresses file is the only database file on the desktop in this case, so it is selected and the data fields it contains are shown in the window at the right. The first field in the database is First Name, so it happens to be highlighted.

□ Click the Merge button to tell Works that the First Name data should be merged at this point. (Because the Merge button has a double line around it, you can select it by pressing the Return or Enter keys instead of by clicking on it—on the Mac, you can select any screen button with a double line around it by pressing Return or Enter.)

You can select only one merge field at a time with the Prepare to Merge command, so after we tell Works to merge the First Name field, the Prepare to Merge dialog box disappears, and the field name and file name appear in a box at the insertion point's position in the letter.

□ Move the insertion point to the right one space by pressing the Spacebar.

□ Choose Prepare to Merge again (or press Command-M) and click on the Last Name field in the dialog box to select it as the data to be merged.

◻ Press the Return key to insert a merge field in the letter.

The Last Name merge field will appear after the First Name merge field in the first line of the address block. Now, we must merge the address.

◻ Press the Return key to move the insertion point from the end of the First Name/Last Name line to the line below.

◻ Press Command-M to display the Prepare to Merge dialog box.

◻ Click on the *Address* field to select it.

◻ Press Return to merge this field on the second line of the address block in the Sales Letter document.

We complete the form letter by merging the City, State, and Zip fields on the third address line, and then merging the First Name field after *Dear* in the greeting. The letter is now ready to print, and the screen looks like this:

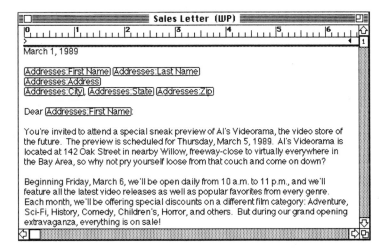

Notice that the name of the field and the name of the database file appear in the box at each merge location. If we want to preview how our data will look, we can choose the Show Field Data command from the Edit menu, and instead of the names of the data fields and file, the letter will show the actual data from the first record in the merged database file. (In this case, the first record contains the name and address of someone in Louisiana—hardly somebody Al would invite to drive to the "freeway-close" Videorama in California. Still, it gives you the idea of how this feature works.) Notice that in the previous illustration, there's a comma and a space between the City and State fields, and a space between the State and Address fields. Merge fields can be treated exactly like text in the word processor: You can move them around by cutting and pasting them, you can delete them as if they were regular words, and you can use tabs, spaces, and periods with them, too.

Printing with Print Merge

When we're ready to print the letter, we use the Print Merge command from the File menu, instead of the Print command. Print Merge tells Works that merged data will be included in the file, and commands it to get that data from the appropriate database file. Works checks to see that the database from which the merged data will be taken is on the desktop. If the proper database file isn't on the desktop, Works will warn you.

If we were to use Print (instead of Print Merge) to print this letter, the letter would be printed with the database file and field data boxes, instead of the actual data, at the insert locations.

Addressing Envelopes

Al has 150 promotional letters printed and ready to go out to the local Couch Potatoes, and now it's time to address the envelopes. There are two ways to do this. He can hand-feed individual envelopes into his LaserWriter II using the Manual Feed option in the Print dialog box, or he can print onto mailing labels and then stick them onto blank envelopes. (For this exercise, we'll assume Al has had standard business envelopes containing his return address and logo printed by a commercial print shop.)

Both of these options require us to set up a new word-processor document containing the address of the person who will receive the mail. So, we'll need to use the merge feature again, but the format of these two documents will be different.

Printing hand-fed envelopes

For the sake of completeness, we'll go through the process of printing addresses on standard 4-inch by 9½-inch business envelopes using a

LaserWriter II and an ImageWriter. (The old LaserWriter doesn't have an envelope feeder.) The difference is that the Page Setup dialog box for the LaserWriter II doesn't have a Custom Size paper option, so we must position the envelope address in the middle of an 8½ by 11 page as if the envelope itself were glued to the middle of the paper. The Page Setup dialog box for the ImageWriter, on the other hand, does have a Custom Size paper option, so we can set the exact size of the envelope as the paper size.

Printing Envelopes on a LaserWriter II

The LaserWriter II has a paper-feeding guide that centers smaller pages between the left and right edges of standard 8½-inch page width. Envelopes only travel through the LaserWriter sideways (with their narrow side first), so we'll have to print sideways on the envelope and assume the envelope is in the middle of an 8½ by 11 space, as shown in Figure 4-6.

Because we're printing this document sideways, we have to remember that margin settings we make will affect the document in ways that

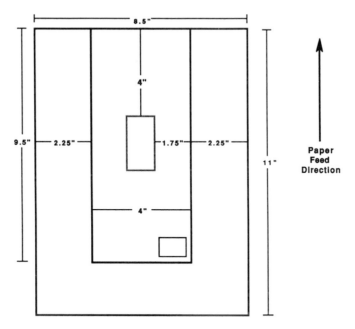

Figure 4-6.
The dimensions of an envelope on an 8½ by 11 page.

are different from standard printing. As you can see in Figure 4-6, the address block on the envelope is 4 inches from the top edge of the paper as it feeds into the LaserWriter. When we print the document sideways, this 4 inch margin will actually become the left margin on the envelope. We'll set the left margin in the Page Setup dialog box to 4. The right edge of the address block will become the top edge when printed sideways. It is also 4 inches from the right side of the page ($2^1/_4$ inches from the right edge of the standard page to the edge of the envelope, plus $1^3/_4$ inches from the right side of the envelope to the top of the address block). So, we'll set the top margin at 4 as well.

After we click the wide-orientation icon in the LaserWriter's Page Setup dialog box and the Manual Feed option in the Print dialog box, we're ready to print. If you don't want to waste paper, you can use the Print Preview feature to see that, indeed, the address will print in the proper position, assuming we're feeding a standard business envelope into the printer. To feed an envelope properly into the LaserWriter, set the paper guides on the manual feeder to the width of the envelope (about 4 inches), and be sure the front of the envelope is facing up, with the pre-printed return address at the leading end of the envelope. Of course, we need to have some text on this document to print. We'll look at address merging from a database file after we see how to print envelopes on an ImageWriter.

Printing Envelopes on an ImageWriter

When printing an address on an envelope with an ImageWriter, think of the envelope as a custom-size document with the address printed sideways. (You could feed an envelope into an ImageWriter with its long side parallel to the platen, but you'll get better results if you feed it from the narrow end.) Because we're feeding the envelope narrow side first, our custom paper will be 4 inches wide and $9^1/_2$ inches long.

□ Choose Page Setup from the File menu.

□ Double-click on the Paper Width box and type *4*.

□ Double-click on the Paper Height box and type *9.5*.

Now, let's determine where the address will actually print on this custom-sized paper. As with the LaserWriter envelope, we want the top of the address block to begin $1^3/_4$ inches from the top edge of the envelope (the flap edge) and about 4 inches from the left-hand narrow edge, as shown in Figure 4-6. Only this time, we're not placing the envelope in the middle of a larger piece of paper.

So, we want to set the top margin to 1¾ inches (because we don't have to add space for the standard-sized paper the LaserWriter expects) and the left margin to 4 inches.

☐ Choose the Page Setup command from the File menu.

☐ Change the Top Margin setting to *1.75*, and the Left Margin setting to *4*.

The last task in setting up this document is to click the wide-orientation icon so that Works knows to print sideways.

When you print envelopes sideways on the ImageWriter, feed the envelope at the left edge of the platen, because the printer thinks your paper is 4 inches wide and the print head will only move out to print the first line 1¾ inches from the right (top) page margin. Use the paper-edge marker on the ImageWriter as your guide and line up the left (bottom) edge of the envelope (the long side opposite the flap edge) along it as you feed it into the printer. As you face the printer, the envelope flap should be facing you, and it should be on the right side of the envelope before you start feeding it in. Finally, feed envelopes into the printer only until the leading edge of the envelope is just under the paper bail — remember, Works will advance the envelope 4 inches to take care of the top (left) margin you set.

Merge printing with envelopes

Now that we've set the right Page Setup specs for envelopes, we can set up the merge fields to print addresses on them. The process is the same no matter which printer you're printing on.

☐ Click OK if the Page Setup dialog box is still visible, to return to the new, untitled document. The insertion point is in the upper-left corner.

☐ Press Command-M to display the Prepare To Merge dialog box. (Be sure the Addresses database file from the Works Tutorial Folder is open.) Click on the First Name field and then press Return. The field will be merged, and a marker will appear in the document.

□ If a person's name appears, choose the Show Field Names command from the Edit menu.

□ Press the Spacebar once (to leave a space between the First Name and Last Name fields) and then merge the Last Name field on the first line.

□ Press Return to move the insertion point down to the second line of the document.

□ Merge the Address field on the second line of the document, and press Return to move the insertion point down to the third line of the document.

□ Merge the City, State, and Zip fields, using a comma and a space to separate City from State, and a space to separate State from Zip.

Placing the merge fields is done, and all that remains is to print the documents. You'll feed each envelope one by one into the printer.

□ Choose Print Merge from the File menu.

□ Click Manual Feed (LaserWriter) or Hand Feed (ImageWriter) in the dialog box.

□ Click OK to print the file.

The printer will print the name and address records, one at a time, as you feed each envelope into the printer. The printer will stop after it prints each address and wait for you to insert another envelope.

Printing mailing labels

You can print one-across mailing labels with any version of Works, whether the labels are continuous with tractor-feed holes for an Image-Writer printer or single-sheet for feeding into a LaserWriter. Because you can't set a custom paper size on the LaserWriter, you must create a full page of merged labels (10 or 11 rows of labels in all) and print a full page of labels at a time. On the ImageWriter, you can print labels individually using the Custom Size paper option in the Page Setup dialog box. Works 2.0 has an added feature that lets you print onto label stock that has labels placed two, three, or more across a sheet.

One-across Labels on the ImageWriter

Setting Works to print continuous labels on the ImageWriter requires some steps that are different from the ones for printing on a LaserWriter, depending on whether you're using one-across label stock or two-or three-across labels. In every case, however, you must determine the vertical size of each label, including the space between one label and the next. You must set this size as the paper size in the Page Setup dialog box. Then, you must set the left margin in the Page Setup dialog box so that the address (on a one-across label) or the left-most address (on stock with two or three labels across) will be printed in the middle of the label, and you must set the top and bottom margins to 0. To set up and print one-across labels, using label stock that is 1 inch high (including space between labels) and $2\frac{5}{8}$ inches wide, use the following procedure.

□ Set the Paper Height in the Page Setup dialog box to 1.

□ Set the Paper Width in the Page Setup dialog box to 2.67 (for $2\frac{5}{8}$ inch labels).

□ Set the Left Margin to 0.5.

□ Set the top and bottom and right margins to 0.

□ Click the No Gaps Between Pages option (an *x* will appear in the box).

□ Click the OK button.

□ Choose the 6 Lines Per Inch spacing option from the Format menu. (This option will space characters so that you can fit exactly six lines of an address on a label.)

□ Merge the name and address fields onto the label, following the procedure presented in the section of this chapter on addressing envelopes.

□ Set the ImageWriter's continuous paper holders so that the left edge of the label stock itself (not the backing paper) will be in line with the alignment mark on the left side of the Image-Writer's paper bail. Then feed the label stock into the paper holders.

□ Choose Print Merge from the File menu, be sure the Automatic Paper Feed option button is selected, and then press Return to print the labels. (Remember, if you choose Print instead of Print Merge, you will print only the first record from the database file or the database file's merged field names, depending on whether you have Show Field Data or Show Field Names selected on the Edit menu.)

In printing one-across labels, we simply treat each label as if it were a separate, albeit small, document. On a full page of such labels, the ImageWriter prints one address on one "document," and then moves down to the next "document" and prints again. This process happens 11 times for each page of 1-inch continuous labels.

Two-across or Three-across Labels

You can also print one-across labels an entire page at a time. Printing one-across labels in this way uses the same process you use to print two-across or three-across labels on the ImageWriter or to print labels of any kind on the LaserWriter. Rather than treat each address as a separate document, you make each document an $8\frac{1}{2}$ by 11 piece of paper that contains 11 stacked address blocks (one per label). Because we're not using a custom paper size, this process is the same on either the Image-Writer or LaserWriter.

The following example uses three-across label stock with the same 1 inch high, $2\frac{5}{8}$-inch wide labels as before, laid out across the page with no space between them. We'll assume that you have the Addresses database file open on the desktop, and a new word-processor document window active on the screen.

☐ Choose Page Setup from the File menu and set a $\frac{1}{4}$ left margin and 0 right, top, and bottom margins for the page. This will space the text of the left column of labels so that it is slightly indented from the left edge of the label. For the ImageWriter, click the No Gaps Between Pages option.

☐ Choose the 6 Line Per Inch spacing option from the Format menu. This will make six lines of text exactly one label high.

☐ Drag the right indent marker out to the 8 inch mark on the ruler.

☐ Click in the blank bar immediately below the ruler's tick marks to set a tab at $2\frac{7}{8}$ inches.

NOTE: If there is horizontal space between labels on the backing paper, you must include this space when you set the tabs.

☐ Set another tab stop at 5³/₄ inches.

☐ Press Command-M to display the Prepare To Merge dialog box. The First Name field is the top one in the list, so it's already selected. Press Return to merge this field.

☐ Choose Show Field Names from the Edit menu, if it is not already selected.

☐ Press the Spacebar once and then merge the Last Name field next to the First Name field.

☐ Choose the Multiple Labels command from the Edit menu.

☐ Drag the mouse over the First Name and Last Name fields, and press Command-C to copy them to the Clipboard.

☐ Place the insertion point at the end of the first line and press the Tab key to move it to the first tab stop.

☐ Press Command-V to paste the First Name and Last Name fields into the second column.

☐ Press the Tab key again and then press Command-V again to copy the two fields into the third column.

☐ Repeat the merge, copy, tab, and paste process for the Address field on the second line and the City, State, and Zip fields on the third line.

☐ Add three blank lines to each label in the row by pressing Option-Spacebar on the three lines below each City, State, and Zip line so that these blank lines will be maintained when the labels print. (If you want to center the text on the labels better, press Option-Spacebar to create a blank line above the first line of text and two below the last line of text.)

Because we're printing on a full page of labels, we must create a document containing a full page of merge fields. We've just done the first row of labels, and now we must fill the other rows on the page. Because we've inserted merge fields and blank line markers for a complete row of labels, we can simply copy this row and paste it into the other rows on the document page to fill it.

☐ Select all six lines of label text (including blank lines) in the first row, and copy them to the Clipboard.

☐ Click at the end of the last blank line in the row to place the insertion point at the end of the first row of label text. Press Return to start a new line.

☐ Paste the copied fields and blank lines from the Clipboard to create the second row of labels.

☐ To fill the page, repeat this process.

The copied text and lines from the first row of labels remain on the Clipboard until you copy something else there, so you can simply paste a row of labels, move the insertion point to the beginning of a new line, paste a row of labels again, and so on down the page. A page of 1 inch high labels contains 11 rows of labels, so you need to paste in 11 rows of merge boxes.

Word Processing Punch

These exercises show that you can be creative and flexible with the Works word processor. The spelling, drawing, and layout features in Works 2.0 make it possible to handle just about any business documentation task with this one versatile program. In Chapter 10, we'll see how to combine the word processing, drawing, and layout features with the other Works tools to produce a newsletter.

Chapter 5

Using the Spreadsheet

In this chapter, we'll look at the Works spreadsheet—what it offers, what makes it special, and how to use it. Spreadsheets (or worksheets, as they're sometimes called) are familiar tools to anyone who works regularly with numbers in business. Before we look at the specifics of the Works spreadsheet, we'll begin with a brief explanation of the basics of these number-crunching tools.

Spreadsheet Basics

Paper spreadsheets have been around for decades, but electronic spreadsheets such as the one in Works didn't appear until 1977, when VisiCalc was introduced. Electronic spreadsheets perform the same basic function as paper spreadsheets, but they use the computer's power to make working with numbers much easier.

A spreadsheet is a matrix of numbers in intersecting rows and columns. By presenting the numbers in rows and columns, spreadsheets let you see the relationships between the individual numbers. A common example is a personal expense budget, such as the one in Figure 5-1, which contains several rows, each of which shows different kinds of expenses (food, rent, and so on), and columns, which show how each type of expense varies monthly.

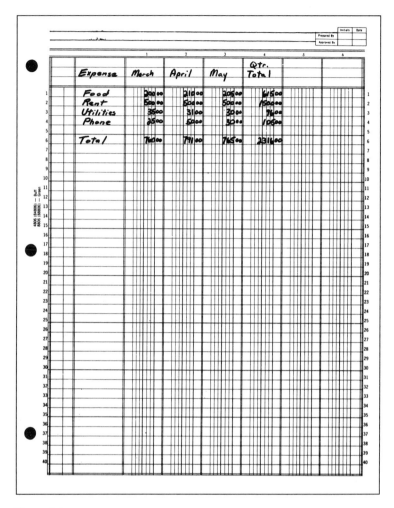

Figure 5-1.
The most common type of spreadsheet is a budget.

As you can see by the sample spreadsheet in Figure 5-1, the spreadsheet shows the results of mathematical calculations. (The total expenses for each month are in the bottom row; the quarter totals for each expense appear in the right-hand column.) But it also shows how each expense contributes to the totals. If you were to use a calculator to add all the expenses for March, for example, you'd end up with merely a total rather than a listing of how each expense contributed to the total.

By showing you the relationship between the numbers and the totals, spreadsheets tell you more about these numbers than you would know if you looked at the totals alone. The budget total in April is higher than in March, for example, and you can see that the higher food and phone costs account for the difference. Knowing this, you know that the food and telephone costs are a good place to cut back if you want to lower your expenses.

Both handwritten and electronic spreadsheets show these relationships between numbers in the same way, but electronic spreadsheets make the calculations much easier. Instead of doing each calculation by hand, you can store formulas in an electronic spreadsheet that make calculations for you. Also, after you enter a formula, you can copy it to other places where you want to perform essentially the same calculation, thereby saving yourself the trouble of entering a formula over and over. (In our sample budget, the same basic addition formula is used to sum each month's expenses.)

Although you can write down numbers anywhere on a paper spreadsheet, electronic spreadsheets are divided into specific cells, which are laid out in rows and columns. Each cell is an area where you can store text labels (row or column titles, for example), numbers, or formulas. In Works version 2.0, you can also attach text notes to cells, as we'll see later in this chapter. The spreadsheet in Works 2.0 contains 16,382 numbered rows and 256 columns (which are labeled A through Z, then AA through AZ, then BA through BZ, then CA through CZ, and so on through IA through IV), for a total of over 4.1 million cells. This is a far larger matrix of cells than you will probably ever need.

As you can see in Figure 5-2, on the following page, each cell is identified by the intersection of a row and column. The first cell in the top-left corner of a spreadsheet is in column A and row 1, so it is known as cell A1.

While this arrangement takes a little getting used to, it allows the electronic spreadsheet user much more power to build relationships between cells (and thus between the numbers or formulas contained in the cells), as we'll see later in this chapter. But first, let's take a look at Works' spreadsheet menus and commands.

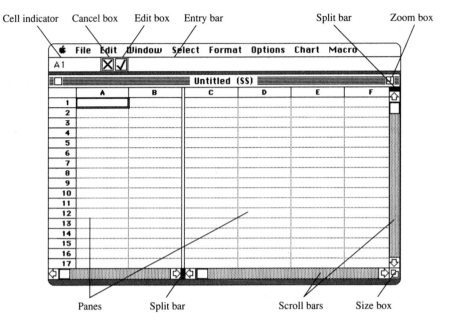

Figure 5-2.

The Works spreadsheet is a matrix of cells surrounded by a cell indicator, an enter box, a cancel box, and an entry bar for displaying the selected cell's contents and entering data; scroll bars for moving around the spreadsheet; split bars for splitting the spreadsheet window into two panes horizontally or vertically; and size and zoom boxes for resizing the window in which a file is displayed. (The enter box and cancel box appear only when you are adding to or changing the contents of a cell.)

A Quick Tour of the Spreadsheet Menus

As mentioned in the tour of the word-processor menus in Chapter 2, the first four menus from the left side of the screen (the Apple, File, Edit, and Window menus) are similar in all the Works applications. However, two of the File menu's printing options become active only when you're using the spreadsheet, and the Edit menu has several commands that are unique to the spreadsheet, as well. Let's start with the printing features.

The File menu: extra printing options

All the commands you see on the File menu in the spreadsheet look like they do in any other Works application, but Works version 2.0 has two options in the Page Setup dialog box that apply only to spreadsheet documents. When you choose the Page Setup command from the File menu, you see two new option boxes: the Print Row and Column Numbers option, and the Print Cell Notes option. You select them by clicking in their boxes. The Print Rows and Column Numbers option prints a spreadsheet file with row and column numbers at the top and left borders. The Print Cell Notes option prints the contents of any cell notes you have created for the spreadsheet. Cell notes are printed on a separate page, following the spreadsheet, and each note's text is identified with the address of the spreadsheet cell to which it is attached. (Cell notes are described in detail later in this chapter.)

The Edit menu

The Cut, Copy, and Paste commands have some special features in the spreadsheet, although their basic functions are the same in every Works application. You can use the Cut command to remove data from a cell or group of cells and place it on the Clipboard. The Paste command takes whatever is on the Clipboard and places it in the cell or group of cells beginning at the insertion point or selection. After you cut or copy data to the Clipboard, the data stays there until you cut or copy something else there. Because of this, you can paste the same Clipboard data into several different places in succession.

- Select the data you want to cut by highlighting it with the mouse. (Click on a cell to highlight one cell, or hold down the mouse button and drag the pointer if you want to highlight a group of cells.)

- Choose the Cut or Copy command from the Edit menu.

- Click on the first cell where you want the data to appear.

- Choose the Paste command to copy the data from the Clipboard to the new location. The data will be pasted from the Clipboard.

- Click on the second cell where you want the data to appear, and choose the Paste command again. The data will be pasted from the Clipboard.

When you paste more than one cell's data from the Clipboard, the data is placed in the same order as it was when you cut it. If you cut five cells from a row, for example, and then select one cell as the place to paste the data, the five cells will appear in the same order, beginning at the cell you selected and extending four more cells to the right. If, however, the data you are pasting will write over existing data in its path (for example, you already have a value in the fourth cell of a row, and you're pasting in five cells of data), Works will warn you that existing data will be lost. You can then decide whether to overwrite the existing data or cancel the paste operation.

One last fact about the Cut command: When you cut an entire row or column from the spreadsheet, both the data and the row or column itself are removed from the spreadsheet. If you cut row 3 from a spreadsheet, for example, that row will be removed to the Clipboard, and the rows beneath it will move up and will be renumbered.

Remember that when you paste from the Clipboard, you are pasting only a copy of the Clipboard's data. The Clipboard retains a copy of the data until you cut or copy new data there. It's especially important to remember this when you have more than one file on the desktop, because Works retains the Clipboard's contents when you switch from one file to another. Thus, if you cut some data to the Clipboard from a spreadsheet file and then move to a word-processor file, the spreadsheet data is still on the Clipboard and will be inserted into your word-processor file at the insertion point if you choose the Paste command.

The Copy command works the same way as the Cut command, except that instead of removing selected data from the spreadsheet, Copy leaves the data where it is, placing a copy of it on the Clipboard.

The Clear command removes selected data completely from a spreadsheet. When you clear a selected cell or cells, the data is deleted. Unlike the Cut command, however, you can't remove rows or columns from the screen when you clear them—you can only remove the data inside those rows or columns. The Clear command does not affect the contents of the Clipboard.

The Select All command selects all 4.1 million cells in the spreadsheet. This command is handy when you want to perform the same formatting operation on the entire document, such as widening columns or changing cell attributes or text formats.

The Paste with Options command allows you to paste formulas and values (which is the default option) or values only from cells you have copied or cut to the Clipboard. Paste with Options also lets you transpose data, so that rows become columns and vice versa.

The Draw On command in Works version 2.0 activates the Draw tool, which, as explained in Chapter 3, lets you add shapes, lines, boxes, and text to enhance the appearance of your spreadsheet. (Drawing is not available in the spreadsheet in Works versions prior to version 2.0.) When the Draw tool is on, the Draw On command on the Edit menu changes to Draw Off. All the drawing features discussed in Chapter 3 are available in the spreadsheet as well as the word processor. We'll see how to use the Draw tool to dress up spreadsheets in Chapter 6.

The Move command is a shortcut for cutting and pasting data, letting you move cells or groups of cells without cutting and pasting them through the Clipboard. When you choose the Move command, you see a dialog box like this:

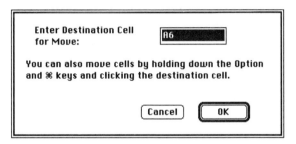

To move a cell or cells, select the cell or cells you want to move, choose the Move command, enter the address of the cell where you want to move the selected cells, and then click the OK button or press the Return or Enter key. The selection simply moves to the new address you entered.

TIP: There's an even faster way to move cells from one place to another than with the Move command.

□ Select the cell or cells you want to move.

□ Hold down the Command and Option keys together, and then click on the cell where you want to move the selection.

The Insert command is used to insert rows or columns into a spreadsheet. When you build a budget spreadsheet, for example, you might find that you forgot to include rows for certain expense items. The Insert command inserts one row or column at the insertion point, depending on whether you have selected a row, a column, or a cell. If you select a row (by clicking on the row number) or a cell, the Insert command inserts an empty row above the selected row or cell. If you select a column (by clicking on the column letter), the command inserts an empty column to the left of the selected column. When you insert a row or a column, all the rows below or columns to the right of it are moved and renumbered. If the rows or columns contain formulas, the formulas adjust themselves to their new locations. We'll learn how they adjust later in this chapter.

The Paste Function command lets you build formulas by selecting one of Works' spreadsheet functions from a list. When you select a cell and choose the Paste Function command, Works displays the following dialog box:

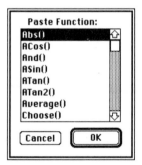

To paste a function, locate the function you want to paste from the list displayed in the dialog box. (You might need to use the scroll bar to find it.) Then double-click on the function name (or click on it and then either click the OK button or press the Return or Enter key). The function appears in the entry bar, followed by two parentheses. When the selected function appears in the entry bar, the flashing entry cursor is between the parentheses. You then enter the actual cell references or numbers you want to calculate inside the parentheses. The spreadsheet in version 2.0 of Works offers 64 mathematical, statistical, financial, logical, date and time, trigonometric, and special-purpose functions. The spreadsheet in earlier versions of Works has 56 functions.

The Absolute Cell Ref command changes the cell references in formulas from relative to absolute or from absolute to relative. The Works spreadsheet always assumes you want to use relative cell references unless you tell it otherwise. A relative cell reference is simply the cell letter and number designation, such as A1 (the top, left-hand cell). An absolute cell reference is indicated with dollar signs in front of the row and column designations, such as $A$1.

In a formula with a relative reference, the cell reference is linked to the location of the formula that contains it. If you enter the formula Sum(A1+A2) in cell A3, for example, and you move the formula to cell B3, the references (A1+A2) will change to (B1+B2), reflecting the formula's new location. Because you entered this formula in the cell directly below the two cells to be summed, Works assumes you want it to always sum the contents of the two cells in the formula, and the addresses of the cells in the formula will change according to the formula's position in the worksheet. This is handy if, for instance, you want to total columns A through F with this formula, because you can simply copy the formula to the right, and the formulas will adjust, each providing a total in its respective column.

In a formula with an absolute reference, however, the cell address remains the same, regardless of where you move the formula. If the formula in the previous example were Sum($A$1+$A$2), for example, that formula would always add those two specific cells, no matter where you moved the formula itself. This is handy if, for example, you have a specific value such as an interest rate that you want to use in a number of different formulas in the spreadsheet. If you decide to copy or move the formula to a new location, the proper cell reference will always be used in the formula.

You don't have to make all the references in a formula absolute or relative; you can mix reference types. In fact, if you like you can make only the row or column part of a cell reference absolute, as in $A1, which means you always want the reference to remain in Column A, but you want the row designation to change if you move the formula.

To change a cell reference to absolute, use the following steps.

- Display the formula in the entry bar (by selecting the cell that contains the formula).

- Select the cell address or group of addresses you want to change by placing the insertion point immediately to the left of the address, holding down the mouse button, and dragging over it.

□ Choose Absolute Cell Ref from the Edit menu or press Command-A. A dollar sign appears in front of each of the row and column designations selected. (Alternatively, you can simply type a dollar sign in front of each row and column designation you want to make absolute.)

There will be times when you'll want to use both types of cell reference, as we'll see later in this chapter and in Chapter 6. There are a few other things to keep in mind, however. The Absolute Cell Ref command is active only when you have selected a cell containing a formula, thus displaying the formula in the entry bar. Also, you can remove an absolute reference or references either by selecting the portion of the formula you want to change and choosing the Absolute Cell Ref command again (or pressing Command-A) or simply by deleting each dollar sign. Although you can create absolute references or change them back to relative references simply by typing or deleting dollar signs in the entry bar yourself, it's easier to use the menu command or key combination when you want to make a series of cell addresses in a formula absolute (or change them back to relative), because you can change them all with one command.

The Fill Right and Fill Down commands let you quickly copy the contents of one cell into one or more selected adjacent cells. Suppose, for example, you have a value in cell A1 and you want to copy the same value into cells A2, A3, and A4. You could copy the value in cell A1 to the Clipboard and then paste it into the adjacent cells one cell at a time, but with Fill Right, you can do it faster.

□ Select cells A1, A2, A3, and A4 by dragging the pointer across them.

□ Select the Fill Right command from the Edit menu, or press Command-R. Cells A2, A3, and A4 will be filled with copies of the contents of cell A1.

The Fill Down command works the same way. Its key combination is Command-D.

The Open Cell Note command is new in Works version 2.0. It lets you attach a text note to any cell in the spreadsheet. Cell notes are handy for explaining where certain numbers came from, how you arrived at certain assumptions, or who is responsible for having created a spreadsheet. When you select a cell and then choose the Open Cell Note command, a small note window appears on top of the spreadsheet.

```
 File  Edit  Window  Macro
                          Untitled (SS)
        A        B        C        D        E        F
  1
  2  ▢≡ Untitled (SS) Note C2 ≡▣≡
  3  |                              ⇧
  4
  5
  6
  7
  8
  9
 10
 11
 12                              ⇩
 13                              ▢
 14
 15
 16
 17
 18
```

Notice that the window's title contains the address of the cell to which it is attached. When the window is open, you can enter text as you normally would in a word-processor document. The following characteristics and restrictions apply to note windows:

- You can use the window's size and zoom boxes to make it as large as your screen.

- Whatever size the window is, the text you type will wrap around to fit the window so that you will always be able to see all of your text.

- You can enter several pages of text into a window.

- If you have selected the Show Notes Indicator command from the Options menu, the upper-right corner of a cell that contains an attached note will display a small black dot. Otherwise, you won't be able to tell which cells have notes attached.

- You can cut and paste text in a note window, but you can't change the text formatting characteristics from the note window, only from the spreadsheet window. The font, size, and style of the note window are the same as they are for the rest of the spreadsheet. Any formatting changes affect the entire spreadsheet.

- You can't select more than one window of text; unlike the word processor's window, the notes window doesn't scroll up or down when you try to click-and-drag past the visible portion of one window. You can, however, place the cursor at the beginning of the text you want to select, scroll to the end of the desired selection while holding down the Shift key, and click at the end of the selection. All text between the two points will be selected.

- When a cell note is open, Works treats it as a document, and its name shows up in the list of open documents on the Window menu.

- To close a cell note, click the close box in its window.

- You can print cell notes only along with a spreadsheet file. To print cell notes, click the Print Cell Notes box in the spreadsheet's Page Setup dialog box. When you print, the notes will be printed on a separate page or pages immediately after the spreadsheet itself, and the text in them will be printed according to the margins set in the Page Setup dialog box, rather than the line widths represented by the sizes of the note windows.

The Sort command lets you rearrange the rows in a spreadsheet, based on the contents of up to three columns, or sort keys. The Sort command works only on highlighted rows or cells in rows, so you can sort some of the rows in a spreadsheet and leave others unsorted. When you use the Sort command, you must select from one to three columns on whose contents the sorting will be based. You can sort data in either ascending (0 to 9 or A to Z) or descending (9 to 0 or Z to A) order. Whether you sort in ascending or descending order, though, Works always places values before labels. If a column contains both values (or formulas) and labels and you sort it in ascending order, for example, Works will place the values and formulas (based on the ranking of the values they

---

TIP: It's nice to be able to open cell notes whenever you want, but it can be distracting to use the Edit menu command to do so. Fortunately, there's a shortcut.

□ Hold down the Command key and double-click on a cell to open its attached note window.

---

produce) in ascending order before it places the labels in ascending alphabetical order.

The next four menus are unique to the spreadsheet, so we'll look at them in more detail.

The Select menu

The commands on the Select menu let you move the selection to specific cells quickly, or let you select either the entire spreadsheet or the last cell in the spreadsheet.

The All Cells command selects all the cells in the working area of your spreadsheet, which is a rectangle containing every row and every column that contains filled cells. If the last filled cell in your spreadsheet is E25, for example, the All Cells command will select the rectangle from column A through column E, and from row 1 down through row 25. The All Cells command is different from the Select All command on the Edit menu, which selects all 4.1 million cells in the spreadsheet matrix. The All Cells command is useful when you want to copy an entire spreadsheet to the Clipboard, widen its columns, or change a value or label format in the active spreadsheet area.

The Last Cell command selects the last cell in the active area of your worksheet, according to the rules for the All Cells command. Thus, it selects the cell in the last filled row and the last filled column. This cell could be an empty cell and still be considered part of the active spreadsheet. Suppose cells A5 and B4 are filled, but cell B5 is not. Cell B5 is selected when you choose the Last Cell command, because it is at the intersection of the last filled row and column.

The Go To Cell command also locates labels or values, but it simply scrolls the spreadsheet window to the area where that cell is located, rather than selecting the cell itself.

The Show Active Cell command scrolls the spreadsheet to the area containing the currently active cell. This command is useful when you are viewing a distant area, and want to return quickly to the area of the spreadsheet containing the active cell.

The Format menu

As you might expect, the Format menu contains commands that affect the appearance of the spreadsheet. Three of the commands, Set Cell Attributes, Borders, and Column Width, affect individual cells or selected groups of cells in the spreadsheet. The Font, Size, and Style commands affect all cells on the spreadsheet.

The Set Cell Attributes command lets you select various number and text formatting options in a dialog box like this:

```
┌─────────────────────────────────────────────────────────┐
│ Set Cell Attributes:                                     │
│                                                          │
│ Display:                      Align:       Style:        │
│ ◉ General    ○ Date Short     ○ Left       ☐ Bold        │
│ ○ Fixed      ○ Date Medium    ○ Center     ☐ Underline   │
│ ○ Dollar     ○ Date Long      ○ Right      ☐ Commas      │
│ ○ Percent    ○ Time                                      │
│ ○ Scientific ☐ Show Day      [2] Decimal Places          │
│                            [ Cancel ]  [  OK  ]          │
└─────────────────────────────────────────────────────────┘
```

As you can see, this box lets you set value formats (the left column of options), date and time formats for use with the spreadsheet's date and time functions, alignment options for text or values, style options (including commas to delineate large numbers), and the number of decimal places in decimal numbers. The default format is General, with two decimal places, and the default text format is plain text.

The Fixed option uses a specific number of decimal places and rounds numbers to that number of decimals, if necessary. The Dollar option shows numbers with dollar signs, followed by the number of decimal places you set. The Percent option multiplies the cell's contents by 100 and then displays it with a percent sign and with the number of decimals you set (thus, .25 becomes 25.00%). The Scientific option shows numbers with exponential notation and the number of decimals you set and is useful when you're working with large numbers. Exponential notation is shown as *Number1* E+*Number2*, where *Number2* is the power of ten to which *Number1* is raised. Figure 5-3 on the following page shows how the options in the Cell Attributes dialog box affect displayed values and text.

You don't need to select the Cell Attributes command from the Format menu whenever you want to reformat a cell. To display the dialog box for a particular cell, double-click on the cell. When you do, the Cell Attributes dialog box appears.

The Borders command displays a sub-menu of options for placing borders around a cell or a group of selected cells. This is useful for setting off a group of cells, such as a title or list of assumptions or variables, from the rest of the spreadsheet. The options are:

- Outline, which places a border completely around a cell or group of cells.

- Left, which places a border only along the left side of the cell or group of cells.

- Right, which places a border only along the right side of the cell or group of cells.

- Top, which places a border only along the top of a cell or group of cells.

- Bottom, which places a border only along the bottom of a cell or group of cells.

The border enhancements look better when you display or print the spreadsheet without its grid lines showing (de-select Show Grid on the Options menu) because the border lines appear on top of the grid lines when the grid is displayed. Also, if you place a border on a cell and then cut or clear that cell from the spreadsheet, the border for that cell will disappear, as well.

The Font, Size, and Color menus contain the same options as in other Works tools. The difference in the spreadsheet is that they affect the entire spreadsheet. You can't change the font, size, or color of only one cell. The defaults in a new spreadsheet are 9-point Geneva text in black. Changing the size of a font makes everything in the spreadsheet bigger or smaller; the columns and rows expand to fit the new type size, but the number of characters in a column's width remains the same.

Option	What You Type	What You See
General	25.00	25
	25.03	25.03
	.25	0.25
Fixed	25.03	25.03
(3 decimals)	25.0356	25.035
Dollar	25	$25.00
(2 decimals)	25.03	$25.03
Percent	25	2500.00%
(2 decimals)	.25	25.00%
	.025	2.50%
Scientific	25	2.50E+01
(2 decimals)	250	2.50E+02
Date Short	3/3/89	3/3/89

Figure 5-3.   *(continued)*
Cell-attribute formats.

Figure 5-3. *continued*

Option	What You Type	What You See
Date Medium	3/3/89	Mar 3, 1989
Date Long	3/3/89	March 3, 1989
Time	1:35	1:35 AM
	13.35	1:35 PM
Show Day (box checked)	3/3/89	Friday, March 3, 1989
Left Align	250	250
Center Align	250	250
Right Align	250	250
Bold	250	**250**
Underlined	250	<u>250</u>
Commas	250000	250,000

Finally, the Column Width command lets you reset the width of a column or a group of selected columns in the spreadsheet. This option is not available unless you have selected one or more cells; it operates on any and all columns containing selected cells. Columns in the spreadsheet can be up to 40 characters wide. You can also widen an individual column by dragging to the right the vertical dividing line located in the column headings area on the right side of each column letter, but for resetting the width of several columns at once, the Column Width command is faster.

The Options menu

The Options menu offers several groups of display and calculation commands. The first group includes the Show Grid and Show Notes Indicator commands. The Show Grid command lets you choose whether to display the grid lines that divide rows and columns in the spreadsheet. When the command has a check mark beside it, the grid is visible. The Show Notes Indicator command lets you see which cells have notes attached by displaying a small black dot in every noted cell's upper-right corner.

The Show Formulas and Show Values commands cancel each other out: Show Formulas displays the formulas entered in cells; Show Values shows the values produced from the calculations of those formulas. The spreadsheet's default mode is to show calculated values, rather than formulas. Show Formulas is handy when you want to examine a group of formulas you have entered. Normally, you can't see the formula in a cell unless you select that cell and look in the entry bar. With Show Formulas, every formula in the spreadsheet is visible in its cell, although you might need to widen some columns to see long formulas completely. You can also use Show Formulas to display formulas and then print them out so that others can see which calculations you've used in a spreadsheet.

The Protected command lets you lock the contents of selected cells so that they can't be deleted, cleared, or changed. After you protect cells, any attempt to change their contents or their formats produces a dialog box that says the cells are protected. You must un-protect any protected cells before changing them. When a cell is protected, the Protected command has a check mark next to it if that cell is selected.

The Set Page Break and Remove Page Break commands let you insert narrower or shorter page breaks than the ones Works uses by default. Page breaks in the spreadsheet appear as heavy dashed lines dividing rows and columns, rather than the faint dotted lines in the normal grid, as shown in the following example.

The page breaks are both horizontal and vertical because a spreadsheet can be both wider than and longer than a standard page. In a new Works spreadsheet, the first page break occurs before row 46, but you might want to reset page breaks so that certain groups of numbers all print on the same page. To set a page break, use the following steps.

    □ Select the cell that you want to be at the upper-left corner of a new page.

□ Choose the Set Page Break command. A new set of dashed page-break lines appear to the left of and above the selected cell.

If, for example, you want only the rectangle from columns A to D and rows 1 through 12 to fall on one page, you can set a new page break by selecting cell E13 (the next diagonal cell outside of that page range) and then choosing the Set Page Break command.

TIP: You can also control what appears on a page by inserting extra rows or columns, or widening columns so that they fill a page. If you have data in columns A-F, for example, but only want the data in columns A-D to print on the first page, you can widen columns A-D. The page-break lines adjust dynamically according to the column widths and the number of rows on a page. Page-break lines also move according to the width or height of the margins you set with the Page Setup command, so you can also move the page breaks by changing the margin values.

To remove a page break, select the same cell you selected when you created the page break (the one in the top-left corner of the page, just inside the page-break markers), and choose the Remove Page Break command.

The Calculate Now, Manual Calculation, and Automatic Calculation commands determine when Works recalculates the formulas in the spreadsheet. Works defaults to automatic calculation, which means that every formula in the spreadsheet is recalculated each time the contents of any cell is changed. With large spreadsheets, however, automatic calculation can slow down your work because the calculation can take a few seconds. If, for example, you enter an entire row of numbers, automatic calculation will cause the spreadsheet to recalculate (and make you wait) after you enter each individual number.

If you know you'll be making a lot of changes or additions to a spreadsheet and you don't need to see the calculation results constantly, it's faster to set the spreadsheet to manual calculation. In that mode, the spreadsheet recalculates only when you tell it to—either by choosing the Calculate Now command from the Options menu or by pressing Command-= (equal sign). That way, you're not interrupted by recalculations you don't care about, and you can recalculate all your changes at once when you're finished making them. The only drawback to manual calculation is that you might sometimes forget to recalculate, and your spreadsheet won't be accurate after any changes unless you do.

The final two commands on the Options menu, Freeze Titles Horizontal and Freeze Titles Vertical, let you freeze row or column titles on the screen so that no matter where you scroll the spreadsheet, the titles are always visible. It's a common problem to scroll to the right or down in a spreadsheet so that the row or column titles (which are typically in the top rows or left columns) are out of view. With no titles visible, it's hard to know which cell is which. Freeze Titles Vertical fixes the column titles at the top of the screen, no matter how far down the spreadsheet you scroll. Freeze Titles Horizontal does the same for row titles, no matter how far to the right you scroll. These commands are available only if you've already divided the spreadsheet into multiple views using the split bars. To freeze a set of vertical (column) titles:

□ Drag the black split bar from its place above the upper scroll arrow at the right of the spreadsheet window down to the row below the column titles. You'll see the window dividing line appear as you drag the bar. Release the mouse button when the bar is on the row where you want it. The spreadsheet window will divide into two "panes," like this:

	A	B	C	D	E	
Home Budget (SS)						
1		January	February	March	April	
8	Rent					
9	Home Insurance					
10						
11	Variable Costs					
12	Electricity					
13	Food					
14	Garbage					
15	Gas					
16	Medical Bills					
17	Entertainment					
18	Donations					
19	Water					
20	Gifts					
21	Misc. Supplies					
22	Repairs					
23	Auto Fuel					
24						

□ Choose the Freeze Titles Vertical command from the Options menu. Now, whenever you scroll down the spreadsheet, the titles and any other rows above the split bar will remain fixed on the screen.

When you use the split bars, each "pane" of the window gets its own set of scroll bars, unless one pane is too small to accommodate a set of scroll bars (as in the previous example), or you have used either of the Freeze Titles commands. After you freeze either horizontal or vertical panes, the corresponding scroll bar disappears, letting you scroll only the pane to the right of the frozen pane, the pane below the frozen one, or the pane below and to the right of the frozen one. By using the split bars, you can scroll different "panes" of the spreadsheet window to view widely different areas of a large spreadsheet.

The Chart menu

The Chart menu is the gateway to making charts from spreadsheet data. When you want to draw a new chart or recall a chart you have defined and stored with a spreadsheet, you use the Chart menu.

You can create charts only from the data in the spreadsheet you are currently working with. To define a chart, you must indicate the cells containing the data you want to chart, select the type of chart you want Works to draw, and, optionally, enter chart titles. You can choose from among line, pie, bar, stacked bar, or combination chart formats to represent your data. (We'll explore these various types of charts in Chapters 6 and 10.)

After you define a chart, Works stores it with the spreadsheet you're currently working on. You can store up to eight chart definitions with each spreadsheet file. If you don't give a chart a name, it is stored with the same name as your spreadsheet. If a spreadsheet is called Budget, for example, the first chart you design will be called Budget Chart 1 unless you specify a different name.

The Draw Chart command produces a dialog box containing a list of previously defined charts you have created for the spreadsheet you are working with. When you select one of the names in the list, that chart is automatically drawn on the screen. If your spreadsheet has no chart definitions, this command is unavailable.

The New Series Chart and New Pie Chart commands produce the dialog boxes in which you define the data sources and chart types and enter the titles for new charts. To define a chart, you choose either the New Series Chart command or the New Pie Chart command from the Chart menu to display a chart-definition dialog box. The chart-definition box for series charts looks like the one on the following page.

```
┌─────────────────────────────────────────────────────────────────┐
│ ▣      ═══════════════ Untitled Chart 1 ═══════════════          │
│ Type of Chart:      Values to be Plotted:    Vertical Scale:     │
│                          1st Row: │3  │      ● Numeric           │
│  ●   ╭╮ ╱╲                                   ○ Semi-Logarithmic  │
│      ╰╯   LINE           2nd Row: │4  │                          │
│                                                                  │
│  ○   ▂▃▅  BAR           3rd Row: │   │     Maximum: │         │  │
│                                                                  │
│  ○   ▃▅▇                4th Row: │   │     Minimum: │0        │  │
│      ▃▅▇  STACK      From Column: │B  │                          │
│                                                                  │
│  ○   ▃▅▇              To Column: │M  │                          │
│      ▃▅▇  COMBO                                                  │
│                   Data Legends in Column: │A  │   ⊠ Draw Grid    │
│                 Horizontal Titles in Row: │1  │   ⊠ Label Chart  │
│                                                                  │
│            Chart Title: │Untitled                             │  │
│     Vertical Scale Title: │Untitled                           │  │
│   Horizontal Scale Title: │Untitled                           │  │
│                                          ( Cancel )  (( Plot It! ))│
└─────────────────────────────────────────────────────────────────┘
```

The chart-definition dialog box lets you select the type of chart, the locations of the data you want to represent (by row and column), and the row and column locations of the titles you want assigned to the data representations in the chart. Also, you can specify vertical and horizontal axis titles (in series charts), and a main chart title at the top of the chart. You'll get more specific information about how to use chart-definition dialog boxes in Chapter 6.

Before you have defined a chart for a spreadsheet, the only commands available are New Series Chart and New Pie Chart, because all other commands on the Chart menu affect existing charts.

The Select Chart Definition command, like the Draw Chart command, produces a list of previously defined charts. When you select a chart name from the list in the dialog box produced by this command, however, Works displays the chart-definition dialog box, instead of drawing the chart itself.

The Duplicate Chart and Erase Chart commands let you duplicate chart definitions and erase chart definitions you have previously created.

The Macro menu

As explained in Chapter 1, the Macro menu works the same in all Works applications. You'll see how to use macros to speed up spreadsheet formatting and data entry later in this chapter and in Chapter 6.

A Sample Spreadsheet

Let's use Microsoft Works to build an electronic version of the budget worksheet in Figure 5-1.

□ Load Microsoft Works.

□ Select the New command from the File menu.

□ Double-click on the spreadsheet icon. A new, blank spreadsheet is displayed.

□ Point to cell A1 and click the mouse button.

Whenever you click the mouse button with the pointer on a cell, that cell becomes the active cell, and you can then enter a label, number, or formula into it.

□ Type the label *Expenses.*

Because this label begins with a letter, the spreadsheet knows that you are entering a label, rather than a value (or number). The spreadsheet stores labels as text—you can't perform calculations on them. If you make a typing mistake at this point, simply use the Backspace key to erase the error and then retype the label.

□ Press the Tab key to enter the label and select cell B1.

When you press the Tab key, Works stores the label or value you've just entered and moves the selection one cell to the right. If, on the other hand, you press the Return key to enter a label or value, the label or value is entered, and the selection moves down to the cell directly underneath. A third way to enter labels or values is to point to the enter box (the box with the check mark, next to the entry bar) and click the mouse button—this enters the label or value and leaves the selection on that cell. To correct a mistake in a cell where you've already entered a label or value, click on the cell to select it, and then edit the entry (using the Backspace key, Spacebar, and other keys) in the entry bar.

□ Type the label *March* and press the Tab key. Enter the labels *April, May,* and *Qtr. Total* in this row.

□ Move the selection back to column A by pointing to cell A3 and clicking the mouse button.

□ Type the label *Food* and press the Return key. Notice that when you press the Return key, the selection moves down to cell A4, instead of to the cell at the right.

☐ Refer to Figure 5-1 to fill in the rest of the labels.

☐ Point to cell B3 and click to make that cell active. Type the number *200*, and press the Tab key. Because the first character in this entry is a number, Works knows that it should treat the entry as a value, instead of a label.

☐ Enter food expenses shown in Figure 5-1 for April and May.

Entering formulas

Now we're ready to enter the first formula on this sample spreadsheet.

☐ Move the selection to cell E3 (if it isn't there already), and then type this formula:

=Sum(B3:D3)

☐ Click the enter box (the box with the check mark, next to the entry bar) when you're done. Notice that the sum of the numbers in cells B3, C3, and D3 appears in cell E3.

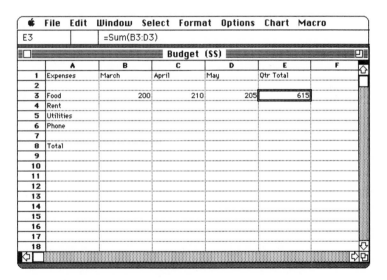

Let's look at how this formula was entered. The first character you typed was the equal sign. This tells the Works spreadsheet you're about to enter a formula, instead of a label or a value. Works treats formulas differently from labels and values, but because all formulas begin with either a number or a letter, you have to type the equal sign to let Works know that you're entering a formula instead of a value or a label.

Following the equal sign, you typed the word Sum. Sum is a spreadsheet function that tells Works to add the values that follow. The Works spreadsheet has 64 built-in functions that do everything from addition to financial calculations. There's an alternate way to enter a function into a formula: Instead of typing the function, you can choose the Paste Function command from the Edit menu and then select a function from a list. As described earlier in this chapter, the Paste Function command inserts the function that you have selected into your formula.

After you enter the function, you must enter the argument—the cell location, value, or range of cell locations to be acted upon (summed, in this case) by the function. Arguments are always enclosed in parentheses. In our example, the argument is B3:D3, which indicates the range of cells B3, C3, and D3. In this example, you could have typed the actual numbers you wanted to sum (200, 210, and 205), but you entered the locations of these numbers instead. Doing this lets you take advantage of the spreadsheet's matrix structure to build a formula that can easily recalculate if you change the values in those cells.

By using cell locations (or references) you're telling Works to sum the contents of the cells B3, C3, and D3. Those cells in our example happen to contain the values 200, 210, and 205. You could change the values in those cells, and the spreadsheet would recalculate the Sum formula to present the new total. If you had used specific numbers instead of cell references in the formula, changing the cell contents would have no effect. To change the result of the formula, you would have to change the formula itself because it is adding specific values.

The argument in this particular formula is a range (a continuous group of cells in the same row or column), so Works adds all the numbers in cells B3 through D3. You indicate a range of cells by typing a colon between two numbers.

After you type the entire formula and click the enter box (or press the Return or Enter key), the spreadsheet calculates the formula and presents the result of the formula in the cell. (Recall that you can display formulas in their cells by choosing the Show Formulas command from the Options menu.)

For now, let's finish entering the expense numbers in the spreadsheet, following the steps outlined earlier: Point to the cell where a value belongs, and then type the number.

□ Enter the rest of the expense numbers — but not the totals — shown in Figure 5-1.

> **TIP:** A faster way to specify a range of numbers in an argument is to hold down the mouse button and drag the pointer across the cells you want to include in the range. As you drag the mouse across cells, an outline appears around the cells. When you release the mouse button to indicate the end of the range, the range is entered into the entry bar in the proper format. Try it with the previous example.
>
> ☐ Click on cell E3 to select it, and choose the Cut command from the Edit menu, or press Command-X to delete the Sum formula from that cell.
>
> ☐ Type *=Sum(* to enter the function and the opening parenthesis that begins the argument.
>
> ☐ Click on cell B3, hold down the mouse button, and drag across cells C3 and D3.
>
> ☐ Release the mouse button. The range is entered in the entry bar.
>
> ☐ Type a closing parenthesis to end the argument, and then click the enter box or press the Return or Enter key to enter the formula.

Using a cell note

When you're through, you're almost ready to enter the rest of the formulas in this worksheet. First, though, let's use the Cell Notes feature in Works version 2.0 to clarify one of the numbers in this matrix. The telephone expense for April (in cell C6) is a lot higher than it is for either March or May. You might wonder why later, so you can attach a note to that cell now to explain the higher cost.

☐ Point to cell C6, hold down the Command key, and double-click on the cell. If you prefer to use a menu to open a cell note, select cell C6 and choose the Open Cell Note command from the Edit menu.

☐ If the note window is covering a part of the spreadsheet you need to see, you can resize it or drag it to a different place on the screen, just as you would a window in the Finder or on the Works desktop.

□ The cursor is blinking at the top of the note, so type in the explanation: *Phone higher this month due to long distance calls: Mom's birthday, Easter calls to relatives.* The Cell Note window now looks like this:

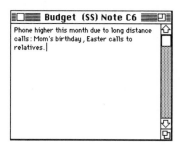

□ Close the note window by clicking its close box. Cell C6 has a black dot in its upper-right corner to indicate that you've attached a note to that cell. If you don't see the mark, choose the Show Notes Indicator command from the Options menu, and the mark will appear.

Now, let's finish this spreadsheet by entering the rest of the formulas, as we did in cell E3. First, we'll enter a formula to produce a monthly total of expenses in cell B8.

□ Select cell B8.

□ Type an equal sign, followed by the formula:

Sum(B3:B6)

□ Click the enter box, or press Return, Enter, or Tab.

The sum of the expense values for March appears in cell B8.

Copying formulas

Now, you can take advantage of having used cell references instead of specific values in the two formulas you copied.

□ Point to cell E3 and hold down the mouse button.

□ Drag the mouse down to cell E6. All the cells in this range are now highlighted.

□ Release the mouse button, and select the Fill Down command from the Edit menu (or press Command-D). Totals appear in cells E4, E5, and E6.

	A	B	C	D	E	F
			Budget (SS)			
1	Expenses	March	April	May	Qtr Total	
2						
3	Food	200	210	205	615	
4	Rent	500	500	500	1500	
5	Utilities	35	31	30	96	
6	Phone	25	50	30	105	
7						
8	Total	760				
9						
10						
11						
12						
13						
14						
15						
16						
17						
18						

As mentioned earlier in this chapter, the Fill Down command tells Works to copy the contents of a cell into the highlighted range of cells below it. In our sample spreadsheet, cell E3 contains the formula Sum(B3:D3), so that formula was copied into the cells in E4, E5, and E6. Notice, however, that the totals in these cells reflect the contents of rows 4, 5, and 6, not the contents of row 3, because the formula in E3 contained relative cell references, rather than absolute cell references.

Unless you specifically tell Works otherwise (by putting dollar signs in front of cell references in a formula to make them absolute), Works uses relative references when you copy formulas and the references are adjusted according to the new position of the formula. If we had used absolute references in the sample formula we copied, Works would have summed the specific values in cells B3, C3, and D3, even if we copied that formula to another location. Because the formula in cell E3 contains relative references, Works will sum the three cells to the left of the formula's location. So, the copy of the formula in cell E4 has summed the contents of cells B4, C4, and D4; the copy of the formula in cell E5 has summed the contents of cells B5, C5, and D5; and so on. Figure 5-4 shows the results of both relative and absolute references. (The columns in these spreadsheets have been widened to show the complete formulas.)

	A	B	C	D	E	
					Budget (SS)	
	A	**B**	**C**	**D**	**E**	
1	Expenses	March	April	May	Qtr Total	
2						
3	Food	200	210	205	=Sum(B3:D3)	
4	Rent	500	500	500	=Sum(B4:D4)	
5	Utilities	35	31	30	=Sum(B5:D5)	
6	Phone	25	50	30	=Sum(B6:D6)	
7						
8	Total	=Sum($B$3:$B$6)	=Sum($B$3:$B$6)	=Sum($B$3:$B$6)		

	A	B	C	D	E	F
					Budget (SS)	
	A	**B**	**C**	**D**	**E**	**F**
1	Expenses	March	April	May	Qtr Total	
2						
3	Food	200	210	205	615	
4	Rent	500	500	500	1500	
5	Utilities	35	31	30	96	
6	Phone	25	50	30	105	
7						
8	Total	760	760	760		

Figure 5-4.

By displaying absolute and relative formulas (top) and then the values they produce (bottom), you can see that the absolute Sum formula in cell B8, when copied to cells C8 and D8, always produces the same result. But the relative Sum formula in cell E3, when copied to cells E4, E5, and E6, produces varying results because it refers to different cells, depending on its new location.

To finish our sample budget worksheet, we could re-enter what is essentially the same Sum formula in cells C6, D6, and E6. But because we've used relative references in the formula, it's much simpler to copy it, and have Works adjust the references for you.

□ Point to cell B8 and hold down the mouse button.

□ Drag the pointer across to cell E8 and release the button.

□ Choose the Fill Right command from the Edit menu (or press Command-R). The formula in cell B8 is copied into cells C8, D8, and E8, and the results of the formulas are shown in these cells.

Entering new values

Now that this simple spreadsheet is complete, you can see the other major advantage of electronic spreadsheets in action. We've entered the formulas, rather than specific numbers, so we can change the values in the locations referred to in the formulas, and the formulas themselves will recalculate automatically.

❑ Click on cell B3, and enter the number *220*.

❑ Press the Return key. The Sum formula at the bottom of this column recalculates the total in cell B8.

By using cell references, rather than specific numbers, to make up formulas, you can take advantage of the fixed relationships between various locations in this spreadsheet. You can change the numbers in the expense rows as you please, and Works will immediately recalculate the formulas that are affected.

Formatting the spreadsheet

Before we file this spreadsheet away, let's make it a little more readable by using Works' formatting commands. Works versions 1.0 and 1.1 limited us to only the 9-point Geneva font for spreadsheet documents, but in version 2.0, we can use any font available on our Mac system. Because this spreadsheet isn't very large and we don't have to worry too much about fitting it on one page, let's use a larger font size.

❑ Choose the Font command from the Format menu, and select the Geneva font, if it is not already selected.

❑ Choose the Size command to display the Size menu and select the 12-point option. The entire spreadsheet is now shown in 12-point Geneva type.

Notice, however, that the page-break marker now falls between columns E and F, which would force the Qtr. Totals column to print on a second page. You can fix this problem in one of two ways.

❑ Choose the Page Setup command and make the left and right margins for this document .5 inch instead of 1 inch.

Or:

❑ Change the font size to 10-point instead of 12-point.

Either way, the page-break marker will move so that all five columns of the document will print on one page.

As another formatting enhancement, we might want to change the row and column titles to boldface and center the column titles in their cells. Because number formats, alignment, and style options are all handled through the same cell-attributes dialog box, we can make all the formatting changes at once to each selected row, column, or cell.

□ Select all of row 1 in the document by clicking on the row number at the left of the screen.

□ Choose the Set Cell Attributes command from the Format menu.

□ Click the Bold option under the Style heading.

□ Click the Center option under the Align heading.

□ Press the Return or Enter key, or click the OK button. The top row of labels are now boldfaced and centered in their cells.

Let's boldface and right align the labels in cells A3 through A6 and in cell A8. Because this isn't a complete row or column, we'll have to drag the mouse pointer across these cells to select them as a group before applying the new cell attributes.

□ Click on cell A3, hold down the mouse button, and drag down to cell A8 to select the block of cells.

□ Choose the Set Cell Attributes command from the Format menu, and then click the Bold Style and Right Align options.

□ Press the Return or Enter key, or click the OK button to make these changes appear in the spreadsheet.

The formatting commands in Works version 2.0 give you much more control over how your finished spreadsheets will look. When combined with the Works Draw tool, you can prepare polished spreadsheet documents for your boss, your banker, or other important audiences.

> **TIP:** If you're changing the attributes of only one cell, you can double-click on the cell to display the Cell Attributes dialog box, rather than having to choose the Set Cell Attributes command from the Format menu.

Making the Most of the Spreadsheet

The basic features of storing, editing, and formatting text, numbers, and formulas in the Works spreadsheet are common to every spreadsheet program on any computer. But Works and the Macintosh can make these tasks a lot easier if you know the shortcuts. On the other hand, the Works spreadsheet isn't a high-powered analytical tool on the order of Microsoft Excel. In most cases, though, there are ways to work around the spreadsheet's limitations. Let's see how to make the most of the Works spreadsheet.

Use the mouse or the keyboard, whichever works best

When you're new to Works, you'll want to use the mouse to help you execute commands and find your way around the spreadsheet. You can enter an entire formula by selecting a function with the Paste Function command and then selecting a cell or range of cells. To enter the formula = Average(B3:D3), for example, use the following steps.

□ Select the cell in which you want the formula to appear.

□ Choose the Paste Function command from the Edit menu.

□ Double-click on the Average function in the list. When you do, the function name and two parentheses appear in the entry bar, and the flashing insertion point appears between the parentheses.

□ Hold down the mouse button while you drag the mouse pointer across cells B3, C3, and D3, and then release the mouse button. The range of cells B3:D3 appears between the parentheses in the entry bar.

□ Click the enter box to enter the formula.

You can also enter individual cells into a formula's argument by clicking on them. Point-and-click formula building helps ensure that you enter the cells you want by eliminating any possibility of mistyping cell references. Even experienced users will find it faster and more accurate to build formulas with the mouse. The only way to select a group of cells for formatting is to use the mouse, but that's also faster and less error-prone than using the keyboard. There are also a few shortcuts available via mouse clicks, rather than selecting an item from a menu or dialog box, as shown in Figure 5-5.

Another activity for which it makes sense to use the mouse is adjusting column widths: When you type in a specific number of characters for a column width, you usually have to guess at the proper number, but if you simply drag the dividing lines between columns using the mouse, you can instantly see when your columns are wide enough.

Action	Shortcut
Move selected data to another cell or cells	Command-Option-click on the destination cell(s)
Display a cell note	Command-double-click on a cell
Display the Cell Attributes dialog box	Double-click on a cell
Paste a function	Double-click on the function name in the Paste Function dialog box.
Specify a range of cells in a formula	Drag the pointer across the cells when a formula is in the entry bar.
Add cell references to a formula	Click on them with a formula in the entry bar
Widen a column	Drag the column dividing line

Figure 5-5.
Mouse shortcuts.

As you gain experience with the spreadsheet, however, you may well find it faster to execute many commands from the keyboard. Figure 5-6 lists all the spreadsheet commands that you can execute with the keyboard.

In situations offering a choice of using the mouse or keyboard, a good rule of thumb is simply to keep using the device you're using at the moment. Don't switch from keyboard to mouse when you can perform the same function with the keyboard, and don't return to the keyboard from the mouse when you can do something just as well with the mouse.

Action	Command	Menu	Keyboard Equivalent
Open a file	Open	File	Command-O
Close a file	Close	File	Command-W
Save a file	Save	File	Command-S
Print a file	Print	File	Command-P
Quit Works	Quit	File	Command-Q
Undo a command	Undo	Edit	Command-Z
Cut text	Cut	Edit	Command-X

Figure 5-6. *(continued)*
Keyboard equivalents for spreadsheet commands.

Figure 5-6. *continued*

Action	Command	Menu	Keyboard Equivalent
Copy text	Copy	Edit	Command-C
Paste text	Paste	Edit	Command-V
Turn on the Draw tool	Draw on	Edit	Command-J
Insert a row or column	Insert	Edit	Command-I
Make a cell reference absolute (toggle)	Absolute Cell Ref	Edit	Command-A
Fill range to the right	Fill Right	Edit	Command-R
Fill a range below	Fill Down	Edit	Command-D
Display on-line help	Help	Window	Command-?
Find a cell	Find Cell	Select	Command-F
Go to a cell	Go To Cell	Select	Command-G
Calculate immediately	Calculate Now	Options	Command-=
Start macro recording	Start Recording	Macro	Option-+
Stop macro recording	Stop Recording	Macro	Option-−
Play back a macro	Playback	Macro	Option-Delete
Stop a macro in progress	—	—	Command-.
Display last document on Window menu	—	Window	Command-,
Make a cell or selection boldface	—	—	Command-B
Make a cell or selection underlined	—	—	Command-U
Make a cell or selection normal text	—	—	Command-N

Use frozen titles and split bars to view different parts of a spreadsheet

The split bars at the lower-left and upper-right corners of the spreadsheet window let you divide your window into as many as four separate, independently-scrolling views. Using the split bars to divide the window lets you view distant areas of the spreadsheet on the screen that you couldn't ordinarily see at the same time in the same window. It's easy to forget the numbers you entered a couple of dozen rows above your current location, but the split bars let you bring that distant row into view so that you can refer to it while continuing to work at your current location. Use the Freeze Titles options on the Options menu to freeze row or column titles in place so that no matter where you scroll, you'll always see where you are.

Use the navigation shortcuts

Spreadsheets usually grow beyond what can be displayed on one Mac screen, and Works has several features that let you move quickly to specific cell locations. The Find Cell and Go To Cell commands on the Select menu can move the selection to a distant cell quickly. You can use the Find Cell command to find text as well as numbers so that you can actually name different sections of your spreadsheet and then move to them easily with this command. The Last Cell and Show Active Cell commands on the Select menu also let you quickly move to a particular cell or section of your spreadsheet. Finally, you can use the scroll bars, although doing so takes a little practice. Each scroll bar's length represents the entire 16,382 rows or 256 columns in the spreadsheet. So if you drag the scroll box to move to a different area, the chances are you'll end up in row 5000 or column CC, when you really wanted to move to row 150 or column AB. It's better to click in the gray area of the scroll bar to view a page of the spreadsheet at a time or to use the Select menu commands to jump to distant locations with more accuracy.

Use macros to speed formatting and data entry

You can store almost any repetitive spreadsheet activity as a macro so that you can handle it quickly by simply pressing a couple of keys. If you regularly produce spreadsheets that cover the same months, weeks, or other time periods, for example, you can record and store a macro that enters the appropriate time periods in adjacent columns. The bigger your spreadsheets, the more useful such a macro will be.

Suppose you regularly do two-year forecasts. Such a forecast might have column labels for each month, with yearly totals and perhaps averages between the two years: There could be as many as 30 column labels in all. If you choose the Start Recording command from the Macros menu before you enter the labels for the first time, you can replay that macro later to enter those labels. You not only save time (because the macro will execute much more quickly than you can type), but you can be sure the labels will be not only identical to your original labels, but also entered with no typing errors, assuming you didn't record any typing errors originally.

You can also use macros to combine several format enhancements under one key combination. Suppose, for example, you always want your row or column titles to be boldfaced and centered in their cells. Without a macro, you must select the row, select the Set Cell Attributes command, click the Bold and Center options, and then click the OK button to apply the changes. With a macro, you could perform all these activities by pressing a single Option-key combination.

Formulas are another candidate for macro recording. Typing function names or selecting them from the Paste Function dialog box, specifying range names, copying formulas, or making a formula absolute instead of relative are other activities you can automate with macros.

Use the copy and move shortcuts

We've seen how the Fill Right and Fill Down commands can speed formula entry, but you can also use these commands to replicate text or divider markers such as a row of dashes or asterisks. If you need to move a group of cells down or to the right a few rows, you can use the Insert command to insert blank columns or rows in front of the group. If you must move the cells without expanding the spreadsheet, you can either use the Move command on the Edit menu or simply select the cell or cells, hold down the Command and Option keys together, and then click on the cell into which you want to move the data. It's also easy to move data from one spreadsheet document to another by means of the Clipboard because you can have up to 14 spreadsheets open at the same time on the Works desktop.

Sometimes, you don't want to copy values and formulas from one spreadsheet area to another or between spreadsheets. The Paste With Options command on the Edit menu lets you choose between pasting values only or pasting both formulas and values. Paste With Options also lets you transpose numbers so that data that was in rows when you copied it to the Clipboard will be placed in columns when you paste it.

Sort rows for clarity

If you're preparing an inventory or budget spreadsheet, you might enter the line items as you happen to think of them and then decide later they would be more useful in alphabetical order. Or, you might enter a series of employee names and employee numbers and then want to sort the list in order of employee number. Works' Sort command lets you sort the rows in a spreadsheet on up to three columns at once. When you choose the Sort command from the Edit menu, Works displays a dialog box like this:

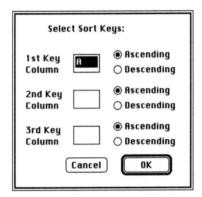

If you select data in a column before choosing the Sort command, that column is entered as the first sort key in the dialog box (column A in the previous example). Otherwise, you type in the columns you want to sort on and then choose either ascending or descending sort order. It's wise to sort a spreadsheet before you enter formulas to calculate data in columns; rearranging the data in a spreadsheet will jumble any formulas pertaining to sorted rows if the formulas contain ranges because the range's rows won't be in the same order after the sort. If you sort a spreadsheet after entering formulas, check the formulas and their totals to be sure they make sense after the sort is completed.

Emphasize points with charts and objects

The charting features in Works let you instantly display data visually so that you and your intended audience can see key relationships between numbers. If charts aren't enough, you can use the Draw tool to circle key numbers, or you can enter text or create boxes or circles to emphasize certain points. You can even use color in an onscreen presentation to make labels or values stand out even more. We'll see these tools in action in Chapter 6.

Format your data to suit your paper and your audience

The Mac's printing and page-setup options let you print a spreadsheet sideways to squeeze more columns of data onto a page; you can also reduce or enlarge the size of print to fit your data on paper. In Works version 2.0, as we've seen, you can also choose any single font and font size in which to display your data. Although the default font size is 9 point, you should always make the font size as large as it can be (depending on how much space you have on your paper) so that those who will read your spreadsheet don't get eyestrain. Other techniques that help you display data effectively include:

- Widening columns to create space between them.
- Turning off the grid lines so that they don't compete with the numbers or borders on a printout.
- Using cell borders to highlight certain labels or numbers.
- Printing row and column numbers on a page to help readers orient themselves.

Printing row and column numbers is particularly important when your spreadsheet contains cell notes because the notes, printed on a separate page, are identified by the address of the cell to which they're attached.

Use the Find command to locate cells

To locate a cell or group of cells quickly, you can simply enter a name above or near the cells you want to be able to locate and then jump to that part of the spreadsheet quickly using the Find Cell command on the Select menu. This approach might take some planning on your part when you design the layout of the spreadsheet. With a large budget spreadsheet, for example, you might divide the individual line items into groups such as fixed expenses, variable expenses, depreciable assets, receivables, and so forth. If you separate each area by one row and then insert the name of the area in a cell above it, you can always move to that area quickly with the Find Cell command.

Use macros to facilitate entering formulas

To facilitate entering references to groups of cells in a formula, you can use a macro to represent the group of cells, and then type the macro key combination whenever you want to enter that range of cells into a formula. To store a range of cells as a macro, use the following steps.

- Select any cell or range of cells.

- Type the beginning of the desired formula using a function, such as =*Sum(*.

- Choose the Macros On command, and then choose Start Recording from the Macros menu. Choose a key to use for invoking the macro, and describe the macro with a name indicating the specific range of cells you want to record.

- Click the Record button and type the address of the range of cells you want to record. (You must type the address of the cell range rather than selecting it with the mouse, otherwise the selection will be relative to whatever happens to be on your screen when the macro is invoked. See the next section, titled ''Tips for working with macros.'')

- Choose the Stop Recording command.

- Finish the formula. To cancel it before entering it, click the Cancel box in the entry bar.

Now, whenever you type the macro key combination you recorded, that cell or range of cells will be inserted in the entry bar.

Tips for working with macros

Macros take you literally—they do only what you specifically tell them to do. When you include a mouse action in a macro, what is recorded has little to do with what you are selecting and everything to do with the exact place on the screen where you clicked, dragged or released the mouse button. For example, if you record a macro that selects a file in the list box of the Open command's dialog box, the macro records the place on the screen where you clicked the mouse, not the name of the file you selected. So if you select a file to open in a macro, you might end up opening the wrong file, if any files have been renamed, or removed from, or added to the list. The file names must be in the same place in the Open command's list box each time you use the macro. One way to ensure this: Create a special folder for these files, be sure it is currently active in the Open dialog box, and remember to never rename, add, or move files in that folder. The file names always appear in alphabetical order in the list box of the Open dialog box, so when you use the mouse to click on each file, their positions will be the same each time you use the macro. Theoretically, you could add more files to the folder as long as they are alphabetically higher than the ones your macro will use. For example, if the files A, B, C, and D are in the folder, and you add file E, the placement of file names A through D will not be affected, but adding file A1 will cause files B through D to move down one space in the list.

Using the mouse to select menu commands works in macros, because the location of each menu command on the screen does not change within an application. The Open command is always in the same place on the File menu, so when the macro records the position of the mouse at the time you choose the command, it will reliably report the action because the menu doesn't move. This is not always the case, however, if you are using a macro to perform operations between Works tools using menus such as the Spell menu, which exists only in the word processor. Invoking a macro that uses the Correct Spelling command while you are in a spreadsheet document will probably cause the macro to choose the Show Grid command, which is in approximately the same place on the screen. So it can be very important to be sure you play back your macros from the same Works application in which they were created.

When you are creating macros, you should also keep in mind that you need to enter references to specific cells using the keyboard, unless you are absolutely sure that the active screen will be identical to the one that existed when you recorded that macro. For example, if you are creating a macro to transfer totals from one Works spreadsheet to another, instead of selecting cells using the mouse, you could use the Find Cell command and enter the specific address of the cell you want to select. In the case of a cell range, you would have to either use the Find Cell command for each cell in the range individually, or include the key combination for another macro that you have created to identify a range of cells within the macro you are currently recording.

You can create several spreadsheets in one file

When you work on a large, complex spreadsheet project, you might want to create separate worksheet files for different aspects of the job. In a corporate budget, for example, you might have individual budget files for each department. Works doesn't let you link spreadsheets. But there is an alternative when you're working on complex tasks. The Works matrix contains over 4.1 million cells, so one spreadsheet file can contain several spreadsheets in different areas of the available grid. Each departmental budget might be in a different part of the matrix for one file, for example, and the consolidated corporate budget could be yet another part of the same file. By putting all of the data in one file, you can use cell references to transfer data automatically from one cell to another.

Let's look at the Budget spreadsheet as an example. Suppose food, rent, utilities, and phone expenses are only the household part of a larger personal budget. We might, for example, have other line items that have to do with long-term debts and short-term debts, as follows:

	A	B	C	D	E
7					
8	Total House Exp.	760	791	765	2316
9					
10	Mortgage	750	750	750	2250
11	Car Loan	185	185	185	555
12	Personal Loan	103	103	103	309
13					
14	Total Long-Term	1038	1038	1038	3114
15					
16	Visa	50	50	50	150
17	Mastercard	25	25	25	75
18					
19	Total Short-Term	75	75	75	225
20	Total Long-Term				
21	Total House Exp.				
22	Total Expenses				
23					
24					

In such a spreadsheet, we might want to duplicate the contents of the household and long-term debt total rows in a summary portion farther down the spreadsheet. We could simply type in the same numbers from these other total rows, or copy them with the Clipboard, but let's duplicate the values in these upper rows by using cell references.

□ Enter the additional labels, values, and Sum formulas.

□ Click on cell B20 to select it.

□ Type the equal sign, followed by the cell designation *B14*.

Press the Return key when you've finished. The value *1038* appears in cell B20.

By using a cell reference, we have told Works to take whatever value is in cell B14, and duplicate it in cell B20. This way, we can change the value in cell B14 (or change the values above it, which affect the total amount that appears in B14), and the value in B20 will change. This is the advantage of using a cell reference to duplicate a value from elsewhere in a spreadsheet, instead of re-entering the value or copying it.

Using this technique, we can transfer totals from departmental budgets to rows in a consolidated budget, as long as all the budgets we are working with are in the same spreadsheet file. This is a good substitute for spreadsheet linking.

Using more than one font or font size in a spreadsheet

You can use Works' integration to apply more than one font and font size to a spreadsheet.

Copy the spreadsheet to the Clipboard, and paste it into a blank word-processor document. You can then use the word processor's multiple fonts and font sizes to format your spreadsheet numbers any way you like.

Now, let's look at some basic tips that will help you as you work.

Basic Spreadsheet Tips

We'll see how the different spreadsheet features work as we perform various types of tasks in Chapter 6, but there are some fundamentals that apply to every type of spreadsheet, no matter what its purpose.

Plan first, execute later

Instead of jumping right into new spreadsheets by entering labels and values, take a few moments to plan what you'll be doing so that you have a reasonable mental picture of how your spreadsheet will look. If you're new to spreadsheets, you might want to draw a rough plan of a spreadsheet on paper before you begin making it with Works. After you gain some experience, you can keep a plan in your head fairly easily. By planning ahead, you can avoid having to rearrange several rows or columns and having to re-enter a number of formulas when you're halfway through a project.

Take a budget, for example. Before you begin, you should have some idea of the kinds of expense items you will be listing and how you will group those items. You might lump household expenses in one set of rows, long-term debt in another set of rows, discretionary income in another set of rows, and so on.

Of course, the general structure of your spreadsheets will depend on what you're trying to accomplish. A budget spreadsheet, for example, will look different from an investment analysis or an amortization table. Whatever the task, though, think before you leap. Consider what you're trying to do, what types of calculations will be necessary, and how best to organize your data so that you can enter formulas easily and make sense out of the results with a minimum of effort.

Format last

As with word processing, you should concentrate on entering the data, labels, and formulas into your spreadsheet first. The usual order of tasks in building a spreadsheet is:

- ☐ Enter row and column labels.
- ☐ Enter values.
- ☐ Enter formulas.
- ☐ Format the spreadsheet.

A classic result of formatting too soon is ruined spreadsheet titles. You might begin a new spreadsheet with a nice, multiple-column title in row 1. But as you enter row and column labels, numbers, and formulas, you may find it necessary to make columns wider or narrower, or to insert, delete, or rearrange columns. Of course, when you do, that lovely title at the top of the spreadsheet is rearranged as well.

This also applies to sorting rows. If you want to sort rows to arrange them in alphabetical or numeric order, do so before you enter formulas so that the formulas will apply to the rows in their final order. Otherwise, rearranging rows can render formulas inaccurate as row positions are changed.

Use a reference area and cell notes

Unless you're making a spreadsheet strictly for your own reading, it's a good idea to begin any spreadsheet with a reference area at the top that describes the document's purpose, the date it was created, and the assumptions it makes about the numbers it includes. If you're assuming a certain interest rate or ratio in an investment analysis or depreciation schedule, for example, enter a line at the top of the spreadsheet that states this. In fact, by entering an interest rate at the top of a spreadsheet, you can then use the cell where that rate is entered as a reference in the formulas you enter below.

Suppose, for example, that you assume sales will grow at a 19 percent annual rate. If you enter a line saying *Assumed annual sales growth, 19%*, being sure to enter the *19%* in its own cell, you can then refer to that cell whenever you need to apply that rate to your calculations. Including this line not only tells readers in advance what you're assuming, but makes it easier to change your assumptions at any time. If you revise your growth estimate to 20%, for example, you can simply change the value in the assumption line at the top, and all the formulas that actually calculate growth (which refer to the cell in the assumption line) will recalculate with the new rate. In Chapter 6, we'll see how to put cell references and reference areas into action.

In cases in which you think you or others might later question where a number in a specific cell came from, use Works' cell note feature to make a note about the number's origin or to state the formula you used to arrive at it so that it will be easy to understand.

Point with the mouse to indicate cell references

Use the mouse whenever possible to indicate the specific cells being entered into formulas or as references elsewhere. When you type, you are far more likely to make a mistake that might mean an improper reference that doesn't show up until much later; but when you point, you are fairly sure of indicating the correct cell. Works makes it simple to indicate the cells you want to include in a formula by pointing to them.

Check all formulas and results

There's a false legitimacy about spreadsheets that makes us trust them too easily. Somehow, we get the idea that an electronic spreadsheet can't be wrong. But remember, a spreadsheet's results are only as good as the formulas and data make them, and the formulas and data entered by a human are subject to errors. It's true that the spreadsheet won't produce an incorrect calculation, but it's quite possible that you could inadvertently specify the wrong cell references or even the wrong functions in a formula.

It's particularly tempting to take a spreadsheet at its word when you've entered and tested one formula and then copied it to a number of other locations. Whether you enter all your formulas by hand or copy them, however, you should check every formula in the file before you sit back and begin relying on the calculations the spreadsheet is producing. Individuals and even large corporations have made serious financial blunders because somebody didn't check every formula in a spreadsheet. Remember, the numbers are only as good as the formulas, and formulas can be wrong.

Save files often

You never know when a software glitch or a power failure will shut down your system, so get in the habit of saving your work by pressing Command-S, or by choosing the Save command on the File menu every few minutes, and certainly whenever you leave your computer. A simple System error could wipe out hours of work if you haven't saved the most current version of your file.

Spreadsheet Specifications

Here are some specifications you may want to refer to as you use the spreadsheet.

Maximum spreadsheet size (rows by columns): 16,382 by 256.

Total number of built-in functions: 64; (56 in version 1.0).

Maximum file size: Approximately 22,500 filled cells (varies depending on specific cell contents).

Maximum number of decimal places in a value: 15.

Calculating precision: 15 decimal places.

Maximum column width: 40 characters.

Maximum length of a value or text: 238 characters.

Maximum length of a formula: 200 characters.

Maximum number of chart definitions per spreadsheet: 8.

Number of chart types available: 5.

Number of fonts available: Any font available to Mac System is available, but only one font can be used per spreadsheet file.

Maximum paper length: 273 inches (with Custom Size selected in the Page Setup dialog box).

Maximum paper width: 273 inches (with Custom Size selected in the Page Setup dialog box).

Minimum paper length: 1 inch (with Custom Size selected in the Paper options of the Page Setup dialog box).

Minimum paper width: 1 inch (with Custom Size selected in the Paper options of the Page Setup dialog box).

Default paper size: US Letter (8½ by 11 inches).

Default Top, Bottom, Left, and Right Margins: 1 inch.

Default Font: 9-point Geneva.

Number of fonts available: 1.

Maximum length of search/replace strings: 80 characters.

Maximum length of headers or footers: 99 characters.

Range of numbered pages in a document: 1 through 2,000.

Chapter 6

Spreadsheet Projects

In this chapter, we'll see several of the spreadsheet's features in action as we help Al Chroma, proprietor of Al's Videorama, do a variety of business and personal projects. To begin, we'll work on a long inventory project that shows how you can enter, copy, sort, and format data in the spreadsheet. Also, we will help Al develop a loan-amortization table and a customer-volume report that includes a chart. And finally, we'll pull all of Al's personal and business finances together on a single, consolidated spreadsheet.

An Inventory

In an effort to offer his customers the very best selection of VCR programming, Al has been stocking videotapes like a madman for a couple of months now. But, for his records, Al has only a stack of videotape order receipts. To avoid digging through those receipts to see how many tapes he has and what they cost him, he wants to set up a spreadsheet that will let him know exactly how much capital he has tied up in his inventory. This spreadsheet will quickly calculate the value of all the tapes in stock and it will show how many copies of each movie are in the inventory. For the purposes of this exercise, we'll work with a small sample spreadsheet that contains only two categories of Al's videotapes. The finished sample spreadsheet is shown in Figure 6-1.

Videorama Inventory

Mar 1, 1989

Title	Quantity	Cost	Total Value
Adventure			
Blazing Bullets	1	$14.95	$14.95
Jungle Fever	2	$11.95	$23.90
Six Gun City	1	$12.95	$12.95
The One-Eyed Assassin	3	$12.95	$38.85
The Spy Who Said No	3	$13.95	$41.85
Two Guys In Trouble	2	$15.95	$31.90
Subtotal Adventure	**12**		**$164.40**
Aerobics			
Aerobic Profit-Taking	4	$14.95	$59.80
George Will's Yoga Fun	1	$12.95	$12.95
King Kong Bundy's Workout	2	$9.95	$19.90
Yoko's Roll-A-Thon	1	$12.95	$12.95
Subtotal Aerobics	**8**		**$105.60**
Grand Totals	**20**		**$270.00**

Figure 6-1.
An inventory spreadsheet for Al's Videorama might look like this.

Entering inventory items and category titles

Let's begin by opening a new spreadsheet file and entering the names of all the videotapes in stock:

☐ Click the spreadsheet icon on the Works opening screen, and then click the New button. A new spreadsheet appears.

☐ Click on cell A1 to select it, and then type the column label *Title*.

□ Press Command-B to make the column title boldface and enter it at the same time.

All of the style commands, such as Underline or Bold, work this way, whether you choose them from the Format menu or use the keyboard. Applying the stylistic enhancement enters the value at the same time.

□ Press the Tab key to move the selection to cell B1, and type the column label *Quantity*.

□ Press Command-B to make this title boldface and enter it at the same time.

□ Enter the title *Cost* into column C and the title *Total Value* into column D, using the preceding two steps.

Now, we're ready to enter the two category titles for the tapes in the sample inventory. The videotapes in this example are divided into two subject areas: Adventure and Aerobics. Let's assume we don't know at this point exactly how many titles we have in each category. We'll skip four rows between each category name for now.

□ Select cell A3 and type the category name *Adventure*. Press Command-B to boldface this category name and enter it at the same time.

□ Press the Return key five times to skip four rows.

□ Enter the category name *Aerobics*, and make it boldface, as you did with the first title.

The spreadsheet now looks like this:

	A	B	C	D	E	F
1	Title	Quantity	Cost	Total Value		
2						
3	Adventure					
4						
5						
6						
7						
8	Aerobics					
9						
10						
11						
12						
13						
14						
15						
16						
17						
18						

Untitled (SS)

Now, we're ready to begin entering tape titles.

☐ Select cell A4 and type the first tape title, *Six Gun City*.

☐ Click on cell A5 or press Return. The label you just typed is entered in cell A4, and cell A5 is selected. Type the second tape title, *Two Guys In Trouble*, and then click on cell A6 or press Return to select the next cell in the column and enter the second label.

Notice at this point that the label *Two Guys In Trouble* is wider than the current column width and that it has extended into column B at the right. When you type a long label into a Works spreadsheet, if there isn't enough room for the whole label in the current column, it extends into columns to the right. In this case, we will want to use column B to enter Quantity numbers later, so we want all of the labels we enter in column A to stay inside that column. To do that, we'll have to widen column A so that there's enough room in it for *Two Guys In Trouble* and other long labels we'll enter.

The easiest way to widen a column in the Works spreadsheet is to drag the column divider.

☐ Move the pointer to the dividing line between the labels for columns A and B at the top of the screen. When the pointer is exactly on top of the dividing line, it becomes a double arrow.

☐ Hold down the mouse button and drag the dividing line to the right about one inch.

☐ Release the mouse button to fix the dividing line in its new location. Column A is now wide enough to hold *Two Guys In Trouble* and other long labels.

☐ Repeat the label-entering process for the titles *Blazing Bullets* and *The Spy Who Said No*.

After you type the second of these titles into cell A7, you're out of room for entering tape titles because the category title for the Aerobics section is in the next row. You need to insert some rows so that you can add two more titles and a blank row in this category.

☐ Click on cell A8 and press Command-I, the keyboard equivalent for the Insert command. A blank row appears above row 8, and what was row 8 becomes row 9.

□ Press Command-I two more times. The Insert command inserts only one row at a time, but if you want to add several rows, simply use the Insert command repeatedly.

□ Type in the final two titles, *Jungle Fever* and *The One-Eyed Assassin*.

We notice after we type these two labels that they appear in boldface, rather than normal text because we inserted rows at the position where a boldfaced label formerly appeared (cell A8). We want these two labels in normal text, like the other tape titles.

□ Click on the cell containing *Jungle Fever* and hold down the mouse button.

□ Drag the pointer down to the cell containing *The One-Eyed Assassin* and release the mouse button. Both A8 and A9 are now selected.

□ Press Command-N to specify the normal text style for these two cells.

□ Click on cell A10 to remove the selection from the labels in A8 and A9. You can see these labels are now displayed in normal text, like this:

	A	B	C	D	E
				Untitled (SS)	
1	Title	Quantity	Cost	Total Value	
2					
3	Adventure				
4	Six Gun City				
5	Two Guys in Trouble				
6	Blazing Bullets				
7	The Spy Who Said No				
8	Jungle Fever				
9	The One-Eyed Assasin				
10					
11	Aerobics				
12					
13					
14					
15					
16					
17					
18					

> **TIP:** To avoid inadvertently assigning the wrong style options to cells when you insert them, insert the rows above a row that has the style you want. In this case, if we had inserted the rows above rows 4 through 7, for example, the labels in the new rows would have been displayed as normal text.

We now have one blank row between the Adventure and the Aerobics categories. Let's insert two more rows at this point so that we can add a row to subtotal the tapes by category.

- □ Select cell A10, if it isn't already selected.

- □ Press Command-I twice to insert two blank rows.

- □ Click on cell A11 and type the title *Subtotal Adventure.* Press the Return key to enter it. (Notice that the label appears in bold because you inserted a row at a location where the existing label had been boldfaced.)

Sorting inventory items

Now we have entered one complete category of tapes. Looking at the order in which the titles were entered, however, we decide the inventory sheet would be easier to use if the list were in alphabetical order (that's the way the tapes are stocked). We can use the spreadsheet's Sort command to rearrange the titles in this section quickly.

- □ Select cell A4.

- □ Hold down the mouse button, drag the pointer down to cell A9, and then release the mouse button. All the tape titles in this category are now selected.

- □ Choose the Sort command from the Edit menu. The Sort dialog box appears. Because the data you selected is in column A, this column is shown as the first sort key. The default sort order is ascending order (A to Z), and that's what you want.

- □ Click the OK button in the Sort dialog box. The titles in rows 4 through 9 are rearranged alphabetically.

> ☐ Using the graphic of the finished spreadsheet in Figure 6-1 as a guide, enter the Aerobics tape titles, along with a label for Aerobics subtotals. Don't forget to make the subtotals label boldface. In row 21 at the bottom, enter the title Grand Totals in column A, and make it boldface.

Now, enter the values for the Quantity and Cost columns in rows 4 through 9 and 14 through 17. (We'll calculate the subtotals, grand totals, and Total Value amounts using formulas a little later.)

> ☐ Enter all the other labels shown in Figure 6-1, and then enter the values shown in columns B and C, rows 4 through 9 and 14 through 17.

We've done a fair amount of work so far, so let's save this spreadsheet. First, though, we'll make sure the titles in row 1 will always appear at the top of the screen when we scroll down below row 18.

> ☐ Point to the pane marker above the top, right-hand scroll arrow, and drag it down until it is between rows 1 and 2.

> ☐ Release the mouse button. The spreadsheet is divided into two panes; one containing only row 1, and the other containing the remaining rows.

Now you can scroll the bottom pane to view areas below row 18 and still have the column labels at the top of the screen in the upper pane. (It isn't necessary to use the Freeze Titles Vertical command to be sure the titles in row 1 stay locked on the screen. The Freeze Titles command removes the scroll bars in the pane containing the titles, but because the top pane in our example is only one row high, there isn't room for scroll bars in it anyway.)

> ☐ Save the spreadsheet with the name Inventory.

Remember, Works files are stored completely in your Mac's memory, so you should save them to disk frequently to avoid losing your work in the event of a power failure or system error.

Entering formulas

Now that we have entered all the video titles, quantities, and costs in the sample inventory, we're ready to enter some formulas. The first formula we'll enter calculates the total value of the tapes by title. That means we'll need a formula for each row that contains a tape title: We want to multiply the Quantity value found in column B by the Cost value in column C and place the result in the Total Value cell in column D. Let's start with the formulas for the Adventure category at the top of the spreadsheet.

□ Select cell D4.

□ Type an equal sign to tell Works that you're beginning a formula.

□ Click on cell B4. Notice that the reference B4 appears in the entry bar at the top of the spreadsheet. (If you prefer, you can type the cell references from the keyboard instead of pointing to cells to enter them into formulas.)

□ Type an asterisk (*) to indicate multiplication. This appears after the B4 reference in the entry bar.

□ Click on cell C4. This reference appears in the entry bar. The formula (cell B4 multiplied by cell C4) is complete, so click the enter box (the box with the check mark in it next to the entry bar). The result of the multiplication appears in cell D4.

File	**Edit**	**Window**	**Select**	**Format**	**Options**	**Chart**	**Macro**

D4   =B4*C4

Inventory (SS)

	A	B	C	D	E
1	Title	Quantity	Cost	Total Value	
2					
3	Adventure				
4	Blazing Bullets	1	14.95	14.95	
5	Jungle Fever	2	11.95		
6	Six Gun City	1	12.95		
7	The One-Eyed Assassin	3	12.95		
8	The Spy Who Said No	3	13.95		
9	Two Guys In Trouble	2	15.95		
10					
11	Subtotal Adventure				
12					
13	Aerobics				
14	Aerobic Profit-Taking	4	14.95		
15	George Will's Yoga Fun	1	12.95		
16	King Kong Bundy's Workout	2	9.95		
17	Yoko's Roll-A-Thon	1	12.95		
18					

Copying formulas

Now we want to copy this formula to all of the other rows containing film title, price, and quantity information in this category. Because all the cells where we want to copy this formula are directly below the formula's original location, we'll use the Fill Down command.

☐ Point to cell D4 and hold down the mouse button.

☐ Drag the pointer down to cell D9 and release it to select this block of cells.

☐ Press Command-D (the keyboard equivalent for Fill Down). The formula in D4 is copied into all the cells between D5 and D9, and the total values appear in these cells. Because the original formula contained relative cell references, the cell references in the copied formulas adjust themselves to reflect the new formula locations. If you click on cell D8, for example, you'll see that the cell references in the formula shown in the entry bar are B8 and C8, instead of B4 and C4.

The film-title rows in the Aerobics category need similar formulas. But we can't use the Fill Down command at this point because the rows we want to fill aren't adjacent to the cells containing the formula. (There are Subtotal and blank rows between the Adventure and Aerobics categories.) Instead, we'll have to copy a formula with the Copy command, and then paste it into its new location.

☐ Select cell D9.

☐ Copy the formula in D9 to the Clipboard by pressing Command-C.

☐ Select cell D14 (the row containing the title, *Aerobic Profit-Taking*).

☐ Press Command-V (the keyboard equivalent for the Paste command). The formula (B14*C14) appears in the entry bar, and the references have adjusted themselves to match the formula's new location. The calculated value from the formula appears in cell D14.

Now we can use Fill Down.

☐ Select cells D14 through D17 by dragging and use the Fill Down command to copy the formula.

Entering subtotal and total formulas

Row 21 at the bottom of the spreadsheet is called Grand Totals and will contain totals of the Quantity and Total Value columns, B and D. We also have category-subtotal rows at the bottom of each category. Let's enter the subtotal formulas for the first category, Adventure. First we want to sum all the Quantity values in cells B4 through B9, and place the result in cell B11.

☐ Select cell B11.

☐ Choose the Paste Function command from the Edit menu.

☐ Scroll down the list of functions to the Sum function. (Be sure to choose Sum, not SSum.) Double-click on it. An equal sign and the Sum function appear in the entry bar, followed by the two parentheses that will enclose the argument (the cells or values on which the function will operate).

☐ To enter the range of cells from B4 through B9, position the pointer on cell B4, press and hold down the mouse button, drag the pointer down through cell B9, and release the mouse button. Notice that the range B4:B9 now appears in the entry bar, and that the range itself is outlined on the spreadsheet.

🍎	File	Edit	Window	Select	Format	Options	Chart	Macro

B11	☒☑ =Sum(B4:B9)

Inventory (SS)

	A	B	C	D	E
1	Title	Quantity	Cost	Total Value	
2					
3	Adventure				
4	Blazing Bullets	1	14.95	14.95	
5	Jungle Fever	2	11.95	23.9	
6	Six Gun City	1	12.95	12.95	
7	The One-Eyed Assassin	3	12.95	38.85	
8	The Spy Who Said No	3	13.95	41.85	
9	Two Guys In Trouble	2	15.95	31.9	
10					
11	Subtotal Adventure				
12					
13	Aerobics				
14	Aerobic Profit-Taking	4	14.95	59.8	
15	George Will's Yoga Fun	1	12.95	12.95	
16	King Kong Bundy's Workout	2	9.95	19.9	
17	Yoko's Roll-A-Thon	1	12.95	12.95	
18					

☐ Click the enter box. The formula is entered, and its result appears in cell B11.

This Sum formula is the same basic formula we need to produce a subtotal for the Total Value column in cell D11. We could enter the formula again, but it's simpler to copy it.

☐ Select cell B11.

☐ Press Command-C, the keyboard equivalent for the Copy command.

☐ Select cell D11.

☐ Press Command-V, the keyboard equivalent for the Paste command. The formula is copied into cell D11, and, because the formula contains relative cell references, the references adjust themselves to the new location of the formula. The subtotaled value now appears in cell D11.

The relative formulas in cells B11 and D11 tell Works to add the contents of the six rows above them. Wherever we copy this formula, Works will adjust the cell references and add the six rows above the formula's location. It would be nice if we could simply copy this same formula into the subtotals row in the Aerobics category, but the Aerobics category doesn't contain six titles—it has four. For this reason, a formula that sums six rows won't work. We need to re-enter the Sum formula in column B for the Aerobics category subtotal and then copy that formula to column D. We know that the formula, except for the cell references, will be the same in both columns of the Aerobics category because both formulas will sum the same number of rows. So, after we enter the revised formula in column B, we can copy it to column D. Let's complete the subtotal formulas for the Aerobics category.

☐ Select cell B19.

☐ Choose the Paste Function command from the Edit menu, and double-click on the Sum function.

☐ Select cell B14, hold down the mouse button, and drag the pointer down to cell B17.

☐ Release the mouse button to enter this range of cells into the Sum formula's argument in the entry bar, and then click the enter box to enter the formula.

- [ ] If cell B19 isn't selected at this point, select it.

- [ ] Press Command-C to copy the formula to the Clipboard.

- [ ] Select cell D19.

- [ ] Press Command-V to paste the formula from the Clipboard. The references in the formula adjust, and the correct sum appears in cell D19.

After the category subtotals are completed, we can enter two formulas to produce the grand totals. We can't drag the mouse over a range of cells to sum them because we want to sum the subtotal cells and they're not in a continuous group. Instead, we'll point to the cells individually to add them together.

- [ ] Select cell B21.

- [ ] Choose the Paste Function command from the Edit menu, and then select Sum from the list of functions. If you forget to type an equal sign before using the Paste Function command, Works will insert one for you.

- [ ] Click on cell B11 (the subtotal of quantities from the Adventure category). This reference is entered in the entry bar.

- [ ] Click on cell B19 to enter this reference into the formula. Works adds a plus sign in front of the second cell reference as you click on it.

** File Edit Window Select Format Options Chart Macro**

B21   ☒☑ =Sum(B11+B19)

Inventory (SS)

	A	B	C	D	E
1	Title	Quantity	Cost	Total Value	
7	The One-Eyed Assassin	3	12.95	38.85	
8	The Spy Who Said No	3	13.95	41.85	
9	Two Guys In Trouble	2	15.95	31.9	
10					
11	**Subtotal Adventure**	12		164.4	
12					
13	**Aerobics**				
14	Aerobic Profit-Taking	4	14.95	59.8	
15	George Will's Yoga Fun	1	12.95	12.95	
16	King Kong Bundy's Workout	2	9.95	19.9	
17	Yoko's Roll-A-Thon	1	12.95	12.95	
18					
19	**Subtotal Aerobics**	8		105.6	
20					
21	**Grand Totals**				
22					
23					

☐ Click the enter box to enter the formula, and the result appears in cell B21.

Now all we have to do is copy this formula to cell D21 to get a grand total of the cost of the tapes. The formula in B21 uses relative references, so we can simply copy the formula from cell B21 and paste it into cell D21. The cell references will adjust.

Formatting the spreadsheet

Now that we've finished the calculations, we'll add a little visual emphasis to this spreadsheet. Works offers two sets of tools to do this: the spreadsheet's own formatting tools and the Draw tool. We'll put both of them to work, starting with a title created with the Draw tool. You might want to refer to Figure 6-1, the finished spreadsheet, as you go through this part of the inventory spreadsheet project.

The Works spreadsheet's own formatting commands limit the entire spreadsheet to one font and font size, but if you use the Draw tool, you can create text boxes that can each have their own fonts, font sizes, and styles. We'll use one now to add the title *Videorama Inventory* to the top of this spreadsheet. Before we do, however, we need to change the font size from the default 9 points to 10 points and turn off the cell matrix grid so that we'll have an accurate idea of how wide the spreadsheet text is. Also, because we've finished entering data, we can remove the pane marker that separates the titles in row 1 from the rest of the spreadsheet.

☐ Drag the upper-right pane marker up to the top of the right-hand scroll bar. The spreadsheet window becomes a single window again.

☐ Choose the Show Grid command from the Options menu. The cell grid becomes invisible.

☐ Choose the Select All command from the Edit menu.

☐ Choose the 10 Point option from the Size sub-menu on the Format menu.

The larger font makes the rows higher and the columns wider, although they still contain as many characters as before. You'll also notice that the page break has moved—it's now between columns D and E, depending on how wide you made column A earlier. (To make your spreadsheet look like the one shown in Figure 6-1, select columns B, C, and D, choose the Column Width command from the Format menu, and change the measurement from 10 to 12 characters wide. You also might want to check column A, which in Figure 6-1 is 22 characters wide.) Let's go ahead and create the title now.

- ☐ Select a cell in row 1 and insert 9 blank rows above it (by pressing Command-I nine times). This will allow plenty of room for the title.

- ☐ Turn on the Draw tool by pressing Command-J, and then select the text tool from the Tools palette.

- ☐ Click about ¼ inch below the top of the window, above the left edge of the *Title* label in row 10. Drag the mouse down and to the right until the text box outline is about ¾ inch high and the right edge of the outline is between the words *Total* and *Value* in the Total Value label. Then release the mouse button.

- ☐ Type the title *Videorama Inventory*. The insertion point is blinking at the end of the title when you've finished, and the text tool is still selected.

- ☐ Drag the pointer across the entire title to select it.

- ☐ Choose a large font from the Font menu. (The one in Figure 6-1 is 24-point Helvetica, but for now, let's use the default Geneva font.) Make it boldface by choosing Bold from the Style sub-menu, and center it in the text box by choosing Center from the Justification sub-menu.

Now the title text is complete. Next we'll put a box around it.

- ☐ Choose the box tool from the Tools palette.

- ☐ Click on the medium line-width option (the third line-width option from the left).

- ☐ Drag a box around the title to make it look like the box in Figure 6-1.

The title, which has a larger font size than the rest of the text on this spreadsheet, is the only part of the project we need to create with the Draw tool. Now, we can use the spreadsheet's own formatting commands to finish the job. First we'll add the date box beneath the title.

- ☐ Press Command-J to turn off the Draw tool.

- ☐ Double-click on cell B6 to display the cell attributes dialog box.

TIP: If cell B6 is obscured by the title or title box, they may be too low on the page. But you can fix the position easily.

- ☐ Turn on the Draw tool again.

- ☐ Click on the edge of the box surrounding the title to display the selection handles.

- ☐ Hold down the Shift key and click on any letter in the title. Both box and title are selected, and you can move them together.

- ☐ Click on the bottom of the box's border in between two selection handles, and hold down the mouse button.

- ☐ Move both box and title up by moving the pointer until the box is ¼ inch below the column letters at the top of the screen. Be careful not to move the box to the right or left. (You can also constrain movement to horizontal, vertical, or 45-degree diagonal directions by holding down the Shift key before clicking on the selected object or objects.)

- ☐ Click the Date Medium, Center, and Bold options to format this cell.

- ☐ Type *3-1-89* (or *3/1/89*, if you prefer). The date will appear as *Mar 1, 1989*.

While we're working with the Cell Attributes command, we might as well change other cell formats to match Figure 6-1. We need to change the alignment of some labels and change the number formats in columns C and D to dollars and cents.

- ☐ Select cell A10.

- ☐ Choose the Set Cell Attributes command from the Format menu.

- ☐ Click the Center button under the Align options, and then press the Return key, press the Enter key, or click the OK button.

- □ Select cells A13 through A18.

- □ Choose the Set Cell Attributes command from the Format menu.

- □ Click the Right button under the Align options, and then press Return, press Enter, or click OK.

- □ Repeat this process for cells A23 through A26, as well as for cells B10 through D10.

- □ Click on the column labels C and D to select these entire columns.

- □ Choose the Set Cell Attributes command again.

- □ Click the Dollar button under the Display options. The Decimal Places box is already set to 2. That is the setting we want. Notice, however, that the Bold box is checked under the Style options because the first row in these columns contains the category titles, and they are boldface. We don't want all the values to be boldface, so click the Bold box to de-select this option.

- □ Click OK to apply the new format. The tape prices, extensions, and value totals now appear as dollars and cents.

- □ Select cells C10 and D10, and press Command-B to return the titles to boldface. The worksheet now looks like this:

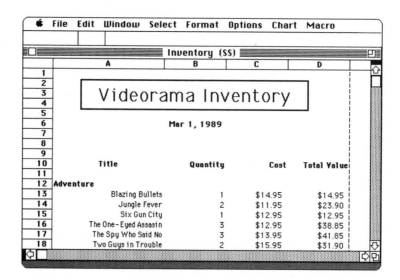

Next we'll make the other totals bold, as they appear in Figure 6-1, and then we'll put borders around the column titles, tape category cells, and Grand Totals row.

☐ Click on the *20* that marks row 20 to select it.

☐ Press Command-B to boldface all the selected cells.

☐ Repeat this procedure for the Subtotal Aerobics and Grand Totals rows (rows 28 and 30).

☐ Select cell B6, choose the Borders command from the Format menu, hold down the mouse button, and select the Outline command from the sub-menu. A box appears around the cell containing the inventory date.

☐ For the borders on row 10, select the cells A10, B10, C10, and D10.

☐ Use the Borders command to put an Outline border around these cells.

☐ Choose the Borders command again, and choose the Right command from the sub-menu. Doing this will insert the vertical dividing lines between the column titles as in Figure 6-1.

☐ Put an Outline border around cells A12 and A22.

☐ Put Outline and Right borders (as in row 10) around the Grand Totals in row 30.

The spreadsheet now looks as it does in Figure 6-1. If it does not, go over the previous steps carefully to see that you've followed them all. To check out the alignment of the title box and text, use the Print Preview feature to see how the document will look when printed.

☐ Press Command-P to display the Print dialog box.

☐ Click the Print Preview check box in the lower-left corner, and then click the OK button. The file is displayed on the preview screen as it will look when printed. If it looks the way you want, you can print it by clicking the Print button on the preview screen or by pressing the Return or Enter key.

If the spreadsheet page looks as if it's not centered on the paper in the preview screen, adjust the margins by entering different top, bottom, left, or right margin values in the Page Setup dialog box. For now, let's assume the page is the way we want. Save the spreadsheet again by pressing Command-S.

Adding items to the inventory

This spreadsheet now contains all the titles in Al's inventory. But as he acquires more videotapes, he'll have to expand it. When it's necessary to add new titles within each of these categories, he can simply insert new rows. The references in all the Sum formulas will adjust themselves to accommodate the new rows. Let's look at an example: Suppose we want to add the title *East Village Exercises* to the Aerobics section.

- □ Click on the title *George Will's Yoga Fun.* We want to add a row above this title.

- □ Press Command-I to insert the new row.

- □ Type the title *East Village Exercises,* and press the Tab key to enter the label and move the selection one cell to the right.

- □ Type *2* for the quantity, and then press the Tab key.

- □ Type the amount *$18.95,* and press the Tab key to enter it.

- □ Select cell D23, and press Command-C to copy the Total Value formula from the row above.

- □ Click on cell D24, and use the Paste command (Command-V) to paste the formula into the new row. The formula calculates the new row's total value, and all of the affected Sum formulas in the subtotal and grand total rows change to reflect the new addition.

As you'll see when you check the formula in the Aerobics category's subtotal row (by selecting either cell B29 or cell D29), the cell references there have changed to accommodate the new row we've inserted.

> **TIP:** To add rows to this spreadsheet, enter the new video titles in alphabetical order when you insert the rows, rather than inserting the rows anywhere and using the Sort command to re-sort the rows. After you enter formulas that calculate a range of rows (as the Sum formulas calculate the category subtotals in this example), re-sorting the range of rows might re-arrange the cells referenced by the formula and render it inaccurate.

An Amortization Table

Al is considering borrowing money to expand the Videorama, and he wants to know what the payments will be. This is a good opportunity to build an amortization table with the Works spreadsheet. If we build the table properly, we'll always be able to change the loan amount, interest rate, and term to determine what a loan will cost.

You can think of each spreadsheet you build as a calculating machine that uses formulas to process numbers in a specific way. As mentioned in Chapter 5, you can use cell references instead of actual values in formulas. That way, you can change the values whenever you want to calculate a different set of numbers. We'll use that technique, to build an amortization table we can use again and again to calculate the cost of loans of various amounts, terms, and rates.

The amortization table consists of two distinct parts: the Loan Summary area and the Loan Activity area. The Loan Summary area spells out the loan amount, term, interest rate, and monthly payment; the Loan Activity area shows how the loan is paid off over its life.

Creating the Loan Summary area

Let's open a new, untitled spreadsheet, and enter the Loan Summary information first. Before entering any data, we'll set up this spreadsheet to match the layout we have in mind. (See Figure 6-2 on page 213.)

- □ Choose the 10 Point font size from the Format menu to make the numbers and values we'll enter a little easier to read.

- □ Select a cell in column A, and then choose the Column Width command from the Format menu.

- □ Type the value *14* in the dialog box, and press the Return key to widen column A.

- □ Select a cell in column B, choose the Column Width command, type *6* in the dialog box, and press Return to make this column 6 characters wide.

- □ Select a cell in column C and make this column 14 characters wide, using the procedure just described.

- □ Select cells in both columns D and E and make these columns 12 characters wide.

Now, we'll enter labels, loan summary information, and a formula to calculate the loan payment.

☐ Select cell A1 and type the label *Loan Summary.*

☐ Press Command-B to boldface this label and enter it at the same time.

☐ In cells C3, C4, C5, and C6, respectively, enter the labels *Loan Amount, Interest Rate, Term,* and *Monthly Payment.*

☐ Select all four cells and type Command-B to make them boldface.

Now we'll complete this area by entering the values and the formula. Let's assume Al wants to borrow $10,000.

☐ Enter the value *10000* in cell D3, next to the Loan Amount label.

For the interest rate in cell D4, we need to enter the monthly interest rate. We'll assume the annual rate is 12 percent, so the monthly rate is 1 percent. This calculation is easy enough to do in our heads, but it won't be so easy when we have interest rates of 13 or 10.85 percent. Fortunately, we can enter a formula that will calculate the correct rate by dividing by 12.

☐ Select cell D4, type *=.12/12,* and then press Return or Enter.

This formula takes the interest rate (0.12, or 12 percent) and divides it by the number of months in a year (12), so the result is 0.01.

Now we'll convert the value 0.01 to a percentage with the Set Cell Attributes command.

□ Double-click cell D4 to display the Set Cell Attributes dialog box.

□ Click the Percent button under the Display options.

The default number of decimal places is 2. That is the number we want, so we can press Return or Enter, or click the OK button to change this cell's format. The resulting percentage is now shown in cell D4.

File	**Edit**	**Window**	**Select**	**Format**	**Options** **Chart** **Macro**

D4 | =.12/12

Untitled (SS)

	A	B	C	D	E
1	Loan Summary				
2					
3			Loan Amount	10000	
4			Interest Rate	1.00%	
5			Term		
6			Monthly Payment		
7					
8					
9					
10					
11					
12					
13					
14					
15					
16					
17					
18					

Whenever you create a payment formula, both the interest rate and the term have to be either monthly or yearly. You can't enter a monthly interest rate and then specify the term in years, for example. We specified a monthly interest rate for Al's three-year loan, so we also need to enter the term of the loan in months.

□ Enter the value *36* in cell D5, to indicate a three-year loan term.

Using the Pmt function to calculate the monthly payment

Now we come to the actual formula that will calculate the payment on this loan. The Works spreadsheet contains eight built-in financial functions that make it easy to analyze investments and debts. You can read more about each of these functions and their uses in the Microsoft Works User's Guide. But for now, we'll focus on the function called Pmt (short for "payment").

As it is structured in Microsoft Works, the Pmt function calculates payments of equal amounts resulting from investments. When you use Pmt to calculate a loan payment, you might find it helpful to look at the loan from the bank's point of view. The bank sees the loan as an investment: The bank spends a fixed amount of money at the beginning of the loan (the loan amount, also known as the investment's present value), and in return it gets back the loan plus interest (at a certain rate) in the form of regular cash flows (your payments) for a specified term (period of time) until the loan is paid off. When the loan is paid off, its value (or balance) is zero. This is the future value of the loan.

Present value, future value, rate, and term are all common financial terms, and these terms are the elements of the Pmt function in Works. To enter a Pmt formula, you must specify the loan's interest rate; the term (abbreviated as nper, which is short for "number of periods"); the loan amount, or present value (pv); and the future value (fv), which usually is zero because you're paying off the loan completely. You must also specify whether each payment comes at the beginning of a period, or at the end (type) because the timing of the payment affects how the interest is calculated. If you don't specify a type in a Pmt formula, Works assumes the first payment comes at the end of the period.

With the abbreviated argument names instead of actual numbers, the Pmt formula in Works looks like this:

Pmt(rate,nper,pv,fv,type)

You must always format the Pmt formula this way, with the various values in exactly this order, and with commas separating them.

With this in mind, let's enter the Pmt formula in cell D6.

☐ Select cell D6.

☐ Choose the Paste Function command from the Edit menu, and scroll down the list of functions until you see *Pmt()*.

☐ Double-click on the Pmt function. The function appears as the beginning of a formula in the entry bar.

☐ Click on cell D4 to enter the monthly interest rate value (rate), and then type a comma.

☐ Click on cell D5 to enter the term value (nper), and then type a comma.

- ☐ Click on cell D3 to enter the present value (pv—the loan amount), and then type a comma.

- ☐ Type a *0* to indicate that the future value (fv) of the loan is 0, meaning we want to pay it off in full.

We could go ahead and type another comma and the last 0 to indicate the type of payment (0 means the payment comes at the end of the first month; 1 means the first payment comes at the beginning of the month), but if we don't enter this value, Works assumes we want the type to be 0, and enters it for us.

- ☐ Click the enter box. Works adds the last 0 to the argument in the entry line, calculates the Pmt formula, and displays the payment amount in cell D6.

	File	Edit	Window	Select	Format	Options	Chart	Macro

D6		=Pmt(D4,D5,D3,0,0)

Untitled (SS)

	A	B	C	D	E
1	Loan Summary				
2					
3			Loan Amount	10000	
4			Interest Rate	1.00%	
5			Term	36	
6			Monthly Payment	-332.1430981	
7					
8					
9					
10					
11					
12					
13					
14					
15					
16					
17					
18					

You'll notice in this example that the payment amount appears as a long decimal number and that it's a negative number because the payments are considered outgoing cash flow, or debits. Of course, you probably will be well aware that loan payments are outgoing cash flow when you start making payments, so you won't need to be reminded by the minus sign. And you'd probably like the amount formatted as dollars and cents. Let's change the formats.

- ☐ Double-click on cell D6 to display the Set Cell Attributes dialog box.

☐ Click the Dollar button under the Display options, and then press the Return key.

The payment is now formatted as dollars and cents, but it appears in parentheses because it's still a negative number.

To make a negative number positive, we must include the Abs (or absolute value) function in the formula. The Abs function will tell Works to present the positive value of the Pmt formula's results.

☐ Select cell D6.

☐ Move the insertion point to the beginning of the Pmt formula in the entry bar by clicking to the left of the *P* in *Pmt.*

☐ Choose the Paste Function command from the Edit menu, and double-click on the Abs function. (It's the first one on the list.) The Abs function appears in the entry bar.

There's one problem with the way Works has pasted the Abs function: A function can't act on anything that's outside the parentheses that follow it, and right now, the Pmt formula is outside the Abs parentheses. We need to move the Pmt formula.

☐ Position the pointer between the parentheses that follow *Abs* and the *P* of *Pmt,* hold down the mouse button, drag the pointer across the Pmt formula, and release the mouse button. Everything in the entry bar from the *P* in *Pmt* to the right is now selected.

☐ Press Command-X to cut the formula from its place in the entry bar.

☐ Click in the space between the two parentheses that follow *Abs* to move the insertion point there.

☐ Press Command-V to paste the Pmt formula into position inside the parentheses.

☐ Click the enter box to enter the modified formula. The payment amount now appears without parentheses around it, indicating that it has been converted to a positive number.

```
 ⌘  File  Edit  Window  Select  Format  Options  Chart  Macro
```

D6		=Abs(Pmt(D4,D5,D3,0,0))			

Untitled (SS)

	A	B	C	D	E
1	Loan Summary				
2					
3			Loan Amount	10000	
4			Interest Rate	1.00%	
5			Term	36	
6			Monthly Payment	$332.14	
7					
8					
9					
10					
11					
12					
13					
14					
15					
16					
17					
18					

Creating the Loan Activity area

The Loan Summary portion of the spreadsheet is all you might need, if you simply want to know how much the payment on a certain type of loan will be. But you might like to see the loan's activity as well. By including a Loan Activity section in this amortization table, you'll be able to see how much principal and interest you're paying each month, and how the remaining balance of the loan is affected after each payment.

Now we'll create the Loan Activity area of the spreadsheet.

☐ Select cell A9 and type the label *Loan Activity*.

☐ Press Command-B to make the label boldface and enter it.

☐ Enter the labels *Month, Interest, Principal,* and *Balance* in cells B11, C11, D11, and E11, respectively, and make them boldface in the same manner.

☐ Select cell A12, enter the label *Loan Begins*, and make it boldface.

☐ Select Cell B12 and enter the value *0* to indicate that this is the beginning month of the loan.

Because the Loan Activity area will contain 36 rows of data (one row for each month's loan calculation), we'll have to scroll down the spreadsheet to see some of the later months. However, it would be convenient to be able to freeze the Loan Summary area at the top of the screen so that it is always visible as well. Let's do this now.

▢ Drag the pane marker from its place above the right-hand scroll bar down to row 7, and release the mouse button.

▢ Choose Freeze Titles Vertical from the Options menu. The upper scroll bars disappear, fixing the Loan Summary area on the screen, like this:

	A	B	C	D	E	
1	Loan Summary					
2						
3			Loan Amount	10000		
4			Interest Rate	1.00%		
5			Term	36		
6			Monthly Payment	$332.14		
7						
8						
9	Loan Activity					
10						
11		Month	Interest	Principal	Balance	
12	Loan Begins	0				
13						
14						
15						
16						
17						
18						

Now we're ready to enter formulas and values by using references to the cells containing the rate, term, and loan amount values we've already entered in the Loan Summary area. There are three formulas to enter this way, plus the beginning loan amount. We'll enter the beginning loan amount first.

▢ Select cell E12 and type an equal sign to begin the formula.

We want to enter the beginning loan amount here, and we can do that by referring to the loan amount value in cell D3.

▢ Click on cell D3 to enter that reference into the formula in cell E12.

▢ Click the enter box or press Return or Enter to complete the formula. The value *10000* appears in cell E12.

Because cell E12 will always contain the value in cell D3 (and the other formulas in the Loan Activity area will also refer to values in the Loan Summary area), we can change the values in the Loan Summary area and recalculate the spreadsheet for different loan amounts, interest rates, and terms.

Now we'll calculate the amount of interest paid each month. This amount is simply the interest-rate figure from cell D4 applied to the previous month's loan balance. The first month's interest will be paid in month 1, which is in row 13.

- ☐ Select cell C13, and type an equal sign to begin the formula.

- ☐ Click on cell D4 to enter the interest rate value.

- ☐ Type an asterisk to indicate that D4 is to be multiplied by the next value.

- ☐ Click on cell E12 to enter the beginning loan amount value.

- ☐ Click the enter box or press Return or Enter to enter the formula. The result *100* appears in cell C13.

The next formula shows how much of each month's payment goes toward reducing the loan's principal. We already know how much the monthly payment is (we've calculated it in cell D6), and we've just calculated how much interest we're paying this month in cell C13. So we only have to subtract the interest from the payment amount to determine the amount of principal paid each month.

- ☐ Select cell D13 and type an equal sign to begin the formula.

- ☐ Click on cell D6 to enter the amount of the monthly payment in the entry bar.

- ☐ Type a minus sign to indicate subtraction.

- ☐ Click on cell C13 to enter that month's interest.

- ☐ Click the enter box or press Return or Enter to enter the formula. The amount of principal appears in cell D13.

Finally, we want to determine the remaining loan balance in Month 1 after deducting the amount of principal paid. We simply subtract the current month's principal from the previous month's loan balance.

- ☐ Select cell E13.

- ☐ Type an equal sign to begin the formula.

- ☐ Click on cell E12 to enter the previous month's loan balance.

- ☐ Type a minus sign to indicate subtraction.

- ☐ Click on cell D13 to enter the month's principal payment.

□ Click the enter box or press Return or Enter to enter the formula. The current month's balance then appears in cell E13.

	A	B	C	D	E
1	Loan Summary				
2					
3			Loan Amount	10000	
4			Interest Rate	1.00%	
5			Term	36	
6			Monthly Payment	$332.14	
7					
8					
9	Loan Activity				
10					
11		Month	Interest	Principal	Balance
12	Loan Begins	0			10000
13			100	232.14309813	9767.8569019
14					
15					
16					
17					
18					

Entry bar: E13 = =E12-D13. Menu bar: File Edit Window Select Format Options Chart Macro. Window title: Untitled (SS).

Notice that we've made all these calculations without typing one number from the keyboard—we've simply been re-using existing cell references by clicking on them.

So far, we've calculated one month's loan activity. However, we want to see the loan's activity over the entire 36 months. To see that, we'll have to copy the three formulas in row 13 down through row 48.

We've copied a lot of formulas before, but in this case, we need to take a different approach because we don't want all the cell references in the formulas to be relative. If you remember, we referred to specific cells in the Loan Summary area (D4 and D6) in our interest and principal formulas, and we want those references to be absolute—that is, we want every copy of these formulas to contain the same D4 and D6 references. Remember, we entered the D4 and D6 references into cells C13 and D13 simply by clicking on them, making the references relative. To make these references absolute, we'll have to change them slightly.

□ Select cell C13. The existing formula in C13 appears in the entry bar.

□ Click between the equal sign and the *D* to move the insertion point there.

□ Type a dollar sign to indicate that the reference to column D is absolute.

□ Click between the *D* and the *4* in the entry bar to move the insertion point there.

□ Type another dollar sign to indicate that the reference to row 4 is absolute.

□ Click the Enter box to enter the modified formula.

As you can see, the results of the formula don't change. We've simply told Works that it should always use the values in cell D4 to calculate this part of the formula, regardless of where the formula itself is copied. Now whenever we make a copy of the formula, the reference will always remain the same.

You'll also notice that we put dollar signs in front of both the *D* and the *4* in the reference. We did this to make both the row and column references absolute. If we had put a dollar sign only in front of the *D*, for example, the reference to row 4 would have remained relative, and it would change to reflect the location of any copies of this formula.

Now we can repeat these same six steps to convert the formula in cell D13. We want to make the reference to cell D6 absolute, in the same way (by selecting cell D13 and inserting dollar signs in front of the *D* and the *6* in the entry bar, and then by re-entering the formula). After we do, we can fill out the rest of the Loan Activity area by copying all three formulas in row 13 down through row 48. (This is a 36-month loan, so we want it to contain 36 rows of calculations—one for each month.)

The simplest way to copy these formulas is to select all three at once, select the 35 rows below them, and use the Fill Down command.

□ Select cell C13, hold down the mouse button, and then drag the pointer across cells D13 and E13 (but don't release the mouse button yet). These three formulas are now selected.

□ Keeping the mouse button down, drag the pointer down to cell E48, and then release the mouse button. Now the area from column C through column E and from row 13 through row 48 is selected.

□ Press Command-D (the keyboard equivalent for the Fill Down command). The three formulas are copied into all the selected cells.

As you can see, you can use Fill Down (or Fill Right, for that matter), to copy formulas, labels, or values in more than one column or row at once.

We only have a month number for Month 0 in cell B12 at this point. We could enter all the month numbers by hand, but we can relieve this tedium by entering a formula in cell B13 and copying it down through cell B48.

□ Select cell B13, and type an equal sign to begin the formula.

□ Click on cell B12 to enter the value *0* from the cell above.

□ Type a plus sign to indicate addition.

□ Type a *1*, and then click the Enter box.

Now cell B13 contains a 1 because we have added a 1 to the value in the cell directly above (which contains a 0). We can now copy this formula down through cell B48.

□ Select cell B13 and hold down the mouse button.

□ Drag the pointer down through cell B48, and release the mouse button to select all these cells.

□ Press Command-D (Fill Down) to copy the formula into all these cells.

Column B will now contain the proper month numbers because a 1 is added to the value in the cell above to calculate the right number in each row of column B.

The finished inventory spreadsheet in Figure 6-2 contains two views: one view showing the calculated values, and one view showing formulas. As you might recall from Chapter 5, you can display the formulas (rather than the values) in a spreadsheet by choosing Show Formulas from the Options menu. This command helps when you want to remember all the formulas you used or when you want to print out the formulas to show someone else how you built the spreadsheet. (You will have to widen column D to show the payment formula in cell D6 completely.)

Now that we've entered all the formulas and copied them, you can see why it was important to build the Loan Activity formulas from references to the Loan Summary area (rather than entering the loan amount, rate, term, and Pmt formula again): We can change any value in the Loan Summary area, and the Loan Activity area recalculates to reflect the change. Since the formulas in row 13 use the cell references

D4 and D6 instead of the values 1% and $332.14, we can easily change the contents of these cells to see how a different loan stacks up.

	A	B	C	D	E
			Amort.Table (SS)		
1	Loan Summary				
2					
3			Loan Amount	$10000.00	
4			Interest Rate	1.00%	
5			Term	36	
6			Monthly Payment	$332.14	
37		25	$37.38	$294.76	$3443.54
38		26	$34.44	$297.71	$3145.83
39		27	$31.46	$300.68	$2845.14
40		28	$28.45	$303.69	$2541.45
41		29	$25.41	$306.73	$2234.72
42		30	$22.35	$309.80	$1924.93
43		31	$19.25	$312.89	$1612.03
44		32	$16.12	$316.02	$1296.01
45		33	$12.96	$319.18	$976.83
46		34	$9.77	$322.37	$654.45
47		35	$6.54	$325.60	$328.85
48		36	$3.29	$328.85	$0.00

	A	B	C	D	E
			Amort.Table (SS)		
1	Loan Summary				
2					
3			Loan Amount	10000	
4			Interest Rate	=.12/12	
5			Term	36	
6			Monthly Payment	=Abs(Pmt(D4,D5	
37		=B36+	=$D$4*E36	=$D$6-C37	=E36-D37
38		=B37+	=$D$4*E37	=$D$6-C38	=E37-D38
39		=B38+	=$D$4*E38	=$D$6-C39	=E38-D39
40		=B39+	=$D$4*E39	=$D$6-C40	=E39-D40
41		=B40+	=$D$4*E40	=$D$6-C41	=E40-D41
42		=B41+	=$D$4*E41	=$D$6-C42	=E41-D42
43		=B42+	=$D$4*E42	=$D$6-C43	=E42-D43
44		=B43+	=$D$4*E43	=$D$6-C44	=E43-D44
45		=B44+	=$D$4*E44	=$D$6-C45	=E44-D45
46		=B45+	=$D$4*E45	=$D$6-C46	=E45-D46
47		=B46+	=$D$4*E46	=$D$6-C47	=E46-D47
48		=B47+	=$D$4*E47	=$D$6-C48	=E47-D48

Figure 6-2.
Two views of the inventory spreadsheet: values and formulas.

Now let's clean up the formatting of this spreadsheet before saving it. We'll reformat columns C, D, and E as dollar amounts, and use Works' Set Cell Attributes and Borders commands to make the spreadsheet more readable. We don't want to reformat the Loan Summary area, because we have one value formatted for percent there, so we'll simply reformat these columns from row 12 down.

☐ Point to cell C12, hold down the mouse button, drag the pointer across to cell D12, and then drag it down to cell E48.

☐ Choose the Set Cell Attributes command from the Format menu, click the Dollar button under the Display options, and then click the OK button or press Return or Enter. The values in this range of cells are now formatted as dollars and cents.

☐ Select cells C11, D11, and E11.

☐ Choose the Set Cell Attributes command from the Format menu, and click the Center button under the Align options to center these titles.

☐ Select cell A1 and choose the Outline command from the Borders sub-menu (on the Format menu) to put a box around this title.

☐ Select cells C3 through D6 and choose the Outline command from the Borders sub-menu. Then choose the Right command from the Borders sub-menu to complete the box around this area.

☐ Select cell A9 and put an Outline border around this title.

☐ Select cells B11, C11, D11, and E11, and put both Outline and Right borders around them.

And now let's add the finishing touches.

☐ Select all the Month numbers (cells B12 through B48), and make them boldface by pressing Command-B.

☐ Double-click on cell D3 to display the Set Cell Attributes dialog box, and click the Dollar button under the Display options.

Saving and printing the table

Let's save this spreadsheet with the name Amort.Table so that whenever we want to check the payments and activity of a loan, we can easily retrieve this file and enter the new figures.

☐ Choose Save As from the File menu.

☐ When the dialog box appears, type *Amort.Table* in the text box and click the Save button.

As it is, this spreadsheet will require two pages when we print it out. (If you scroll down to row 45, you can see the page break marker between rows 45 and 46.) The simplest way to fit the entire table on one page is to change either the Top Margin or Bottom Margin setting in the Page Setup dialog box to ½ inch. Shortening one of these margins by ½ inch will allow enough extra room to print the entire table on one page. Alternatively, you could set a new page break on row 7 and print the Loan Summary data on one page and the table on another. Let's set this page break.

☐ Select cell F8, which is the row below where you want the horizontal page break to appear and one column to the right of where you want the vertical page break to appear. (Actually, you want the vertical page break to stay where it is, but because Works inserts both horizontal and vertical page breaks at the same time in the spreadsheet, you need to select the cell immediately below and to the right of where you want the new horizontal and vertical page breaks to intersect.)

☐ Choose the Set Page Break command from the Options menu.

☐ A new horizontal page break appears between rows 7 and 8, and the vertical page break stays where it was before, between columns E and F.

Finally, you might want to turn off the grid lines (using the Show Grid command on the Options menu) before you print; the borders you placed around some of the labels and the Loan Summary area will stand out more if you print the file without grid lines dividing every cell.

Customer Volume Report

Al Chroma is monitoring the traffic in his store, and he's using the spreadsheet shown in Figure 6-3 on the following page to keep track of the results. The spreadsheet stores the weekly customer volumes and the number of new video-club members. It also tracks the advertising source that brought each customer in. We'll use this spreadsheet and Works' charting feature to help Al visualize the data.

In this project, we're mainly interested in the charting features of the spreadsheet. Before we can explore Works' chart functions, however, we need to create a spreadsheet like the one in Figure 6-3.

	A	B	C	D	E	F
1		WEEKLY VIDEORAMA TRAFFIC −			MARCH	
2						
3		3/13/88	3/20/88	3/27/88	Totals	
4	Source					
5						
6	Walk-In	35	65	75	175	
7	Word of Mouth	2	10	20	32	
8	Bugle Ad	20	42	35	97	
9	Gazette Ad	30	40	37	107	
10	Flyer	27	35	40	102	
11						
12	Total Customers	114	192	207	513	
13	New Club Members	80	130	167	377	
14	Percent Video Club	70.18%	67.71%	80.68%		
15						
16						
17						
18						

Figure 6-3.
A spreadsheet for keeping track of the number of customers in the video store each week.

No techniques are used to create this spreadsheet that haven't been used in the previous projects, but the following are the steps to do it.

☐ Open a new spreadsheet file.

☐ Using the Column Width command on the Format menu, make column A 18 characters wide and columns B, C, D, and E 10 characters wide.

☐ Select cells B3, C3, and D3, and choose the Date Short option in the Set Cell Attributes dialog box.

☐ Select cells E1 and E3 and choose the Right alignment option using the Set Cell Attributes command.

☐ Select cells B14, C14, and D14, and choose the Percent format with 2 decimal places, using the Set Cell Attributes command.

☐ Enter the labels in column A and rows 1 and 3 as shown in Figure 6-3, making them boldface by pressing Command-B to enter them or by selecting them after you enter them and then pressing Command-B.

☐ Enter the values in the ranges B6:B10, C6:C10, D6:D10, and B13:D13.

☐ Hold down the Command key and double-click cell B3. A cell-note window appears. Type the note *3/13 is first week because store opens this week.* (Otherwise, someone might wonder later why the first week of March isn't included in this spreadsheet.)

☐ Close the cell-note window.

☐ In cell B12, type *=Sum(B6:B10)*, and enter this formula.

☐ Copy the formula in cell B12 into cells C12 and D12.

☐ In cell B14, type *=B13/B12*, and enter this formula.

☐ Copy the formula in cell B14 into cells C14 and D14.

☐ Enter the formula *=Sum(B6:D6)* in cell E6, and then copy this formula into cells E7, E8, E9, E10, E12, and E13.

☐ Save the spreadsheet as Store Traffic.

Now we're ready to display this data in a few chart formats that will reveal Videorama's customer growth trends.

Creating a chart that tracks store traffic and new members

Suppose we first want to get a visual picture of how customer traffic fluctuates from week to week and how the traffic total compares with the number of new video-club members during March. We want to see how the numbers change over time (in this case, three weeks), so we want to make a series chart. (Figure 6-4 on page 220 shows the completed chart, if you want to refer to it as we go along.)

☐ Choose the New Series Chart command from the Chart menu. A new chart-definition window appears.

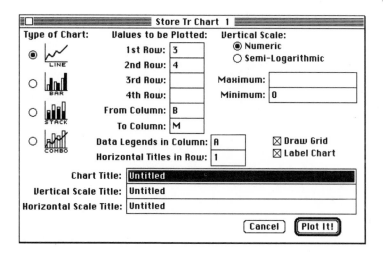

We want to represent not only the total number of customers each week, but also the number of new video-club members, so that Al can see how these two values stack up against each other. The best way to show this comparison is with a bar chart. If we select the two appropriate data rows (Total Customers and New Club Members), Works will draw a bar for each value.

□ Click on the button next to the bar-chart icon in the chart-definition window.

Now we need to specify the rows from which Works will take the charted data. Unfortunately, the chart-definition window is covering the Store Traffic spreadsheet at this point, and it's hard to remember the exact number of the rows containing the data we want to graph. Let's move the chart-definition window to uncover the spreadsheet.

□ Point to the title bar at the top of the chart-definition window.

□ Hold down the mouse button and drag the window toward the bottom of the screen, until rows 12 and 13 are revealed on the spreadsheet.

	File	**Edit**	**Window**	**Macro**			

Store Traffic (SS)

	A	B	C	D	E	F
1		WEEKLY VIDEORAMA TRAFFIC –			MARCH	
2						
3		3/13/88	3/20/88	3/27/88	Totals	
4	Source					
5						
6	Walk-In	35	65	75	175	
7	Word of Mouth	2	10	20	32	
8	Bugle Ad	20	42	35	97	
9	Gazette Ad	30	40	37	107	
10	Flyer	27	35	40	102	
11						
12	Total Customers	114	192	207	513	
13	New Club Members	80	130	167	377	

Store Tr Chart 1

Type of Chart:	Values to be Plotted:	Vertical Scale:
◯ ⌇ LINE	1st Row: 3 2nd Row: 4	◉ Numeric ◯ Semi-Logarithmic

Now we can enter the value locations for our chart in the chart-definition window.

- Double-click in the 1st Row box, and enter the number *12*. This tells Works to get the data for the first bar in the bar chart from row 12 of the spreadsheet. Do not press Return yet—pressing Return at any time while the chart-definition window is displayed tells Works to plot the chart according to the current definition.

- Double-click in the 2nd Row box and enter the number *13* to indicate the second row of data. Again, don't press the Return key yet.

If you press Return by mistake and the chart is plotted, you can display the chart-definition window again by closing the chart window and redisplaying the chart-definition window, using the following steps.

- Click the close box in the upper-left corner of the chart window. The chart disappears, and the spreadsheet from which you made the chart is displayed again.

- Choose the Select Chart Definition command from the Chart menu. A list of currently defined charts appears.

- Double-click on the name of the chart you want to redefine (or choose New Series Chart). That chart-definition window opens again (either the previously stored window you selected or a new window).

Rows 12 and 13 contain all the data we want to chart, so now we must specify the range of cells in these rows that we want to chart. First, we need to make the appropriate portion of the chart-definition window visible.

- Drag the chart-definition window up toward the top of the screen until the From Column and To Column boxes are revealed. When you do this, you'll see that the default reference, column B, is already entered in the From Column box.

Because our weekly traffic data runs from column B through column D, we don't have to change the From Column value. We do, however, have to change the To Column value.

- Double-click in the To Column box, and enter the value *D*.

We have now defined two different bars—one representing data in row 12 and another representing data in row 13—for each of three weekly periods. The data is in columns B through D in those two rows. Next, we must tell Works which spreadsheet labels to use to identify the bars it will draw. Works will visually differentiate the two bars in each period by filling them with a different pattern, as you can see in Figure 6-4, but we need to tell Works how to label each pattern so we know which bar represents which data. The Data Legends In Column box lets us do this. As you can see, the box contains the default value A, which tells Works to use the labels found in column A of the spreadsheet to identify data legends. Because we're plotting rows 12 and 13, Works will use the labels Total Customers and New Club Members to identify the bars it draws. This is exactly what we want, so we don't need to change this value.

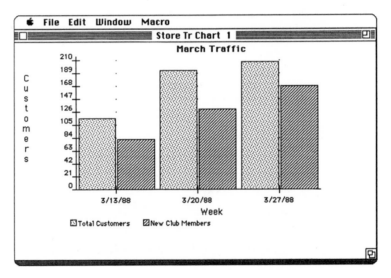

Figure 6-4.
A chart of customer traffic, based on data from the spreadsheet in Figure 6-3.

We also need to tell Works where to find the horizontal titles that will identify each set of bars on the chart. We are charting three weekly periods, so we want to identify each group of bars by the week. These titles are located in row 3 of our spreadsheet, as you can see in Figure 6-3. Works' default value for the Horizontal Titles In Row box is row 1. But we want the horizontal titles taken from row 3.

◻ Double-click on the Horizontal Titles In Row box and change this value to *3*.

Now we can adjust the formatting of this bar chart before we plot it. The Chart Title box lets us enter a name that will appear at the top of the chart.

❑ Double-click in the Chart Title box and enter the name March Traffic. Remember, don't press Return after typing the name.

The Vertical Scale Title box lets us enter a title to identify the numbers on the chart's vertical scale (the scale running up and down the left side of the chart). Our numbers indicate the number of customers, so we'll enter the title *Customers*.

❑ Double-click in the Vertical Scale Title box and enter the name *Customers*.

Likewise, the Horizontal Scale Title box lets us identify the numbers on the chart's horizontal scale (the scale running across the bottom of the chart). In our case, the numbers are weekly periods, so we'll enter the title *Week*.

❑ Double-click on the Horizontal Scale Title box and enter the name *Week*.

Finally, we must decide which scaling method Works will use to increment the vertical scale, whether the chart should appear on a grid, and whether a chart label should be included. The Vertical Scale section in the upper-right corner of the chart-definition window lets us choose between straight numeric and semi-logarithmic scales. A numeric scale is divided into 10 regular increments, depending on the minimum and maximum values found in the data being graphed. If the minimum value is 0 and the maximum value is 200, for example, the scale would show 20, 40, 60, and so forth up to 200. In a semi-logarithmic scale, on the other hand, the distances between the increments decrease geometrically as the numbers become larger. For example, a data sample from 0 to 200 might be scaled as 0, 100, and 1000. Generally, you'll want to use the numeric scaling unless your data sample contains both very large and very small numbers.

The Maximum and Minimum boxes below the scaling options let you specify maximum and minimum scale values. The default setting in the Minimum box is 0, which means chart scales will begin with the value 0. If you're graphing values between 10,000 and 50,000, you would probably want to reset the minimum value to 10,000.

The Draw Grid box lets you choose to either display or not display a grid underneath the data you chart. Grids often help you determine exactly which values are being represented on a chart, and this option is selected by default, meaning a grid will be drawn. The Label Chart box lets you either display or not display all the text labels on a chart, including horizontal and vertical scale titles, data legends, and the chart title. Usually, you'll want to display titles, so this box should have an X in it.

The completed chart-definition window looks like this:

Let's draw the chart we've just defined.

□ Press the Return key or click the Plot It! button. The chart appears, as shown in Figure 6-4.

Now that we've defined this chart, Works will store it with the Store Traffic spreadsheet. When we add or change the numbers in the spreadsheet, the chart will reflect the changes whenever we draw it. Although we had to make a chart definition to draw this chart originally, we can simply tell Works to draw the chart any time in the future. When we use the Draw Chart command from the Chart menu, we can choose from a list of charts we've already defined and then select a chart to be drawn. If, on the other hand, we want to modify a chart's definition, we can use the Select Definition command to re-display any chart's original definition window.

This finished chart could use a little graphic enhancement. To enhance a chart with the Draw tool, we must first copy it into a word-processor document. We'll see how to do this in Chapter 10.

Creating a chart that tracks traffic by advertising source

One other chart might be useful for this spreadsheet. Because the number of customers visiting the store is broken down by advertising source, it might be useful to draw a pie chart that shows how each of these sources contributed to the total customer base during March. Each Works spreadsheet can store up to eight chart definitions at once, so we can make this chart without losing the bar chart we've just drawn.

To begin a new chart, we'll click the close box at the upper-left corner of the bar-chart window we now have on the screen. This closes that chart window and returns us to the spreadsheet. Then, we'll make a pie chart by using the following steps.

☐ Choose the New Pie Chart command from the Chart menu. The Pie Chart Definition window appears.

```
┌────────────────────────────────────────────────┐
│ ▣ ▤▤▤▤▤▤▤▤▤ Store Tr Chart  2 ▤▤▤▤▤▤▤▤▤ │
│  Pie Chart Definition:                          │
│                                                 │
│  Chart Title: ▐Untitled▌                        │
│                                                 │
│  Plot Values in Column:  │B│                    │
│             From Row:  │3│                      │
│          Through Row:  │7│                      │
│  Column of Value Titles:  │A│                   │
│                                                 │
│                        ( Cancel ) (( Plot It! ))│
└────────────────────────────────────────────────┘
```

Pie charts represent the contents of only one column in a spreadsheet, and because the chart has no horizontal or vertical legends, the definition window is much simpler. First, we'll give the chart a title.

☐ Enter the title *Traffic Sources* in the Chart Title box. Remember, don't press the Return key after typing the title.

Next, we have to identify the column from which Works will take the chart's values. We could chart any column from B through D to plot one week's traffic, but let's plot the entire month's traffic instead.

☐ Double-click in the Plot Values In Column box, and enter the letter *E*. Column E contains the March totals.

☐ Double-click in the From Row box, and enter the number *6*. Row 6 is the first row of traffic-source figures.

□ Double-click in the Through Row box, and enter the number *10*. Row 10 is the last row of the traffic-source data.

When the chart is plotted, each individual cell in column E from row 6 through row 10 will represent a slice of the pie. We want these slices identified by the row labels in column A. The Column Of Value Titles box already contains the letter A (the default), so we're now ready to plot the chart.

□ Click the Plot It! button or press the Return key, and the chart is plotted.

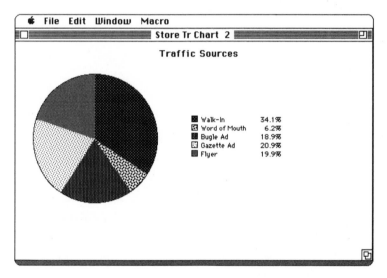

You can use the size box to resize charts on the screen, so that the spreadsheet underneath them is showing and you can refer to the original data while you look at the chart. For example, we might want to resize the pie chart so that we can consult the totals, change them, and then instantly see the results of those changes.

□ Resize the pie-chart window by dragging the size box up and to the left.

□ Click on the spreadsheet to activate the spreadsheet window, and change the Walk-In total in cell D6 from *75* to *150*. The spreadsheet recalculates the Sum formula in cell E6, and the total in that cell changes to *250*.

When you click on the spreadsheet to activate its window, the chart window disappears, but you can bring it back quickly by choosing it from the Window menu. To redisplay the chart, use the following steps.

☐ Select the chart's name from the Window menu. The chart now appears on top of the spreadsheet again. It has changed to reflect the changed value in cell E6.

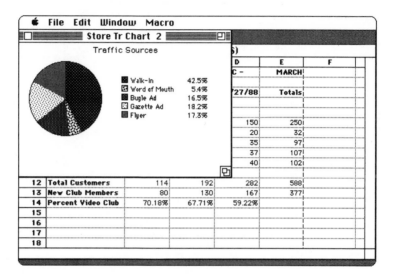

A Consolidated Spreadsheet

Suppose our friend Al wants to consolidate all of his personal and business financial information in one spreadsheet file. Having all the data in one file will make it easier for Al to copy and compare data. He could put all of his data in one large matrix, but that would get messy: Because Al has a number of income and expense items, both personal and business, the bottom line figures would be widely separated, making quick comparison difficult. So, instead of doing all these expense and income items in one big matrix, we'll divide the spreadsheet file into five different areas: Business Income, Personal Income, Business Expenses, Personal Expenses, and Summary, in the placement shown in Figure 6-5. Then, we'll copy the totals from each area into one summary area.

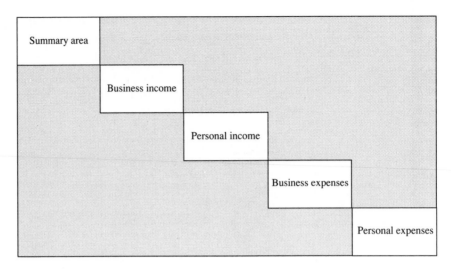

Figure 6-5.
A diagonal layout for a consolidated spreadsheet.

Creating the summary area

To begin, we'll put the summary area of the spreadsheet at the top of a new spreadsheet file, beginning in column A and row 1. The summary is what we'll probably want to see most often, so it makes sense to place it here. Because this is a summary area for values that will come from other areas we'll create later, right now we'll enter only labels for the summarized expense or income items and the months of the year.

☐ Open a new spreadsheet and create a summary area like this:

	Income/Expense (SS)				
	A	**B**	**C**	**D**	**E**
1	**Income-Expense Summary**				
2					
3		Jan	Feb	Mar	Apr
4	**Income**				
5	Videorama				
6	Personal Income				
7					
8	**Total Income**				
9					
10	**Expenses**				
11	Videorama				
12	Personal - Fixed				
13	Personal - Discretionary				
14					
15	**Total Expenses**				
16	**Total Income**				
17	**Cash Flow**				
18					

This example shows column A formatted 24 characters wide, with the rest of the columns 12 characters wide. Be sure to include columns for every month, not only through April as shown here.

Now we want to create the detail areas that will contribute totals to the summary area. Instead of placing these areas beneath or to the right of the summary area, we'll place them below and to the right, on the diagonal, as shown in Figure 6-5.

When you have more than one detail area in a spreadsheet file, it's best to place each area in a diagonal layout. A diagonal arrangement lets you add or delete rows or columns or make columns wider or narrower in one area without affecting the other areas. (If you had two areas, one underneath the other, adding or deleting columns in one of them would affect the other one as well.)

Creating the first detail area

To place our first detail area on the diagonal with the summary area, we have to locate the last cell (the one in the lower-right corner) of the summary area. Whenever you build a spreadsheet, Works considers the last cell to be the one at the lower-right corner of the matrix of cells you've filled. We've filled columns A through M and rows 1 through 17 in our summary area, so the last cell is M17. We could scroll down to find M17 manually, but Works offers an easier way.

◻ Select the Last Cell command from the Select menu. The spreadsheet scrolls and cell M17 is selected.

To begin a new area on the diagonal with the summary area, then, we want to select the next cell on the diagonal, which is cell N18.

First, we'll enter the label *Business Income* in the upper-right corner of this area (cell N18). Make the label boldface. (You'll have to widen column N about ½ inch to make room for this label.) That way, we'll be able to use the Find Cell command whenever we want to move quickly to this area. We'll simply ask Works to find the label *Business Income*. Then, working as we would with any new spreadsheet, we'll enter row labels for each expense item and column labels for each month. The column labels are the same as the ones we already entered in the summary area, so, to save time, we can copy them.

◻ Click on cell B3, and drag the pointer across row 3 to cell M3. All the month columns and the totals column are highlighted.

□ Press Command-C to copy these labels to the Clipboard.

□ Choose the Last Cell command from the Select menu. The spreadsheet scrolls down to cell N18 and that cell is selected.

□ Click on cell O19 to select it. (We want the column labels to be in the row below the area label.)

□ Press Command-V to paste the column labels into row 19, beginning at column O and extending to the right.

	M	N	O	P	Q	R
17						
18		Business Income				
19			Jan	Feb	Mar	Apr
20						
21						
22						
23						
24						
25						
26						
27						
28						
29						
30						
31						
32						
33						
34						

Income/Expense (SS)

Now, we can enter the labels in column N, beginning in row 20.

□ Complete the Business Income area so that it looks like this:

	M	N	O	P	Q	R
17						
18		Business Income				
19			Jan	Feb	Mar	Apr
20		Club Memberships				
21		Videotape Rentals				
22		Videotape Sales				
23		Accessory Sales				
24		VCR Rentals				
25						
26		Total Income				
27						
28						
29						
30						
31						
32						
33						
34						

Income/Expense (SS)

Adding a formula that transfers totals to the summary

As Al determines his monthly income totals at the Videorama, he can enter them in the cells in this spreadsheet area. A Sum formula in the Total Income row (row 26) will calculate his total business income each month, and we can use cell references to transfer these totals to the appropriate row in the summary area at the top of the spreadsheet file. Let's do one column of income totals to see how this works.

☐ Enter the value *2000* in cell Q20 (Club Memberships for March).

☐ Enter the following values in the following cells: *2500* in Q21; *125* in Q22; *140* in Q23; and *385* in Q24.

☐ Select cell Q26 and enter *=Sum(* to begin a formula. Drag the pointer across cells Q20 through Q24 to select this range and enter it in the entry bar, and then type *)* and press Return or Enter to complete the formula.

The summary portion of the spreadsheet now looks like this:

	N	O	P	Q	R	S
17						
18	**Business Income**					
19		Jan	Feb	Mar	Apr	May
20	Club Memberships			2000		
21	Videotape Rentals			2500		
22	Videotape Sales			125		
23	Accessory Sales			140		
24	VCR Rentals			385		
25						
26	**Total Income**			5150		
27						
28						
29						
30						
31						
32						
33						
34						

Now, we'll transfer this total to the summary area using a cell reference.

☐ Press Command-G (the Go To Cell command), type *A1* in the cell window, and then press Return or Enter. The spreadsheet scrolls up to the summary area.

☐ Select cell D5 (Videorama Income for March), type *=Q26*, and press Return or Enter to enter this formula.

Works now will copy the total March income from the Videorama from cell Q26 in the Business Income detail area to the Videorama Income cell for March in the summary area. If the Videorama income figures in the detail area change, the total in Q26 will change as well.

To complete the Business Income detail area, copy the Sum formula in cell Q26 into the other cells for monthly totals in row 26, and then enter the cell references for the other row 26 totals in their matching monthly income cells in the summary area (row 5). After you enter these formulas, Works will calculate business income totals and copy the totals to the summary area as you enter them each month.

Creating additional detail areas

By now, you probably get the idea of how to create a consolidated spreadsheet.

When you want to use separate detail areas and consolidate them in a summary, remember a few major points:

- Build the spreadsheets on the diagonal so that the insertion of rows or columns in one area doesn't affect other areas.

- Use the Last Cell command to find the lower-right corner of each area so that you know where to begin the next area below and to the right of it.

- Label each spreadsheet area, so you can jump there quickly using Works' Find Cell command.

- Enter the cell references from the total rows of each detail area in the appropriate row in the summary area so that Works transfers the total values from the detail areas to the summary area.

Using this simple approach, you can build extremely complex spreadsheets without using one huge matrix in which it is difficult to find your way around. And you can create charts of individual detail areas, or of the summary area.

Adjusting page breaks

The only consideration that remains is where the pages break. Unlike a word-processor document, in which page breaks occur horizontally between pages only, a spreadsheet's page breaks divide it both horizontally and vertically. It's quite possible that you'll have more columns than can fit across one page of paper, and you might also have more rows than will fit on the length of one piece of paper. So page breaks for both width and height are necessary.

As mentioned in Chapter 5, in the Works spreadsheet, page breaks are indicated by horizontal and vertical dashed lines that take the place of the normal, solid row and column dividers. To get an idea of how these page breaks occur, you can scroll a blank spreadsheet to see the first default page breaks between columns F and G, and between rows 45 and 46. Every Works spreadsheet starts out with these default page breaks, but you can change them by using the Set Page Break command on the Options menu.

When you specify a new page break, Works inserts both horizontal and vertical page breaks directly above and to the left of the currently selected cell. Thus, if you were to select cell D29 and then use the Set Page Break command, a new horizontal break would appear dividing rows 28 and 29, and a new vertical break would appear between columns C and D. In other words, cell D29 would become the upper-left cell in a new spreadsheet page.

If we were to print our consolidated spreadsheet file, we would probably want each detail area printed on its own separate page. To ensure that, we'll have to adjust the page breaks. Whenever you adjust page breaks in a Works file, it's best to start from the top of the file and work your way down. Changing a page break near the top of a file can change the locations of the page breaks that follow it.

Unless you specify otherwise, each worksheet page contains the same number of rows and columns, as determined by the margins you set with the Page Setup command. A blank spreadsheet with the default margin settings contains pages with 6 columns and 45 rows, for example. If you reset a page break on such a spreadsheet so that the first page contains only 20 rows, the next page will begin on row 21 (instead of row 46), and will end on row 66 (instead of row 90). Because you usually want to have specific information included on specific printed pages of a spreadsheet, you should check the contents of pages and adjust page breaks beginning at the top of the spreadsheet and working your way down.

☐ Scroll to the top of the spreadsheet file so that cell A1 is showing.

A page will hold about 45 rows and the summary area is only 17 rows deep, so we know that it will print easily on one page. When we scroll to the right, however, we see that a page break (the vertical dashed line) occurs after column E (April). We'd prefer that all the months in this area were printed on one page, if possible. To do that, we will have to adjust the page setup and change the way the spreadsheet is printed.

☐ Choose the Page Setup command from the File menu. The Page Setup dialog box appears.

```
┌──────────────────────────────────────────────────────────────────┐
│ ImageWriter                                    v2.6   ┌─────────┐  │
│                                                       │   OK    │  │
│ Paper:  ⊙ US Letter        ○ A4 Letter                └─────────┘  │
│         ○ US Legal         ○ International Fanfold     ┌─────────┐  │
│         ○ Computer Paper   ○ Custom Size               │ Cancel  │  │
│                                                        └─────────┘  │
│ Orientation    Special Effects:  ⊠ Tall Adjusted                  │
│  ┌──┐ ┌──┐                       ☐ 50 % Reduction                 │
│  │  │ │  │                       ☐ No Gaps Between Pages          │
│  └──┘ └──┘                                                        │
│                                              Paper Width:  ┌────┐  │
│  ☐ Print Row and Column Numbers                           │8.5 │  │
│  ☐ Print Cell Notes                          Paper Height:┌────┐  │
│                                                           │11  │  │
│  Header:  ┌──────────────────────────────────────────────────┐   │
│           │ |                                                 │   │
│           └──────────────────────────────────────────────────┘   │
│  Footer:  ┌──────────────────────────────────────────────────┐   │
│           └──────────────────────────────────────────────────┘   │
│  Left Margin: ┌────┐            Right Margin: ┌────┐              │
│               │1   │                          │1   │              │
│               └────┘                          └────┘              │
│  Top Margin:  ┌────┐            Bottom Margin:┌────┐              │
│               │1   │                          │1   │              │
│               └────┘                          └────┘              │
└──────────────────────────────────────────────────────────────────┘
```

Because our spreadsheet area is much wider than it is long, it makes sense to change the printing orientation here.

☐ Click on the wide icon in the Orientation section of the dialog box to print sideways so all columns fit.

☐ Click the OK button.

Scrolling to the right in the spreadsheet now, we see that the page break has moved from column E (April) to column G (June). Changing the printing orientation helped a little, but not enough.

At this point, we have a couple of alternatives. We could either make all the month columns narrower (either by dragging the column dividers individually, or by specifying a new column width with the Column Width command on the Format menu), or we can reduce the size of the print. Either alternative will let us print more data across a page. For the sake of this example, we'll reduce the print size.

☐ Choose the Page Setup command from the File menu.

□ Click the 50% Reduction option in the Special Effects section if you're using an ImageWriter, or type *50* in the Reduce Or Enlarge box if you're using a LaserWriter.

□ Click the OK button to return to the spreadsheet.

Now if we scroll to the right, we see that the page break has moved over to column O. That means the entire area will fit on one page. But even though the 50-percent reduction has solved the problem in our example, you might want to test-print in this mode before you print one of your own spreadsheets: The default font used for spreadsheet data is small (9-point) to begin with, and when you reduce it by 50 percent, the results can be very difficult to read, especially if you're printing on an ImageWriter.

If you're printing on a LaserWriter, you might try different reduction levels, say about 70 percent, and see how this reduction affects your ability to fit the entire summary area on one page. (Works' Print Preview feature will show how large this reduced-print spreadsheet will be on a page, but you can't see how the type will actually look on paper.)

If you do use the reduced print mode, you could also try increasing the spreadsheet's font size from 9-point to 10-point or 12-point. Larger type will be larger and easier to read when reduced. For this example, let's assume we can live with a 50-percent reduction and 9-point type. The problem now is that the page break is actually two columns farther to the right than we want it—the page will include the first two columns of the Business Income area as well. We'll have to insert a new page break so that only the summary area is included on the first page.

Remember, when you insert a page break in the spreadsheet, you insert both horizontal and vertical page breaks simultaneously. This means we'll have to select the cell that's immediately below the bottom row of the summary area (row 18), and immediately to the right of the December column in the summary area (column N).

□ Select cell N18.

□ Choose the Set Page Break command from the Options menu. A new page break appears.

	M	N	O	P	Q	R
			Income/Expense (SS)			
12						
13						
14						
15						
16						
17						
18		Business Income				
19			Jan	Feb	Mar	Apr
20		Club Memberships			2000	
21		Videotape Rentals			2500	
22		Videotape Sales			125	
23		Accessory Sales			140	
24		VCR Rentals			385	
25						
26		Total Income			5150	
27						
28						
29						

Now the entire Business Income area will be printed on a new page. We can scroll down the spreadsheet into the other detail areas and insert page breaks in them to be sure each area prints on a new page.

Adding page headers

The final touch before printing is to insert a page header. Because this will be a multiple-page printout, it would be nice to have a page header that identifies the project and numbers the pages.

☐ Choose Page Setup from the File menu. When the Page Setup dialog box appears, you'll notice that the insertion point is blinking in the Header box.

☐ Type the header *Al Chroma Expense/Income Report,* but don't press the Return key. (Pressing Return accepts the settings in the Page Setup dialog box and returns you to the spreadsheet.)

We've entered the text of the header now, but we need to tell Works how to format the header. You have to enter special formatting commands in the header window if you want to specify how a header is justified, how pages are numbered, and whether a date and time are included in the header. All the formatting commands begin with an ampersand (&) sign. The following are the commands.

Command	Results
&L	Left justifies the header or footer text
&R	Right justifies the header or footer text
&C	Centers the header or footer text
&P	Prints page numbers in the header or footer
&D	Prints the current date (as supplied by the Macintosh clock) in the header or footer
&T	Prints the current time (as supplied by the Macintosh clock) in the header or footer
&F	Prints the file name in the header or footer
&B	Prints the text following this command in boldface
&I	Prints the text following this command in italics

Because the ampersand symbol begins formatting commands, you also have to use it if you want to print a single ampersand in a header. If you wanted Works to print *Expense & Income* in a header, you would have to enter *Expense && Income* in the Header box.

All these commands and procedures apply to both headers and footers. If you want, you can have both a header and a footer in a document. In this case, we'll simply finish the header. We've typed the basic header text, but we also want to right-justify the text, make it boldface, and include a date and page number.

- □ Click at the beginning of the text in the Header box to move the insertion point there.

- □ Type *&R&B* to specify that you want the header text right-justified and boldfaced.

- □ Click at the end of the header text, type a space, and then type *- &D - Page &P*. This formatting command tells Works to enter the date, followed by the word *Page* and then the page number.

So, the entire header text looks like this:

&R&BAl Chroma Expense/Income Report - &D - Page &P

The header commands that cause text to be added (the date, time, and page number commands) will place those bits of text exactly where you put the command. So if you want spaces around a date or page number, for example, you must add a space in front of and behind that command. Here, we've set off the date and page number from the header text with dashes. Also, it's a good idea to include the word *Page* in a header before the page number command so that other readers of the document will know that the number that appears there is the page number.

When this header is printed, it will appear in the top, right-hand corner of each page, and will look like this, depending on the date you print:

Al Chroma Expense/Income Report - March 31, 1989 - Page 1

These projects have shown you most of the basic features of the Works spreadsheet in action. (If you want more information about specific functions or operations, consult the Microsoft Works User's Guide.) Now let's look at the basic features of the Works database.

Chapter 7

Using the Database

Just as the Works spreadsheet can store, sort, calculate, and otherwise manipulate numbers, the database can store, sort, calculate, and otherwise manipulate facts. Facts can be text, such as names, addresses, or product descriptions, or they can be numbers, such as dates, times, part numbers, or prices. The Works database lets you easily store a wide variety of data, and then retrieve, sort, print, or even calculate it.

Database Basics

All database programs work fundamentally the same way. You use a database file to store information about people, places, or things. In such a file, you almost always want to store more than one fact about each person, place, or thing. A simple telephone list, for example, would contain two facts about each person: the person's name and the person's telephone number. In a database file, each fact or item of information is stored in a field, and each collection of facts about an individual person, place, or thing is stored in a group as a record.

Before you can store information in any database file, you must structure it in a specific way to accept your data—you must define the fields, or information categories, for your data. After you define fields for a database file, you can enter your data into them, and then you can retrieve, arrange, or display the data in a variety of ways.

You can display data from a Works database file in two ways. In the form window, shown at the top of the next page, you can look at all the data from individual records, one record at a time.

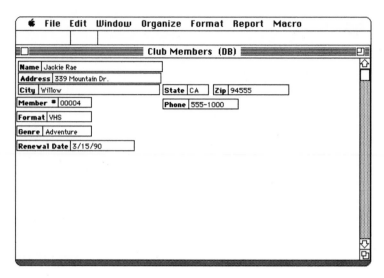

In the list window, you can look at data from several records at a time, like this:

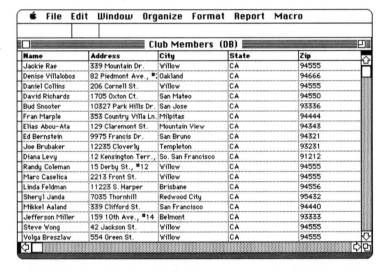

The list window lets you view a lot of information from different records, but it might not show you every field of data in each record it displays. As you'll see later, you can scroll to the right in the list window to view other fields in records, and you can scroll down to view other records or groups of records in the file. In the form window, you see every field in a record, but only one record at a time. You can switch from a form window to a list window by selecting the Show List or Show Form command from the Format menu. These two commands alternate on the Format menu, depending on which type window is active: When a form window is displayed, the Show List command appears on the menu; and when the list window is being displayed, the Show Form command appears on the menu. Pressing Command-L is the keyboard equivalent of these two commands; it toggles between the two views.

To print information from a Works database file, you create a report using the database's Report menu. Reports are designed with a report window, which appears on top of the open database file you're working with and looks like this:

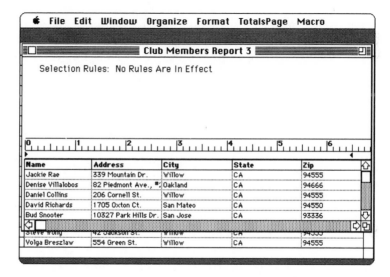

Using the report window, you can select certain records, or you can select fields of data within records to be included in a printed report. You can also specify calculations in the report, such as the addition of numeric fields. We'll explore these features in detail later in this chapter. First, let's look at the various commands available on the database menus.

A Quick Tour of the Database Menus

When you are working with data or creating a new database file, there are eight menus of commands available in the menu bar at the top of the screen. Unlike in the other Works applications, the commands listed on some of the database menus change, depending on whether you're working with a database file in general or whether you're working with a specific report. (We'll look at these differences as we go through the descriptions of each of the menus.)

As mentioned in previous chapters, the Apple menu is the same, no matter which Works application you're working with. So, we'll start our tour with the File menu.

The File menu

The commands on the File menu have the same names in every Works application, but in the database, there are a couple of differences in how they work. When you're defining a file, entering data, or manipulating data with the database, the Page Setup, Print, and Print Merge commands are dimmed. (Dimmed letters in a command mean it's not available.) The Page Setup and Print commands are available only when you're working with a database report and have a report window open. The Print Merge command is active only in the Works word processor.

The Edit menu

The Edit menu is another menu you'll find in every Works application, but it contains some commands that are specific to the database, and some command names are dimmed (not available). The only Edit menu commands that are available when you're working on a database report are Copy Totals and Change Report Title.

As in the other Works applications, you can use the Undo command to cancel a previous action. If you delete a record and then decide you didn't mean to do that, you can choose the Undo command. Undo will cancel your previous command (the command to delete the record), and the record will reappear.

You can use the Cut command to remove data that's in a field, record, or group of records from a file and place it on the Clipboard. When you use the Cut command to remove a record or group of records, those records disappear from the file and any records beneath them move up and are renumbered.

You can use the Copy command when you want to place a copy of a field, record, or group of records on the Clipboard without removing the data from the file. When you're working with a database report, the Copy Totals command, mentioned earlier, replaces the Copy command.

Copy Totals lets you copy the field totals from a report to the Clipboard for transfer into another document so that you can see a report's totals without printing the report. (You can't see the totals in a report window; you must either print the report on paper, use Print Preview and the magnifying glass to see the totals, copy the totals to a word-processor document or spreadsheet, or copy the totals to the Clipboard and use the Show Clipboard command on the Window menu to view them. (See the discussion of the Window menu later in this chapter.)

The Paste command lets you move data from the Clipboard into a database file, beginning at the selected field or record's location. If you have only one field's data from one record on the Clipboard, that data will be inserted into the field you have selected when you use the Paste command. If you cut or copy data from two fields of one record to the Clipboard, the data will be inserted beginning at the field you select and extending to the right into the adjacent field.

Whenever you cut or copy data, a copy of that data remains on the Clipboard until you cut or copy another selection of data. Thus, you can cut all or part of one record to the Clipboard, and then paste it into several different locations in a file by using the Paste command repeatedly. If you were putting data into an address file, for example, and several records had the same city and state data, you could enter this data in the first record, copy it to the Clipboard, and then quickly paste it into several other records.

The Clear command removes data from a field, record, or group of records without eliminating the records themselves. When you clear an entire record in a list window, for example, the data in that record is deleted, but the blank record remains.

The Select All command selects all the fields and records in a database file. This command works only in the list window. Select All is useful if you want to cut or copy all of a file's records to the Clipboard.

The Insert Record command inserts a new, blank record above the currently selected record in a list window, or in front of the current record in a form window. You can insert only one blank record at a time with this command.

The last three commands on the Edit menu let you change field names, add fields, or delete fields.

To use the Change Field Name command, you must select an entire field by clicking on its name. When you select a field and choose the

Change Field Name command, the Field Name box appears, letting you enter a new name for that field.

When you choose the Add New Field command, the Field Name box also appears, letting you type the name for a new field. The new field is added to the right of any existing fields in the list window or below any existing fields in the form window.

To use the Delete Field command, you must select a field by clicking on its name. After you select a field, you can delete it by choosing the Delete Field command. When you delete a field, you lose all the data stored in that field.

These three commands aren't available when you're working with a database report. Instead, there is a command called Change Report Title, which lets you change the name you've given to a report.

The Window menu

As in other Works applications, the Window menu contains commands that let you view the contents of the Clipboard (Show Clipboard), access Works' built-in Help file (Help), or activate one of the documents open on the desktop. The Show Clipboard command is particularly handy when you want to see the results of a field total you've copied from a database report, when you aren't yet ready to print the report. By using the Copy Totals command on the Edit menu, you can copy a report's calculated totals to the Clipboard and then view them using the Show Clipboard command.

The Organize menu

The Organize menu contains the commands for locating, selecting, or sorting data in the database.

The Find Field command finds data in any field in any record, according to comparison information you enter. When you choose the Find Field command or press Command-F, a dialog box appears, letting you enter the matching information to locate the data you want. If you want to find all occurrences of the name Bob, for example, you would type *Bob* in the Find Field dialog box as the comparison information. Find Field finds the first record that contains the comparison information and presents it on the screen (in a form window) or highlights the matching data (in a list window). To find the next occurrence of the data, you must choose the Find Field command again and click on the Find Next button. To save time, you can limit the search to text fields only so that Works doesn't spend time searching fields that contain numbers, times, or dates. The Find Field command isn't available when you're working with a database report.

The Match Records command (Command-M from the keyboard) also searches for data that matches comparison information you type into a dialog box, but instead of presenting records one at a time, it presents all the matching records in the list window at the same time. (If there are more matching records than will fit in the list window, you can scroll the window to see them.) This command isn't available when you're working with a database report.

The Record Selection command is a more sophisticated way of selecting certain records from a database file and listing them on the screen. Unlike the Match Records command, which locates all of the records that contain your comparison data in any field, the Record Selection command selects records only if the comparison information is in a specific field and the data meets logical conditions, or selection rules, that you specify, such as a zip code beginning with a certain number or a date falling between two other dates. After you define record-selection rules, the command finds all the records meeting those rules and then displays them all at the same time. You can use the Record Selection command to select certain records to view in a list window, or you can use it to select records to include in a database report. The Record Selection dialog box looks like this:

```
┌─────────────────────────────────────────────────────────────┐
│                      Record Selection:                        │
│  ┌──────────────────────────┐  ┌──────────────────────────┐  │
│  │ Name                  ⬆️ │  │ equals                ⬆️ │  │
│  │ Phone                 █  │  │ contains              █  │  │
│  │ Address               █  │  │ begins with           █  │  │
│  │ City                  █  │  │ is greater than       █  │  │
│  │ State                 ⬇️ │  │ is greater than or equal to ⬇️ │  │
│  └──────────────────────────┘  └──────────────────────────┘  │
│                                                               │
│  Record Comparison Information: │                           │ │
│                                                               │
│  Selection Rules: No Rules Are In Effect                      │
│                                                               │
│  ○ And   ○ Or                                                 │
│  ○ And   ○ Or                                                 │
│  ○ And   ○ Or                                                 │
│  ○ And   ○ Or                                                 │
│  ○ And   ○ Or                                                 │
│  ┌──────────┐  ┌─────────────┐  ┌─────────────┐  ┌────────┐   │
│  │  Cancel  │  │ Delete Rule │  │ Install Rule │  │ Select │  │
│  └──────────┘  └─────────────┘  └─────────────┘  └────────┘   │
└─────────────────────────────────────────────────────────────┘
```

After you use the Record Selection command, if you want to display all the records in the file again, you must choose the Show All Records command. You can also use Show All Records to cancel record-selection rules you've set for a database report.

The Sort command lets you arrange records in a database file in alphabetical, numerical, or chronological order. However, you can sort only in alphabetical order in a text field; in numerical order in a numerical field; and in chronological order in a date or time field. The Sort command isn't available when you're working with a database report.

The Format menu

The Format menu contains a variety of formatting options for the form and list windows when you're working with an entire file, but it has far fewer options when you're working with a database report.

The Show Form/Show List command toggles the display between the form window and the list window. (As was mentioned earlier in this chapter, Show Form appears when you're in the list window, Show List when you're in the form window.) You can also toggle the display by double-clicking in the record-selector boxes or the deselector box located to the left of the records in the list window, by double-clicking anywhere in the form window except on a field box, or by pressing Command-L.

The Font, Size, and Color menus contain the same options as they do in other Works applications. But in the database, as in the spreadsheet, they affect the entire document. You can't change the font, size, or color of one field or record. The defaults in a new database document are 9-point Geneva text in black. Changing the size of a font makes everything in the database file bigger or smaller; the field widths and record heights expand to fit the new type size, but the number of characters in a field's width remains the same.

The Show Grid command lets you choose to display or not to display the matrix of lines that separate fields and records in both the list window and in the report window. The Show Grid command is checked when the grid is showing; when you select it to eliminate the grid, the check mark disappears.

The Set Field Attributes command, available in either the list or form window, lets you select the type of data a field can contain; it lets you align the data to the left, right, or in the center of the field; and it lets you underline or boldface the data. To use this command, you must first select a field. Otherwise, the command is dimmed on the menu. As a shortcut, you can double-click on a field name to select this command. The Set Field Attributes command isn't available in database reports.

The Report menu

The Report menu is the gateway to all reports in the database. It is not available when you're working with a database report.

The Select Report command produces a list of reports you have defined and lets you choose one to work with.

If you have a new database file and you haven't defined any reports yet, the New Report command is the only one available on the Report menu. You can define and store up to eight reports with each file.

You can use the Duplicate Report command to produce an exact copy of a previously defined report. This command is helpful when you want to create a complex report that is substantially similar to an existing report—you can duplicate the existing report and then make the changes you want.

The Erase Report command lets you delete reports you have defined before.

The TotalsPage menu

The TotalsPage menu replaces the Report menu in the menu bar when you're working with a database report. It does not appear when you're working in any other type of database window.

The Sum This Field command produces a total for all of the data in any numeric field. To use this command, you select the numerical field you want to sum, and then choose the Sum This Field command from the TotalsPage menu. Field totals appear only when you print a report, or when you use Copy Totals to move them to the Clipboard. You can then see the totals by using the Show Clipboard command or pasting the totals into another document.

The Take A Sub-Total On Field Change command works in conjunction with the Sum This Field command to produce subtotals of numerical fields whenever the name or number in another field changes. If you had an inventory that was divided into several classes of parts, for example, and you wanted a subtotal of the number of parts in each class, you would use the Sum This Field command on the field containing the part quantities, and then use the Take A Sub-Total On Field Change command on the field containing the names of parts classes. This way, the database would produce a subtotal in the quantity field whenever the data in the class field changed. We'll see how this works in Chapter 8.

The Take A Sub-Total On 1st Char is similar to the Take A Sub-Total On Field Change command. Take A Sub-Total On 1st Char produces a subtotal only when the first character in a field changes. This command is useful when the first digit of a part number is a code that divides an inventory into classes. A company's widgets, for example, might be numbered X-1, X-2, X-3, and so on, while its doodads might be numbered Y-1, Y-2, and Y-3. If you wanted to produce subtotals of all widgets or doodads, you would use the Take A Sub-Total On 1st Char Field command, and the database would wait until it had printed all the product codes beginning with the same letter or number before it produced a total.

The New Page After Total command causes Works to begin a new page after it prints each subtotal in a database report. To use the command, you simply choose it while working in a report window.

The Macro menu

As explained in Chapter 1, the Macro menu works the same in all Works applications. We'll put the macro feature to work on database projects in Chapter 8.

A Sample Database

To see how to set up and use a Works database file, let's look at a quick example.

Creating the database

Suppose we want to store several names, addresses, and telephone numbers in the Works database.

- ☐ Load Microsoft Works.

- ☐ Select the New command from the File menu.

- ☐ Double-click on the database icon. A Field Name window will appear.

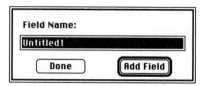

We want a field and label for each category of information for our file. The file will contain names, telephone numbers, and addresses, so let's use these categories as our field names.

☐ Type the field name *Name* and press the Return key. A new field with this name appears in the database-file window. (Pressing Return is the same as clicking the Add Field button in the Field Name window.)

☐ Type the field name *Phone* and press the Return key. This new field is added to the database-file window.

☐ Enter the field names *Address, City, State,* and *Zip.* Press Return after you type each name.

☐ Click the Done button in the Field Name window to tell Works you are finished naming fields for this file. The Field Name window disappears, and the form window appears, ready to store information.

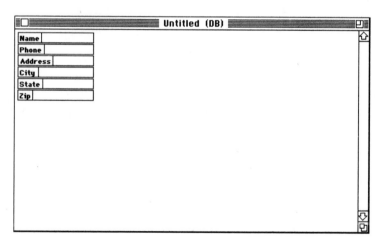

Now, we can enter a few names and addresses.

☐ Click on the Name field to select it, if it isn't already selected.

□ Type the name *Joe Jones,* and press the Return key. The name is entered in the Name field and the Phone field is selected.

□ Type the phone number *555-1111,* and press the Return key. The number is entered, and the Address field is selected.

□ Enter *12 Main St., Belmont, CA* and *94444* in the Address, City, State and Zip fields, respectively, pressing Return, Enter, or Tab after each entry.

You'll notice that after entering the Zip information and pressing the Return, Enter, or Tab key, a new record is displayed. Whenever you fill in the last field in a Works database record in the form window and press the Return, Enter, or Tab key, that record is stored away and a new, blank record is displayed. This lets you enter a lot of records into the file easily because you're always presented with a new record when you finish filling in the last field of the current record.

Most database programs keep track of information by numbering the records in each file. In the Works database, the number of the current record is always shown in the upper-left corner of the entry bar, as long as one of the fields in the record is selected.

□ Point to the upper right-hand scroll arrow and click on it to display the record you previously entered. The record appears in the form window, like this:

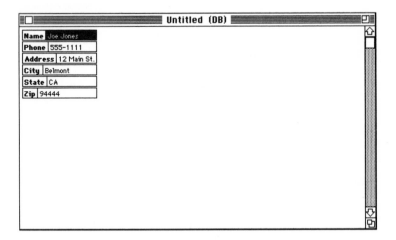

The form window displays all the fields in a record one record at a time. As we'll see, you can rearrange the layout of the fields, add new fields, or change field names or attributes all from this screen. Sometimes, however, you want to see more than one record at a time.

☐ Choose the Show List command from the Format menu (or press Command-L), and the list window appears, like this:

Name	Phone	Address	City	State
Joe Jones	555-1111	12 Main St.	Belmont	CA

In this window, fields are arranged in columns, and each record is a row. Some files you create might contain more fields than can be displayed in columns on the screen, but as we'll see, you can easily display other fields when you want.

Adding, deleting, and renaming fields

Most people don't have a clear idea how they want to store data when they first create a database file. Works lets you change your mind after you've begun storing information. You can add, delete, or rename fields in a file any time you want. The action you take depends on whether you're working in the form window of the list window.

In the form window, you can add a field simply by pointing to a blank area of the form, holding down the mouse button, and dragging. As you drag the pointer, a field outline appears. When you release the mouse button, the Field Name dialog box is displayed.

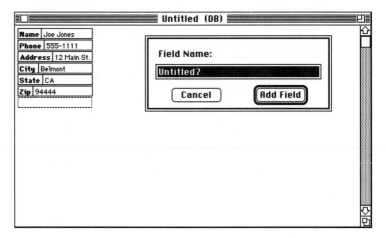

Simply type in the field name you want, click the Add Field button (or press the Return or Enter key), and the field will be added in the place where you drew it.

In the list window, you must choose the Add New Field command from the Edit menu. The list window also displays the Field Name dialog box. After you enter the field name and click the Add Field button, the new field appears as a new, blank column to the right of any existing fields in the file. (If you have more fields than can be displayed on the screen at once, you will have to scroll to the right to see the new field.) You can name up to 60 fields in a Works database file.

To delete a field in either the form window or the list window, you must use the Delete Field command on the Edit menu. If the field you want to delete contains data, all data in that field will be lost.

When you choose the Change Field Name command on the Edit menu, a dialog box lets you enter a new name.

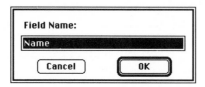

You can also display this dialog box by double-clicking on the field name you want to change. This shortcut works in both the list and the form windows.

Browsing through a file

So far, we've been using the Return, Enter, or Tab key to advance the selection from one field to the next (or from the last field in a record to the first field in the next record), but there are other ways to move the selection through a file. You can always select a field by pointing to it and clicking the mouse button. You can use the scroll bars to move from record to record or to see off-screen fields in the list window of a file. You can also use the keyboard. Figure 7-1 contains a table of the various keyboard navigation options available in the Works database. As you can see, some options work only in either the list window or the form window and others work in both.

Action	Keys	View
Move down one field	Return	Form
Move up one field	Shift-Return	Form
Move down in same field, next record	Return or Down Arrow	List
Move up in same field, previous record	Shift-Return or Up Arrow	List
Move right one field	Tab or Right Arrow	Both
Move left one field	Shift-Tab or Left Arrow	Both
Advance to next record from last field	Return or Down arrow	List
Back up to previous record from first field	Shift-Return or Up arrow	List

Figure 7-1.
Keyboard navigation options.

When you use a key combination to move the selection to an off-screen field in the list window, the part of the file containing that field scrolls into view. Pressing the Return key or the Down Arrow key when the selection is in the last record in the list moves the selection to the first record in the list. Similarly, if you press the Tab key or the Right Arrow key when the last field in a record is selected, the selection moves to the first field in the next record.

Changing the layout

Works displays a database file in the form window when you first create the file, and new fields are arranged vertically. But after you've created a file, you can resize or rearrange the fields in either the form window or the list window to view the information in different ways.

In the form window, you move fields around by dragging them with the pointer.

◻ Place the pointer on top of a field name. The arrow turns into a hand symbol like this:

◻ Hold down the mouse button, drag the field anywhere else on the screen, and then release the mouse button. The field is now fixed in its new position.

The only restriction on moving fields in the form window is that you can't place a field on top of another field. To move a field in the list window, you drag the entire column representing the field.

◻ Point to the field name at the top of the column. The arrow turns into a hand symbol.

◻ Hold down the mouse button, and then drag the field to the left or right.

As you drag the field across other fields in the list window, the name of the field being overlapped darkens to show that it is beneath the field you're dragging. When you release the mouse button, the field you have been dragging is placed to the right or left of the field beneath it, depending on which direction you are moving it.

◻ Release the mouse button.

Fields are composed of two areas: the field name and the field data. Field names in the Works database can be up to 64 characters long; field data can be up to 250 characters long. Any data you type into a field (up to the 250-character limit) will be stored in the field. But when you first create a new field, the data area is large enough to display only about 10 characters. To make a field wider, you again use the mouse.

In the form window, use the following steps.

☐ Point to the right edge of the field data area. The arrow pointer turns into a double arrow.

☐ Hold down the mouse button, and drag the edge of the field to the right or the left to make it larger or smaller.

A field data area can stretch almost to the edge of the form window itself; if you're using a large-screen monitor (so the file's window is bigger) the field can be even wider on the screen. But no matter how large your screen, a field can hold only 250 characters of data.

In the list window, you widen fields in much the same way as you do in the spreadsheet.

☐ Point to the line dividing the field name you want to widen from the field name on its right. The selection pointer turns into a double arrow.

☐ Hold down the mouse button, and drag the line to the right or left, to make the field wider or narrower.

Another way to change the appearance of a database file is through the field attributes you assign to each field. The Field Attributes dialog box, which appears when you choose the Set Field Attributes command from the Format menu, looks like this:

```
┌─────────────────────────────────────────────────────────────┐
│  Set Field Attributes                                        │
│                                                              │
│  Type:         Display:       Align:        Style:           │
│  ● Text        ○ General      ● Left        ☐ Bold           │
│  ○ Numeric     ○ Fixed        ○ Center      ☐ Underline      │
│  ○ Date        ○ Dollar       ○ Right       ☐ Commas         │
│  ○ Time        ○ Percent      ┌──┐                           │
│                ○ Scientific   └──┘ Decimal Places            │
│  ☐ Computed  ☐ Show Day       ( Cancel )  (  OK  )           │
│                                                              │
└─────────────────────────────────────────────────────────────┘
```

As you can see, you can use this dialog box to vary the data type, numerical display type, alignment, or style of the data in any field. Most of these are the same options available in the Works spreadsheet. (For a fuller explanation of how the Field Attributes options affect the appearance of text or numbers in a file, see the discussion of the Format menu in Chapter 5.)

> **TIP:** You can also display the Field Attributes dialog box by double-clicking on the data area of any field in either the list or form window.

The database Field Attributes dialog box also lets you create a computed field. A computed field is one that creates its data by performing a calculation on the data in other fields. After you select the Computed field option in this dialog box and click the OK button, Works inserts an equal sign in the entry bar, followed by the flashing insertion point, indicating that you must type in a formula to make the calculation required to produce the data for this field. We'll see how this works in Chapter 8. The Field Attributes dialog box also lets you include the actual day in a date field.

Manipulating data

The Works database has tools that let you locate, sort, and select data in a variety of ways. To find an individual record in the database, use the Find Field command on the Organize menu. This command produces a dialog box that lets you enter the data you want to search for, like this:

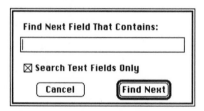

Simply type in the data you want to find. Works will search the file for it and then display the selected field and its record on the screen if there's a match. Notice that this dialog box has a check box that tells the program to search only text fields, rather than numerical, time, or date fields. This option allows for faster text searches, because Works doesn't waste time searching fields that don't contain text information. If more than one record contains a match for the search data you enter, you must continue using the Find command to locate each additional occurrence of the data. Fortunately, the search data you enter in the Find Field dialog box remains there until you type something else. To find additional occurrences of the same matching data, you can simply press

Command-F to display the Find Field dialog box, and then press the Return key or the Enter key to search for the next occurrence.

If you want to find a certain record, but the only search data you can remember is common to many records, use the Match Records command. This command uses the same search key dialog box as the Find Field command, but it searches the file and then displays a window containing all the records that match your search data. You can then scroll through the window and find the exact record you want. You can also print the window using the Print Window command on the File menu, and you can save the group of selected records with a different name using the Save Selected Records Only option in the Save As command's dialog box.

Finally, if you want to select a group of records from your file based on a complex set of search rules, use the Record Selection command on the Organize menu.

By selecting field names and selection operators such as "equals" or "contains" and then by typing in matching data, you can select data on up to six combined rules. The Record Selection command lets you be extremely precise in searching for records. Like the Match Records command, it displays all the records that match its criteria in a window, and you can print or save only the selected records, if you like.

TIP: You can use the Record Selection command to select a large group of records from a file and then use the Match Records command to select a subset of the selected records. Simply create the selection rules and apply them to the file, and then perform a Match Records operation on the set of selected records. Both the Match Records command and the Record Selection command retain their search criteria until you replace them with something new, so it's easy to use them to quickly display the same subset of records at any time.

Also, the Match Records command and the Record Selection command are toggles: After you use either command, a check mark appears next to the command's name on the Organize menu, indicating that you are working with only a selected set of the file's records. After using the Record Selection command, you must select the Show All Records command to view the entire file again. After using the Match Records command, choosing the same command again returns you to the previously selected list.

Finally, you can sort the data in a database file. Sorting a file on the Name field in alphabetical order, for example, makes it much easier to find a certain person's record as you scroll through the file. The Sort command, also found on the Organize menu, produces this dialog box:

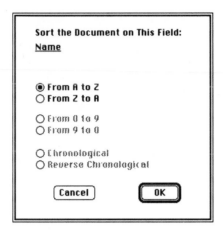

As you can see, you can sort on only one field at a time. (The field name is shown at the top of the dialog box.) You can sort in either ascending or descending alphabetical order (for text fields), numerical order (for number fields), or chronological order (for date and time fields). When you sort, you must sort every record in the file; unlike the spreadsheet, you can't select a group of records (or rows) in the list window and sort only those.

We'll put these various selection options to work on business projects in Chapter 8.

TIP: The Sort command works independently of the Match Records and Record Selection commands. If you like, you can use Match Records or Record Selection to select a subset of records, and then sort those records. However, after you have sorted a subset of a file in this way, you will find that the entire file has also been sorted when you choose the Show All Records command or turn the Match Records toggle off.

Printing data

Printing a database file starts with creating a report, using the Report menu. Database reports always take a form similar to the list window, with fields in columns and records in rows. As with the list window, you can change the arrangement or width of columns in a report. You can also choose the Record Selection command with a report format displayed to produce a report containing only a subset of a file's records.

If you want to arrange data for printing onto labels, business forms, or other documents for which a row-and-column format is inappropriate, you can merge the data from a database file into a word-processor document. In Chapter 10, we'll see how Works can combine data from the word processor and the database for a variety of printing and data-handling needs.

Making the Most of the Database

By now, you should have a general idea of how the Works database lets you manipulate and format data. This section offer some suggestions for making the best of both.

Use the selection options to aid manual data validation

If others will be entering data in your Works database files, you need to be able to set rules about the format of data in certain fields. This process is known as data validation, or validation of data types. Works will check the field-type attribute: If you set a field's attribute as numerical, for example, and then try to enter text into that field, Works will warn you that the entry isn't valid. (On the other hand, Works does allow you to enter times, dates, and numbers in "text" type fields—it simply treats the entries as text.) But you'll have to check manually for other data-entry errors by visually checking files.

You can inspect data in Works in two ways. The simplest is to display the file in the list window, sort it on various fields, scrolling through the file between sorts, looking for odd entries or duplications. If you're scanning a Zip Code field, for example, you can easily pick out zip codes that have been mistakenly entered with four or six digits instead of five. Sorting the file first lets you locate duplicate records easily because duplicates will fall next to each other in the list.

Another way to inspect data is with the Record Selection command. Using the selection dialog box, you can create rules that look for mistakes in your data. Suppose you have a numerical field in your file called Part Number, in which the data should always contains six digits. Using the Record Selection rules, you could search the file for records in which the Part Number field contains fewer than six digits or more than six digits by searching for ranges. If you want to find numbers larger than six digits, for example, you could search for numbers larger that 999999. Or you could look for records containing six-digit numbers that fall outside of a specific range (200001 through 499999, for example).

With six rules allowed per record selection, you could also search for very specific mistakes in more than one field at a time.

Use Works' flexibility to approximate relational features

The Works database is what's known as a "flat file" database, which means that each file you create is entirely separate and the program doesn't support any commands or operations that allow one database file to interact with another. Some stand-alone database programs are what's known as "relational" databases. A relational database lets you create a set of separate files (sometimes called relations) that can compare or even transfer information among one another. Comparing or transferring data between files is useful to people and businesses that often need to store the same pieces of data in more than one file.

In Microsoft Works, you can perform operations like this manually. You can also copy data between files to create the information set that you want without a lot of redundant data entry. Let's look at some situations you might run into and how to handle them in Works.

You might want to give a subset of the records in your file to somebody else. Perhaps you're dividing up sales territories, and you want each salesperson to have only the records in his or her territory. Perhaps you're having a clerk work on personnel records, but you don't want him or her to see the records of your management team.

To create a new file with a subset of records, use the following steps.

☐ Open the original file.

☐ Use Match Records or Record Selection to select only the records you want to move to the new file.

- Use the Save As command with the Save Selected Records Only option to save the selected records as a new file.

- If you want to hide one or more fields of data in the new file, delete them by using the Cut or Clear commands, and save the edited file again.

- Distribute the subset file.

One of the reasons to distribute such a file is to have somebody update or add to the data in it. The preceding steps are fine for that, but what if you want to enter the changes into your original file?

- Open both the original file and the subset file.

- Copy all the records from the subset file into the original file.

- Sort the original file on a field in which the information in each record should be unique, such as Customer Name. The sorted file will arrange the records so that the duplicate records (the updated records you copied into the file) will appear next to the original copies of those records in the list window.

- Delete the original copies of the records (so that only the updated copies remain), and save the original file again to preserve the new information.

- Delete the subset file from your disk.

Because Works files are limited in size by the amount of memory in your Mac, it might also be necessary to divide large files into two or more smaller files. You can simply use the Record Selection command to select a group of records to split off from the original file, and then save the subset with a similar name, or (if you can't select records logically), you can cut records from the list window in one file and paste them into the list window of a new file. In both cases, the names of the original and of the new file should be similar, such as Data1 and Data2.

It's much easier if you can split records between files logically using the Match Records or Record Selection command. You simply select all the records you want, for example, records in which the data in the Name field begins with the letters M through Z, and then save the selection as a new file.

If you plan to cut records from the original file and paste them into a new file in order to split the data between two files, you must first create a duplicate file to receive the copied records. The following procedure will save you the trouble of having to redefine your fields and attributes, as you would if you simply opened a new file.

☐ Open the original file. (Let's assume it's called Data1.)

☐ Be sure there's a copy of it on your disk.

☐ Delete all the records from the file.

☐ Rename the desktop file Data2, and save it to disk. You now have two files with the same structure.

☐ Select half the records in the original file, cut them to the Clipboard (thereby removing them from the original file), and paste them into the new file.

In most cases, you'll be able to split a file by using the Record Selection command. If you can't, it's a sign that you haven't structured your database file logically.

Using the Clipboard, Works also lets you combine information from two files into one file.

Suppose that we have a separate file containing names and employee numbers (in a field called Employee Number), and we want to merge the employee numbers with our existing address file.

TIP: Before splitting a file in two to work with a larger database, sort the file on a field with unique data, such as Name, so that you can divide the records logically. Sorting on a Name field, for example, would let you select all the records with names beginning with the letters M through Z to copy to the second file.

Before copying records to the duplicate file, be sure the fields in the list window are arranged in the same order as in the original file so that the data you paste in falls into the correct fields.

☐ Open the file containing the employee numbers.

☐ Click on the Name field to select it.

☐ Choose the Sort command from the Organize menu, select the A–Z option, and then press the Return key so that the entire file is sorted by name.

☐ Select all the data in the Employee Number field by clicking on the field name. (Note that this doesn't select the field name itself, only the data contained in that field.)

☐ Choose the Copy command from the Edit menu to copy the data to the Clipboard.

☐ Open the address file.

☐ Double-click on the screen to switch to the list window.

☐ Sort the file on the Name field with the A–Z option.

☐ Choose the Add New Field command from the Edit menu. The Field Name box appears.

☐ Type *Employee Number* (or another name, if you like) as the new field name, and press the Return key. The new field is added at the right of the existing fields in the list window.

☐ Click in the bottom scroll bar to move the Employee Number field into view, if it isn't in view already.

☐ Click on the Employee Number field in the first record.

☐ Choose the Paste command from the Edit menu. The employee numbers are pasted from the Clipboard, and because both of the files are sorted in the same order, the numbers match the correct employees.

Use the keyboard commands or the mouse to save time

Many of the database operations can be accomplished with keyboard commands as well as with the mouse. If you're in the middle of typing data into your file, it will be faster to use the keyboard commands to execute various database operations. Figure 7-2 contains a list of keyboard commands available in the Works database.

Action	Command	Menu	Keyboard Equivalent
Open a file	Open	File	Command-O
Close a file	Close	File	Command-W
Save a file	Save	File	Command-S
Print a file	Print	File	Command-P
Quit Works	Quit	File	Command-Q
Undo a command	Undo	Edit	Command-Z
Cut data	Cut	Edit	Command-X
Copy data	Copy	Edit	Command-C
Paste data	Paste	Edit	Command-V
Insert a record	Insert Record	Edit	Command-I
Access on-line Help facility	Help	Window	Command-?
Display last document on Window menu		Window	Command-,
Find a field	Find Field	Organize	Command-F
Match records	Match Records	Organize	Command-M
Sort records	Sort	Organize	Command-A
Show form or list format	Show Form/ List	Format	Command-L
Start macro recording	Start Recording	Macro	Option-+
Stop macro recording	Stop Recording	Macro	Option-–
Play back a macro	Playback and	Macro	Option-Delete
Stop a macro in progress			Command-.
Copy data from the field above			Command-'

Figure 7-2.
Database actions, commands, and keyboard equivalents.

On the other hand, if you're scrolling through a file with the mouse, you can accomplish other operations with a mouse click faster than using the keyboard. Figure 7-3 contains a short list.

Action	*Shortcut*
Display the Field Name change box	Double-click on field name
Display the Field Attributes dialog box	Double-click on field data
Widen a field	Drag field dividing line
Add field references to a computed field formula	Click on them with a formula in the entry bar
Change from list to form window	Double-click on selector boxes (to the left of records)
Change from form to list window	Double-click on blank area of form

Figure 7-3.
Mouse shortcuts in the database.

Use efficient field names to maximize screen space

You create a Works database using the form window, and because there's a lot of room on that screen, you might not think about the length of field names you assign. But a lot of the real data entry and browsing is done in the list window, and in that window, the length of field names can affect the number of fields you see on the screen.

A good example is the name State. In most cases, the data you would store in a State field would be two-letter state name abbreviations, such as CA, NY, or TX. If you use the name State, the field name will be twice as long as the field data, and when you display records in the list window, the State field will be wider than it needs to be. You could just as easily use the abbreviation ST, in which case the field name would be no longer than the field data, and you wouldn't waste any extra screen space. As a rule, try to keep field names as short as, or shorter than, the data you'll be storing.

Use field names to divide your data in useful ways

Although Works lets you add and delete fields from a database file whenever you want, you can help minimize such changes by planning ahead. When you decide how many fields your file will have and what the field names will be, think about how you might want to sort or select data in the future. Suppose you want to be able to sort or select records based on a person's last name. If you only create one field called Name, you'll have to enter the last names first (Smith, John, instead of John Smith) in order to sort on last names because Works sorts text fields by the first letter in the field. To make life easy for a sort like this, it would be better to specify two fields, First Name and Last Name. That way, you could always sort on the Last Name field easily. You might also want to separate area code and telephone number data into two fields so that you could sort on area codes as well as on telephone number prefixes.

> **TIP:** If you find you've made a mistake in dividing up data into different fields, all is not lost. You can create a new field to hold part of the data that is currently stored in another field, and then use the macro feature to have Works cut part of the information from the original field and copy it into the new field. If you've created a Name field and want to split the information into First Name and Last Name fields, for example, you could create the Last Name field, rename the Name field as First Name, and then record the steps involved in cutting the last name from the original (First Name) field and pasting it into the Last Name field. We'll see a similar technique in action in Chapter 8.

Customize the form window for easy data entry

Although fields are simply placed one on top of the other in the order in which you define them in the form window, you can drag fields around the screen to relocate them. By relocating fields, you can place them in the most logical order for your data-entry needs.

If you usually only fill out half of the fields in a new record, you should place those fields in the same part of the form window so that you can move easily from one field to the next. You can rearrange fields any time, so you can adjust the layout of a form window as your data-entry needs change. You might also want to rearrange fields in a form window to match a paper form you are using. If the form window is laid out like the paper form, you can fill in data in the same way you're used to filling it in on paper.

Database Specifications

Here are some specifications you may want to refer to as you use the database.

Maximum file size: Approximately 6,000 records on a Mac Plus, Mac SE, or Mac II with 1 MB of RAM. File size increases proportionally with larger amounts of memory.

Maximum field length: 250 characters.

Maximum number of fields in a record: 60.

Maximum number of stored reports per database file: 8.

Maximum number of record selection rules: 6.

Maximum paper height: 273 inches (with Custom Size paper option).

Minimum paper height: 1 inch.

Maximum paper width: 273 inches (with Custom Size paper option).

Minimum paper width: 1 inch.

Default paper size: US Letter ($8\frac{1}{2}$ by 11 inches).

Default top, bottom, left, and right margins: 1 inch.

Default font: 9-point Geneva.

Number of fonts available: Any font available to the Mac System is available to the database, but you can use only one font per database file.

Maximum length of search strings: 80 characters.

Maximum length of headers or footers: Limited by font size, page margins, and paper size.

Range of numbered pages in a document: 1 through 1,999.

Chapter 8

Database Projects

The Works database is extremely flexible when it comes to arranging, selecting, and even calculating data. In this chapter, we'll see how flexible the database can be, as we help Al Chroma with a variety of business and personal projects.

A Calendar

With all the activity involved in getting the Videorama off the ground (personal appointments, employee interviews, due dates for various license fees and bills, and vendor appointments), Al has found that he has far more things to do than he can remember, and he's having trouble organizing his day-to-day activities. A calendar is the obvious answer, and with the Works database, Al can make a calendar that will quickly produce daily "to do" lists and lay out his schedule for the weeks and months ahead. Because he can have up to 14 Works files on the desktop at a time, Al can load his calendar file every day and leave it on the desktop so that it's instantly available whenever he needs it.

Creating the calendar file

The calendar file we'll create is really quite simple: It contains few data fields. The secret lies in formatting the fields and creating useful reports. Let's begin by creating the file itself.

☐ Load Microsoft Works.

☐ Click on the database icon, and then click the New button.

The Field Name window appears, ready for you to enter field names for the new file.

Before we enter field names, we need to think about the types of data we'll want to store in the calendar file. Calendars store dates and times of events, along with descriptions of the events themselves. So let's begin this file with three field names: Date, Time, and Event.

☐ Type the field name *Date* in the Field Name window, and press Return or Enter, or click the Add Field button to add this field to the database file. The field appears in the form window, and the Field Name window reappears, ready for the second field name.

☐ Type the field name *Time* in the Field Name window, and press Return or Enter to add it to the file.

☐ Type the field name *Event* and press Return or Enter to add it to the file. This is the final field you want to add to the file at this point, so click the Done button in the Field Name window. The Field Name window disappears, and the form window is displayed with these three fields in it.

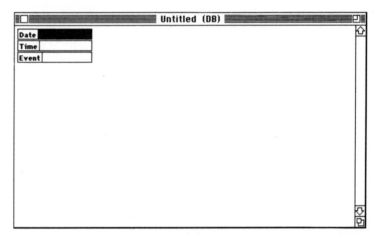

Before we begin entering appointment information into this file, we need to adjust each field so that the file is as useful as possible. The file contains date and time information. By using the Set Field Attributes command, we can tell Works that the Date and Time fields contain date and time information. This will let us sort these fields in chronological order, and it will let us specify certain formats for the dates and times we enter.

❑ Double-click on the data area in the Date field to display the Set Field Attributes dialog box.

```
┌─────────────────────────────────────────────────────┐
│  Set Field Attributes For Date                      │
│                                                     │
│  Type:        Display:      Align:      Style:      │
│  ⦿ Text       ○ General     ⦿ Left      ☐ Bold      │
│  ○ Numeric    ○ Fixed       ○ Center    ☐ Underline │
│  ○ Date       ○ Dollar      ○ Right     ☐ Commas    │
│  ○ Time       ○ Percent     ┌──┐                    │
│               ○ Scientific  │  │ Decimal Places     │
│                             └──┘                    │
│  ☐ Computed  ☐ Show Day      ( Cancel )  ( OK )     │
└─────────────────────────────────────────────────────┘
```

❑ To tell Works that the Date field will contain date information, click the Date option in the Type area. When you do, the options in the Display area change to Short, Medium, and Long.

The Short, Medium, and Long options are three different formats in which Works can present dates. The formats are as follows.

Format	*Example*
Short	3/24/89
Medium	Mar 24, 1989
Long	March 24, 1989

Because this is a calendar file, we'll want fairly descriptive dates, so we'll select the Medium option.

❑ Click the Medium button.

You can also tell Works to calculate the day of the week for a date you enter and to display it along with the date in a field. You specify this format by clicking the Show Day box at the bottom of the Set Field Attributes dialog box. Works will display the day with a date only when you have selected either Medium or Long as the date format. When you click the box next to Show Day, the day will be displayed in the date format you have selected.

Format	*Example*
Medium	Fri, Mar 24, 1989
Long	Friday, March 24, 1989

❑ Click the Show Day box.

TIP: You can use the Show Day option to determine the day of the week on which any past or future date falls. Simply enter the date you want to know about in a date field formatted with the Show Day option activated. With Apple System version 6.0.2 (the current version at this writing), you can choose any date between the beginning of 1904 and the end of 2039.

The other options in the Set Field Attributes dialog box control how data is aligned in a field and whether or not the data is enhanced with underlining and other style options. The default alignment option is Left, meaning data is aligned with the left edge of data fields. Left alignment is fine for a calendar, so we don't need to change it. The only Style options available in this dialog box when you set the data type to Date are bold and underline. Let's leave the Style options alone for now. (If you want to make all the data in every field of a file appear in boldface all the time, you can select Bold Field Data from the Format menu.) To confirm these field-attribute settings, either click the OK button in the lower-right corner of the dialog box or press Return or Enter.

The next field in the file will contain time data, so you'll want to set the field attributes for it as well.

☐ Click on the Time field to select it, and then choose the Set Field Attributes command from the Format menu.

☐ Click the Time option in the Type area.

☐ Press Return or Enter to confirm this change and return to the form window.

The third field will contain only text, and the default field data type is text; so we don't have to change this field's attributes. Now we're ready to enter some data into the file. Let's suppose Al has made an appointment with his dentist for 9:00 in the morning on March 24.

☐ Click on the Date field to select it, and type 3/24/89. Press Return or Enter. Works converts this entry to the Medium date format and displays it in the window.

When you specify a certain data type for a field, Works expects you to enter that data in a particular format. Because we specified Date data for this field, Works will accept dates in any of the following formats.

- 03/24/89

- 3-24-89

- 3.24.89

- 03/24/1989

- Fri, Mar 24, 1989

- Mar 24, 1989

- March 24, 1989

- Friday, March 24, 1989

Works will convert any of these formats to the display format you selected in the Set Field Attributes dialog box.

When we enter this date in our first record, however, there's a problem: Works converts the date to the Medium format, but the field isn't wide enough to display the entire date.

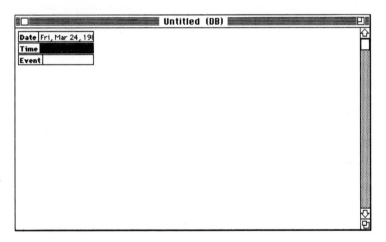

To see the entire date, we'll widen this field.

□ Place the pointer on the right edge of the Date field. The pointer changes to a double arrow.

□ Hold down the mouse button and drag the edge of the field to the right about two inches.

□ Release the mouse button. The entire date is displayed.

You can make any field wider or narrower at any time in the form window by dragging the field's right edge. While we're at it, we might as well widen the other two fields in this file.

☐ Drag the right edge of the Time field about an inch right.

☐ Drag the right edge of the Event field to the right edge of the screen. (This field will sometimes contain a lot of data, so you'll want all the room you can get.)

Now we can enter the other two items of information.

☐ Click on the Time field, enter *9:00*, and press Return. Works converts this entry to 9:00 AM and selects the Event field.

Works uses a 24-hour clock to convert times, so if you enter any time up to 12:00 without specifying either AM or PM, Works assumes you mean AM. To enter times after noon, you can either use military (24-hour clock) time or type *PM* after them.

If you type:	Works shows:
9:00	9:00 AM
21:00	9:00 PM
9:00 PM	9:00 PM
9:00	9:00 AM
09:0	9:00 AM

The best course is to specify AM or PM when you enter times.

Finally, you can enter the text describing the calendar event itself. The Event field should already be selected.

☐ Type *Dentist Appointment-Dr. Hesselschwerdt, 12th & Broadway, 6th Floor.*

Notice that this entry is longer than the space in the database's entry bar will allow. When you type more data than will fit in the entry bar, the entry bar expands to reveal an extra line below.

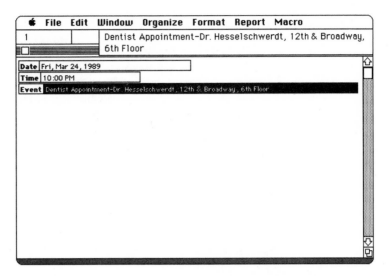

You can enter up to 250 characters of data into any database field. The entry bar can expand to be up to four lines deep. When a data field is not wide enough to display an entry, Works still stores the entry (up to 250 characters), but displays only what fits in the field. You can view the full entry by selecting the field and looking at the entry bar, where all the field's data is displayed.

☐ Press the Return key to enter this data.

From here on, entering data into this file is simply a matter of typing in each appointment as we make it. If you have trouble reading the database's default 9-point Geneva type, you can use the Format menu as you do in the other Works applications to change the font, font size, or even the color of the type used in the database. Remember, however, that font, size, and color changes apply to all the type that appears on the database screen; only the bold and underline styles can be applied to individual fields.

☐ Choose the Save command from the File menu. A dialog box appears, prompting you to type a name for the new file.

☐ Type the name *Calendar,* and then either click the Save button or press the Return key. The file will be saved to the current disk drive.

Using the calendar file

Now let's assume that Al has made a couple of weeks' worth of appointments and entered them into the Calendar file. He entered the appointments as they were made, which means they weren't always entered in the order in which they will occur. Now he wants to see how his calendar shapes up for the next few months. To do that, he will want to look at several appointments at once and then sort them chronologically.

The form window is showing because we were working with the form window when we saved the file. We want to see the list window, however.

- □ Double-click in a blank part of the form window. The display changes to the list window.

Double-clicking in a blank part of the screen is a fast way to change from the form window to the list window. Of course, you can also use Show Form or Show List from the Format menu to change displays, or you can press Command-L.

In a list window, the file looks like this:

Date	Time	Event	
Fri, Mar 24, 1989	9:00 AM	Dentist Appointment – Dr. Hesselschwerdt, 12t	
Tue, Apr 4, 1989	9:00 AM	3-day sale begins	
Mon, May 15, 1989		Anna's Birthday	
Mon, Mar 27, 1989	6:30 PM	Dinner with the Jacksons, their house	
Sun, Jun 4, 1989	1:00 PM	Felicia's wedding, St. Mary's	
Fri, Mar 31, 1989	2:00 PM	Income Tax preparation, Bud Rosen	
Sat, Mar 25, 1989	10:15 AM	Interview VCR technician	
Sun, Mar 26, 1989	12:00 PM	Lunch with cousin Lou, Antoine's	
Sat, Mar 25, 1989	4:00 PM	MCA Video salesman	
Fri, Mar 31, 1989		Payroll Tax installment due	
Fri, Sep 29, 1989		Payroll Tax installment due	
Sun, Apr 2, 1989	12:00 PM	Projectionist's Union picnic	
Fri, Sep 1, 1989	12:00 PM	Tony's retirement lunch, Bingo's	
Mon, Apr 3, 1989	3:00 PM	UA Video salesman	
Sat, Aug 12, 1989		Vacation begins	
Mon, Aug 21, 1989		Vacation ends	
Sat, Mar 25, 1989	3:30 PM	Video Listing To Printer	

Calendar (DB)

- □ Enter the rest of the appointments as shown.

With the list window showing, we can see that the appointments are out of order. We also notice that not much of the first Event entry is visible because the Event field is too narrow. To make the most of our screen space, we'll make the Time field narrower (because it has more room than it needs) and then make the Event field as wide as possible.

□ Point to the vertical line that divides the Time field name from the Event field name. The pointer changes to a double arrow.

Date	Time	+Event	
Fri, Mar 24, 1989	9:00 AM	Dentist Appointment – Dr. Hesselschwerdt, 12t	
Tue, Apr 4, 1989	9:00 AM	3-day sale begins	
Mon, May 15, 1989		Anna's Birthday	

Calendar (DB)

□ Hold down the mouse button, drag the line to the left until there is just enough room to display the longest time entry (10:15 AM) in the records below, and then release the mouse button.

□ Point to the line dividing the Event field name from the blank field to its right.

□ Drag this line over to the right edge of the window to make it as large as possible.

Now that we can see more of the Event data, let's sort the file so that the records are in chronological order by date.

□ Click on the Date field name (or any date entry in a record) to select that field.

□ Choose the Sort command from the Organize menu. The Sort dialog box appears.

When you sort a Date-type or Time-type field the only options available are Chronological and Reverse Chronological. The Chronological option is the default, so it is selected.

□ Click the OK button or press Return or Enter. The records are sorted chronologically on the Date field.

```
┌─────────────────────────────────────────────────────────────────────────┐
│ ▢ ▦▦▦▦▦▦▦▦▦▦▦▦▦▦▦▦▦▦▦ Calendar (DB) ▦▦▦▦▦▦▦▦▦▦▦▦▦▦▦▦▦▦▦ ▣│
├──────────────────┬──────────┬───────────────────────────────────────────┤
│ Date             │ Time     │ Event                                      │
├──────────────────┼──────────┼───────────────────────────────────────────┤
│ Fri, Mar 24, 1989│ 9:00 AM  │ Dentist Appointment – Dr. Hesselschwerdt, 12th & Broadway, 6th Floor.│
│ Sat, Mar 25, 1989│ 10:15 AM │ Interview VCR technician                   │
│ Sat, Mar 25, 1989│ 4:00 PM  │ MCA Video salesman                         │
│ Sat, Mar 25, 1989│ 3:30 PM  │ Video Listing To Printer                   │
│ Sun, Mar 26, 1989│ 12:00 PM │ Lunch with cousin Lou, Antoine's           │
│ Mon, Mar 27, 1989│ 6:30 PM  │ Dinner with the Jacksons, their house      │
│ Fri, Mar 31, 1989│ 2:00 PM  │ Income Tax preparation, Bud Rosen          │
│ Fri, Mar 31, 1989│          │ Payroll Tax installment due                │
│ Sun, Apr 2, 1989 │ 12:00 PM │ Projectionist's Union picnic               │
│ Mon, Apr 3, 1989 │ 3:00 PM  │ UA Video salesman                          │
│ Tue, Apr 4, 1989 │ 9:00 AM  │ 3-day sale begins                          │
│ Mon, May 15, 1989│          │ Anna's Birthday                            │
│ Sun, Jun 4, 1989 │ 1:00 PM  │ Felicia's wedding, St. Mary's              │
│ Sat, Aug 12, 1989│          │ Vacation begins                            │
│ Mon, Aug 21, 1989│          │ Vacation ends                              │
│ Fri, Sep 1, 1989 │ 12:00 PM │ Tony's retirement lunch, Bingo's           │
│ Fri, Sep 29, 1989│          │ Payroll Tax installment due                │
└──────────────────┴──────────┴───────────────────────────────────────────┘
```

At this point, Al can scan the list window to see all his appointments on a certain date. There's still one problem, however. Works will sort only one database field at a time, and although we've sorted dates, some of the times within those dates aren't in chronological order. For instance, you can see that on March 25, some of the times are out of order. To arrange the records so that both fields are in chronological order by date and time, you have to sort the file twice—once by time and once by date.

□ Click the Time field name to select this field.

□ Choose the Sort command from the Organize menu, or press Command-A.

□ Press Return to select the default option to sort in chronological order. The records will be sorted by time of day.

□ Click the Date field name to select this field.

□ Sort the Date field in chronological order. The records are now sorted by date, and within each date, they remain sorted by time.

Now these records are useful to look at in the list window. But it might also be handy to print out a report for a certain day so that Al can carry a list of his daily appointments with him. Ordinarily, you would create a report format to print out selected records from a database file. But because there are only a few appointments in any given day on this calendar, you can do something a little simpler, especially because the file is already sorted in chronological order. Suppose we want to print out a list of Al's appointments for March 25.

☐ Choose the Match Records command from the Organize menu. A dialog box appears.

☐ Type the information you want to match (in this case, *Mar 25*).

☐ Click the Search Text Fields Only box to remove the check mark. (Works assumes you want to search only text fields. The Text Fields Only box is checked when you first use the Match Records or Find Field command. Because we are searching a date field, we don't want to limit the search to text fields.) The Match Records dialog box should now look like this:

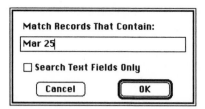

Match Records That Contain:

Mar 25

☐ **Search Text Fields Only**

[Cancel]   [OK]

☐ Press Return or Enter, or click the OK button. The records that contain the date Mar 25 are selected from the file and displayed on the screen.

Date	Time	Event
Sat, Mar 25, 1989	10:15 AM	Interview VCR technician
Sat, Mar 25, 1989	3:30 PM	Video Listing To Printer
Sat, Mar 25, 1989	4:00 PM	MCA Video salesman

Calendar (DB)

This list has been shortened because the file contains only three records that are dated March 25. Now we can print these three records quickly using the Print Window command.

□ Select the Print Window command from the File menu. The entire window (including the field names and grid lines) is printed.

If you want to print using the Print Window command without printing grid lines, choose the Show Grid command from the Format menu to remove its check mark before printing. To redisplay all the records in a file, choose the Match Records command again.

The Print Window command is a quick way to print only the records that are showing on the screen. On the built-in Mac Plus or SE screen, the window size limits you to printing 17 or 18 database records in a list window; a Mac II or third-party external monitor will allow a larger database window and thus let you display and print more records in one window.

This basic calendar file can be further enhanced with a Notes field that lets you add driving instructions, reminders, or other miscellaneous bits of text to your appointment records. In Chapter 10, we'll see how to merge this calendar data into a word-processor document to print out custom-formatted daily appointment schedules.

A Video Club Member File

Al wants to keep track of everyone who joins the Videorama's video club, so he's set up a simple file that does this. In the list window, Al's file looks like the screen display in Figure 8-1.

Name	Address	City	ST	Zip	Phone	Memb #	Renew
Jackie Rae	339 Mountain Dr.	Willow	CA	94555	555-1000	00004	3/15/90
Denise Villalobos	82 Piedmont Ave., #	Oakland	CA	94666	555-1001	00001	3/15/90
Daniel Collins	206 Cornell St.	Willow	CA	94555	555-1002	00002	3/15/90
David Richards	1705 Oxton Ct.	San Mateo	CA	94550	555-1003	00003	3/15/90
Bud Snooter	10327 Park Hills Dr.	San Jose	CA	93336	408-555-1222	00005	3/16/90
Fran Marple	353 Country Villa Ln.	Milpitas	CA	94444	408-555-1345	00006	3/16/90
Elias Abou-Ata	129 Claremont St.	Mountain View	CA	94343	555-1609	00007	3/16/90
Ed Bernstein	9975 Francis Dr.	San Bruno	CA	94321	555-1900	00008	3/16/90
Joe Brubaker	12235 Cloverly	Templeton	CA	93231	408-999-9999	00009	3/16/90
Diana Levy	12 Kensington Terr.,	So. San Francisco	CA	91212	555-1323	00010	3/16/90
Randy Coleman	15 Derby St., #12	Willow	CA	94555	555-9898	00011	3/16/90
Marc Caselica	2213 Front St.	Willow	CA	94555	555-9790	00012	3/16/90
Linda Feldman	11223 S. Harper	Brisbane	CA	94556	555-5454	00013	3/16/90
Sheryl Janda	7035 Thornhill	Redwood City	CA	95432	555-3536	00014	3/16/90
Mikkel Aaland	339 Clifford St.	San Francisco	CA	94440	555-2121	00015	3/16/90
Jefferson Miller	159 10th Ave., #14	Belmont	CA	93333	555-2398	00016	3/16/90
Steve Wong	42 Jackson St.	Willow	CA	94555	555-0023	00017	3/16/90
Volga Breszlaw	554 Green St.	Willow	CA	94555	555-9001	00018	3/16/90

Club Members (DB)

Figure 8-1.
A video club membership file.

Creating the membership file

To follow along with this exercise, you need to create a sample file such as the one shown in Figure 8-1, using the procedures outlined for the Calendar file. The following is a summary of the steps.

- ☐ Open a new database file.

- ☐ Create fields titled Name, Address, City, ST, Zip, Phone, Memb #, and Renew Date.

- ☐ Type in the data shown in Figure 8-1 or your own data.

- ☐ Drag the field dividing markers to the left so that the list window of the file looks like the one in Figure 8-1.

- ☐ Choose the Save As command from the File menu, type the file name *Club Members*, and press Return to save the file to disk.

Now, you're ready to continue.

After some preliminary rearranging of the form window, the file looks like this:

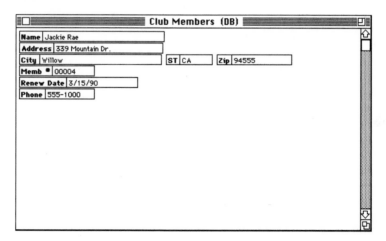

We've already seen how to change the length of a field; now we'll see how to rearrange fields on the screen.

Rearranging the fields

After entering a few records, Al discovers a few problems with this file. For one, a couple of employees have suggested that the Phone field should be next to the Name field so that they can find phone numbers more easily when they call a member about a reserved videotape. Fortunately, this is an easy modification to make in the form window.

□ Place the pointer on top of the Phone field name. The pointer turns into a hand.

□ Hold down the mouse button and drag the Phone field until it is to the right of the Name field.

As you hold down the mouse button, you'll notice that an outline appears around the field name and data, like this:

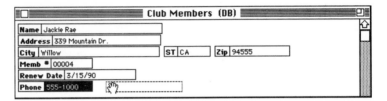

The outline shows you the overall size of the field you're moving. This is important because you can't place one field on top of another field on the screen. If you try to, Works will display a warning that says you can't. By seeing the field outline, you can determine exactly where the edge of a field is, and you won't place part of it over another field when you move it.

□ When the Phone field is to the right of the Name field, release the mouse button. The field moves to its new position, like this:

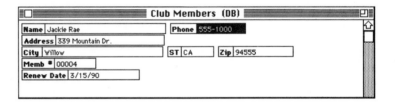

Adding fields

Now that the form is a little more useful, Al has something else he wants to do. Because a lot of storage space remains in this file, he wants to add more fields to store other useful information. One field will specify a customer's videotape format. Adding this field will help Al decide how many Beta-format tapes and how many VHS-format tapes to stock.

Another field that will help Al in his purchasing decisions is one that records the favorite film genre of each customer. Let's add these fields to the file in the form window.

- ☐ Point to the blank area directly below the Memb # field and hold down the mouse button. The pointer changes to a right-pointing arrow.

- ☐ Drag the pointer to the right. As you drag, a dotted outline of a new field appears.

- ☐ Drag the pointer until the field outline is about two inches long, then release the mouse button. The Field Name box appears, ready for you to type in the new field name.

- ☐ Type the field name *Format,* and press Return, press Enter, or click the Add Field button to add the new field. The new field appears in place of the outline on the screen.

- ☐ Place the pointer to the right of the Format field, and repeat the steps for adding a new field.

- ☐ Type the field name *Genre,* and press Return or Enter. The second new field is added to the file.

Now Al can record these added bits of information with each new video club member, and he can also add the information to existing records. To add information as easily as possible, Al will use the list window.

- ☐ Double-click in a blank area of the form window, and the display changes to the list window.

Splitting a field with a macro

At this point, Al notices that because he's entered customer first and last names in one field called Name, he won't be able to address form letters to individuals by their first or last name only. Because he would have to specify the name field, the greeting in his letters would contain text something like *Dear Jackie Rae* when he merged this file with a form letter. Al decides he'd like to split the first and last names into two different fields so that he can specify only the first name field in a greeting and have letters that begin, *Dear Jackie.*

The following steps are the basic procedure for splitting up this information.

☐ Change the Name field's name to LastName.

☐ Add a new field named FirstName to the file.

☐ Cut each customer's first name from the LastName field to the Clipboard.

☐ Paste each customer's first name into the FirstName field for their record.

With a large database file, manual entering and deleting is a slow and tedious process. But after we have created the proper fields, we can automate much of the operation with the macro feature built into Works version 2.0.

☐ Be sure the form window is displayed.

☐ Drag the Phone field (which is now next to the Name field) to the right about 2 inches, to make room for the new FirstName field.

☐ Place the pointer on top of the Name field until the hand symbol appears, and drag this field to the right, until its right edge is almost touching the Phone field.

☐ Double-click on the word *Name* in the Name Field to display the Field Name dialog box, type *LastName,* and press Return or Enter to change this field's name.

☐ Point to upper-left corner of the form (where the Name field used to be), hold down the mouse button, drag a new field outline to the right until it almost touches the left edge of the LastName field, and then release the mouse button.

☐ Type the name *FirstName* into the Field Name dialog box that appears, and press Enter or Return to add this field to the file.

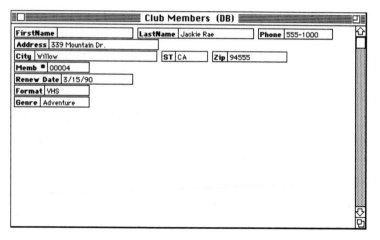

Now we have two different fields, properly named and positioned in the form window, and we're ready to divide up the first and last names into their proper fields. Here's where the macro feature comes in. The idea is to manually transfer the first name data from the LastName field to the FirstName field, and record our actions with the macro feature so that Works can perform them at the touch of a key on the other the records in the file.

□ Choose the Macros On command from the Macro menu.

□ Choose the Start Recording command, or press Option-+ (plus). The Start Recording dialog box appears, like this:

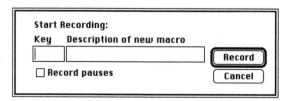

□ Type *S* for the macro key and *Split Names* for the description. Press Return or Enter to begin recording. (Don't click the Record Pauses box because we don't want to record them.)

□ Click on the name *Jackie Rae* in the LastName field.

□ Move the pointer to the entry bar, and double-click on the name *Jackie* to select it.

☐ Press Command-X, or choose the Cut command from the Edit menu.

☐ Click on the blank data area in the FirstName field.

☐ Press Command-V, or choose the Paste command from the Edit menu.

At this point, you have placed the first and last names of this record in their proper fields, like this:

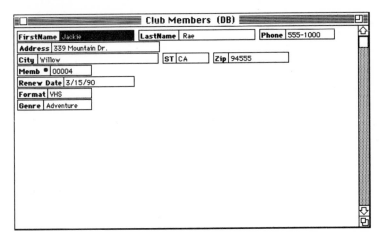

However, there's still one more operation to record in our macro. Notice that there's a space in front of the name *Rae* in the LastName field. That's because we double-clicked on the name *Jackie* to select it, and selecting a name like this selects the name or word only, not the space before or after it. We don't want a space in front of the name *Rae*, so we'll remove it.

☐ Click on the name *Rae* to select this field data. The name appears in the entry bar.

☐ Move the insertion point directly in front of the *R* in *Rae*, and press the Delete key to remove the leading space.

☐ Press Return or Enter, or click the Enter box to enter the name without the space.

Now the FirstName and LastName fields contain exactly the right information. The macro is complete, and we can turn the macro-recording feature off.

☐ Press Command-– (hyphen), or choose the Stop Recording command from the Macro menu. The Currently Recording box appears.

☐ Click the Stop button or press Enter or Return to stop recording.

With the macro recorded, it's a simple matter to change all the rest of the records in the file.

☐ Press the Down Arrow key until the second record in the file is displayed. (If your Mac keyboard doesn't have a Down Arrow key, press Return or Enter repeatedly until the second record appears.)

☐ Press Option-S to activate the macro, and watch as the names are split into the proper fields.

☐ Repeat the preceding two steps until you finish the last record in the file.

Ordinarily, Works asks you if you want to save changes to the macro file when you quit the program. This file, called Microsoft Works(keys), stores every macro you create in any Works application. Because you might want to store a different Option-S macro in the spreadsheet, word processor, the Draw tool, or communications application in the future, you can save this database macro in its own file.

☐ Choose the Save Macro File As command from the Macro menu.

☐ Type the name *Database Keys*, and then click the Save button.

Now, let's change the view to the list window and see how to view widely separated fields there.

TIP: We recorded this macro in the form window because that's the only way it would work. When Works records mouse clicks, it records the position of the pointer when you click it, rather than the name of the field on which it is clicked. If we had recorded this macro in the list window, the macro would have worked only on the specific fields and the specific record on which it was recorded. Using the macro key after it was recorded would have acted only on the Jackie Rae record. By recording the macro in the form window, it acts on the LastName and FirstName fields and will convert whatever data is in those fields. Because we are displaying a different record each time we use the macro, that particular record's data is changed.

We selected only the first name when we cut it to the Clipboard, rather than the name and the space after it also because of mouse-position recording. The act of selecting the name Jackie and the space after it would be recorded as selecting the first seven characters in the entry bar, and although this act would work for the name Jackie, it wouldn't work for names such as Fred, David, or Ed. In these latter cases, the seven-character selection would select either part of the first name only or the whole first name, the space, and part of the second name. By recording the macro as we did, we created a macro that works for every record in the file.

Viewing wide files

The FirstName field we've added appears at the far right of the list window. Let's move this field so that it appears to the left of the LastName field.

- ☐ Scroll all the way to the right in the list window, and select the FirstName field by clicking on its name.

- ☐ Hold down the mouse button, and drag the field to the left until it is on top of the LastName field.

- ☐ Release the mouse button to place the FirstName field to the left of the LastName field.

❑ While you're at it, drag the field dividing marker between the FirstName and LastName fields to eliminate the extra space in the FirstName field.

Now that we have added some fields to the list window, we can't see the new Format and Genre fields—they're off the screen to the right. And, if we scroll to the right so that we can see them, we can no longer see the FirstName and LastName fields at the left. This arrangement will make it hard to match each club member's name with the proper Format and Genre information.

We could rearrange the fields as we did with the FirstName field, but there's another way to see both the left and right parts of a file in a list window at the same time: Split the window into two panes.

❑ Point to the split bar in the lower-left corner of the list window (the black bar to the left of the left-hand arrow in the bottom scroll box), and hold down the mouse button.

❑ Drag the split bar to the middle of the list window. As you drag, a vertical dotted line appears.

❑ When the dotted line is at the middle of the list window, release the mouse button. The dotted line is replaced by two solid lines, and the screen divides into two side-by-side panes.

FirstName	LastName	Address	City	ST	Zip	Phone	Memb
Bud	Snooter	10327 Park Hills Dr.	San Jose	CA	93336	408-555-1222	00005
Fran	Marple	353 Country Villa Ln.	Milpitas	CA	94444	408-555-1345	00006
Elias	Abou-Ata	129 Claremont St.	Mountain View	CA	94343	555-1609	00007
Ed	Bernstein	9975 Francis Dr.	San Bruno	CA	94321	555-1900	00008
Joe	Brubaker	12235 Cloverly	Templeton	CA	93231	408-999-9999	00009
Diana	Levy	12 Kensington Terr.,	So. San Francisco	CA	91212	555-1323	00010
Randy	Coleman	15 Derby St., #12	Willow	CA	94555	555-9898	00011
Marc	Caselica	2213 Front St.	Willow	CA	94555	555-9790	00012
Linda	Feldman	11223 S. Harper	Brisbane	CA	94556	555-5454	00013
Sheryl	Janda	7035 Thornhill	Redwood City	CA	95432	555-3536	00014
Mikkel	Aaland	339 Clifford St.	San Francisco	CA	94440	555-2121	00015
Jefferson	Miller	159 10th Ave., #14	Belmont	CA	93333	555-2398	00016
Steve	Wong	42 Jackson St.	Willow	CA	94555	555-0023	00017
Volga	Breszlaw	554 Green St.	Willow	CA	94555	555-9001	00018
Millard	Cuvee	233 Portnoy St.	Burlingame	CA	94435	555-0878	00019
Madelyn	Korbut	957 Oak Park Dr., #4	Willow	CA	94555	555-0978	00020
Toni	Walker	5050 Camino Diablo	San Mateo	CA	94550	555-5555	00021

Club Members (DB)

You can also divide the list window horizontally by pulling down the split bar located at the top of the right-hand scroll bar. Splitting the window horizontally lets you view two separate groups of records on the screen at once. You can also use both split bars at once to view four different parts of a file on the screen at a time.

Now we can scroll the two windows independently to display two different parts of the file. The names in the records are already displayed in the left window, so scroll the right window until the Format and Genre fields appear. With all the pertinent fields displayed for each record, it will be easy to enter the new Format and Genre information into the existing records.

Creating a report

Let's assume that Al has updated all the records in this file and that he's ready to take advantage of Works' sorting and reporting features.

To continue this project, fill in the Format and Genre information for each record. It doesn't really matter which customer has which format and genre. The formats are VHS and Beta, and the genres are Adventure, Classics, Horror, Sci-Fi, Children's, and Comedy. Fill in these designations for each record.

Al has an opportunity to acquire a special collection of classic comedies in VHS format, and he wants to find out if he has enough club members who like classics or comedies (and whose tape format is VHS) to support the purchase.

◻ Choose the New Report command from the Report menu. A report window appears.

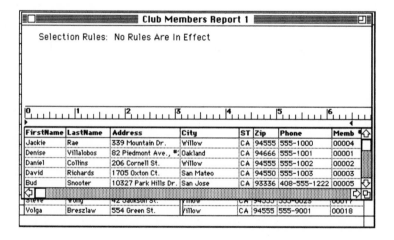

TIP: To enter duplicate information quickly, enter the information once, press Return to move to the field below, and press Command-' (apostrophe) to duplicate the entry. This way, you can enter a lot of data quickly by simply pressing Return and pressing Command-' repeatedly.

First, we need to decide which fields of data should appear in the report. Al wants to know how many people like comedies or classics in VHS format, so the address, telephone number, renew date, and member number information is irrelevant for this report—the report should include only the FirstName, LastName, Format, and Genre fields.

You can tell which fields will be included in a database report by looking above the field names at the ruler in the report window. This ruler is like the one in a normal document window, and the left and right edges of the report as it will print are indicated by the left and right edge markers, the black triangles below the 0 and 6½-inch ruler marks.

We can see that this report already includes the FirstName and LastName fields, but the Format and Genre fields will not print because they're off the screen to the right. Let's move the Format and Genre fields so that they're next to the LastName field.

☐ Scroll the window to the right, and click on the Format name above this field to select it.

☐ Hold down the mouse button, drag the field to the left until it is on top of the Address field, and then release the mouse button. The Format field is inserted between the LastName and the Address field.

☐ Repeat these steps with the Genre field to insert it to the right of the Format field.

TIP: You can change the position of the right edge marker by dragging it with the mouse. The left edge marker is always under the 0 in the ruler. To change the left margin, use the Page Setup dialog box. The 0 mark in the ruler will always begin at the left margin, as defined in the Page Setup dialog box.

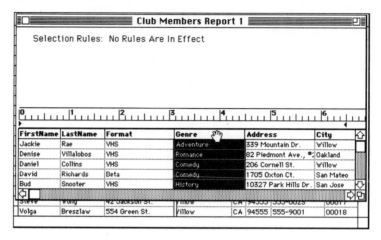

Now the four fields we want in the report are next to each other in the window. As you can see, however, the report still contains the Address field and part of the City field, which we don't want included. To eliminate these fields from the report, we could adjust the margins in the Page Setup dialog box or narrow the report by dragging the right edge marker to the left, but it's easier simply to widen the Genre field by dragging its right-hand dividing line farther to the right.

- ☐ Place the pointer on the dividing line between the Genre and Address field names.

- ☐ Hold down the mouse button, and drag the dividing line until it is beneath the right edge marker.

- ☐ Release the mouse button. The Genre field now extends all the way to the edge of the report.

Now that the report contains only the fields that interest us, we need to select specific records. We'll use Works' record-selection rules to do this.

- ☐ Choose Record Selection from the Organize menu. The Record Selection box appears.

```
┌─────────────────────────────────────────────────────────────┐
│ ┌─────────────────────────────────────────────────────────┐ │
│ │              Record Selection:                           │ │
│ │ ┌─────────────────────────┬─┐ ┌───────────────────────┬─┐│ │
│ │ │LastName                 │⬆│ │equals                 │⬆││ │
│ │ │Address                  │ │ │contains               │ ││ │
│ │ │City                     │▓│ │begins with            │▓││ │
│ │ │ST                       │▓│ │is greater than        │▓││ │
│ │ │Zip                      │⬇│ │is greater than or equal to│⬇││ │
│ │ └─────────────────────────┴─┘ └───────────────────────┴─┘│ │
│ │                                                           │ │
│ │ Record Comparison Information: ┌───────────────────────┐ │ │
│ │                                 └───────────────────────┘ │ │
│ │                                                           │ │
│ │ Selection Rules: No Rules Are In Effect                  │ │
│ │                                                           │ │
│ │  ○ And   ○ Or                                             │ │
│ │  ○ And   ○ Or                                             │ │
│ │  ○ And   ○ Or                                             │ │
│ │  ○ And   ○ Or                                             │ │
│ │  ○ And   ○ Or                                             │ │
│ │                                                           │ │
│ │ ┌──────────┐  ┌─────────────┐  ┌─────────────┐ ┌────────┐│ │
│ │ │  Cancel  │  │ Delete Rule │  │ Install Rule│ │ Select ││ │
│ │ └──────────┘  └─────────────┘  └─────────────┘ └────────┘│ │
│ └─────────────────────────────────────────────────────────┘ │
└─────────────────────────────────────────────────────────────┘
```

The Record Selection box contains a list of the field names in the file from which you're reporting and a list of logical operators. You choose the field upon which you want record-selection criteria to be based, and then you choose the logical operator. Finally, you enter the comparison information that will determine whether a record is selected. (A record is selected if the field you choose matches the criteria you've specified.) You can have up to six record-selection rules in a report, so you can be very specific in selecting data from a file. The first rule we want to use in Al's tape report will select only the records in which the Format field contains the entry VHS.

□ Scroll down the list of fields in the Record Selection box until the Format name is showing.

□ Click on the Format name to select it.

We want the Format field's data to equal VHS (to use Works' own terminology). The equals operator is already selected in the list of logical operators, so we can skip the second part of the rule-making process this time and go on to the third part.

□ Enter the comparison information *VHS* in the window below the logical operator box. Do NOT press the Return key. Doing so selects the records according to the current rules, and you aren't finished entering rules yet.

□ Click the Install Rule button at the bottom of the box. The rule is now installed, and you can see it spelled out in the Record Selection box.

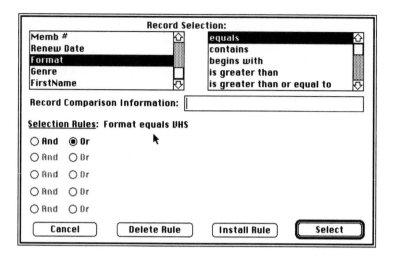

We've now installed one rule, but we're not ready to select records yet. We also want the selection based on the Genre field—that is, we want only records in which the Genre field contains either Comedy or Classics. You'll notice that below the first rule are some And and Or buttons. These are connectors that link rules. The first group shows the Or button selected, meaning the selection would be based on either the first rule (Format equals VHS) or a second rule you specify. But we want Works to use both the first rule and a second rule.

□ Click the And button to select it.

Now we can specify the second rule.

□ Scroll through the field list until the Genre field is showing, and then click on it to select it.

Again, the equals operator is the one we want, so we don't have to change that selection in the operator list.

□ Type the comparison information *Comedy.*

□ Click the Install Rule button. This second rule is installed beneath the first one. The complete set of rules now reads *Format equals VHS and Genre equals Comedy.*

We also want to select records in which the Genre field contains Classics. In this case, the Or connector is appropriate (we want records that contain either Comedy or Classics). The Or connector is already selected. Next, we can install the last rule.

□ Be sure the Genre field is still selected.

Again, we want Genre to equal Classics, and the equals operator is already selected.

□ Type the comparison information *Classics.*

□ Click the Install Rule button. All three rules are now displayed.

□ Click the Select button or press Return or Enter to actually select records based on these rules.

The report now contains only the records in which the Format field contains VHS and the Genre field contains either Comedy or Classics. All other records are left out. We've also formatted the report so that only the Name, Format, and Genre fields are included.

Now we'll sort the data so that all records with the same Genre data are together and we can easily count the number of records for each genre. (The report we've created contains only a few records, so it will be easy to count the different genre totals manually. But as you'll see in the next project, you can also use the TotalsPage menu to have Works sum the sorted entries in a field.)

Works doesn't allow data-sorting in a report window, so we'll have to select the database file window from the Window menu and sort the data there.

□ Choose the Club Members file from the Window menu.

□ Click on the Genre field name to select that field.

□ Choose the Sort command from the Organize menu. The default sorting method is from A through Z, which is what we want. Press the Return key to sort the file this way. The records will be sorted on the Genre field from A through Z, placing all records with the same genre data together.

□ Display the report window again by selecting the report from the Window menu.

> **TIP:** When a report is short, as this one is, you can use the Print Preview feature to print it to the screen, and count the records there.

Naming the report

The report is almost ready to print out, but let's change the name so it's more descriptive. That way, it will be easy to remember what the report is for when we want to use it again.

☐ Choose the Change Report Title command from the Edit menu.

☐ Type the name *Comedy & Classics in VHS,* and press Return or Enter. The report is renamed. The report window now looks like this:

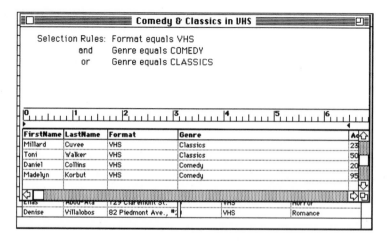

The report will be stored with this name when you close and save the Club Members file. You can recall the report any time the file is open by choosing Select Report from the Report menu and then selecting this report from the list of stored reports.

Printing the report

To print the report, press Command-P or choose the Print command from the File menu. If you've been using the Print Preview feature to view the report on the screen, be sure to click the check box to remove the X mark so that the report will print on paper. The report will be printed with the margins you set with the Page Setup command.

A Tax Ledger

Now that Al is in business for himself, he has a lot of expenses that could be tax-deductible. One way to track deductible expenses along with income is to store a record of each transaction in a database file. The database's sorting and reporting features will then make it easy to zero in on tax-deductible expenses and taxable income when tax time rolls around.

To be useful, this file must contain enough fields so that Al can include information about each type of expense or income, its purpose, its amount, and the date. The list window of this file is shown in Figure 8-2.

Date	Type	Account	Description	Amount
3/10/89	Expense	Advertising	Lippi Sign Company – Front window sign	$195.00
3/3/89	Expense	Inventory	UA Video – rental videotape selection	$3496.90
3/8/89	Expense	Phone	Deposit on Videorama phones	$125.00
3/15/89	Expense	Rent	March	$1250.00
3/6/89	Expense	Stationery	ABC Printers – Printing	$200.00
3/8/89	Expense	Utilities	Deposit on Videorama electricity	$75.00
3/18/89	Income	Accessory Sales	Week of March 12	$94.50
3/25/89	Income	Accessory Sales	Week of March 19	$156.25
4/1/89	Income	Accessory Sales	Week of March 26	$250.00
3/7/89	Income	Pension	Projectionists' Union pension check	$402.87
3/1/89	Income	Social Security	Monthly check	$335.00
3/18/89	Income	VCR Rentals	Week of March 12	$78.50
3/25/89	Income	VCR Rentals	Week of March 19	$225.00
4/1/89	Income	VCR Rentals	Week of March 26	$250.00
3/18/89	Income	Video Rentals	Week of March 12	$847.50
3/25/89	Income	Video Rentals	Week of March 19	$1562.35
4/1/89	Income	Video Rentals	Week of March 26	$1804.40

Figure 8-2.
A simple ledger of taxable income and expenses.

Creating the database file

To follow along with this exercise, you must create a database file like the one Al has.

☐ Open a new database file.

☐ Define fields named Date, Type, Account, Description, and Amount.

☐ Double-click on a data entry in the Date field column to display the Field Attributes dialog box, and set this field to the Date format. The Short display option is selected. Click the OK button or press Return or Enter.

☐ Double-click on a data entry in the Amount field column to display the Field Attributes dialog box, and set this field to the Numeric format and the Display option to Dollar. The Decimal Places option is set at 2. Click the OK button or press Return or Enter.

☐ Type in the 17 records of information shown in Figure 8-2.

☐ Choose the Save As command, and save the file to disk with the name Tax Ledger.

Now you're ready to continue.

With these fields, Al can sort or select tax-related data in many ways. The Type field separates income from expenses so that he can generate reports that total only expenses or only income. The Account field breaks up expenses or income by purpose or source so that he can produce reports that list only utilities expenses or only Social Security income. The Description field lets him zero in on specific transactions. By using the Set Field Attributes command, Al has identified the Date field as a date field (so that he can sort or select records chronologically), and he's identified the Amount field as a numeric field with the Dollar format (so that he can total expense amounts).

Most of the transactions to be recorded in this file will be transferred from a checkbook. Al can go through his checkbook every week or so and update the file with all the expenses that are deductible. When he has cash expenses, he can get the information from receipts. As for income, he can use bank-account and savings-account statements as a source of deposit information, or he can use cash-register tapes from the Videorama. As he gathers information, Al can manipulate the data in this file in a number of useful ways. Let's look at a couple of examples.

Viewing selected records

Suppose Al wants to determine quickly how much money he has spent on the videotapes he rents. Because he's been careful to specify the videotape rental in the description of expenses related to it, all he has to do is select all the records that contain those words.

☐ Choose the Match Records command from the Organize menu. A dialog box appears, asking you to type in comparison information Works will use to match records.

□ Type the word *videotape*, and then press Return or Enter. The dialog box disappears, and only the record that contains the word videotape appears on the screen.

Date	Type	Account	Description	Amount
3/3/89	Expense	Inventory	UA Video – rental videotape selection	$3496.90

Tax Ledger (DB)

Notice that the Match Records command displays only records from the file that match the criteria you type in. When you're ready to view the entire file again, choose the Match Records command a second time to display the entire file's records as before.

If you want to locate comparison information as it appears in the file (rather than displaying only records that match that information), use the Find Field command from the Organize menu. This command finds any field that contains the comparison information you type and highlights that field, one record at a time. The records are not selected out of the file and displayed separately. You can use Find Field in either the list or form window. If we had used the Find Field command with the videotape comparison information, the list window would have looked like this:

Tax Ledger (DB)

Date	Type	Account	Description	Amount
3/10/89	Expense	Advertising	Lippi Sign Company – Front window sign	$195.00
3/3/89	Expense	Inventory	UA Video – rental videotape selection	$3496.90
3/8/89	Expense	Phone	Deposit on Videorama phones	$125.00
3/15/89	Expense	Rent	March	$1250.00
3/6/89	Expense	Stationery	ABC Printers – Printing	$200.00
3/8/89	Expense	Utilities	Deposit on Videorama electricity	$75.00
3/18/89	Income	Accessory Sales	Week of March 12	$94.50
3/25/89	Income	Accessory Sales	Week of March 19	$156.25
4/1/89	Income	Accessory Sales	Week of March 26	$250.00
3/7/89	Income	Pension	Projectionists' Union pension check	$402.87
3/1/89	Income	Social Security	Monthly check	$335.00
3/18/89	Income	VCR Rentals	Week of March 12	$78.50
3/25/89	Income	VCR Rentals	Week of March 19	$225.00
4/1/89	Income	VCR Rentals	Week of March 26	$250.00
3/18/89	Income	Video Rentals	Week of March 12	$847.50
3/25/89	Income	Video Rentals	Week of March 19	$1562.35
4/1/89	Income	Video Rentals	Week of March 26	$1804.40

Creating a monthly income report

Now let's help Al create a monthly income report. Al's income comes from a few different sources, but let's assume he simply wants a quick way to total each month's income and view it without printing out the report. In this report, let's say he wants to create a total of all the income transactions for the month of March. That means we'll have to use Works' record-selection rules to select only records for which (in Works' terminology again) the Type field equals Income and for which the Date field is greater than or equal to March 1 and less than or equal to March 31. After you select the records, you'll want to sum the Amount field to produce an income total from all the selected transaction records. Also, it would be nice if all the transaction records were in chronological order.

You can't sort records in a report window—you have to do your sorting with the database file itself. So, we'll start by arranging the records in the Tax Ledger file.

- ☐ Click on the Date field name to select that field in the list window.

- ☐ Press Command-A (a shortcut for selecting the Sort command from the Organize menu). The Sort dialog box appears.

Because we selected a date field (and the field's attributes identify it as containing date-type data), the Sort dialog box option is set to sort the file in chronological order. This is the order you want.

- ☐ Press the Return key to sort the file.

Now, we can create the report.

- ☐ Choose the New Report command from the Report menu. The report window opens.

There is no scroll bar at the bottom of the report window because all the fields in this report fit on the screen. We don't have to rearrange any fields—we can simply include every field in the report. (If the Amount field in your version of this file extends slightly past the right-hand edge marker, drag its right dividing line to the left a little bit to make the field a little narrower.)

- ☐ Choose Record Selection from the Organize menu. The Record Selection box appears.

We want to create a rule that says: "Type equals Income and Date is greater than or equal to 3/1/89 and less than or equal to 3/31/89."

☐ Following the steps detailed for the video club member file earlier in this chapter, complete the Record Selection box like this:

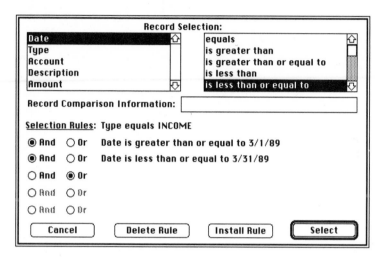

☐ After installing these rules, press the Return key to select the records.

With the records selected, you can now sum the income amounts to produce a total for the month.

☐ Click on the Amount field name to select this field.

☐ Choose Sum This Field from the TotalsPage menu. A check mark appears next to this command, letting you know it is in effect. (To see this, try selecting another field and looking at the TotalsPage menu. You'll see that Sum This Field is not checked.) Because we've chosen this command with the Amount field selected, Sum This Field tells Works to add all the Amount values to produce a total at the end of the report.

☐ Choose the Change Report Title command from the Edit menu, and type the new title *Monthly Income.* Then press the Return key.

Monthly Income is a more descriptive name for this report and will make it easy to remember what the report is for.

This report is now ready to print. But let's assume we want to get a quick look at the total income without actually printing the report on paper. There are two ways to do this: We can use the Copy Totals command to copy the total amount from the report to the Clipboard and then view it there, or we can use the Print Preview command to print the entire report to the screen and view the total there. Let's use the Copy Totals method.

☐ Choose the Copy Totals command from the Edit menu (or press Command-C as a shortcut). This copies all field totals you've specified in the report to the Clipboard.

☐ Choose the Show Clipboard command from the Window menu. The Clipboard window opens, and the report total is shown in a one-line record. To view the total, either scroll the Clipboard window to the right or make the window larger.

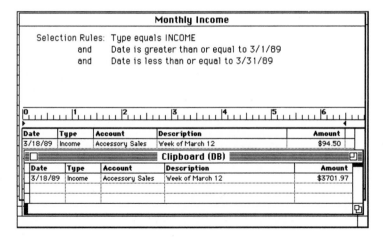

To view the totals with Print Preview, use the following steps.

☐ Press Command-P, or choose the Print command from the File menu.

☐ Click the Print Preview box, and then click the OK button or press Return or Enter. The first page of the report is displayed on the screen.

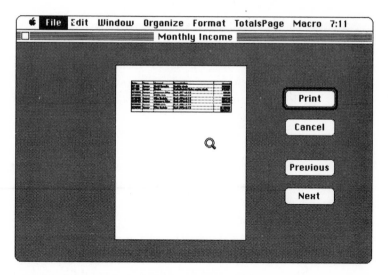

□ Because this is a one-page report, move the magnifying-glass pointer over the bottom line of the report and click the mouse button. The print zooms to actual size, and you can see the report total there, like this:

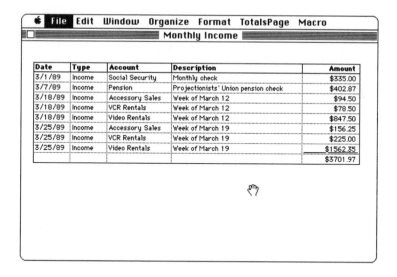

Preparing an income and expense report

Now let's suppose Al wants to get ready for tax time. This will involve printing a report that shows each of his expense and income categories, with subtotals for each account type. We don't need to use record-selection rules here because we want to include all the records in the file. But we'll have to arrange the totals a little differently in this report. Before specifying the totals, though, we have to re-sort the records in this file.

When you print a report from a Works database file, the records are printed in the order that they occupy in the file at that time. In this income and expense report, we want the records printed in two groups: all the expense records in one group and all the income records in another group. This way, we can produce separate totals for each group. Also, we want all the records grouped by account so that we can produce subtotals of expenses or income by account name. And finally, it will be most useful if we arrange the records in chronological order within each account.

What this amounts to is a three-level sort of the file: We want records sorted by transaction type (expense or income), within types by account, and within accounts by date. Works sorts only one field at a time, so we'll have to sort the Tax Ledger file three times on three different fields. Remember, in a multi-level sort, you sort the least important field first, and the most important field last. In this case, the least important field is Date, and the most important field is Type.

- □ Click on the Date field name.

- □ Press Command-A (a shortcut for choosing the Sort command from the Organize menu). Since this is a date-type field, the sort selection is chronological, which is what you want.

- □ Press the Return key to sort the file chronologically.

- □ Click on the Account field name.

- □ Press Command-A, and then press the Return key to sort the Account field from A to Z. This will group all the records by account.

- □ Click on the Type field name.

- □ Press Command-A, and press the Return key to sort the Type field from A to Z. This will separate all the records into two groups: Expense and Income.

Now that the records are arranged properly, you can create the report itself.

☐ Choose the New Report command from the Report menu.

☐ As before, all the fields should fit between the edge markers in this report. (If not, drag the right-hand field dividing line on the Amount field to the left a bit so it fits completely.)

☐ Click on the Amount field name to select this field.

☐ Choose the Sum This Field command from the TotalsPage menu.

At this point, the report will produce a grand total of all the expenses and income amounts for the entire year because Works will add together all the values in the Amount field. Naturally, we don't want income and expenses added together, so we'll have to specify subtotals that will show sums of each account.

You can control when Works generates a subtotal using the Take A Sub-Total On Field Change command, which tells Works to insert a subtotal in a field whenever the contents of a second field change. In this file, we want subtotals to appear at the end of each account group (so that the report shows subtotals for rent, utilities, advertising, and other expense categories). To create these subtotals we'll use the Take A Sub-Total On Field Change command for the Account field.

☐ Click on the Account field name to select this field.

☐ Choose the Take A Sub-Total On Field Change command from the TotalsPage menu.

Now the report will produce a subtotal whenever the contents of the Account field change. Because the records are sorted into account groups, a subtotal will appear at the end of each group.

The report is almost ready to print out, but we need to take care of some final formatting chores. First, the report could use a more descriptive name.

☐ Choose the Change Report Title command from the Edit menu.

☐ Type Income/Expense Report and press the Return key to change the report name.

Because this report will eventually contain an entire year's transactions, it will cover several pages. Accounts containing only a few transactions will occupy only a few lines, but other accounts (such as the weekly income records) will occupy more than one page. You could set up the report so that a new printed page begins after each subtotal. This would make it easier to keep each account's printed records separate. To do this, you would choose the New Page After Total command from the TotalsPage menu. But for our purposes in this example, we'll let several totals appear on the same printed page.

The only other thing left to do is specify a header for the report. Because the report will cover several pages, a header will help identify the separate pages as belonging to the same report, and it will also let you number the pages and date the report.

□ Choose the Page Setup command from the File menu. The Page Setup dialog box appears.

The Paper and Margin settings are the way we want them, but we need to supply header information.

□ The insertion point is already blinking in the header entry line, so type *&LIncome/Expense Report - &D - Page &P* as the header.

The ampersand commands in the header information tell Works to do certain things. The *&L* tells Works to left justify the header text, the *&D* tells Works to print the current date, and the *&P* tells Works to print the current page number. Thus, this header will contain the title Income/Expense Report, followed by the date, followed by the word *Page*, and the page number. The Page Setup box now looks like this:

```
┌──────────────────────────────────────────────────────────┐
│ LaserWriter Page Setup                      5.2    ┌─────┐ │
│ Paper: ⦿ US Letter  ○ A4 Letter  ○ Tabloid         │ OK  │ │
│        ○ US Legal   ○ B5 Letter                    └─────┘ │
│        Reduce or ┌───┐%    Printer Effects:        ┌──────┐│
│        Enlarge:  │100│     ⊠ Font Substitution?    │Cancel││
│                  └───┘     ⊠ Text Smoothing?       └──────┘│
│        Orientation         ⊠ Graphics Smoothing?   ┌──────┐│
│                            ⊠ Faster Bitmap Printing?│Options││
│                                                    └──────┘│
│                                                    ┌──────┐│
│                                                    │ Help ││
│                                                    └──────┘│
│  ☐ Print Row and Column Numbers      ☐ Print Cell Notes   │
│  Header:  ┌──────────────────────────────────────────────┐│
│           │&LIncome/Expense Report - &D - Page &P         ││
│           └──────────────────────────────────────────────┘│
│  Footer:  ┌──────────────────────────────────────────────┐│
│           │                                               ││
│           └──────────────────────────────────────────────┘│
│  Left Margin: │1│           Right Margin: │1│             │
│  Top Margin:  │1│           Bottom Margin:│1│             │
└──────────────────────────────────────────────────────────┘
```

☐ Press the Return key or click the OK button to store these changes to the page setup.

Now let's print the report.

☐ Choose the Print command from the File menu. The Print dialog box appears.

☐ Select the options you want.

☐ Press Return or click the OK button to print the report.

When the report is printed, all the accounts will be subtotaled, and the Income and Expense groups will have totals. A sample page from the printed report is shown in Figure 8-3 on the next page.

Although we've set up this report for a year-end summary, you could also use the record-selection rules in Works to prepare reports like this for each month, quarter, or six-month period. All you would have to do is to specify record-selection rules that match information in the Date field with the dates you want to report on.

Another useful way of setting up this report (or a separate report) might be to use the Take A Sub-Total On Field Change command on the Type field rather than the Account field. This would give you subtotals of all income and all expenses, rather than subtotals on individual accounts.

☐ Click on the Account field name to select this field.

☐ Choose the Take A Sub-Total On Field Change command to de-select it (remove the check mark from it) for the Account field.

☐ Click on the Type field name to select this field.

☐ Choose the Take A Sub-Total On Field Change command.

☐ Choose the Print command and press the Return key. (Use the Print Preview option, if you want.)

If you printed the report at this point, it would look like the one in Figure 8-4 on page 307.

Expense/Income Report - April 1, 1989 - Page 1

Date	Type	Account	Description	Amount
3/10/89	Expense	Advertising	Lippi Sign Company - Front window sign	$195.00
				$195.00
3/3/89	Expense	Inventory	UA Video - rental videotape selection	$3496.90
				$3496.90
3/8/89	Expense	Phone	Deposit on Videorama phones	$125.00
				$125.00
3/15/89	Expense	Rent	March	$1250.00
				$1250.00
3/6/89	Expense	Stationery	ABC Printers - Printing	$200.00
				$200.00
3/8/89	Expense	Utilities	Deposit on Videorama electricity	$75.00
				$75.00
3/18/89	Income	Accessory Sales	Week of March 12	$94.50
3/25/89	Income	Accessory Sales	Week of March 19	$156.25
4/1/89	Income	Accessory Sales	Week of March 26	$250.00
				$500.75
3/7/89	Income	Pension	Projectionists' Union pension check	$402.87
				$402.87
3/1/89	Income	Social Security	Monthly check	$335.00
				$335.00
3/18/89	Income	VCR Rentals	Week of March 12	$78.50
3/25/89	Income	VCR Rentals	Week of March 19	$225.00
4/1/89	Income	VCR Rentals	Week of March 26	$250.00
				$553.50
3/18/89	Income	Video Rentals	Week of March 12	$847.50
3/25/89	Income	Video Rentals	Week of March 19	$1562.35
4/1/89	Income	Video Rentals	Week of March 26	$1804.40
				$4214.25
				$11348.27

Figure 8-3.

A printout of the income and expense report.

Expense/Income Report - April 1, 1989 - Page 1

Date	Type	Account	Description	Amount
3/10/89	Expense	Advertising	Lippi Sign Company - Front window sign	$195.00
3/3/89	Expense	Inventory	UA Video - rental videotape selection	$3496.90
3/8/89	Expense	Phone	Deposit on Videorama phones	$125.00
3/15/89	Expense	Rent	March	$1250.00
3/6/89	Expense	Stationery	ABC Printers - Printing	$200.00
3/8/89	Expense	Utilities	Deposit on Videorama electricity	$75.00
				$5341.90
3/18/89	Income	Accessory Sales	Week of March 12	$94.50
3/25/89	Income	Accessory Sales	Week of March 19	$156.25
4/1/89	Income	Accessory Sales	Week of March 26	$250.00
3/7/89	Income	Pension	Projectionists' Union pension check	$402.87
3/1/89	Income	Social Security	Monthly check	$335.00
3/18/89	Income	VCR Rentals	Week of March 12	$78.50
3/25/89	Income	VCR Rentals	Week of March 19	$225.00
4/1/89	Income	VCR Rentals	Week of March 26	$250.00
3/18/89	Income	Video Rentals	Week of March 12	$847.50
3/25/89	Income	Video Rentals	Week of March 19	$1562.35
4/1/89	Income	Video Rentals	Week of March 26	$1804.40
				$6006.37
				$11348.27

Figure 8-4.
Income and expense report with subtotals on the Type field.

Note that the grand total at the bottom of each version of the report is the sum of all income and expenses, which is marginally useful in an accounting sense. But if you want to see any totals at all, including subtotals, you must use the Total This Field command, which will always produce a grand total at the bottom.

A Videotape Inventory

One final example will expand on the simple inventory-valuation spreadsheet we looked at in Chapter 6. By maintaining inventory data in the database instead of on the spreadsheet, you can store text information more easily, and you can search for or sort the data in more ways.

Let's assume Al has the inventory file shown in Figure 8-5.

Tape Inventory (DB)					
Title	**Format**	**Qty**	**Price**	**Stock #**	**Distributor**
Blazing Bullets	Beta	1	$34.95	A001B	Adventure Video
Blazing Bullets	VHS	1	$34.95	A001V	Adventure Video
Six Gun City	VHS	1	$22.95	A003V	Western
The One-Eyed Assassin	Beta	1	$34.95	A004B	Western
The One-Eyed Assassin	VHS	3	$34.95	A004V	Western
Bonzo Gets Long Pants	VHS	1	$26.95	C001V	Apex Distributors
Forgotten Dreams	Beta	1	$34.95	C002B	Apex Distributors
Forgotten Dreams	VHS	2	$34.95	C002V	Apex Distributors
Aerobic Profit-Taking	Beta	1	$34.95	E001B	Topshows
Aerobic Profit-Taking	VHS	4	$34.95	E001V	Topshows
Galaxy Zappers	VHS	3	$28.95	S001V	Adventure Video
My Brother The Microbe	Beta	1	$32.95	S002B	Adventure Video
My Brother The Microbe	VHS	4	$32.95	S002V	Adventure Video
Bored To Death	VHS	3	$22.95	T002V	BestVid
Closet Noises	VHS	2	$22.95	T003V	Apex Distributors

Figure 8-5.
A database inventory.

To follow along with this exercise, you must create a database file like the one shown in Figure 8-5.

- ☐ Open a new database file, and create fields named Title, Format, Qty, Price, Stock #, and Distributor.

- ☐ Enter the data shown in Figure 8-4.

- ☐ Double-click on any data entry in the Format field to display the Field Attributes dialog box, and click on the Right button under Align.

- ☐ Double-click on a data entry in the Qty field to display the Field Attributes box, and click on the Numeric button under Type.

- ☐ Using the Field Attributes dialog box as described in the preceding step, set the Price field to Numeric type with the Dollar display format, and set the Stock # field to right alignment.

- ☐ Choose the Save As command from the File menu and save this file to disk with the name Tape Inventory.

Now you're ready to proceed.

The file shows each tape title, format, quantity, price, stock number, and distributor, but one item of information is missing. As it is, this file can't possibly produce a report that shows how much Al's videotape inventory is worth—it shows the quantity of tapes and their prices, but it doesn't calculate their values.

When you want to calculate new values from existing values in a database file, you have to create a special kind of field – called a calculated field. Calculated fields contain information that comes from calculating data in two or more other fields. To calculate the value of tapes in the inventory, we have to create a new field. Let's call it Value.

□ Choose the Add New Field command from the Edit menu. The Field Name box appears.

□ Type the name *Value*, and press the Return key. The new field is added to the file, to the right of the Distributor field.

This new field doesn't contain any data yet, and we won't have to type any data into it. We want the Value field to contain the total value of the tapes in each record. Therefore, in each record, we want to multiply the contents of the Qty (quantity) field by the contents of the Price field to produce the total value of tapes. To do this, we have to specify that the new Value field is a computed field, and then we'll enter a formula that tells the database how to arrive at the values to be stored there.

□ Double-click on a blank entry in the Value field to display the Set Field Attributes dialog box.

□ The Value field will contain a dollar value computed from the Qty and Price fields, so click on the Numeric button and Dollar button. The default number of decimal places is 2, which is what you want.

□ To tell Works this will be a computed field, click the Computed box at the bottom of the Set Field Attributes dialog box. The settings now look like this:

```
┌─────────────────────────────────────────────────────┐
│  Set Field Attributes For Value                      │
│                                                      │
│  Type:        Display:      Align:      Style:       │
│  ○ Text       ○ General     ○ Left      ☐ Bold       │
│  ◉ Numeric    ○ Fixed       ○ Center    ☐ Underline  │
│  ○ Date       ◉ Dollar      ◉ Right     ☐ Commas     │
│  ○ Time       ○ Percent     [2] Decimal Places       │
│               ○ Scientific                           │
│  ☒ Computed ☐ Show Day      [ Cancel ] [[  OK  ]]    │
└─────────────────────────────────────────────────────┘
```

□ Press the Return key to confirm these Set Field Attributes settings.

Since we specified a computed field, we still have to enter the formula for the calculation. Works is expecting this, and the insertion point is blinking next to an equal sign in the entry bar at the top of the file window.

	Format	Qty	Price	Stock#	Distributor	Value
	Beta	1	$34.95	A001B	Adventure Video	$0.00
	VHS	1	$34.95	A001V	Adventure Video	$0.00
	VHS	1	$22.95	A003V	Western	$0.00
ssin	Beta	1	$34.95	A004B	Western	$0.00
ssin	VHS	3	$34.95	A004V	Western	$0.00
nts	VHS	1	$26.95	C001V	Apex Distributors	$0.00
	Beta	1	$34.95	C002B	Apex Distributors	$0.00
	VHS	2	$34.95	C002V	Apex Distributors	$0.00
ing	Beta	1	$34.95	E001B	Topshows	$0.00
ing	VHS	4	$34.95	E001V	Topshows	$0.00
	VHS	3	$28.95	S001V	Adventure Video	$0.00
crobe	Beta	1	$32.95	S002B	Adventure Video	$0.00
crobe	VHS	4	$32.95	S002V	Adventure Video	$0.00
	VHS	3	$22.95	T002V	BestVid	$0.00
	VHS	2	$22.95	T003V	Apex Distributors	$0.00

Tape Inventory (DB)

🍎 File Edit Window Organize Format Report Macro

We want Works to multiply the Qty field by the Price field, so enter the formula that way, using the field names in place of values in the formula.

☐ Click on any entry in the Qty field. The word Qty appears as the first part of the formula in the entry bar.

☐ Type an asterisk (*) to indicate multiplication in the formula in the entry bar.

☐ Click on any entry in the Price field to enter the word Price in the formula in the entry bar.

☐ Click the Enter box or press Return or Enter to enter the formula. Works multiplies the Qty entry by the Price entry in each record, and puts the result in the Value field for that record.

TIP: You can type the formula directly instead of clicking on fields to select them. In this case, you would type *Qty*Price.*

```
  🍎 File  Edit  Window  Organize  Format  Report  Macro
  1    |        | =Qty*Price
```

Tape Inventory (DB)

	Format	Qty	Price	Stock*	Distributor	Value
	Beta	1	$34.95	A001B	Adventure Video	$34.95
	VHS	1	$34.95	A001V	Adventure Video	$34.95
	VHS	1	$22.95	A003V	Western	$22.95
ssin	Beta	1	$34.95	A004B	Western	$34.95
ssin	VHS	3	$34.95	A004V	Western	$104.85
nts	VHS	1	$26.95	C001V	Apex Distributors	$26.95
	Beta	1	$34.95	C002B	Apex Distributors	$34.95
	VHS	2	$34.95	C002V	Apex Distributors	$69.90
ing	Beta	1	$34.95	E001B	Topshows	$34.95
ing	VHS	4	$34.95	E001V	Topshows	$139.80
	VHS	3	$28.95	S001V	Adventure Video	$86.85
crobe	Beta	1	$32.95	S002B	Adventure Video	$32.95
crobe	VHS	4	$32.95	S002V	Adventure Video	$131.80
	VHS	3	$22.95	T002V	BestVid	$68.85
	VHS	2	$22.95	T003V	Apex Distributors	$45.90

Now the formula is stored with this file, and its results will always be placed in the Value field. If we change an entry in the Qty or Price field in a record, the calculated value in the Value field in the affected record will change as well. The general rules for calculating fields in a database file are:

- The fields being calculated must be numerical-type fields, as indicated with the Set Field Attributes command.

- You can specify fields to be calculated either by clicking on them or by typing their exact names.

- You can use arithmetic operators or spreadsheet functions to calculate fields. (The operators are +, −, *, and / for adding, subtracting, multiplying, and dividing.) When you use spreadsheet functions, you must use the same formula format as in the spreadsheet, except that you specify field names instead of cell coordinates. You can type the function names into calculated fields by hand, or you can use the Paste Function command on the Edit menu, as you do in the spreadsheet, to select a function from a list and add it to a formula. (See Chapters 5 and 6 for details about using spreadsheet formulas and functions.)

With the calculated field added, this file becomes much more useful. We can now determine how much the entire inventory is worth by specifying a field total on the Value field. We can also count the total number of tapes by specifying a field total on the Qty field.

The Stock # field will let us produce subtotals of tape amounts and values by tape genre (Adventure, History, Classics, and so on). The stock number entries are coded to indicate each tape's genre (the letter at the beginning of each stock number indicates which genre group the tape belongs to).

Let's create a report that shows total quantities and values of tapes by genre and that includes grand totals for the entire report. First, we'll sort the file on the Stock # field so that the records are arranged in groups by genre.

- ☐ Click on the Stock # field name to select this field.

- ☐ Choose the Sort command from the Organize menu, or press Command-A. The Sort dialog box appears.

- ☐ The Stock # field is a text field, and the default sort order is from A to Z, which is what you want, so press the Return key to sort the file.

Now, let's create the report.

- ☐ Choose the New Report command from the Report menu. A report window opens.

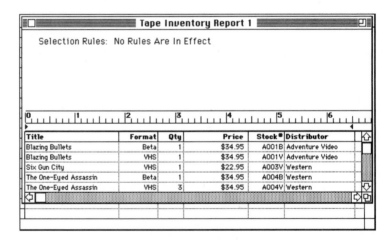

As you can see, the report format doesn't contain all the fields we want in this report (the Value field is off the screen to the right, beyond the right-hand edge marker). We could change the margin settings in the Page Setup dialog box to make everything fit, but it's as easy to make all the fields narrower.

☐ Drag the right-hand field dividing lines on the Format, Qty, Price, Stock #, Distributor, and Value fields to the left, making each of these fields narrower. After you do this, all the fields fit inside the right-hand edge marker.

Now we're ready to calculate sums and subtotals for the report.

☐ Click on the Value field name to select this field.

☐ Choose the Sum This Field command from the TotalsPage menu. Works will now total the values in this field at the end of the report. Remember, Works doesn't show report totals on the screen in a report window—you have to either print the report to the screen with the Print Preview option or use the Copy Totals command to put the totals on the Clipboard, and then view them there.

☐ Click on the Qty field name to select this field.

☐ Choose the Sum This Field command from the TotalsPage menu. Works will now total the tape quantities in this field at the end of the report.

We've set up this report to calculate grand totals of tape quantities and values, but we also want it to produce subtotals by genre group. (Genre groups are determined by the first character in the stock numbers.) We've already sorted the file on the Stock # field, so the tapes are arranged in genre groups. All we have to do now is give Works some subtotaling instructions.

☐ Click on the Stock # field name to select this field.

☐ Choose the Take A Sub-Total On 1st Char command from the TotalsPage menu.

We used the Take A Sub-Total On 1st Char command—rather than the Take A Sub-Total On Field Change command (which we used in the Tax Ledger report earlier in this chapter) because we want Works to produce a subtotal each time the first character in the Stock # field changes. If we used the Take A Sub-Total On Field Change command to produce subtotals, Works would print a subtotal after each record (because each stock number is different).

Finally, let's specify a header with the Page Setup command.

☐ Choose the Page Setup command from the File menu.

☐ Type *&CInventory Report-&D-Page &P* as the header information. This tells Works to center the header on the page (the
&C), print the date between two dashes (the *&D*), and print the
page number after the word *Page* (the *&P*).

☐ Click the OK button or press Return or Enter to store the page
setup changes.

The report is now complete. We can either print it on paper, or use
Print Preview or Copy Totals to see a quick summary of the inventory's
value on the screen. Let's do a quick check.

☐ Choose the Copy Totals command from the Edit menu. The
report totals are copied to the Clipboard.

☐ Choose the Show Clipboard command from the Window menu.

☐ Enlarge the Clipboard window and scroll it to the right so that
both the Qty and Value fields are showing. You'll see that all
the subtotals and grand totals are there.

			Clipboard (DB)			
itle	Format	Qty	Price	Stock*	Distributor	Value
lazing Bullets	Beta	7	$34.95	A001B	Adventure Video	$232.65
onzo Gets Long Pants	VHS	4	$26.95	C001V	Apex Distributors	$131.80
erobic Profit-Taking	Beta	5	$34.95	E001B	Topshows	$174.75
alaxy Zappers	VHS	8	$28.95	S001V	Adventure Video	$251.60
ored To Death	VHS	5	$22.95	T002V	BestVid	$114.75
		29				$905.55

Title	Format	Qty	Price	Stock*	Distributor	Value
Blazing Bullets	Beta	1	$34.95	A001B	Adventure Video	$34.95
Blazing Bullets	VHS	1	$34.95	A001V	Adventure Video	$34.95
Six Gun City	VHS	1	$22.95	A003V	Western	$22.95
The One-Eyed Assassin	Beta	1	$34.95	A004B	Western	$34.95
The One-Eyed Assassin	VHS	3	$34.95	A004V	Western	$104.85

One way to see if you have narrowed the fields in the report enough
to fit inside the right-hand edge marker is to check the Clipboard when
you use the Copy Totals command. If the Value field isn't shown on the
Clipboard, even after you scroll the Clipboard window to the right,

that field isn't included in the report. Any field in a report that is either partially or completely to the right of the right-hand edge marker will not be included in the report when you print it.

In this way, the Copy Totals command is just like printing—you only copy the portion of the database report that falls within the edge markers. To include more fields in the report, make the fields narrower by dragging their dividing lines to the left, or change the margin settings in the Page Setup dialog box. If you change the Left and Right margin settings to 0.5 inch instead of 1 inch, for example, the report can be one inch wider.

Although the Copy Totals command only shows subtotals and the grand total in the report, rather than each record, the printed report itself will show all the records, with subtotals and grand totals included, as shown in Figure 8-6.

Inventory Report - April 1, 1989 - Page 1

Title	Format	Qty	Price	Stock#	Distributor	Value
Blazing Bullets	Beta	1	$34.95	A001B	Adventure Video	$34.95
Blazing Bullets	VHS	1	$34.95	A001V	Adventure Video	$34.95
Six Gun City	VHS	1	$22.95	A003V	Western	$22.95
The One-Eyed Assassin	Beta	1	$34.95	A004B	Western	$34.95
The One-Eyed Assassin	VHS	3	$34.95	A004V	Western	$104.85
		7				$232.65
Bonzo Gets Long Pants	VHS	1	$26.95	C001V	Apex Distributors	$26.95
Forgotten Dreams	Beta	1	$34.95	C002B	Apex Distributors	$34.95
Forgotten Dreams	VHS	2	$34.95	C002V	Apex Distributors	$69.90
		4				$131.80
Aerobic Profit-Taking	Beta	1	$34.95	E001B	Topshows	$34.95
Aerobic Profit-Taking	VHS	4	$34.95	E001V	Topshows	$139.80
		5				$174.75
Galaxy Zappers	VHS	3	$28.95	S001V	Adventure Video	$86.85
My Brother The Microbe	Beta	1	$32.95	S002B	Adventure Video	$32.95
My Brother The Microbe	VHS	4	$32.95	S002V	Adventure Video	$131.80
		8				$251.60
Bored To Death	VHS	3	$22.95	T002V	BestVid	$68.85
Closet Noises	VHS	2	$22.95	T003V	Apex Distributors	$45.90
		5				$114.75
		29				$905.55

Figure 8-6.
An inventory report.

The extent to which you can use the database to handle personal and business projects is limited only by your imagination. If you are careful when you define database fields, you can usually sort, select, or report information in any way you need it. You can also merge database data into word-processor documents. This is an extremely powerful feature that lets you use database files in many other ways. We'll look at some of these applications in Chapter 10.

Chapter 9

Using the Communications Application

Creating and storing Works spreadsheet, database, and word-processor files for your own use is fine most of the time, but sometimes you'll want to share your files with other computer users, or you'll want access to files or information stored in another computer. The communications module in Microsoft Works lets you use your Macintosh to communicate with other computers over standard telephone lines. Just as you use a telephone to exchange spoken information with other people, your Mac can use the telephone to exchange digitized data with other computers. With the communications part of Works, you can send your spreadsheet, word-processor, or database files to other computers. You can also transmit files you've created with other Macintosh programs, such as MacPaint. And you can use Works to access other computers so that you can read files stored in those computers and sent to you electronically. Before we get into the specifics of communications with Microsoft Works, let's look at personal-computer communications in general.

How Computers Use the Telephone

Telephones are designed to transmit spoken sounds, which is fine for allowing people to talk to each other. But computers store and represent information as silent electrical impulses. In order to communicate over a telephone line, a computer must be given a "voice" with a device called a modem. A modem (short for MOdulator/DEModulator) translates the electrical data stored in a computer into sounds that can be transmitted via telephone lines. In order to use the communications module in Works to transmit data, you must have a modem connected to your Macintosh. You can buy a modem from your Apple dealer or from any computer specialty store.

At first glance, communications looks like a simple application for a computer because communications programs don't require as many commands and options as spreadsheet, database, or word-processor programs. But, despite outward appearances, communications is very complex because it involves more potential trouble spots than other applications. If something doesn't work right in a database, spreadsheet, or word-processor file, you know that you have a problem with one of only two types of interaction: Either you have given a wrong command (the interaction between you and your software) or there is a problem in the interaction between your hardware and software. With communications, these two types of interaction are only the beginning.

Using a communications program and modem to exchange data with another computer involves five types of interaction:

- You interact with the communications software.

- The communications software and your computer interact.

- The computer and software interact with the modem.

- The modem interacts with the telephone line.

- Your computer and modem interact via the telephone line with another computer and modem.

When the modem is properly connected and turned on, it receives instructions from you (through the software) about how to format and send data to other computers. These instructions (or protocols) can include:

- The speed at which data is sent from the computer to the modem.

- The speed at which data is sent from the modem to the telephone line.

- The data format—that is, the number of electrical impulses it takes to transmit each piece of data (a number in a spreadsheet or a character in a word-processor file, for example), and the method by which each individual piece of data is separated from the others.

- The data type—that is, whether a file being sent is a text file, which can contain only characters, or a binary file, which can also contain graphics or program instructions.

- The presence or absence of special error-correcting routines that help verify the accuracy of data sent.

The quality of the telephone connection also plays a part in communications. Because the modem is translating computer data into sounds, a noisy telephone line can be a problem—one of the communicating modems may not be able to "hear" the other modem's tones properly because of interference on the line. When this happens, some of the data is garbled, or the transmission may be broken off.

Even if you have set up your software and modem to send data properly, the modem and computer at the other end of the line must be set to match your transmission rate and other protocols. Otherwise, the two modems can exchange tones, but they can't understand each other. It's like having your modem transmitting in English while the modem at the other end of the line is set to receive in Spanish.

To communicate effectively, all of these types of interaction must work smoothly. Fortunately, today's modems, computers, and communications software automate much of the process. Most modems, for example, can adjust their transmission speeds to match the transmission speed of the modem at the other end of the line. Most communications programs have error-checking facilities, which help compensate for noisy telephone lines and ensure accurate data transmission by verifying each piece of data as it is sent and by retransmitting data that was garbled. And the transmission protocols (data size and so forth) are fairly standard, so the number of possible settings is limited.

To see how you can control some of these facets of communications with Works, let's look at the menu commands.

A Quick Tour of the Communications Menus

The first four menus from the left edge of the menu bar are either identical or similar to the same menus in other Works applications. However, on the File menu, the Page Setup, Print, and Print Merge commands are dimmed because you can't print an entire file directly from a communications document.

And on the Edit menu, the Undo command is dimmed when you're using a communications document because it's not active. After you issue an editing command, such as Cut, Copy, or Clear, you can't undo it. The Select All command selects all the text in a communications document.

The Communications menu

The Communications menu is the real control center of the communications application in Works.

The Echo On and Echo Off commands determine whether information you are sending is displayed (echoed) on your screen. The type of echo depends on how the other (or remote) computer's echo (or duplex) function is set. If you type data to transmit and don't see it on your screen, change the setting to Echo On. On the other hand, if each character you type is displayed twice on the screen, change the setting to Echo Off.

The Dial command displays the telephone list you've stored for the current communications document. When the telephone list is displayed, you can click the Dial button next to any of the numbers to have Works dial the number for you.

The Hang Up command disconnects the modem from the telephone line, just as hanging up a telephone receiver disconnects a regular call. Use this command when you have finished communicating.

The Answer Phone command sets your modem to answer the telephone when it rings. Use this command when you are expecting some other computer to call your computer and you want your Mac to answer the phone.

The Capture Text command lets you receive and save a text file as a Works word-processor file. The Send Text command lets you transmit text files. You can also use these commands to send or receive standard Works word-processor, spreadsheet, or database files, as well as standard text files created by other programs. When you begin receiving a text file, the Capture Text command changes to End Text Capture. You must choose the End Text Capture command to save the file to disk.

The Receive File and Send File commands let you receive and send binary files. Use these commands when you want to send or receive Mac-Paint files, BASIC programs, Scrapbook files, and other non-text files. When you use the Send File or Receive File command, you have the choice of using either the MacBinary or the Xmodem error-correcting protocol. Xmodem is a common error-checking protocol, and it can be used to communicate with a variety of other computers. Works has two Xmodem protocols: Xmodem Text and Xmodem Data. You use the Xmodem Text protocol when you're sending or receiving text characters only, and you use Xmodem Data when you're sending or receiving text characters and formatting information. The MacBinary protocol can be used only when you're communicating with another Mac that is also using this protocol. When you use the Receive File command and open a receiving file on disk, the Receive File command changes to Cancel Receive, and you must choose Cancel Receive before the file will be saved to disk.

The Settings command displays a dialog box in which you indicate communications settings, such as the transmission speed (or baud rate), data size, stop bits, parity, and other protocols.

The Keypad menu

Two of the communications settings you can specify with the Settings command make your Mac and the Works communications program act like, or emulate two standard types of terminals used to communicate with minicomputers and mainframe computers: Digital Equipment's model VT-52 and VT-100. The Keypad menu displays a graphic keypad for use when you're communicating with a larger computer using VT-52 or VT-100 terminal emulation.

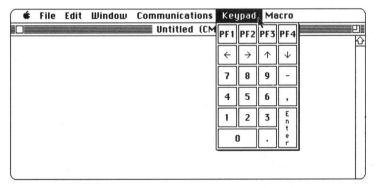

If you're using a Mac that doesn't have a numeric keypad on its keyboard, you can click the keys on the Keypad with the mouse to send instructions to the remote computer. See Appendix H of the Microsoft Works User's Guide for a list of VT-52 and VT-100 commands you can send with the keypad.

The Macro menu

As explained in Chapter 1, the Macro menu works the same in all Works applications. You can use macros in the Communications application to automate log-on sequences to remote computer services. We'll put some macros to work later in this chapter.

Keyboard shortcuts

Just as in the other Works applications, the Communications module has many keyboard equivalents you can use to issue other special commands directly from the keyboard. The keyboard equivalents are shown in Figure 9-1.

Action	Command	Menu	Keyboard equivalent
Open a file	Open	File	Command-O
Close a file	Close	File	Command-W
Save a file	Save	File	Command-S
Quit Works	Quit	File	Command-Q
Cut data to Clipboard	Cut	Edit	Command-X
Copy data to Clipboard	Copy	Edit	Command-C
Paste data from Clipboard	Paste	Edit	Command-V
Access on-line Help facility	Help	Window	Command-?
Display last document on Window menu		Window	Command-,
Display the phone list	Dial	Communications	Command-D
Hang up the modem	Hang-Up	Communications	Command-=
Start macro recording	Start Recording	Macro	Option-+

Figure 9-1. *(continued)*
Keyboard equivalents for Works' communications commands.

Figure 9-1. *continued*

Action	Command	Menu	Keyboard equivalent
Stop macro recording	Stop Recording	Macro	Option-–
Play back a macro	Playback and	Macro	Option-Delete
Stop a macro in progress			Command-.
Send Break code			Command-Option-3
Send Delete code			Command-Option-Delete
Send Escape code			Command-Option-[

Using many of these shortcuts is the same as choosing a menu command with the mouse, as you can see. But five commands are special. The commands to send Break, Escape, and Delete codes let you send these codes to other computers or information services that require them. There is no Break key on the Mac keyboard, and you can't always send the proper Escape and Delete codes simply by pressing these keys on the Mac keyboard when you're using the Works communications module. Another special command lets you stop a macro in the middle of its playback. The last special command displays the last document listed on the Window menu—using this command lets you toggle through the documents on the Window menu quickly by pressing Command-, (comma).

Now, let's look at how to set up your modem and use some of these commands.

Hooking Up a Modem

Before you can use Works to communicate, you need to get a modem and hook it up to your Mac. You can choose from several brands of modems. Basically, however, all modems let your Mac communicate with other computers—the differences lie in the variety of transmission speeds you can use, the types of software commands each modem understands, and the presence or absence of extra convenience features.

Modem transmission speeds are measured in bits per second (bps, also called baud). Today's personal computer modems transmit at speeds from 110 to 19,200 bps. Most personal-computer communication takes place at 300, 1200, or 2400 bps. If you buy a modem that transmits at 300 and 1200 bps, you will be able to communicate with virtually every other personal-computer modem.

Modems are programmed internally to accept certain control commands from the communications software you use. These commands instruct the modem about its transmission speed, data format, and so forth. The most common set of commands in use for personal computers is called the Hayes command set. (Hayes Microcomputer Products of Norcross, Georgia, was the first major supplier of microcomputer modems, and most subsequent manufacturers have used its command set.) Microsoft Works uses the Hayes command set, so be sure that the modem you buy uses Hayes commands.

Beyond these two essential considerations, you can choose from a variety of modems, depending on the price and extra features you want. Some modems, for example, contain built-in memories that let you capture incoming data in the modem itself or store outgoing transmissions so that they can be sent later. Other modems have built-in error-correcting circuitry.

You hook up a modeum using the following steps.

□ Connect one end of the data cable to the modem and the other end to the Mac's telephone port (the one on the rear of the Mac with the telephone handset icon above it).

□ Connect one end of the telephone cable to the modem and the other end to a standard modular telephone jack. If your phone location doesn't have a standard modular jack, you can buy an adapter from a telephone supply store.

□ Connect the modem's power-supply cord to a standard AC electrical outlet.

□ Check your modem's manual to see if you need to set any switches on the modem.

That's all there is to setting up the modem. Now, you must set up the Works communications software.

Specifying communications settings

As with every other Works application, you begin communications by opening a new document.

◻ Load Microsoft Works.

◻ Click on the Communications icon.

◻ Click on the New button.

When you open a new communications document, the Communications Settings dialog box appears.

```
┌─────────────────────────────────────────────────────────────┐
│  Communications Settings:                                     │
│  Type:        ⦿ TTY ○ VT-100 ○ VT-52  ☐ Auto-wrap  ☐ Newline  │
│  Baud Rate:   ○ 300  ○ 2400  ○ 9600   Delete Key Means:        │
│               ⦿ 1200 ○ 4800  ○ 19200      ○ Delete             │
│  Data Size:   ⦿ 8 Bits    ○ 7 Bits     ⦿ Backspace            │
│  Stop Bits:   ⦿ 1 Bit     ○ 2 Bits    Number of screens: [4]  │
│  Parity:      ⦿ None      ○ Odd        ○ Even                 │
│  Handshake:   ○ None   ⦿ Xon/Xoff ○ Hardware    ○ Both        │
│  Phone Type:  ⦿ Touch-Tone®            ○ Rotary Dial          │
│  Line Delay: [0]          Character Delay: [0]                │
│  ☒ Capture Text When Document Opens                           │
│  Connect To:  ⦿ 📞  ○ 🖨    ( Cancel )  ( OK )                │
└─────────────────────────────────────────────────────────────┘
```

This box is where you indicate all the basic settings that let Works interact properly with your modem. You can re-display this dialog box at any time by choosing Settings from the Communications menu.

Beginning at the top of the dialog box, you click the option in each area to set the program so that it instructs your modem to transmit properly. When the settings are the way you want them, click OK.

The Type setting lets you choose the type of computer terminal you want your Mac to emulate. For communicating with other personal computers or computer services, such as CompuServe or MCI Mail, choose the TTY setting. The VT-52 and VT-100 settings are only for communicating with a minicomputer or mainframe that is set up to communicate with these specific types of terminals.

The Auto-wrap box is an option only when you choose VT-52 or VT-100 emulation. Choosing Auto-wrap causes Works to wrap text of one line to the next line when the first line is full.

The Newline box is another VT-52 or VT-100 option. It makes the insertion point move to the beginning of the next blank line when the remote computer sends a command to begin a new line.

The Delete Key Means options are also for VT-52 or VT-100 use only. These options let you change the actual ASCII text codes Works sends when you press the Delete key on your keyboard. Toggling one or the other of these options will cause Works to send either the ASCII code for Delete or the ASCII code for Backspace when you press the Delete key.

The Baud Rate setting is the speed at which you'll transmit your data. There are two things to remember about the Baud Rate setting: You and the person you're communicating with must transmit data at the same rate, and your modem must be capable of handling the rate you select. If you choose the 9600 baud rate, for example, and your modem transmits only up to 1200 baud, then you will transmit data at 1200 baud. The most common transmission rate is 1200 baud, so Works selects this setting when the dialog box appears. Clicking any other option tells Works to instruct your modem to send data at that rate instead.

The Data Size, Stop Bits, and Parity settings indicate the form each item, or character, of data will take as it is transmitted. These settings must be the same on both the sender's and receiver's software for the communication to take place. The Data Size is the size (in bits, or electrical impulses) of each character of information. Data can be represented in either 7-bit or 8-bit groups. The Stop Bits setting specifies the presence and number of bits that indicate where one character ends and the next one begins. The Parity setting lets you specify the presence and number of bits used to check for transmission errors. The most common settings for these three items are 8 Bits for Data Size, 1 Bit for Stop Bits, and None for Parity, so the dialog box contains these default selections when it first appears. You can set these options any way, as long as the computer with which you're communicating is set the same way. When you communicate with an information service, such as MCI Mail or Dow Jones News/Retrieval, you will have to set your Works settings to match the settings of that service.

When you're receiving data from a remote computer, the data appears on your screen a line at a time. When the Works screen is full, the text scrolls up as new text is added at the end of what you've already received. Works versions 1.0 and 1.1 had no way to re-display the text that had scrolled off the top of your screen, but the Number Of Screens option in Works 2.0 lets you do this. Number Of Screens lets you specify how many screens of information Works will store in your Mac's memory and lets you scroll up to have another look at text that has scrolled past.

The default setting for Number Of Screens is 4, which means Works will retain the last four screens of text in memory. After you receive the fifth screen of text, the first screen you received is dumped from memory, leaving always only four screens available at a time.

You can opt to save up to 100 screens in memory, if you like, but each time you ask Works to save an additional screen, you are setting aside a portion of your Mac's memory to hold those screens, and that memory can't be used for anything else while you have that communications document open. To give you an idea of how much memory you use when you save screens, a blank Communications document with four screens saved uses 17 KB of memory; a blank Communications document with 8 screens saved uses 33 KB of memory. Works will warn you if you don't have enough memory to specify a certain number of saved screens.

The Handshake setting determines how Works and the computer with which you communicate will indicate when each computer, in turn, has stopped transmitting and is waiting for an answer. Most personal computer applications use Xon/Xoff, or software, handshaking (each computer sends a special character to indicate when it's finished sending), and Works defaults to this option when the dialog box first appears with each new document. Use Hardware Handshake when you transmit by means of a cable hooked directly to another computer.

The Phone Type setting lets you specify whether your telephone line uses rotary or Touch-Tone dialing. Most telephone systems support Touch-Tone dialing now, so that is the default setting. If your system uses rotary dialing, you'll have to change this option.

The Line Delay and Character Delay options let you place pauses in the transmission so that your computer will wait a specified number of seconds after transmitting each line or character. Normally, no line or character delay is needed, so the default entries here are 0. To enter a delay value, double-click in the Line Delay or Character Delay box to select it and then type the number of seconds you want. DO NOT press the Return key until you've finished changing settings; pressing Return confirms all the settings and makes the dialog box disappear.

The Capture Text When Document Opens option lets you tell Works to save the text it receives to a file on your disk. If you check this box when you store the communications settings, Works will display a dialog box that lets you specify the name and location of the file where you want to store the captured text.

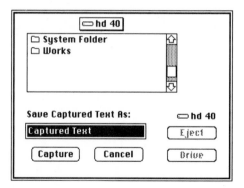

Works will display a dialog box like this one each time you open this communications document. If you don't check this option, Works won't ask you to name a captured text file when you open the document, but you can still capture text to a file at any time by choosing the Capture Text command from the Communications menu.

The Connect To area lets you specify which port your modem is using. Works assumes you connected your modem's data cable to the telephone port, and defaults to this option. If you connected your modem's data cable to the printer port (the one with the printer icon over it), click that option in the Connect To area.

To review, then, if you accept all the default settings in the Communications Settings dialog box, Works will instruct the modem to act like a TTY terminal, to send data at 1200 baud, using a format of eight data bits, one stop bit, and no parity bits, with Xon/Xoff handshaking, using a Touch-Tone phone system, with no line or character delays, and connect to the modem port on the Mac. Works will also set aside enough memory to save four screens of text, and it will ask you to name a file into which to save captured text each time you open the document.

To save these settings, click OK or press Return or Enter. When you do, the Settings dialog box disappears, and the file selection box is displayed, giving you a chance to name and specify a location for the captured text file. (If you have changed your mind and don't want to capture text from the session, click the Cancel button.)

When you decide about the captured text file, a blank communications document appears.

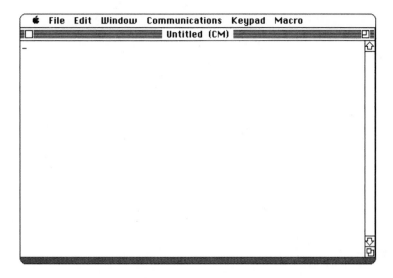

Calling another personal computer

Now you're ready to communicate. Let's assume you want to call a friend's computer. Be sure your modem is on and connected.

☐ Press Command-D or choose the Dial command from the Communications menu. A list of telephone number blanks appears.

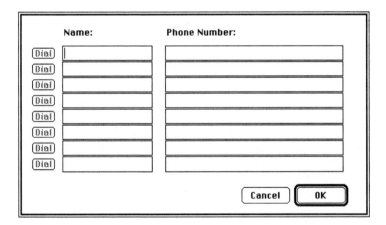

The telephone list can store up to eight names and phone numbers. When the phone list first appears, the insertion point is blinking in the first Name blank on the list, waiting for you to enter the name of the person or information service whose number you want to store. (If you want to follow along on your own computer with the example in this chapter, you'll need to enter a phone number—either an actual number of a friend with a modem or the fictitious number used in the example.) After you type in a name and telephone number and press the Return key, Works stores the name and number.

- Type the name *Joe Jones*, and press the Tab key. The insertion point moves to the Phone Number blank to the right.

- Type the phone number *5554545*, and press the Tab key. The insertion point moves to the Name blank in the second row, and the Dial button for the first name/number entry is no longer dimmed, indicating that you can now click this button to dial that number.

Notice that you didn't include a dash to separate the prefix in the phone number. When you enter phone numbers in Works, you don't need to use dashes between prefixes and area codes—simply type all the numbers one after another.

At this point, you could continue entering names and telephone numbers, or you could put the phone list away by clicking the OK button in the lower-right corner of the dialog box or by pressing the Return key. Instead, you want Works to dial Joe Jones's number.

- Click the Dial button next to Joe Jones's name. The phone list disappears, and the blank communications document screen is displayed again. Works reports that it is dialing the telephone number by displaying the message on the screen.

If Joe Jones's computer answers the phone (and his computer software is using the same settings as yours), his modem and your modem will exchange acknowledgment signals, and the message CONNECT will appear on your screen. You can then type messages on your Mac, and Joe's computer will receive them. If Joe types a message, you'll see it on your screen. Of course, typing messages while you're connected is a tedious process, so you may well want to send text files you have stored on disk. After you are connected, you can use some of the Communications menu's other options to send or receive data.

If you call Joe Jones or someone else frequently, you can store a macro that displays the telephone list and selects Joe's number to dial.

- ☐ Choose the Macros On command from the Macro menu.

- ☐ Press Option-+ (plus) to begin recording. The Start Recording dialog box is displayed.

- ☐ Type the letter *O* as the macro key and *Dial Joe Jones* as the description.

- ☐ Press Return or Enter to begin recording.

- ☐ Press Command-D to display the telephone list.

- ☐ Click on the Dial button next to Joe Jones' name.

- ☐ Press Option-– (hyphen) to display the Currently Recording dialog box, and then press Return or Enter to stop recording.

This macro is now stored. You can now dial Joe's number simply by pressing Option-O.

Calling an information service

For most individuals, commercial information services, such as CompuServe, Dow Jones News/Retrieval, or MCI Mail, are the main reason for communicating by means of a personal computer. These services are large mainframe computers that store thousands of computer files and programs, as varied as magazine excerpts, stock quotations, games, special-interest bulletin boards, and shop-at-home services. You can also use many commercial information services to communicate with other personal computer users, either in an online, interactive mode (in which you type a message, and the other user reads the message as you type and then responds to it), or through electronic mail (in which you send a message to another user's electronic mailbox to be read later).

To call a commercial information service, you need Works and a modem, of course, but you also need a password or other information that identifies you as a subscriber. Commercial services require you to have a subscription before you can use them, and the password or other user identification number you get when you subscribe lets you access, or log-on to, that system.

After you receive your password or other access information, look it over to familiarize yourself with how the information service works. In particular, learn how to issue commands to see various types of information, what to type to access the service, and how to exit the service when you've finished. When you're ready, use the following steps.

- ☐ Check your modem and cables to be sure everything is plugged in and turned on.

- ☐ Load Microsoft Works.

- ☐ Click on the Communications icon, and then click the New button. A blank communications document appears, with the Communications Settings dialog box displayed.

The information kit you get from the service to which you've subscribed will tell you how to set up your modem and communications program for proper communications. Most services let you transmit at either 300, 1200, or 2400 bps, and most services use 8-bit data with one stop bit and no parity bits. Every service accepts calls from TTY-type terminals. When you open a new communications document with Works, the Communications Settings box contains the default settings of TTY type, 1200 baud, eight data bits, one stop bit, and no parity bits, so you don't have to change these settings on the screen.

- ☐ The Handshake setting in the dialog box is automatically set to Xon/Xoff. This is also the type of handshaking commercial services use, so leave this setting as it is.

- ☐ Set the Phone Type option to match the type of telephone service you have, as in the previous example.

- ☐ With most information services, you don't need to specify a line delay or character delay when you transmit—the service can receive your data as fast as you can send it. These two delay options are set to zero automatically, so you don't need to change them.

- ☐ The Number of Screens setting defaults to 4 screens. Leave this setting as it is, unless you have a specific reason for increasing or decreasing it.

- ☐ The Capture Text When Document Opens setting is always checked when you open a new communications document. It's a good idea to capture what you receive from an information service, and with this box checked, Works will capture the data by default. You can then review the captured text file at your own pace after you disconnect from the service and are no longer paying its connect charges.

□ Set the Connect To option to match the port to which your modem is connected, as in the previous example.

□ Click the OK button or press Return or Enter to store these communications settings. The dialog box disappears, and you're ready to begin communicating.

□ Press Command-D or choose the Dial command from the Communications menu. The telephone list appears.

□ Type the name of the information service in the first name blank, and press the Tab key.

□ Type the telephone number of the information service in the Phone Number blank. Your information service might have different access telephone numbers for different parts of the country, so choose the one that is in your local dialing area.

□ After you type the phone number, the Dial button next to the top name/phone number line is shown in normal text (instead of gray text), indicating that you can now dial this number. Click the Dial button. The telephone list disappears, and Works dials the number you entered in the first blank.

If everything is working properly and your modem is equipped with a speaker, you will hear a dial tone, followed by the sound of the telephone number being dialed. When the commercial information service answers, you will hear a high-pitched acknowledgment signal. Your modem will respond with a similar sound, and you will be connected.

Just as we created a macro to dial the phone number for Joe Jones, you can follow the same procedure to store a macro that dials any information service.

At this point, the information service will prompt you to enter a user name, user number, or password. The prompt will look something like this:

User Name?

□ Type the user name you received in the service's information packet when you subscribed. You should be able to see the user name on your screen when you type it. If you can't see it, choose Echo On from the Communications menu. If, on the other hand, you see double letters (JJOONNEESS instead of JONES, for example), choose the Echo Off command from the Communications menu.

□ After you type the name, press the Return key. The information service will evaluate your entry to be sure it is valid, and then it will probably ask you for a password with a prompt something like this:

Password?

□ Type the password you were given when you subscribed to the information service. Usually, you can't see the password on your screen when you type it. This is to prevent someone from looking over your shoulder and learning your password. (If you can see your password on the screen as you type, choose the Echo Off command from the Communications menu.)

□ After you type the password, press the Return key.

After a few seconds, the information service will respond. If your user name and password are valid, you will see a message something like the following:

Welcome to MCI Mail

You are now connected to the system, and you can proceed to select options from the system's menus or issue commands to access information on the system.

TIP: You can record macros to store all or part of any information service log-on sequence. Depending on the service and how it presents its demand for your user name and password, you have to store your user name and password as separate macros, or you might be able to store them as one text string. Storing this log-on information as a macro assures that you will enter the information properly every time. Otherwise, if you type in a user name and password by hand and make an error, you'll have to go through the log-on sequence again. To store a user name macro, simply start recording the macro, type the text followed by a carriage return, and stop recording the macro.

If the system is particularly busy when you call, it might take some time for you to get a response to your typed commands or log-on information. Information services and other mainframe computers can handle dozens of users at the same time, but the more people using the computer, the longer it takes for the computer to respond. Be patient. It doesn't do any good to re-type information if you aren't getting a response as fast as you'd like—you'll only be transmitting those same characters again, and the system will have to respond to the second set of characters after it responds to the first set.

Sending files

You can transmit files with Works in one of two ways: You can send text, which is a stream of characters, symbols, or numbers without any formatting, or you can send a file, which is everything in a file, including formatting and program instructions. If you want to send only the data in a Works word-processor, spreadsheet, or database file, use the Send Text command. You can also send files created in other programs and then converted to text files, which allows you to send regular-text files to a different kind of computer or to another Macintosh that isn't using Works. Most word-processing programs have utilities that let you convert files from the program's standard format to regular-text format. If you want to send a word-processor file including its format commands or a spreadsheet or database file complete with its formulas and formatting, use the Send File command.

To send a text file, use the following steps.

☐ Choose the Send Text command from the Communications Menu. A list of files on the current disk drive is displayed, like this:

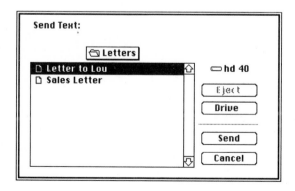

☐ Double-click on the name of the file you want to send. The file's contents are displayed on your screen as it is transmitted. When you see the last of your file displayed, you can then type further messages or send another file.

You can also send a formatted Works file, a Works word-processor file that contains a drawing, a MacPaint file, a BASIC program, another Mac program, the contents of a Scrapbook file, or another non-text file.

☐ Choose the Send File command from the Communications menu. A list of all the files on the current disk drive will be displayed, like this:

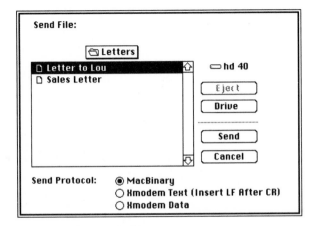

☐ Click on the Send Protocol option you want. The MacBinary protocol, the default, ensures error-free transmission of files between Macs using MacBinary. If you want to communicate with a computer other than a Mac or with one that isn't running software that has the MacBinary option, you need to use the Xmodem Text or Xmodem Data protocol. The Xmodem Text protocol is for transmitting text only; the Xmodem Data protocol is for transmitting text and formatting information (such as the specific layout of a word-processor, spreadsheet, or database file).

☐ Double-click on the name of the file you want to send, and the file will be sent. Instead of displaying the contents of the file on the screen, Works displays a status box that shows how much of the file has been transmitted.

```
Transmitting Letter to Lou with MacBinary Protocol

Press "⌘" plus "." to cancel the transfer.

Total Blocks:          34
Blocks Completed:       0    Retransmissions:      0
```

As the file is sent, the number of blocks transmitted increases until the number of blocks completed matches the total number of blocks to be sent. When the transmission is finished, you can type further instructions or send another file.

Receiving files

In addition to sending files, you can set up your Mac to receive files from another computer. Because you receive text and binary files using different protocols, you can use one of two different commands for receiving files in Works: Capture Text and Receive File. As explained earlier, in the section on setting up a communications document, you can set Works to ask you to name a captured text file (and then open that file) whenever you open a communications document. A captured text file can store the text data that is displayed on your screen as your Mac receives it. If you don't set up a captured text file when you open a communications document, you can always do it during a communications session with the Capture Text command.

To capture a text file, use the following steps.

☐ Choose the Capture Text command from the Communications menu. A dialog box will appear, asking you to type the name of the file in which you want to save the captured text.

☐ Type a name for the file. If you don't type a file name, Works will save the file with the name Captured Text.

☐ Click the Capture button or press the Return key. The dialog box disappears, and you're returned to the communications screen. Everything that appears on your screen from this point on will be saved to a file on disk under the name you specified.

Works won't begin saving the text it receives until you choose the Capture Text command, name the file, and then click the Capture button in the dialog box. Any data that was on your screen before you perform these steps will not be saved on disk (although you might be able to scroll back up to it, select it, and copy it to the Clipboard if you have

Works set to save screens). Still, it's important to open a captured-text file before you begin receiving the data you want to store. If you're about to look at the text of an article on an information service, for example, be sure to open a captured-text file before you give the command that starts displaying the article's text on your screen. As mentioned before, it's best to simply open a captured-text file as soon as you open your communications document whenever you call an information service. That way, you'll always have a disk file that contains whatever text you receive. You can delete unwanted material from the captured-text file later.

After you capture all the text you want (after you receive all of an article or electronic mail message, for example), you must close the captured-text file. The file can then be opened as a Works word-processor file, letting you review or edit its contents. To close a captured-text file, do the following.

□ Choose the End Text Capture command from the Communications menu. Works closes the text file and lets you continue with your communications session.

Closing a captured-text file does not end a communications session. If you wanted, you could capture some text, end the text capture, capture text to a new file, end the text capture, and so on, without disconnecting. If you wanted to capture three separate articles from an information service, for example, you might want to save each article in a file with a different name. You can open and close one captured-text file after another without ending the communications session. However, you can't open a captured-text file with the Works word processor until you have ended the text capture with the communications program.

Sometimes, you might want to receive a non-text file, or a text file that includes formatting, spreadsheet formulas, or database layouts. A friend might want to send you a BASIC program or a MacPaint drawing, for example. To receive a non-text file, use the following steps.

□ Before the other computer begins sending the file, choose the Receive File command from the Communications menu. A dialog box appears, letting you specify the name of the file in which you want to save the incoming information.

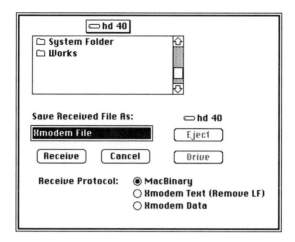

□ Type a file name for the receive file, and choose a Receive Protocol option.

□ Click the Receive button.

□ After you specify the file name, a status box appears, showing the total number of blocks in the incoming file and the number of blocks received as they come in.

When you've finished receiving a file, you must end the receive operation by choosing the Cancel Receive command from the Communications menu or by pressing the Command and period (.) keys at the same time.

□ Choose the Cancel Receive command from the Communications menu (or press Command-.). The receive file will be closed.

As with capturing text, you can't work with a received file until you close it. Also, closing a receive file doesn't disconnect you from the remote computer.

Ending a communications session

To end a communications session, you must hang up the phone, just as you do at the end of a telephone conversation.

□ Press Command-= (equals) or choose the Hang Up command from the Communications menu. The screen shows the message Hanging Up..., and then displays the message OK after the phone line is disconnected. Whenever the phone line is disconnected, for whatever reason, the screen displays the message NO CARRIER, to let you know that you're no longer in contact with the remote computer.

When you're calling another personal computer, ending the session is simply a matter of hanging up. However, when you call a commercial information service or electronic-mail utility, it's best to log off the service before you hang up. Each commercial service has a special log-off command (such as BYE, EXIT, LOGOFF, or QUIT) that lets the remote computer know you are ending your session. Most services have a time-out feature that disconnects if you have not issued any commands for a few minutes. But if you don't log off such a service, you might be charged for the few minutes between the time you hang up and the time its time-out feature tells it to disconnect from you.

Answering an incoming call

You can set your Mac to answer a phone call from somebody else's computer.

□ Choose Answer Phone from the Communications menu.

The following message will appear on the screen:

Setting modem to answer calls

This message tells you that your modem will answer the phone.

Maximizing Works Communications

The Works communications tool is a fairly basic Macintosh communications program. By combining the communications program's features with Works' integrated power and its macro feature, you can handle most of your communications tasks. The following are a few tips for making the most of the communications module.

Store several phone numbers in one document

Each Works communications document has room for eight telephone numbers. Because the communications settings are the same for many commercial information services and other personal computers, you can store several phone numbers in one document's phone list and use the common group of settings for any of them.

If you spend much of your online time communicating with different types of computers, it might make sense to create separate communications documents that store groups of phone numbers: perhaps one for information services, one for business associates, one for bulletin boards, and so on. However, Works lets you have only one communication document open at a time.

Use macros to automate operations

We've already seen how you can create macros that dial certain telephone numbers or enter your user name or password after you're connected to an information service. But that's only the beginning of what you can do with macros in the communications application. If you regularly issue the same commands to an information service after you log on, you can store those commands as a macro, too. If you always scan your mailbox for new mail when you log onto MCI Mail, for example, you can create a macro to scan for your mail, and thereby avoid having to type the command each time.

Another useful type of macro is one that simply displays the telephone list and dials a certain number. Unlike many other communications programs, Works doesn't re-dial phone numbers that are busy or don't answer. If you've defined a macro to dial a certain number, however, you can quickly re-dial the number when you need to.

After you begin creating macros for communications, be sure to save them in a separate macro file. Having a separate file lets you use any of the available macro keys for new macros, rather than having to share the keys with macros you might have defined for the spreadsheet, word processor, Draw tool, or database. In fact, you might want to store sets of macros specific to individual information services in different macro files, if you end up defining a lot of macros for each service.

You can't create a macro that will turn the macro feature on or one that opens a macro file. You'll have to remember to perform these functions manually to access the group of macros you want before you can begin using them.

Use other applications during long file transfers

Works' communications application will continue to operate in the background if you activate another document. If you start sending a file to another computer, for example, and you know it will take 5 or 10 minutes to complete the transfer, you don't have to sit and wait: You can open a database, spreadsheet, or word-processor document and work on something else while the communications application continues transferring the file behind the scenes. It's a simple matter to activate the communications document from the Window menu periodically to check the progress of the file transfer so you know when it is complete.

Use the MacBinary protocol for formatted file transfers

The MacBinary transfer protocol in Send File or Receive File dialog box lets you transfer files in their native format between your Mac and another Mac which is also using the MacBinary protocol. Rather than transferring only text characters, you can send graphics files, programs, spreadsheets or databases (complete with all their reports, formatting, and formulas intact), and other complete files. Even if you're simply transferring a word-processor file to another MacBinary-compatible computer, it makes sense to use MacBinary because it saves the person receiving the file from having to re-format it when it arrives.

MacBinary is also a far more reliable transfer method than Xmodem. Even normal noises on a telephone line can cause some of the text characters in a file to become garbled when you send by using Xmodem, but sending with the MacBinary protocol will eliminate such errors by retransmitting any blocks of data in which errors are found.

Use the Clipboard to store incoming text

If you've forgotten to set up a captured-text file and find you want to save some text that has just scrolled across your screen during a communications session, all is not lost. Assuming you've left the Number Of Screens option set to 4 in the settings of the document you're using, you'll be able to scroll the communications window back up to view the text again. When the text is in view, select it and copy it to the Clipboard, and then open a new word-processor document and paste the text into it. With the text safely stored in a word-processor document, you can continue with your communications session. And because the communications tool runs in the background, you don't have to worry about disconnecting from the remote computer when you copy the text to a word-processor document: When you return to the communications document, you'll still be connected.

Reformat communications text in the word processor

Unlike the other Works applications, communications documents only display text in one font, 9-point Geneva. After you receive text, however, you can either copy it to the Clipboard (as described earlier) and then into a word-processor document, or you can open a captured-text file with the word processor directly. When your communications data is in the word processor, you can change the font, style, and formatting in a variety of ways.

Use special software when it has special advantages

The Works communications application is fairly versatile and has the decided advantage of being integrated with other productivity tools, but sometimes you might need software specifically designed for communicating with a particular remote computer. Desktop Express, for example, is a program for dialing MCI Mail, and it does far more than simply dial a telephone number. Desktop Express lets you create MCI Mail messages before you're connected and then send them automatically after you log on. It retrieves any messages you have waiting on the service. Finally, it can send programs, graphics files, and formatted spreadsheet, database, and word-processor files intact to MCI Mail, where they can be retrieved intact by other Mac owners using Desktop Express. (Works' MacBinary protocol can also send files with their formats intact, but MCI Mail doesn't support this protocol.)

Other services, such as CompuServe, Dow Jones News/Retrieval, and MacNet, have their own special terminal programs as well, and these offer the same types of advanced features as Desktop Express. In some programs—such as CompuServe Navigator, the software for CompuServe—the special program can send and receive files using a proprietary error-correcting protocol that Works doesn't support.

Essentially, however, the main advantage of all such programs is that they let you plan your interaction with the information service before you log on, and then they execute that plan. The software can issue commands to the information service more quickly than you can (and without errors), minimizing the amount of time you're actually connected to the service, and reducing your communications charges.

But despite the automated features of these special programs, there are times when you can use Works to better advantage. If you use MCI Mail or CompuServe's EasyPlex regularly, for example, and are waiting for a message from one person in particular, you could use Works to log onto the service, scan your mailbox for a message from that person, and quickly retrieve only that message. If you used Desktop Express or CompuServe Navigator instead, those programs would retrieve all the mail you had waiting.

Test your connection before transferring data

If you plan to send or receive a file from another personal computer, test the connection first by typing *Hello* or some other text, and then wait for the person at the other computer to respond. This lets you know that you're both sending and receiving properly before you send a file.

Don't forget to activate the file-capture or file-receive feature

Remember, you can't save incoming data to disk unless you set up a captured-text file or turn on the Receive File feature in Works. Be sure you do this before the transfer begins, and be sure to choose the End Text Capture or the Cancel Receive command to close the receiving file before you close the communications document.

Stick to a troubleshooting plan

Personal computer communications are ripe with the potential for problems because of all the different levels of interaction described at the beginning of this chapter. The following is a troubleshooting sequence that will help you isolate the particular problem you're having.

- □ Check your modem. Be sure the modem-to-Mac cable is securely connected to the modem and the telephone port on your Mac. Be sure the telephone cable is connected from the proper jack on the modem (the one labeled Line, if there are two jacks) to the wall. Be sure the modem's power cable is plugged in and that the power switch is on.

- □ Check your telephone line. Hook a normal telephone up to your modem's phone line and dial your own or a friend's number to ascertain that the line is, in fact, working.

- □ Check your modem settings in the communications document. In particular, be sure you have selected the phone port on your Mac and either TouchTone or Rotary Dial service, depending on the type of telephone you have. Be sure you've set the baud rate to a rate your modem supports.

If you've checked these three items, you should at least be able to make your modem dial a telephone number and connect with another computer. If you can't, you are probably using a modem that is not a Hayes compatible, and whose internal command set is so different from the Hayes command set that Works can't communicate with it.

If you can dial the remote computer but get garbled text, no response, or are abruptly disconnected, try the following steps.

☐ Check the Data Size, Stop Bits, Parity, and Handshake settings. These are almost always the culprit when the data you send to or receive from another computer is garbled. You will probably have to disconnect from the remote computer, change the settings, and dial again to establish proper contact. If you can, consult the information service's manual or call the owner of the remote computer to find out which data size, stop bit, and parity settings his or her computer is set for.

☐ Check the Echo On and Echo Off settings on the Communications menu. You might be connected properly and are simply unable to see what you're typing because you have the wrong echo setting.

If you've done all of these steps and are still having problems, the problem probably isn't with your Mac or with Works. You might have a noisy telephone line that is preventing you from sending or receiving data reliably, or the remote computer itself might be having problems. If so, try the call again later.

Communications Specifications

The following are some specifications you may want to refer to as you use the communications module:

Maximum size of sent and received files: Limited by the amount of available disk space.

Maximum number of saved screens: 100, but limited by the amount of available RAM.

Maximum number of stored telephone numbers per document: 8.

Error-correcting protocols available: MacBinary, Xmodem Text, Xmodem Data.

Default font: 9-point Geneva.

Number of fonts available: 1.

Chapter 10

Using Works As a System

Each of the Works applications is powerful by itself, but you can use these applications together to perform more complex tasks. You can easily move data from one Works application to another—or between Works and other programs—to create a data-handling environment that lets you work with information in the format and with the tools that best suit you. In this chapter, we'll cover the basics of moving data between applications, and then we'll look at several examples that show how this capability can help you.

Moving Data with Works

You can move data from one Works application to another or between Works and other programs in three ways: by cutting and pasting data through the Clipboard; by merging database data into the word processor; and by exporting or importing files. Let's look at each of these methods in general before we see how they can be used to perform a variety of personal and business tasks.

Using the Clipboard

The simplest way to move data from one Works application to another is to use the Clipboard. The general procedure is the same, no matter which two applications you're using.

- Open the file from which you want to copy data (or activate that file, if it's already open on the desktop).

- Select the data you want to copy by holding down the mouse button and dragging the pointer across it.

- Press Command-C or choose the Copy command from the Edit menu. This copies the data to the Clipboard.

- Open or activate the file to which you want to copy the data.

- Move the insertion point or selection to the place in the file where you want the data to appear.

- Press Command-V or choose the Paste command from the Edit menu. The data will be inserted into the file.

You can use either the Copy or Cut command to place data on the Clipboard (except in spreadsheet charts, where only the Copy command is available). As mentioned in earlier chapters, the Copy command places a copy of the selected text on the Clipboard, leaving the original data intact in the file. The Cut command removes the original data from the file and places it on the Clipboard. Each Works application handles data copied from other applications a little differently, as we'll see next.

Moving Data to the Word Processor

The word processor is the most logical place to integrate or combine data from other Works applications because it has the most formatting flexibility. When you paste spreadsheet, database, or communications data into the word processor, the data appears in the format it had in the original file. For example, the word processor inserts tab stops to separate columns of numbers or data from the database or from the spreadsheet.

When you insert data between two blocks of word-processor text, the lower block of text moves down to accommodate the inserted data. Inserted data always appears in the font, size, style, and (for color Mac users) color it had in the document from which you copied it. So, if the surrounding text is in a different font, size, or style, and you want the inserted data to match, you need to reformat it.

After data is pasted into a word-processor file, you can edit it as you would any other word-processor text. The data you paste becomes text, and any mathematical relationships, formulas, data attributes, or calculated fields from spreadsheet or database documents disappear when the data is moved to the word processor. If you copy a column of spreadsheet numbers containing a Sum formula into the word processor, for example, the formula will disappear, and the column will no longer recalculate automatically if you change one of the column's values, as it would in the spreadsheet.

Along with this change in the nature of the data, the format of pasted data is a consideration in the word processor. Data you paste into the word processor from the spreadsheet or database file may be wider than the word processor's current line-width settings allow. (After all, spreadsheets of database files can be dozens of columns or fields wide.) If you paste spreadsheet or database data into the word processor, the data will be inserted, and the line-width setting in the word processor will change to accept the new data. If you have a word-processor document set for 6½-inch-wide lines and you paste in spreadsheet or database data that is 11 inches wide, for example, the formatting in the section containing the inserted data will adjust itself to an 11-inch line.

However, the word processor allows documents only up to 15 inches wide. So, if the spreadsheet or database data you insert is wider than 15 inches, the data will wrap around on the screen. Here's what spreadsheet data wider than 15 inches looks like when pasted into a word-processor document:

The Dec label and total, which should be on the same line as the rest of the monthly labels and totals, have wrapped down to the next line because this selection from the spreadsheet is wider than 15 inches.

If the data is wider than the maximum width of a word-processor document, you can't make more room for it by widening the line. To make the data fit, you have to reformat the data itself so that it takes up less space. You might be able to delete some of the space between columns. But in some cases, there will simply be too much data to fit into the word-processor document properly, and you'll have to delete some data from the pasted selection.

To delete space between columns, move the insertion point into the line in which you want to eliminate space between columns, and then drag the tab stops in the ruler closer together. (The word processor inserts tab stops to maintain the original columnar formatting of the spreadsheet data.) As you drag the tab stops closer together, the columns will move closer together.

When you copy database data to the word processor, it's best to copy from the list window, where you can select several records or several fields by highlighting them before you use the Copy command. You can copy only one field of data at a time from a form window. When you copy data from a database file, the data from each field appears with the appropriate field name above it in boldface, like this:

Club Members (DB)

FirstName	LastName	Address	Date	Format	Genre
Jackie	Rae	339 Mountain Dr.		VHS	Adventure
Ed	Bernstein	9975 Francis Dr.		VHS	Adventure
Joe	Brubaker	12235 Cloverly		VHS	Adventure
Randy	Coleman	15 Derby St., #12		VHS	Adventure
Marc	Caselica	2213 Front St.		VHS	Adventure
Mikkel	Aaland	339 Clifford St.		VHS	Adventure

Untitled (WP)

FirstName	LastName	Address	City	ST	Zip	Phone	Mer
Jackie	Rae	339 Mountain Dr.	Willow	CA	94555	555-1000	0000
Ed	Bernstein	9975 Francis Dr.	San Bruno	CA	94321	555-1900	0000
Joe	Brubaker	12235 Cloverly	Templeton	CA	93231	408-999-9999	0000
Randy	Coleman	15 Derby St., #12	Willow	CA	94555	555-9898	000
Marc	Caselica	2213 Front St.	Willow	CA	94555	555-9790	000
Mikkel	Aaland	339 Clifford St.	San Francisco	CA	94440	555-2121	000
Jefferson	Miller	159 10th Ave., #14	Belmont	CA	93333	555-2398	000

You can also paste individual cells, columns, rows, or blocks of spreadsheet data into the word processor. In addition to spreadsheet data, you can also copy spreadsheet charts to the Clipboard for use in the word processor. To copy a chart, follow these steps.

□ Open or activate the spreadsheet file.

□ Create a new chart or use the Draw Chart command from the Chart menu to draw a chart.

□ Press Command-C or choose the Copy command from the Edit menu. (You can't use the Cut command in a chart window.) This action copies the chart to the Clipboard.

□ Open or activate the word-processor file.

□ Move the insertion point to the place in the word-processor document where you want the chart to appear.

□ Press Command-V or choose the Paste command from the Edit menu. The chart is inserted into the word-processor document, like this:

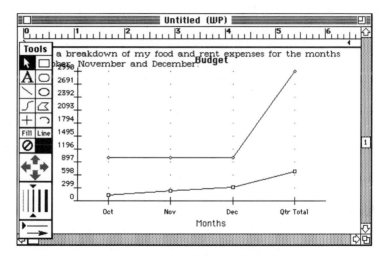

Unlike spreadsheet data, spreadsheet charts are not converted to word-processor text when you paste them from the Clipboard. Instead, they're pasted as complete drawings, and they activate the Draw tool in the word processor after you paste them in. You can use the Draw tool to move or resize a chart, but the only way to edit a chart's contents is to draw something different on top of the items you want to edit.

When you paste a spreadsheet chart into a word-processor document, Works tries to place the chart so that you can see as much of it as possible on the screen. On a Mac Plus or Mac SE screen, this requirement might necessitate placing part of the chart on top of the text in the document, as shown in the preceding example. But because the chart is a drawing, it is stored independently of the text, and you can select the chart with the Draw tool on and then drag the chart down lower in the document so that it doesn't obscure any text.

Pasting to the Spreadsheet

In most cases, you'll want to paste only spreadsheet data into a spreadsheet. But at times, you'll want to move database or word-processor data to the spreadsheet format. If you begin a file in the database and then realize you want the additional calculating flexibility the spreadsheet offers, for example, you can move the data to the spreadsheet.

When you paste any kind of data into the spreadsheet, Works always inserts the data at the selected cell (or in the upper-left corner of a selected block), extending down and to the right of the selected cell. For example, if you select cell B3 in a spreadsheet file before pasting data, Works will insert the data into cell B3 and will fill some of the cells below and to the right of B3 with the data, depending on how much room is necessary. Of course, you can also select rows, columns, or blocks in a spreadsheet as the destination for pasted data.

One possible complication with pasting data into the spreadsheet, unlike pasting into the word processor, is that existing data doesn't move out of the way to accommodate data you're pasting in. If you select an occupied cell as the place for inserting data or if cells are filled in the area where pasted data will appear, Works will display this warning message:

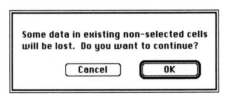

If you proceed with the paste operation, the existing data will be overwritten (replaced by the pasted data). When you paste data into the spreadsheet, therefore, be sure enough empty cells exist in the area where you're pasting.

When you copy data from the word processor to the spreadsheet, text is treated as label data, and numbers are treated as values. Because you are copying from a file that has lines containing words of varying lengths into a spreadsheet with strict cells, rows, and columns, you have to format the word-processor data so that the spreadsheet knows where to place it. Word-processor text separated by tab stops is placed in separate cells in the spreadsheet, and text separated by carriage returns is placed in separate rows in the spreadsheet. Suppose you copy text and three columns of numbers from a word-processor document like this:

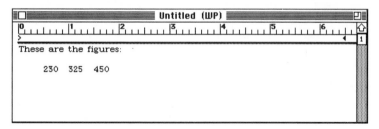

If you select cell A1 in the spreadsheet and then paste the data from the Clipboard, the spreadsheet will arrange the data like this:

	A	B	C	D	E	F
1	These are the figures:					
2						
3		230	325	450		
4						
5						
6						
7						
8						
9						

The first line of text is treated as one label entry, so it all goes into one expanded cell. Long lines of pasted text will expand into as many spreadsheet cells as are necessary. Because two carriage returns separate the text line from the numbers, the numbers are inserted two rows down. And because the numbers have tab stops between them, each number is placed in a separate column. Also, there's a tab stop before the row of numbers in the word-processor document, so the spreadsheet begins inserting the numbers in column B.

When copying data from the database, be sure the list window is showing before you select the data. As mentioned earlier, the list window lets you select any combination of fields or records from the file, and its row-and-column setup matches that of the spreadsheet. When you paste database data into a spreadsheet, each entry in a field fills one cell, and each record becomes a row in the spreadsheet. The database data appears along with the boldface field names. You can delete the field names by selecting the cells in which they appear and using the Clear command. Information that was text in the database becomes label data in the spreadsheet, and numbers from the database become values.

Pasting to the Database

The database treats incoming data from other applications as text, unless you've specified a particular data type (using the Set Field Attributes command) for a certain field. If you have specified alternate data types (date, time, or numbers), the incoming data must match that data type. If you are pasting spreadsheet numbers into a database file and two of the fields are set up for date and time data, for example, Works will display a dialog box saying the transfer of data into fields with different data types did not take place, and those fields will remain blank.

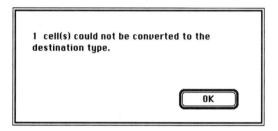

When you paste data into a database file, the data also is accepted or rejected according to the amount of room available. Data from spreadsheet columns is placed in fields in a database file, and data from rows is placed in records. If there aren't enough fields in a database file, not all of the pasted information will transfer. If you try to copy five columns of spreadsheet data into a database file that contains only three fields, the rightmost two spreadsheet columns won't be transferred. And, if you try to paste data into a place where it will overwrite existing data in a database file, Works will display a warning.

You can inadvertently arrange a database file so that not enough fields are available for the pasted data, even if the file contains enough fields. Suppose you want to copy these three columns of numbers from a word-processor file:

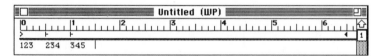

And let's suppose that the database file where you want to paste these numbers contains three fields, like this:

First Number	Second Number	Third Number	

If you select the First Number field in the list window as the insertion point before pasting the data, then all three numbers will be pasted into a new record in order. The number 123 will go into the First Number field, 234 will go into Second Number, and 345 will go into Third Number. But if you select the Second Number field, the first two numbers will go into the Second Number and Third Number fields, and the third number will be left out.

When you move word-processor text to a database file, the database treats the text exactly as the spreadsheet does: All text separated by tab stops is placed in separate fields, and text separated by carriage returns is placed in separate records. If you had a database file containing two fields (Name and Phone), for example, you would have to format word-processor text like this to transfer it properly:

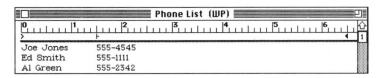

Here, the names and phone numbers are separated by a tab stop, and each name/phone number (or record) is on a separate line (separated by a carriage return). You have to be careful about how word-processor text is formatted if you want it to transfer properly to the database file.

Merging database data with the word processor

The second way to move data from one Works application to another is by merging. This feature is available only for merging data from a database file into a word-processor document. To merge data, you must have two files open on the desktop—both the database file from which you want to get the data and the word-processor file into which you want to merge the data. You select fields from the database file to merge with the word-processor document, and all the work is done in the word-processor document by the Prepare to Merge command. The procedure is described in detail in Chapter 4.

As we'll see in the examples that follow this overview, the merge feature can be quite powerful. You can merge data from several database files at once (provided that they're all open on the desktop), and you can use the database's record-selection features to merge data only from certain records. If you want to send a form letter to all of your customers who are past due in their payments, for example, you can merge the name, address, and payment amount fields from a database file and then use the database file's record-selection features to merge data only from the records of delinquent customers.

Importing and exporting text files

The Works applications can make use of files created by other programs by importing them, and you can format Works files so that they can be used by other programs by exporting them. The word processor and database can both import and export text files. Along with files saved in text format from any other Mac program, the word processor can import files from MacWrite (versions 5.0 or earlier) or Microsoft Word (version 1.0 only). The database can import standard text files or files from Microsoft File. The importing procedure in the word processor is simple.

□ Choose the Open command from the File menu.

□ Click the Word Processor icon.

□ Click the Import File box. You will see a listing of all the text files, MacWrite files, and Microsoft Word version 1.0 files on the current disk.

□ Double-click on the name of the file you want to import. The file will be converted to a new, untitled Works word-processor file, which will then be displayed.

In the database, this procedure is a little more complicated. The database also works with text files, but text files don't have a row-and-column format like the database. So you must tell the database how to treat the incoming text data. When you try to import a text file into a new database file, Works displays a dialog box that asks you to specify the format of the incoming text file, like this:

```
┌─────────────────────────────────────────────┐
│  Separate Database Fields By:                 │
│                                               │
│  ⊙ Tabs (Each Record Ended By A Return)       │
│  ○ Two Or More Spaces (Treated As A Tab)      │
│  ○ Returns    [      ]   Field(s) Per Record  │
│                                               │
│                     ( Cancel )  (( OK ))      │
└─────────────────────────────────────────────┘
```

As you can see, Works separates text information into fields and records according to how each word or group of words is separated from the others. The Tabs option tells Works that data separated by tab stops in the text file should be placed in separate fields in the database file. The Two Or More Spaces option tells Works that groups of data separated by two or more spaces should be placed in separate database fields. The Returns option means that groups of data separated by carriage returns should go in separate fields. When you use the Returns option, you must tell Works how many database fields to create from the information. When a file's data is separated by carriage returns, the database needs some way of determining where one record ends and the next one begins. To see why, let's look at the following list of two addresses:

Joe Jones
123 1st St.
Morris, CA 95003
Fred Smith
383 Alvin Dr.
San Carlos, CA 94504

Each line in this list ends with a carriage return, so Works will put each line into a separate field if you don't tell it otherwise. In this case, you want two records with three fields in each record, so you need to specify the number of fields in the Field(s) Per Record box.

In many cases, you won't know the exact format of a text file you're importing. If you don't, try the three different format options. If the format of the resulting database file isn't right when you choose one format option, close the file without saving it and try another format option.

For exporting text files, the word processor offers two file format options (standard text and Rich Text); the database offers only one (standard text). The general procedure is the same in either case:

- Choose the Save As command from the File menu. The Save As dialog box appears.

- Click the Export button (and then click the Export As Rich Text Format box if you want to use this option with a word processor file).

- Type a name for the file that is different from the name of the standard Works file.

□ Press the Return or Enter key. The file is saved as text (or Rich Text), and it can be loaded by another program that uses that format.

Saving a word-processor file as standard text stores it as a stream of characters in which carriage returns retain their original positions. Saving a word-processor file as a Rich Text Format (RTF) file stores it with all the characters as well as its original formatting information. RTF is a format that several other Macintosh and MS-DOS programs, including other Microsoft programs such as Word, can read.

When you save a database file as text, Works separates field entries with tab stops, and it separates records with carriage returns. Also, the database saves the field names as the first record (or first line of text) in the file. By clicking the Save Selected Records Only box in the Save As dialog box, you can save only the selected records currently shown in the document (using the Record Selection or the Match Records command) when you export a database file.

Importing and Exporting Spreadsheet Files

You can import or export spreadsheet files either as SYLK files or as text files. SYLK is a special file-transfer format developed by Microsoft for its products that lets you exchange data between Works and other Microsoft software, such as Multiplan and Microsoft Excel. SYLK files contain text and numbers, but they also contain formulas. Thus, you can import a SYLK file made from a Microsoft Excel spreadsheet, for example, and begin working with it right away, as if it had been created with Works.

Microsoft Excel and Multiplan have some features that Works doesn't, however. If you've used some of these extra features in files you've imported from Microsoft Excel or Multiplan, they won't work in the Works spreadsheet. When Works is unable to use a Multiplan or Microsoft Excel formula, it places quotation marks around the formula and presents it as a label. Appendix B of the Microsoft Works User's Guide has more information about the limitations of using Multiplan or Microsoft Excel SYLK files with Works.

Text files can contain numbers, words, and formulas. If you import a text file, Works will place all the data separated by tab stops in separate columns and all the data separated by carriage returns in different rows. Numbers are converted to values in the spreadsheet; text becomes labels. If text is written in exactly the same format as a formula, such as =C3+C4, Works converts such text into a formula in the spreadsheet.

To import a text file or a SYLK file into the spreadsheet, use the following steps.

☐ Choose the Open command.

☐ Click on the Spreadsheet icon.

☐ Click the Import File box. A list of SYLK and text files on the current disk drive is displayed.

☐ Double-click on the name of the SYLK or text file you want to load. A dialog box appears, asking whether you are importing a SYLK file or a text file. Click the appropriate option.

☐ Press Return or click the OK button. A new Works spreadsheet file containing the converted text or SYLK data opens.

When you export a file from the Works spreadsheet, you have three options. You can export the file as a SYLK file, for use in Microsoft Excel or Multiplan; you can export it as a text file with labels and values only; or you can export it as a text file with labels, values, and formulas. To export a file, use the following steps.

☐ Choose the Save As command from the File menu.

☐ Click the Export File box.

☐ Type a name for the file that is different from the original Works file's name.

☐ Click the Save button. A dialog box appears, asking you to choose one of the three possible formats for the file.

☐ Click the export format option you want (SYLK, text with values only, or text with values and formulas).

☐ Click the OK button or press the Return key to save the file.

Importing AppleWorks files

Microsoft Works version 2.0 comes with a utility program, called the Works-Works Transporter, which can convert AppleWorks files into Microsoft Works files. To use the Works-Works Transporter, you must first convert the original AppleWorks file to a Macintosh-compatible file format on a 3.5-inch disk, using the Apple File Exchange utility program. After you convert the AppleWorks file with Apple File Exchange, you can use the Works-Works Transporter to convert AppleWorks word processor, spreadsheet, or database files into files compatible with these applications in Works. For further information, see Appendix B of the Microsoft Works User's Guide.

Now, let's look at some examples of Works' data-movement techniques in action.

Exchanging Word-Processor Files Between Works and MacWrite

Suppose Al Chroma and a friend are working on a screenplay together. Al is using the Works word processor, and his friend is using MacWrite version 5.0. If Al wants to use his friend's MacWrite files in Works, he'll have to import them.

- ☐ Load Works.

- ☐ Click on the Word Processor icon.

- ☐ Click the Import File box. A list of MacWrite, Word, and other text files on the current disk appears. If the file you want isn't on this disk, either click the Eject button and insert the correct disk or click the Drive button to view the directory of the disk in the other drive.

- ☐ Double-click on the name of the file you want to import. Works loads the file and opens it as an untitled word-processor document.

If Al wants to save one of his Works word-processor files in a format that his friend can use in MacWrite, he can export the file.

- ☐ Open the file you want to export.

- ☐ Choose the Save As command from the File menu. The Save As dialog box appears, asking you to type a name for the file.

If you want to save the exported file on a disk other than the one in the current drive (you might put the file on a blank disk so that you can mail the disk to your friend, for example), you can insert another disk or change drives and save the file with the name it already has. But if you're saving the exported file on the disk containing the original file, give the file a different name so that you don't overwrite the original.

- ☐ Type a name for the file.

- ☐ Click the Export File box.

□ Click the Save button, press Return, or press Enter to save the file. The file is saved in a text format that can be read by MacWrite.

You can share your Works files with many other word-processing programs on the Macintosh or with other computers by exporting them. If you are sharing the file with a person who has a modem, you can transmit the file as a communications document with the Send Text command. Word-processor files you transmit by using the Send Text command have the same format as files you export onto a disk.

Using a Text File in the Database

Now let's suppose Al Chroma has been elected secretary/treasurer of the Classic Film Club. When he took over his duties with the club, he had to get the membership file from Ed Green, the outgoing secretary/treasurer, who had maintained them with a database program on a different kind of computer. Al wants to use Ed's database so that he doesn't have to type the membership list into his Mac. Fortunately, Ed has stored the file as text, so he can transmit it to Al by means of a modem. For the purposes of this exercise, we'll simulate the file Ed transmits to Al by creating a text file that's much like a file Ed might transmit to Al by modem. We'll create this file by exporting data from a database file. After we create the text file, we'll use it to create a new database file. The original database file we'll use is shown in Figure 10-1.

Name	Last Dues Paid	Address	City	ST	Zip	Phone	Member #
Marc Caselica	Nov 27, 1988	2213 Front St.	Willow	CA	94555	555-9790	00012
Mikkel Aaland	Sep 18, 1988	339 Clifford St.	San Francisco	CA	94440	555-2121	00015
Jefferson Miller	Oct 14, 1988	159 10th Ave., #14	Belmont	CA	93333	555-2398	00016
Fran Marple	Nov 18, 1988	353 Country Villa Ln.	Milpitas	CA	94444	408-555-1345	00006
Millard Cuvee	Sep 19, 1988	233 Portnoy St.	Burlingame	CA	94435	555-0878	00019
Toni Walker	May 15, 1988	5050 Camino Diablo	San Mateo	CA	94550	555-5555	00021
Daniel Collins	May 30, 1988	206 Cornell St.	Willow	CA	94555	555-1002	00002
David Richards	Jun 15, 1988	1705 Oxton Ct.	San Mateo	CA	94550	555-1003	00003
Steve Wong	Jun 12, 1988	42 Jackson St.	Willow	CA	94555	555-0023	00017
Madelyn Korbut	Nov 22, 1988	957 Oak Park Dr., #4	Willow	CA	94555	555-0978	00020
Linda Feldman	Nov 30, 1988	11223 S. Harper	Brisbane	CA	94556	555-5454	00013
Bud Snooter	Dec 5, 1988	10327 Park Hills Dr.	San Jose	CA	93336	408-555-1222	00005
Elias Ata	Dec 16, 1988	129 Claremont St.	Mountain View	CA	94343	555-1609	00007
Denise Villalobos	Dec 22, 1988	82 Piedmont Ave., #24	Oakland	CA	94666	555-1001	00001
Diana Levy	Nov 23, 1988	12 Kensington Terr., #3B	So. San Francisco	CA	91212	555-1323	00010
Sheryl Janda	Sep 19, 1988	7035 Thornhill	Redwood City	CA	95432	555-3536	00014
Volga Breszlaw	Sep 21, 1988	554 Green St.	Willow	CA	94555	555-9001	00018

Figure 10-1.
A membership database file.

☐ Create a new database file, and define fields for Name, Last Dues Paid, Address, City, ST, Zip, Phone, and Member #.

☐ Type in the 17 records shown in Figure 10-1.

☐ Choose the Save As command from the File menu, click the Export button, type the file name *Members.text,* and then click the Save button to save the file to a disk.

☐ Save the new database file you created with the name *Members,* and close it.

We'll use the Members file again later.

☐ Choose the Open command, click the Word Processor icon, click the Import File box, and then select *Members.text* from the list of files that appears. The database data will open into a word-processor file, like this:

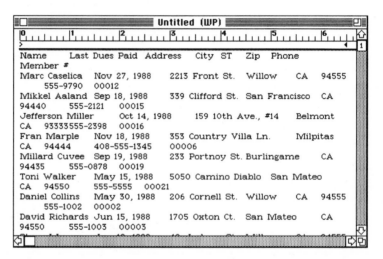

This new text file is much like the one Al Chroma would receive by modem from Ed Green, so we can use it to continue this exercise. Before we do, however, let's go over the steps Al would take to actually receive the text file using Works' communications function.

☐ Open a new communications document.

☐ Be sure the communications settings match those being used by the other computer.

☐ Click the option to capture text when the document opens, if it is not already selected. The captured text dialog box appears.

☐ Accept the default file name, Captured Text, by clicking the Capture button.

☐ Turn on your modem, and be sure it's connected to the telephone line and your Mac.

☐ If your communications partner is calling you, set your Mac to receive the call by choosing the Answer Phone command from the Communications menu. Otherwise, press Command-D or choose the Dial command, enter the other person's phone number, and then click the Dial button.

☐ When you make contact with the other computer, the message *CONNECT* appears. You and your partner should type a few words back and forth to be sure you're communicating properly.

☐ Type a request for the other person to begin transmitting the text file.

☐ When you've received all of the text file, choose the End Text Capture command from the Communications menu.

☐ Type a sign-off message to let the other person know you're about to hang up, and then press Command-= or choose the Hang Up command from the Communications menu.

☐ Click the close box on the communications document.

Now we're ready to convert the text file for use in the database. When we open the file, we'll open it as a word-processor document, remember. So we'll need to open the document, export it as a text file onto our disk, and then import that text file into the database.

☐ Open the file Captured Text. It opens as an untitled word-processor document, just like the one we created for this exercise. If that file isn't on your screen now, display it.

Notice that there's very little formatting in this document. Depending on the computer that sent the file, the formatting of a data file you receive might look different from this example. The individual entries in the original database file (name, date, address, and so on) are separated by tab stops, rather than by spaces or carriage returns. Notice, too, that the end of each record is indicated by a carriage return (each Name entry begins on a new line). The method used to separate the entries is important: You have to tell Works which method was used when you convert the file to a database file.

- ☐ Choose the Save As command from the Edit menu.

- ☐ Click the Export button.

- ☐ Type a new name for the file.

This is only a temporary file (you won't need this exported file once the data is converted to a database file), so give it the simple name Text.

- ☐ Press the Return key to save the file.

- ☐ Close the untitled word-processor document without saving it.

Now the communications file you received and opened as a word-processor document has been saved in text format again, and you can use it to create a new database file.

- ☐ Choose the Open command from the File menu.

- ☐ Click on the database icon.

- ☐ Click the Import File box.

- ☐ Double-click on the file name Members.text. A dialog box opens, asking you how Works should identify individual entries in the imported file. The Tabs button is already selected, so press Return to open the file.

- ☐ The new database file opens, with the entries divided into appropriate fields. (In this case, we created the text file from an exported Works database file, so the first record in the file is the field names, rather than the data.)

As you can see in the following illustration, each entry separated by a tab in the original text file has been placed in a field in the database. In the list window, each record is separated properly, too. Now we can rename the fields with the Change Field Name command, make the fields wider so that they show all the data they contain, and then add more fields or arrange the information to suit ourselves. If we had actually created this file from a transferred communications file, we would want to save this new database file with a descriptive name. (As it is, we have already saved a copy of this database file as Members.) Now we can delete the exported database file (Members.text) and the exported word-processor file (Text) because we don't need them anymore.

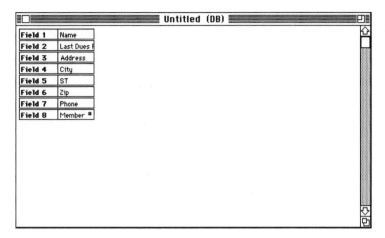

Text files created by different database programs will have their individual entries separated in different ways. Remember, if you choose one option for separating entries when you open a database file and the data isn't formatted properly, simply close the file without saving it and try another option. If none of the three options produces a properly formatted database file, you'll have to open the text file with the word processor and put the data into a format that is acceptable to the Works database, by separating the entries either with tab stops or with spaces.

The Film Club Report

Al has decided to prepare a monthly newsletter reporting on the Classic Film Club's activities. Because Al has a Macintosh with Works, he can combine data from several files into one document. He plans to create the report itself in a new word-processor document, using the Draw tool to arrange data in a two-page newsletter layout. The source data will come from a financial spreadsheet, the membership database he got from Ed Green, and a database that's a calendar of club events. In this month's report, Al wants to discuss the club's finances for the first three months of the year, and he wants to remind delinquent members to pay their annual dues. After that, he'll add a list of upcoming club events.

☐ To start, create or load all the necessary files to the desktop: the Club Finances spreadsheet shown in Figure 10-2, the membership database file you created in the previous exercise, and the Club Calendar database file shown in Figure 10-3.

Classic Film Club - 1989 Finances				
	Jan	Feb	Mar	Qtr. Totals
Income				
Dues	360	120	180	660
Film Rentals	500	275	350	1125
Events	0	335	260	595
Total Income	860	730	790	2380
Expenses				
Projector rentals	120	120	120	360
Popcorn	35	85	125	245
Utilities	28	34	30	92
Soda Pop	15	35	52	102
Candy	20	40	35	95
Office supplies	75	121	68	264
Total Expenses	293	435	430	1158
Total Income	860	730	790	2380
Profit (Loss)	567	295	360	1222

Figure 10-2.

The Club Finances spreadsheet.

Club Calendar (DB)		
Date	**Time**	**Event**
Mon, Jan 2, 1989	7:30 PM	Club Meeting – San Carlos Clubhouse
Sat, Jan 21, 1989	11:00 AM	Fox Theatre Tour, San Jose, 11-5
Mon, Feb 6, 1989	7:30 PM	Club Meeting – San Carlos Clubhouse
Fri, Feb 17, 1989	1:30 PM	Private Screening of Potemkin, San Carlos Clubhouse
Sat, Feb 25, 1989	7:30 PM	Public Screening of Intolerance, San Carlos Clubhouse
Mon, Mar 6, 1989	7:30 PM	Club Meeting – San Carlos Clubhouse
Sat, Mar 25, 1989	7:30 PM	Public Screening of Greed, San Carlos Clubhouse
Mon, Apr 3, 1989	7:30 PM	Club Meeting – San Carlos Clubhouse
Wed, Apr 12, 1989	11:00 AM	Paramount Theatre Tour, Oakland, 11-5
Wed, Apr 19, 1989	7:30 PM	Public Screening of The 39 Steps, San Carlos Clubhouse
Fri, Apr 21, 1989	8:00 PM	Disney Studios Weekend Begins
Mon, May 1, 1989	7:30 PM	Club Meeting – San Carlos Clubhouse
Sat, May 27, 1989	7:30 PM	Public Screening of Dr. Caligari, San Carlos Clubhouse

Figure 10-3.

The Club Calendar database.

(The Club Finances spreadsheet is simply values with Sum formulas to calculate the Income and Expense totals. The Total Income row at the bottom copies the values from the Total Income row 11 rows above using references such as =A9. The Profit (Loss) row uses formulas that subtract the Total Expenses value two rows above from the Total Income values one row above.)

☐ Open a new word-processor document and press Return or Enter until the insertion point is below the first page-break marker on the screen. (Or open a blank drawing page document, if you saved one from the exercise in Chapter 3.)

Before we begin creating the newsletter on the Mac, we'll draw a layout on paper like the one in Figure 10-4 so that we can get an idea of how the finished product will look. Al wants a two-column layout on the first page. He'll begin with an introduction, followed by a financial report, a membership report, and finally a calendar of upcoming club events. In the layout, we'll block out these sections on the pages.

Figure 10-4.
A diagram of the newsletter layout.

Now we have a general plan for how the finished product ought to look. Because we don't know at this point how much space our text and data will occupy, these blocks of data will probably shift around a little by the time we're finished.

Although the Works Draw tool lets you create text boxes and then copy text into them from a standard word-processor document (Al could have written all the text before and then pasted it into the layout), we'll use the text tool from the Tools palette to enter all the text of this newsletter as we go.

☐ To begin the newsletter, create a banner like the following one by using the Draw tool.

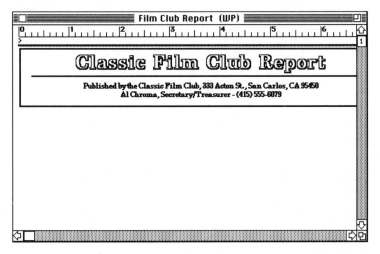

☐ First, change all the document's margins in the Page Setup dialog box from 1 inch to 0.5 inch.

☐ Drag the right margin marker in the ruler to the right until it's under the 7⅜-inch mark.

☐ Turn on the Draw tool, click on the text tool, hold down the mouse button, and drag a text box about 1¼ inch high from the left edge of the screen to just inside the right margin marker on the screen.

☐ Type *Classic Film Club Report*, and then press the Return key twice.

□ Type *Published by the Classic Film Club, 333 Acton St., San Carlos, CA 95450* as the second line of text, press the Return key, and then type *Al Chroma, Secretary/Treasurer - (415) 555-6079* as the third line of text.

□ Select all the text inside the box, choose the Justification command from the Format menu, and center the text.

□ Select only the first line of text, and change its format to 24-point bold and shadowed text using the Style command on the Format menu.

□ Select the lower two rows of text, and use the Style command to change their format to bold.

Because Al has a LaserWriter II NT, he used 14-point New Century Schoolbook, one of the resident fonts on the LaserWriter. To do this, select the font you want to use most often in the document while the arrow tool is selected in the Tools palette. Doing this will change the default font for the current session, or until you quit Works.

If you're using a Mac Plus or SE, you can't see all of the second row of text because it extends past the edge of the screen window, but it's there: Scroll to the right and see for yourself.

□ Now select the square tool, and then choose the No Fill pattern from the Fill Pattern menu.

□ Drag a rectangle surrounding all three lines of text. The right edge of the rectangle should fall right under the 7¼-inch mark on the ruler.

□ Choose the straight-line tool and draw a line dividing the newsletter title from the bottom two lines of text.

The banner is now complete. Next, we'll create two columns that divide up the remaining space on this page below the banner.

□ Click the lower-right scroll arrow to scroll the page down until only the bottom line of the banner's border is showing.

□ Choose the text tool, hold down the Option key, and hold down the mouse button as you drag a text box from below the left edge marker (in line with the left edge of the banner's border), out 3½ inches to the right, and down until the outline of the text box is just above the bottom of the page. The page scrolls as you drag the outline of the text box down.

□ Release the mouse button and the Option key. Because you held down the Option key, Works recognizes this text box as a column, and places a column header above it. Scroll back up the page to see the column header, which looks like this:

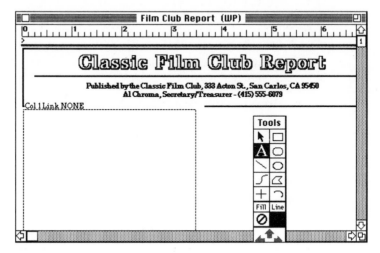

You'll notice that the column header is displayed on top of the banner's border. Don't worry about it: The header doesn't print out on paper.

□ Move the pointer to the right of the top edge of this column until it's just under the 3¾-inch mark on the ruler.

□ Hold down the mouse button and the Option key, and drag a second text box to the right until it lines up with the right edge of the banner's border and down until it is as long as the first column.

□ Release the mouse button and the Option key, and the second text column is defined.

If this were a plain two-column layout, we would link the two columns so that text in one column could flow into the second column. But in this case, we know that we're inserting graphics and that the lengths of these two columns will vary, perhaps causing us to insert extra text boxes above or below these two existing ones. So, we'll leave these columns unlinked for now.

TIP: You could also duplicate the first text column by selecting it with the selection tool, copying it to the Clipboard, and then pasting it into the space next to the first column. You would need to drag this second column around a bit to place it in the proper location. Also, because you had made a copy of the first column, both column headers would read *Col 1*, and you wouldn't be able to link the two columns until you had edited the second column header to read *Col 2* or a number other than *1*.

With the columns defined, we're ready to type some text into them. But before we do, let's save this layout. It's a good idea to save drawing projects frequently because they are more likely to cause memory-usage problems and system errors than other projects in Works. We'll save this file in two ways: once as a standard word-processor document called Film Club Report and again as stationery so that we can call up this layout as an Untitled document for next month's newsletter.

□ Press Command-S, enter the name *Club Report Template*, click the Stationery button, and press Return or Enter.

Because we saved the document as stationery, our document on the desktop remains untitled.

□ Press Command-S again, enter the name *Film Club Report*, and press Return or Enter.

Now we're ready to begin entering the text.

□ Select the text tool and click inside column 1. The insertion point appears at the upper-left corner of the box.

□ Type the introductory text shown on the next page.

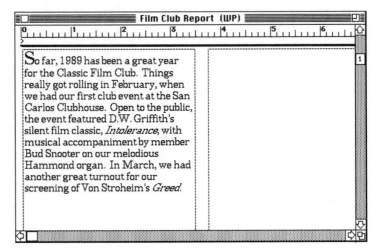

One point about entering text with the text tool needs to be mentioned: The page doesn't scroll down as you reach the bottom of the screen. The text you type is entered, but you must manually scroll the page down to see it.

TIP: Al has formatted the *S* in *So* as 24-point type so that it looks like the large initial capital letters used in magazines. He's also formatted the titles of the films in italics. You can change the style of individual characters or lines with the text tool.

We'll continue to use the same font we have been using (14-point New Century Schoolbook), but this is the time in the project to decide which font and font size you want to use. Making changes in the font or font size after you've pasted in graphics might require major changes in the layout later.

Next, Al wants to use the Club's financial report.

□ Place the insertion point at the end of the introductory paragraph, and press Return twice.

□ Type *Financial Report,* and press Return twice.

□ Type the following text:

The first three months show us in good shape. As the table below indicates, our income this quarter has outpaced our expenses, providing for a healthy surplus.

□ Select the line containing *Financial Report*, and choose Bold from the Style sub-menu.

□ Move the insertion point back to the end of the introductory financial text, and press Return twice.

Now we want to insert a small table from the Club Finances spreadsheet. Scrolling down the page shows that over 3 inches of space remain in this column, so we should have plenty of room for the table.

□ Select the Club Finances spreadsheet from the Window menu.

As it is, the last three rows of this spreadsheet contain the data we want, but we want to paste only the labels in column A and the quarter total values in column E into the newsletter layout. Because these items are not in adjacent cells, let's copy them to a new area of this spreadsheet temporarily so that they are adjacent and we can copy the entire block at once.

□ Select the Total Expenses, Total Income, and Profit (Loss) labels, and press Command-C to copy them to the Clipboard.

□ Scroll the spreadsheet down until row 30 is showing at the bottom of the screen. You should still be able to see the last three filled rows in the spreadsheet, and there should be several empty rows below them.

□ Click on cell A27 and press Command-V to paste the labels into cells A27, A28, and A29.

□ Select the Qtr. Totals values in the last three rows of column E, and copy them to the Clipboard.

□ Select cell B27, choose the Paste With Options command from the Edit menu. A dialog box appears, offering the option to paste either values only or formulas and values. The Values Only button is already selected, so press Return or Enter or click the OK button.

We must use the Paste with Options command here because we want to paste values that have been calculated by formulas. This command lets us paste the values resulting from the formulas, rather than the formulas themselves. If we simply pasted in what we copied to the Clipboard from the quarter total in the Total Expenses row, for example, we would be pasting the formula in that cell. The formula—which is =Sum(E12:E17)—would then try to calculate the sum of cells

B20:B25 directly above its new location. But no values exist in rows 22 through 26, so the formula would display the incorrect value, 1427.

Properly copied, the values and formulas that will make up our table in the newsletter layout look like this:

	A	B	C	D	E	F
Club Finances (SS)						
13	Popcorn	35	85	125	245	
14	Utilities	28	34	30	92	
15	Soda Pop	15	35	52	102	
16	Candy	20	40	35	95	
17	Office supplies	75	121	68	264	
18						
19	**Total Expenses**	293	435	430	1158	
20	**Total Income**	860	730	790	2380	
21	**Profit (Loss)**	567	295	360	1222	
22						
23						
24						
25						
26						
27	**Total Expenses**	1158				
28	**Total Income**	2380				
29	**Profit (Loss)**	1222				
30						

Now we can copy these two columns of data to the Clipboard and paste them into the newsletter layout. We have the following two alternatives here:

- We can paste the data directly into the text box in the layout (where we'll be subject to the text-handling limitations of the text tool).

- We can shorten the text box to create space on the word-processor document itself, and paste the data directly into the word processor.

Let's use the first option. You'll see why we're better off with the second method when we're finished.

- Select the values and labels from the new spreadsheet and copy them to the Clipboard (cells A27:B29).

- Activate the Film Club Report. Be sure the text tool is still active, and the insertion point is at the beginning of the second blank line below the end of the financial text.

□ Press Command-V to paste the spreadsheet data from the Clipboard. (The Draw tool is off in the following example to show the page better.)

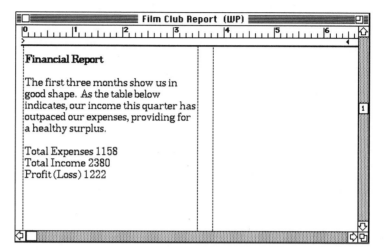

As you can see, the data from the spreadsheet was pasted in without tab stops to separate the values and labels from each other. That's because the text tool doesn't recognize or let you enter tab stops. You could separate these labels and values manually by inserting spaces between them, but because these are proportionally spaced characters, it will be hard or impossible to get the numbers to line up neatly in a column. The situation gets even worse when you have more than one column of numbers to line up.

We're much better off at this point if we shorten the text box in this column and paste the data into the word-processor document layer. Because we'll be pasting into the word processor, Works will recognize the tabs from the spreadsheet. First, let's delete the unformatted spreadsheet text and shorten the column.

□ Be sure the text tool is still active, and then select the spreadsheet data you just pasted. Press the Delete key to remove it from the column.

□ Choose the selection tool, and click on the border of column 1 to select that column.

- ☐ Scroll to the bottom of the page and point to the middle handle in the bottom edge of column 1's outline, hold down the mouse button, drag the line up until it is immediately below the last line of text, and then release the mouse button.

- ☐ Press Command-J to turn off the Draw tool. (Remember, we want to paste data into the word processor part of the document, so we can't have the Draw tool on.)

If you haven't used the Clipboard for anything else, the spreadsheet data will still be there, ready to paste again. Otherwise, copy the data to the Clipboard again before you proceed:

- ☐ Activate the Film Club Report document.

- ☐ Click the insertion point below the bottom of the text in column 1.

- ☐ Press Command-V to paste in the spreadsheet data.

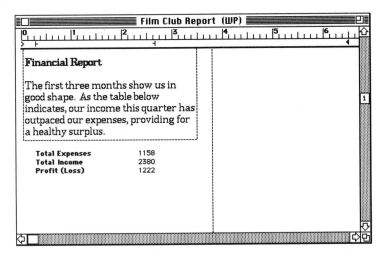

This time, you can see that the word processor has inserted tab stops that correspond to the positions of the labels and values you pasted from the spreadsheet. You can now move these tab stops by dragging them; change the size, font, or style of the text; insert some spacing lines; and otherwise arrange it so that it fills this space nicely. The illustration on the next page shows the reformatted text with a box around it. The box was added with the Draw tool.

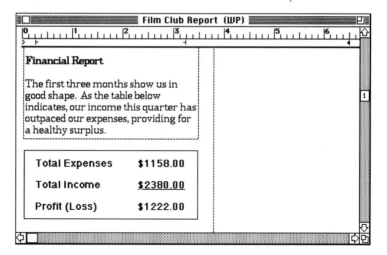

We can check the overall look of our work at this point with the Print Preview command.

☐ Press Command-P to display the Print dialog box.

☐ Click the Print Preview box, and then press Return or Enter or click the OK button to print. A reduced display of the entire page appears on the screen, and you can see how the layout looks.

☐ You can see any part of the page in actual size by clicking anywhere on the page with the magnifying glass, and dragging the page around in the window with the hand. If anything looks out of alignment, make a note of it and fix it by dragging with the selection tool when you return to the normal view of the document.

☐ Click the close box on the zoomed page display, and then click the Cancel button on the Page Preview screen to return to the normal view of the document.

☐ If the document is what you want at this point, save it by pressing Command-S. Otherwise, fix the alignment problems first, and then save it.

The next step is to fill up the rest of the space in the first column of the layout with more text. There's only about 1½ inches of vertical space remaining in this column, so we'll draw a second text box to continue with Al's financial report.

☐ Press Command-J to activate the Draw tool. Using the text tool, hold down the mouse button and the Option key and draw a new text box. Start at left edge of the screen immediately below the table and drag the outline out to the 3½-inch mark on the ruler and then down until the bottom of the box lines up with the bottom of the column on the right.

In this case, we'll link this text box with the column box on the right, because text might well overflow from this box into the next one.

☐ Choose the selection tool, hold down the Option key, and click in the new text box.

☐ With the Option key still held down, click inside the text box on the right side of the page. When you do this, you see a dialog box warning you that you have created a circular link. To fix this, scroll to the top of the column on the right, and with the text tool, change the Column 2 Link to NONE. The columns are now linked.

☐ Choose the text tool, and place the insertion point at the top of the new text box you just created, and then type the following text:

Our monthly expenses were in line with what we'd expect, except for a disturbing trend in popcorn costs. As the following chart shows, popcorn expenses for March accounted for a significant portion of our total outlay that month. I'm not sure at this point just what the problem is, but the food committee is looking into it. I expect their report in time for next month's newsletter.

When you finish typing, choose the selection tool and scroll to the top of the document. You'll see that the text has overflowed the bottom of the left-hand column, and has continued in the text box on the right. Now it's time to insert a pie chart showing how the popcorn expenses for March contribute to the month's total expenses. We can create this chart from the Club Finances spreadsheet, and then copy it into the newsletter layout. But first, let's save the document again.

☐ Press Command-S to save the current version of the Film Club Report.

Works won't let you paste a spreadsheet chart or other graphic inside a text box, so we must shorten the right-hand text box until it stops immediately below the end of our text, creating blank space into which to paste the chart.

□ Scroll down to the bottom of the page.

□ Using the selection tool, select the right-hand text box by clicking on its border, and then drag the center handle at the bottom of the box up until it is immediately below the end of the text introducing the chart. The display scrolls up as you drag the bottom of the box up.

Now we'll draw the expenses chart.

□ Activate the Club Finances spreadsheet, and choose New Pie Chart from the Chart menu. The chart definition box appears. The exact rows in your version of this spreadsheet might differ, but here's what the pie chart definition looks like based on the file that was printed to produce Figure 10-2:

```
╔═══════════════ Club Fin Chart 1 ═══════════════╗
║  Pie Chart Definition:                          ║
║  Chart Title: │March Expenses            │      ║
║                                                 ║
║  Plot Values in Column: │D │                    ║
║          From Row: │12 │                         ║
║         Through Row: │17 │                       ║
║  Column of Value Titles: │A │                    ║
║                                                 ║
║                          ( Cancel )  ║Plot It!║  ║
╚═════════════════════════════════════════════════╝
```

□ Press Enter or Return to plot the chart. The chart window fills the screen.

We know we'll need to resize this chart so that it will fit into the space in our layout, but how can we tell exactly? First, we can reduce the chart window to about a quarter of its full size, and then we'll display the newsletter document. After that, we'll be able to activate the chart window again and drag it under the bottom of the right-hand column to get a good idea of how large the chart should be.

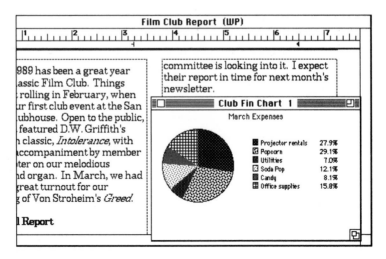

Now we can resize the chart in its own window to make it the correct size. Be sure to measure the size of the chart itself, not the chart and the blank space between the chart and the edges of its window. When the chart looks to be the correct size, use the following steps.

- Press Command-C to copy it to the Clipboard.

- Activate the Film Club Report file.

- Choose the selection tool from the Tools palette, and click in the blank space below the text box in the right-hand column.

- Press Command-V to paste the chart into the blank space.

The chart appears in the space with selection handles around it.

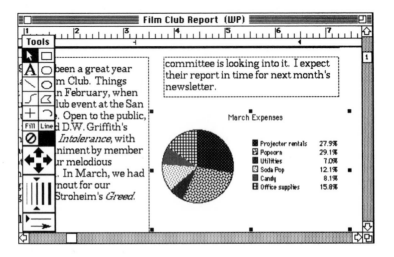

To move the chart so that it fits in the center of the space, point the selection tool in the middle of the chart, hold down the mouse button, and drag the chart to the proper position. If you need to make the chart larger or smaller, drag the left, right, top or bottom selection handles to enlarge or reduce the chart.

Notice in the preceding example that the actual handles for this chart are almost on top of the outline for column 1. It's alright if a graphic's selection handles cross borders, or even page-break markers, as long as the graphic itself doesn't cross them. You can always check to see if you've made a graphic too large by using the Print Preview feature to view the document on the screen.

After this chart is pasted in, Al wants to move to a new section called Member Notes. Now, however, we must create a fourth text box beneath the chart to continue the text in this column.

□ Scroll the display to the right so that you can see both edges of the column on the right.

□ Choose the text tool, hold down the Option key and mouse button, and then drag a text box the same width from immediately under the pie chart to the bottom of the page.

Now we can begin typing the text for the next section of the newsletter, the Member Notes.

□ Type the subheading *Member Notes,* then select it and make it boldface. Press the Return key twice.

□ Type the following text:

Our 1989 membership drive continues to swell the ranks of the Classic Film Club. During March, the club welcomed three new members: Ed Hastings, Julia Morgan, and Sharon Ott. If you haven't met these new members yet, be sure to introduce yourself at our next meeting.
But among our more established members, I'm sad to report that a few of us have yet to pay our 1989 dues, which were due the first of the year. Here's the list:

Here, Al wants to copy a selection of membership records from the Members database file and paste it into the column. The record selection in the database will show all members who haven't yet paid their dues for 1989. (Al figures that members who haven't paid dues since before September, 1988 are delinquent.) Use the following steps to select the proper records.

☐ Activate the Members database file.

☐ Choose the Record Selection command from the Organize menu.

☐ Install a record-selection rule that says "Last Dues Paid is less than 9/1/88," and then select these records. Four records will be displayed on the screen.

☐ Copy the name data from the four selected records to the Clipboard.

With the names of delinquent members ready to paste into the newsletter, we must again decide whether it's better to paste them directly into the column's text box or to shorten the text box and paste them into the word processor part of the page. This time, let's paste the names directly into the text box. Because only one column of names exist, it will be easy to center them all in the text box by using the Spacebar.

☐ Activate the Film Club Report file. Be sure the text tool is still selected.

☐ Place the insertion point two lines below the bottom of the text.

☐ Press Command-V to paste in the names from the Clipboard. Because you copied data from a database field, the names appear along with the name of the field from which they came, like this:

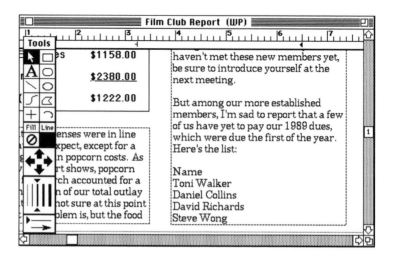

All that remains to finish this page is to align the database names in the center of the text box and delete the field name.

☐ Select the word *Name* with the text tool, and press the Delete key twice (once to delete the name, and the second time to delete the extra space between the names and the last line).

☐ Place the insertion point in front of the first name, Toni Walker, and press the Spacebar 22 times (if you are using the 14-point New Century Schoolbook font) to move this name to the middle of the column. (We can't use the Justification submenu to center the names, because all of the text in the column would take on the same format.)

☐ Repeat the preceding step with the last three names in the column, or select the inserted spaces, copy them to the Clipboard, and insert them before each name with the Paste command.

Now press Command-S to save this newsletter page. We've placed all the text and graphics on this page, but now we should check to see that everything is aligned properly before we print it on paper. Use the Print Preview option to inspect the page, and use the zoom feature to check the vertical alignment of the text in the right and left columns: Does the text in the left column appear on the same horizontal line as the text in the right column? To make the necessary adjustments, use the following steps.

☐ Cancel the Print Preview to return to the document.

☐ Choose the selection tool, and drag the text boxes or graphics on the page up or down slightly so that the text aligns properly from one column to the next. The finished newsletter page is shown in Figure 10-5 on the next page.

Referring to the second newsletter page in the hand-drawn layout of Figure 10-4, you can see that the layout of the first page looks almost the same as the diagram. We won't go through all the steps of creating the second page, but the following steps describe the general process.

☐ Open the stationery file named Club Report Template, which contains the newsletter banner and two column boxes.

☐ Delete the column boxes.

☐ Activate the Club Calendar file, and make a record selection that will display only the activities for the month of April.

Classic Film Club Report

Published by the Classic Film Club, 333 Acton St., San Carlos, CA 95450
Al Chroma, Secretary/Treasurer - (415) 555-6079

So far, 1989 has been a great year for the Classic Film Club. Things really got rolling in February, when we had our first club event at the San Carlos Clubhouse. Open to the public, the event featured D.W. Griffith's silent film classic, *Intolerance*, with musical accompaniment by member Bud Snooter on our melodious Hammond organ. In March, we had another great turnout for our screening of Von Stroheim's *Greed*.

Financial Report

The first three months show us in good shape. As the table below indicates, our income this quarter has outpaced our expenses, providing for a healthy surplus.

Total Expenses	$1158.00
Total Income	<u>$2380.00</u>
Profit (Loss)	$1222.00

Our monthly expenses were in line with what we'd expect, except for a disturbing trend in popcorn costs. As the following chart shows, popcorn expenses for March accounted for a significant portion of our total outlay that month. I'm not sure at this point just what the problem is, but the food

committee is looking into it. I expect their report in time for next month's newsletter.

March Expenses

■	Projector rentals	27.9%
▨	Popcorn	29.1%
■	Utilities	7.0%
⊡	Soda Pop	12.1%
▨	Candy	8.1%
⊞	Office supplies	15.8%

Member Notes

Our 1989 membership drive continues to swell the ranks of the Classic Film Club. During March, the club welcomed three new members: Ed Hastings, Julia Morgan, and Sharon Ott. If you haven't met these new members yet, be sure to introduce yourself at the next meeting.

But among our more established members, I'm sad to report that a few of us have yet to pay our 1989 dues, which were due the first of the year. Here's the list:

> Toni Walker
> Daniel Collins
> David Richards
> Steve Wong

Figure 10-5.

A printout of the first page of the newsletter.

- □ Copy the selected records to the Clipboard.

- □ Paste the records into the portion of the second newsletter page below the banner.

- □ Reformat the data, change the column spacing, and style the text the way you want.

- □ Insert the title *April Calendar of Events* above the three columns of data.

- □ Turn on the Draw tool and put a box around the title. When you're finished, the second newsletter page will look something like the one in Figure 10-6.

Classic Film Club Report

Published by the Classic Film Club, 333 Acton St., San Carlos, CA 95450
Al Chroma, Secretary/Treasurer - (415) 555-6079

April Calendar of Events

Date	Time	Event
Mon, Apr 3, 1989	7:30 PM	Club Meeting - San Carlos Clubhouse
Wed, Apr 12, 1989	11:00 AM	Paramount Theatre Tour, Oakland, 11-5
Wed, Apr 19, 1989	7:30 PM	Public Screening of *The 39 Steps*, San Carlos Clubhouse
Fri, Apr 21, 1989	8:00 PM	Disney Studios Weekend Begins

Figure 10-6.
A printout of the second page of the newsletter.

A Daily Calendar

In Chapter 8, we created a database file called Calendar, which is used to list daily appointments. We found that by sorting the file on its Time and Date fields and then by using record selection rules, we could select only the appointments for one day and print them in a database report. The sorted calendar file looks like this:

Date	Time	Event
Fri, Mar 24, 1989	9:00 AM	Dentist Appointment – Dr. Hesselschwerdt, 12t
Sat, Mar 25, 1989	10:15 AM	Interview VCR technician
Sat, Mar 25, 1989	3:30 PM	Video Listing To Printer
Sat, Mar 25, 1989	4:00 PM	MCA Video salesman
Sun, Mar 26, 1989	12:00 PM	Lunch with cousin Lou, Antoine's
Mon, Mar 27, 1989	6:30 PM	Dinner with the Jacksons, their house
Fri, Mar 31, 1989	2:00 PM	Income Tax preparation, Bud Rosen
Fri, Mar 31, 1989		Payroll Tax installment due
Sun, Apr 2, 1989	12:00 PM	Projectionist's Union picnic
Mon, Apr 3, 1989	3:00 PM	UA Video salesman
Tue, Apr 4, 1989	9:00 AM	3-day sale begins
Mon, May 15, 1989		Anna's Birthday
Sun, Jun 4, 1989	1:00 PM	Felicia's wedding, St. Mary's
Sat, Aug 12, 1989		Vacation begins
Mon, Aug 21, 1989		Vacation ends
Fri, Sep 1, 1989	12:00 PM	Tony's retirement lunch, Bingo's
Fri, Sep 29, 1989		Payroll Tax installment due

Calendar (DB)

If you're not sure how to create this file and sort it, refer to Chapter 8. In this project, we'll merge the data from the Calendar file into a custom layout prepared in the word processor. Using the word-processor's formatting flexibility and the Draw tool, we can create an attractive, useful daily calendar page that lists our scheduled appointments and provides space for new appointments and notes. The finished calendar page is shown in Figure 10-7.

We'll start by merging all the necessary data from the Calendar file into a new word-processor document, and then we'll arrange and format the page.

□ In the sorted Calendar file, select the second record (a Saturday, March 25 date and the 10:15 appointment).

□ Double-click on this date, or choose the Set Field Attributes command from the Format menu.

□ Click the button to display the date in the long format. The Show Day box is already checked.

Saturday, March 25, 1989

Scheduled Appointments

Time	Event
10:15 AM	Interview VCR technician
3:30 PM	Video Listing To Printer
4:00 PM	MCA Video salesman

New Appointments

8:00 AM	1:00 PM
9:00 AM	2:00 PM
10:00 AM	3:00 PM
11:00 AM	4:00 PM
12:00 AM	5:00 PM
Evening:	

Notes:

Figure 10-7.
A daily calendar.

☐ Press Return or Enter to change the date field's format.

☐ Open a new word-processor document.

☐ Press Command-M, or choose Prepare to Merge from the Edit menu. The merge dialog box appears, and if the Calendar is the only database file open on the desktop, the dialog box looks like the one on the next page.

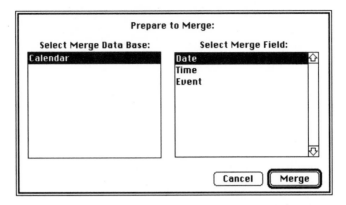

☐ If the Calendar file name in the database list isn't selected, click it to select it, and then select the Date field from the merge field list.

☐ Press Return or Enter, or click the Merge button. The date of the selected record appears in the document, like this:

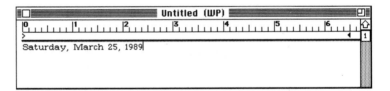

The date is displayed as it appears in the selected database record, with the day showing and the long date format. We could display the database file and field name instead by choosing the Show Field Names command from the Edit menu, but we'll want to see how actual data will fit in this form, so we'll leave the file the way it is.

☐ Press the Return key four times and type *Scheduled Appointments*.

☐ Press the Return key three times and type *Time*.

☐ Press the Tab key three times, type *Event*, and press the Return key two more times.

In using this calendar page, we will want to merge one set of Time and Event data for each appointment in any given day. The current day we have selected on Al's calendar has three scheduled appointments, so we need to merge three sets of Time and Event data. But Al may have days when he has more than three appointments, and we'd want room and merge markers to include those extra appointments as well. So, we'll merge six sets of Time and Event data into the Scheduled Appointments portion of the calendar page. Then, Works can merge up to six appointments from any day, and if there are fewer than six appointments, the program will simply leave blank space.

To merge data from more than one record onto the same page, we must use the Multiple Labels command. And because we're merging more than one set of merge markers from the same fields in the file, we'll switch the display to show the field names, rather than the data before merging these fields.

□ Select the Multiple Labels command from the Edit menu.

□ Select the Show Field Names command from the Edit menu.

□ Press Command-M, select the Time field, and merge this data into the document.

□ Press the Tab key, press Command-M, select the Event field, and merge this data into the document. Select the line containing the two merge markers and click once in the Ruler just below the 1½-inch mark to set a tab stop at this position. The two merge markers now look like this:

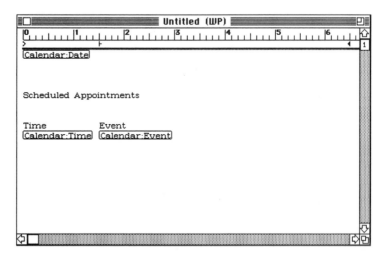

Notice also that because we changed the display to Show Field Names, the date merge marker above no longer shows the actual date from the selected record in the Calendar file. We could use the Prepare to Merge command 10 more times to merge the other five sets of Time and Event data, but because Works lets us treat merge markers the same as text, we can simply copy the line containing the Time and Event markers already in the document and then paste them in below it five times.

☐ Select the line containing the Time and Event merge markers and press Command-C to copy it to the Clipboard.

☐ Place the insertion point on the line below the two merge markers, and press Command-V to paste in another copy.

☐ Repeat this operation four more times to paste in the last four sets of merge markers. The page now looks like this:

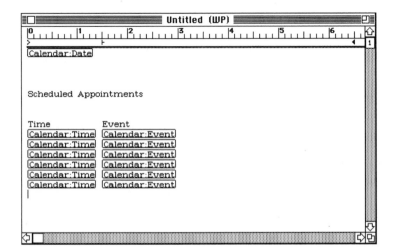

That's all we need to do with the merged data in this document. The rest of the page is simply text that we type in and enhancements with the formatting commands and the Draw tool.

☐ Press the Return key four times and type *New Appointments.*

☐ Press the Return key three times and type *8:00 AM.*

☐ Press the Tab key five times, type *1:00 PM,* and press the Return key twice.

☐ Using the previous two steps as a guide, enter the other times and the label *Evening:* as shown in the completed Calendar Page in Figure 10-7.

☐ Press the Return key five times and type *Notes:.*

With the text and data-merging for this calendar page complete, we're ready to adjust the formatting. We'll start at the top and work our way down. (Al has chosen to format the entire document with the Palatino font at this point, to take advantage of his LaserWriter's resident font capability.)

☐ Place the insertion point immediately before the date at the top of the page and press Return to add space for a box.

☐ Select the date, and change its size and style to 24-point bold using the Format menu.

☐ Center the date by choosing the Justification command on the Format menu.

☐ Turn on the Draw tool, select the rectangle tool, and draw a box around the date, extending from under the ¼-inch mark to the 6¼-inch mark on the ruler.

After you draw the box, the date disappears (unless you have already chosen the no-fill pattern) because the default fill pattern for a rectangle is white and the rectangle is covering the date. Be sure the box is still selected, and choose the no-fill pattern from the Fill Pattern menu. The date reappears.

☐ Select the text *Scheduled Appointments* and make it 14-point, bold, and underlined. Repeat this step for the text *New Appointments.*

☐ Select the Time and Event text and make it 12-point bold.

☐ Select the text *Notes:* and make it 14-point bold.

All that remains now is to draw the lines separating the time and notes areas of the page.

☐ Activate the Draw tool, select the straight-line tool with the finest line thickness, hold down the Shift key and the mouse button, and draw a line between the text *8:00 AM* and *9:00 AM*, from the left edge of the screen out to the right until it's under the 6¼-inch mark on the ruler.

☐ Repeat this step to insert the lines between the other times in the New Appointments area.

☐ Finally, select the next-thickest line and halfway between the text *Evening* and the text *Notes,* draw a line the same length as those above.

This page is finished, and you can save it as Calendar Page on your disk. This page is designed for standard-sized paper, and you can use a hole punch to insert it into a binder. If you want to use a smaller notebook, you can easily print half-size sheets (5½ by 8½) by laying out two such pages in smaller type, side by side, and then printing with the horizontal orientation option. You can also reduce the size of the print with the print reduction options in the ImageWriter or LaserWriter Page Setup dialog boxes.

In only a few seconds a day, you can select the appointments for each day and print them out onto this calendar page by using the Print Merge command. But whether you use this calendar page or not, this project gives you an idea of the formatting versatility you can gain by merging database data into a word-processor document.

Converting an Inventory Spreadsheet to a Database File

The main reason for pasting spreadsheet data into a database file (or database data into a spreadsheet, for that matter) is to be able to work with data in the different ways that another application allows. For example, the spreadsheet is fine for totaling numbers in columns, but it isn't very good at producing reports of selected inventory items and their values. When you look at a spreadsheet file, you look at the whole file; when you look at a database file, however, you can look at selected groups of records.

To illustrate these two different ways of looking at data, let's suppose Al has the inventory spreadsheet shown here:

	A	B	C	D
	Title	Quantity	Cost	Total Value
10	Title	Quantity	Cost	Total Value
11				
12	Adventure			
13	Blazing Bullets	1	$14.95	$14.95
14	Jungle Fever	2	$11.95	$23.90
15	Six Gun City	1	$12.95	$12.95
16	The One-Eyed Assassin	3	$12.95	$38.85
17	The Spy Who Said No	3	$13.95	$41.85
18	Two Guys In Trouble	2	$15.95	$31.90
19				
20	Subtotal Adventure	12		$164.40
21				
22	Aerobics			
23	Aerobic Profit-Taking	4	$14.95	$59.80
24	George Will's Yoga Fun	1	$12.95	$12.95
25	King Kong Bundy's Workout	2	$9.95	$19.90
26	Yoko's Roll-A-Thon	1	$12.95	$12.95
27				

Inventory (SS)

You might recognize this spreadsheet—it's the same inventory spreadsheet we created in Chapter 6. If you've already created this spreadsheet, use it to do this exercise. Otherwise, refer to the inventory exercise in Chapter 6 and create the spreadsheet before continuing.

By looking at this file, Al can quickly tell the value of videotapes in a certain genre subgroup. But the file leaves out a lot of information, such as the format of each tape and the distributor. Al wants to transfer this information to a database file, where he can add fields to display more types of data and then sort records out of the file with more flexibility.

□ Open the Inventory file. Make a note of the number of columns in the file and the type of information they contain.

Remember, Works will transfer all the data in each spreadsheet column into a field in the database, and it will make each row of spreadsheet data a separate record in the database. The Inventory file has four columns (called Title, Quantity, Cost, and Total Value), but we don't need the Total Value column in the new database file. (We can calculate the total value of each tape title with a calculated field in the database.)

□ Open a new database file, and specify three fields: Title, Quantity, and Cost. Then, click the Done button in the Field Name window. The list window in the new file looks like this:

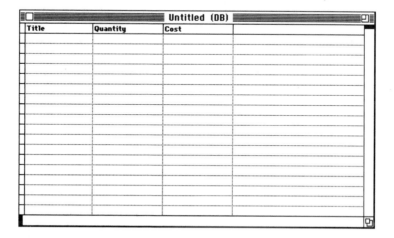

Before we transfer the data from the spreadsheet, we need to use the Set Field Attributes command to make the Quantity and Cost fields numeric. We also need to make the Quantity field General in format, and format the Cost field for Dollars with two decimal places. This way, the data will be properly formatted when we paste it in, and (by identifying the data as numerical) we can use these fields to create a calculated field that shows the total value of each title in inventory.

□ Double-click on the first blank field below the Quantity field name to display the Field Attributes dialog box.

□ Click on the Numeric and General buttons, and then press the Enter or Return key to make these changes.

□ Double-click on the first blank field below the Cost field name to display the Field Attributes dialog box. Click the Numeric and Dollar buttons, and then press Enter or Return to make these changes.

To move the data from the spreadsheet, use the following steps.

□ Choose the Inventory spreadsheet from the Window menu.

□ Select all the titles, quantities, and costs of the tapes in the Adventure category (cells A13:C18).

□ Press Command-C or choose the Copy command from the Edit menu to copy this data to the Clipboard.

□ Activate the new database file you've just created and select the Title field in the first blank record at the top of the window.

□ Press Command-V or choose the Paste command from the Edit menu. The spreadsheet data is pasted to the database file, and the data is formatted properly, as you can see here:

Title	Quantity	Cost
Blazing Bullets	1	$14.95
Jungle Fever	2	$11.95
Six Gun City	1	$12.95
The One-Eyed Assas:	3	$12.95
The Spy Who Said No:	3	$13.95
Two Guys In Trouble	2	$15.95

Untitled (DB)

Some of the titles aren't completely visible in the Title field.

☐ Drag the field boundary between the Title and Quantity fields to the right until all the titles are showing.

☐ Paste in the rest of the videotape titles, quantities, and costs.

After we have transferred all the data from the spreadsheet, we need to save the database file.

☐ Choose Save As from the File menu, type the name *Tape Inventory*, and click the Save button.

Now we can add new fields to store more specific information about each tape, such as the genre category, the format, the distributor, the copyright date, the rental price, and so on. Using the database's reporting features, we can create reports with subtotals that show the number and value of tapes in each category, as we did in Chapter 8.

When you paste data from the database to a spreadsheet file, the procedure is much the same, except you don't have to specify a certain number of fields for the spreadsheet file. Each field of data copied from a database file's list window will become a column of data in the spreadsheet. So, it's easy to move data between these two applications whenever you want to work with text or numbers a little differently.

Integration Tips

Taking advantage of Works' integration features is largely a matter of using the Clipboard, the import/export and merge features, and some imagination. The following are some general tips to keep in mind as you work with several files on the desktop at the same time and move data between them.

Group files in folders by project

The disks on the Macintosh can hold dozens of files, so it can be hard to locate a specific file if the files are jumbled together in one window. By organizing your files into folders, you can reduce the number of items in a disk window and make it easier to locate individual files. If you use several files for a specific project, for example, you can find them more easily if you group them together in a folder on a disk and then label the folder with the project's name. If Al Chroma works with a newsletter layout, a calendar database, a membership database, and a financial spreadsheet in his duties for the Classic Film Club, for example, he can put all these files into a folder called Film Club. To create a new folder in a disk window, choose the New Folder command from the File menu in the Finder.

Make custom Works desktops

Another organizational tool you can use in Works is the Works Desktop feature. The Works Desktop is a special file that stores a particular desktop containing certain open files. This feature lets you pick up where you left off when you last quit Works. It remembers which files you had open on the desktop when you chose the Quit command from the File menu, and opens Works along with that specific collection of files when you double-click on the Works Desktop icon in the Finder. If you've closed all your files before quitting, double-clicking the Works Desktop icon in the Finder will load only the Works program itself. The Works Desktop file is always stored on the same disk containing the System Folder from which you started your Mac.

You can make any number of Works Desktop files while you're working with the program by choosing the Make Works Desktop command from the File menu. This command creates a Works Desktop file that remembers which files you have open at the time, and it lets you save the Works Desktop file with a different name or to a different disk. So, for example, Al could make a Works Desktop file called Film Club Newsletter while he had the appropriate database, word-processor, and spreadsheet files open, and then simply double-click this icon to load those files the next time he worked on that project.

Of course, because Works Desktop files are treated the same as any other files in the Finder, you can always rename them in the Finder. With a little imagination, you can create several Works Desktop files that will load all the files you need for different projects. The only limitation is that the Works Desktop file will remember and load only 14 files (the maximum number of open files Works allows at a time), or as many files as your Mac's memory can store at a time, whichever is less.

Avoid disk clutter

If you import and export a lot of files or capture a lot of text files with the communications module, you should keep in mind which files are meant to be stored permanently and which ones represent data that's merely in transit from one program or application to another. If you receive a file from a friend by modem, for example, that file might be named Captured Text. But if you open that file with the word processor, you'll create a new, untitled file, and the Captured Text file will still be on disk. After you save the word-processor file, you no longer need the Captured Text file, and you can delete it from your disk.

Every now and then, you should examine your disk's contents and delete any temporary files. By keeping your disk free of needless clutter, you'll be able to find the files you want more easily.

Check data destinations in the spreadsheet and database

When you paste data into a word-processor document, any existing data in the file moves to make room for data you're inserting. In the spreadsheet and database, however, the data you paste in will overwrite any existing data in its path. Works will warn you when you're about to overwrite data in the spreadsheet or database when you try to paste from the Clipboard. You will avoid the warning message, though, if you get into the habit of pasting data at the end of a database file, or at the bottom or right edge of your existing spreadsheet data.

Save your work frequently

You should always save your work frequently to avoid losing data in the event of a power failure or system error, but it's especially important when you're working with several files on the desktop. It's easy to become involved in a project, switching among several open files and forgetting to save as you go. It's a good habit to save each file every time you work with it, just before you activate a different file. And, if you regularly work with several files at a time, check the About MS-Works command on the Apple menu from time to time to be sure you have plenty of memory. When the Memory Free indicator at the bottom of the Works trademark window falls below 20 percent, think about closing one or more files to free up some memory. Otherwise, you might run out of memory when you copy a large amount of data or a graphic to the Clipboard.

The Rest Is Up to You

Armed with the explanations and exercises in this book, you should now have a solid understanding of how to use Microsoft Works and some ideas about what you can do with this program to simplify your business and personal life. The more you put these tools to your own use, the more you'll understand about how to use them better. You might be at the end of this book, but you're only at the beginning of what promises to be a long and productive partnership.

Appendix

This appendix describes hardware products for your Mac that will help you get more out of Microsoft Works. Specific products and prices change constantly, so this listing includes only the names of manufacturers who offer such products in each group, rather than names and prices of specific products. These descriptions are meant to give you the basic knowledge you'll need to further explore specific products in any of these categories.

Hard Disks

A hard disk drive is almost a necessity on a Macintosh these days, and it will make using Works much more convenient and enjoyable. A hard disk can store 20 million bytes (megabytes, abbreviated MB) or more of data or programs in one place—the equivalent of 25 standard Mac floppy disks, which hold 800 KB, or kilobytes, of data each. Even the newer Apple FDHD high-density floppy disk drive holds only 1.4 MB of data per disk. And 20 MB is the bottom of the range for hard disk sizes: You can buy hard disks that hold 100 MB, 300 MB, or even more.

With a hard disk connected to your Mac, you can start up Works or other programs and store all your files without ever having to insert a floppy disk at all.

If we look at "hard disk" as a generic term used to describe any device that stores several megabytes of data in one unit, we'll find several types of these mass storage devices on the market.

Internal and external Winchester hard disks

The most common type of hard disk is the Winchester hard disk, a sealed box containing a rotating metal disk that stores several megabytes of data. Winchester hard disks have the speed and convenience advantages described previously, but because they are sealed, their capacity is fixed—when you fill up a Winchester hard disk, you are out of space until you buy another Winchester hard disk. You can connect up to seven hard disk drives to your Mac at a time.

Most Mac hard disks are external units that fit beside or beneath your Mac, but a growing share of buyers are opting for internal hard disks, which are made to fit inside a Mac SE or Mac II. With a Mac SE, an internal hard disk has the added advantage of maintaining the Mac's portability while adding a lot of storage.

My recommendation is to stick with an external hard disk on the Mac Plus or Mac SE, especially because many external units are so small and light that you can easily carry one along with your Mac. If it breaks down, you can simply unplug it and send it in for repairs, and you can continue to use your Mac. On the Mac II, which is much easier to open than an SE and which has hard disks that are easy for normal people to remove and install, an internal hard disk is preferable, particularly because the Mac II's own hardware takes up so much desk space.

The current price for a 20 MB Winchester hard disk is about $500 and a 40 MB drive is about $900, but prices and products change frequently. See your local Apple dealer for up-to-date information on the best Winchester disk drive.

Removable cartridge Winchester hard disks

As previously mentioned, unlike a removable floppy disk, the capacity of a Winchester hard disk is finite. However, a few manufacturers offer removable cartridge Winchester hard disks. These units act more like a floppy-disk drive: The metal disk on which the data is stored is encased in a removable plastic cartridge. You can swap these cartridges in and out of the drive just as you can swap disks in a floppy-disk system. The individual disk cartridges on such current systems hold about 45 MB of data, although this capacity is certain to rise over time as better technology emerges.

Removable hard disks in the 45 MB range sell for about $1,500 at this writing. The cartridges are over $100 each, so the cost of entry is almost twice what it would be for a standard 45 MB Winchester drive. On the other hand, you can increase your storage space in 45 MB increments inexpensively compared with adding a second hard-disk drive.

A removable hard disk makes the most sense if you create large amounts of data (graphics files, databases, or whatever) that must be backed up or transported easily. It's much easier and less expensive to mail or deliver a data cartridge than an entire hard disk, and removable cartridges make fast and convenient backup disks for your data. If you don't create a lot of new data regularly, however, and you expect most of your data to stay by your computer, a standard hard disk makes more sense. Current manufacturers of removable hard disks include Peripheral Land and Mass Micro.

Bernoulli boxes

One high-capacity alternative to the Winchester technology is the Bernoulli-type disk, which is a removable, flexible disk that stores 10, 20, or even 40 MB of data. Bernoulli-type disks work in almost the opposite way from Winchester disks. A Winchester disk spins at about 3500 rpm, creating an air current on the top side of the disk upon which the disk's read/write head floats. A Bernoulli-type disk spins in a way that creates an air current on the bottom of the disk, pushing the disk up close to the read/write head. The difference is safety: If the column of air in a Winchester drive is disturbed by dirt, dust, smoke, or movement, the read/write head falls down (or crashes) to the surface of the disk, possibly wiping out the data written there. If the column of air in a Bernoulli-type disk is disturbed, the disk itself falls safely away from the read-write head, back to the position it occupies when the drive isn't running.

Bernoulli-type drives have received high marks for reliability and compatibility, but like removable-cartridge Winchester drives, they are more expensive initially than standard Winchesters. Expect to pay about $2,000 for a 20 MB Bernoulli-type drive from a vendor such as Iomega (the originators of the Bernoulli drive), Bering, or others.

High-density floppy disks

At least one company sells a floppy-disk drive using disks that simply hold a lot more data. These high-density floppy disks are larger than standard Mac floppies, but they usually hold 10 or 20 MB of data each. These disks aren't as speedy as Winchester or Bernoulli disks, but they are less expensive and they offer the convenience of removable media and the ability to expand storage by simply buying more disks. Jasmine is the best-known company that sells a high-density floppy-disk drive at this writing. These devices cost about $700 for a 10 MB unit and $1,000 for a 20 MB unit. Extra floppy disks cost about $30 each.

Modems

If you want to use the communications features of Microsoft Works, you'll need a modem. All modems use much the same technology: They all connect to your Mac the same way, and they all work the same way. One big difference is speed. A couple of years ago, 1200-baud modems were all priced at $500 or more, and many people bought 300-baud modems, because they were cheaper.

Now you can buy a 1200-baud modem for about $100, and almost everyone communicates at this speed. In fact, 2400-baud modems are now available for around $200, and a growing number of Mac owners are buying these faster units as commercial information services such as CompuServe, MCI Mail, and MacNet offer service at this speed. The next widespread jump in modem speed will probably be to 9600 baud, although modems in that category are still too expensive (around $800 to $1,000) to be popular yet. Today, I recommend that you shop for a 1200-baud modem at the minimum, and go with a 2400-baud modem if you can afford it. You can always use the 2400-baud modem to transmit at 1200 or even 300 baud to friends with slower equipment, but you'll be able to transmit faster (and thereby cut down on your telephone and information-service connect-time charges) with the faster speed.

Even if you have a lot of money, it doesn't make sense today to buy a 9600 baud or faster modem unless you have a specific remote computer to which you want to send a lot of data. You can send at a given speed only if the other computer can also send and receive at that speed, and none of the commercial information services these days can handle anything faster than 2400 baud. But if, for example, you have an office across the country and you send dozens of 500 KB files between them daily, the extra expense of 9600 baud modems will be paid back in reduced telephone charges within a short time.

Most modems for personal computers are external boxes that connect to your Mac with a serial cable, to the telephone line with a standard phone cord, and to the wall with an electric plug. One or two internal modems are available for Mac II models. The only advantage of internal modems over external ones is that you don't have an extra box on your desk. But because modems are small devices anyway, this isn't a very compelling advantage. On the other hand, although any modem will connect your computer to another over the telephone, some distinguishing features set models and brands apart.

Although all modems dial telephone numbers and answer calls automatically, for example, some more-expensive models also have built-in memory buffers. A memory buffer in a modem can capture and store incoming data even if your Mac isn't running, and it can store outgoing data from your Mac and transmit it later when telephone rates are lower. Some modems, such as those from Microcom or the Hayes V-series, have built-in error-correcting circuitry. Other companies make tiny, portable modems that run on batteries and fit in a shirt pocket.

Among the companies that make and sell modems are (in alphabetical order) Anchor Automation, Apple Computer, Avatex, Hayes, Microcom, Practical Peripherals, Prometheus Products, Racal-Vadic, and Ven-Tel.

Printer Adapters

Your Mac was designed to print either on an Apple ImageWriter or on a LaserWriter. For one reason or another, though, you may want to print on a different brand of printer. For instance, you may want the typewritten look of a daisy-wheel printer, or you may have another brand of dot-matrix printer that you also use with another computer. As it is, you'll have a hard time printing on a non-Apple printer with your Mac and Microsoft Works. But there are products that help you make the connection. Start Software and Orange Micro are two companies that make hardware or software products that can link your Mac to non-Apple printers.

Printer Buffers and Spoolers

When you print from Microsoft Works, your Mac sends data to your printer much faster than your printer can print it. So there's a bottleneck while your Mac waits to send additional data until your printer catches up with what's been sent. And while your Mac is waiting, you can't use it for anything else. To eliminate this bottleneck, you can use a printer buffer or spooler.

A printer buffer is a box containing external memory. Your Mac sends the data to be printed into the buffer's memory, and the buffer's memory feeds the data slowly to your printer. In the meantime, your Mac has emptied its own memory of the data to be printed, so you're free to do other things.

A print spooler does much the same thing, except that a spooler is a software program that uses part of your Mac's own memory or disk space to store the data to be printed, but leaves the rest of the Mac's memory for other jobs. Because some print spoolers use part of your Mac's own memory, they diminish the amount of available memory when you use them. And because print spoolers are software programs rather than hardware, they are far less expensive than printer buffers. Printer buffers, on the other hand, do not use up any of your Mac's memory, and they can usually store larger documents than spoolers can.

A spooler called PrintMonitor comes free as part of MultiFinder in Apple's system software version 6, but PrintMonitor works only if you're printing to a LaserWriter. Other manufacturers sell print-spooler software that works with the ImageWriter or other dot-matrix printers, or which spools print jobs more quickly than PrintMonitor. Some third-party spoolers have extra features as well, such as the ability to set different priority levels for different jobs waiting to be printed. (For example, one job might be printed first even though others were waiting to be printed before it.) The two largest makers of spooler software are Super-Mac Technology and Symantec.

Printer buffers are available with from 32 KB to as much as 1 MB of memory, so you can choose the size of buffer that matches the size of the files you typically print. Two manufacturers of printer buffer hardware for Macs are Ergotron and Practical Peripherals.

Index

About MS-Works command 5, 397
Abs function 206
Absolute Cell Ref command 145, 146
absolute reference 145
Add button 35, 95
Add Field button 247, 250
Add New Field command 242, 250, 309
Adobe Illustrator 50
Aldus PageMaker 77
Aligning objects 78, 111
Align options 197, 214
All Cells command 149
All check box 35
amortization table 201
ampersand 234, 304
Answer Phone command 320
Apple Font/DA Mover program 29
Apple high-density floppy-disk FDHD drive 399
Apple icon 5
Apple menu 5, 65, 76, 140, 397
Apple System Software Version 6.0 77
AppleTalk network 13
Application Memory Size entry box 7
applications 2
arcs 53, 57, 64
arithmetic operators 311
arrow pointer 252, 253
arrows 53, 54
ASCII code 326
ASCII format 18
asterisk 190, 209, 310
attributes, setting 257
Automatic Calculation command 154
Automatic Paper Feed option button 133
Auto-wrap check box 325

B

bar chart 218, 223
baud rate 321

Baud Rate setting 326
Bering 401
Bernoulli box 401
Best-quality option 30
black dot (in a cell) 162
Bold command 31, 85
Bold Field Data command 270
Bold option 166
bold type 30
Borders command 149, 150, 199, 213
Borders sub-menu 214
Bottom Margin setting 105, 215
Bottom option 151
Bring To Front command 67, 68

C

CAD programs 50
Calculate Now command 154
cancel box 140
Cancel button 11, 90, 102, 117
Cancel Receive command 321, 339, 344
Capture Text command 320, 328, 337
Capture When Document Opens option 327, 332
caret symbol 46
Cell Attributes command 150–51, 196–97
cell indicator 140
cell notes 141, 161, 179
    window 148, 216, 217
cell references 145, 165, 176, 179, 210
cells
    correcting mistakes in 158
    locking the contents of 153
    moving 143
Center button 197
Center option 85, 166
Change Field Name command 241, 242, 250, 364
Change function 28

Change Report Title command 240, 242, 294, 299, 303
changing spacing between letters 64
Character Delay options 327
Chart menu 156, 217, 222, 351
Chart Title entry box 223
charting features 172
charts
  chart-definition window 218, 219
  defining 156
Clear command 13, 25, 142, 241, 353
Clipboard 13, 17–18, 22, 24, 25, 38, 63, 75, 108, 115, 116, 135, 136, 142, 171, 176, 177, 228, 337, 342–43, 347–55, 371, 374, 394
  copying text from 62
  copying to 390
  pasting from 382
  using 347–55
  viewing the contents of 14
Clipper, The 76
Close All command 8, 9
Close command 8
CloseView utility 77, 89
Color-Black Dots command 65–66
Color command 29
Color menu 31, 151
color monitor 65
Color-White Dots command 65–66
Column feature 72
columns 59, 60
  changing order of linking 61
  creating text 59
  deleting space between 350
  editing 60
  linked 59
  renaming 60
  selecting 60
Column of Value Titles entry box 224
column width, resetting 152
Column Width command 149, 152, 196, 201, 216, 232
Command-key combinations 22, 45–46, 168–69, 262
commands
  About MS-Works 5, 397
  Absolute Cell Ref 145, 146
  Add New Field 242, 250, 309

commands *(continued)*
  All Cells 149
  Answer Phone 320
  Automatic Calculation 154
  Bold 31, 85
  Bold Field Data 270
  Borders 149, 150, 199, 213
  Bring To Front 67, 68
  Calculate Now 154
  Cancel Receive 321, 339, 344
  Capture Text 320, 328, 337
  Cell Attributes 197
  Change Field Name 241, 242, 250, 364
  Change Report Title 240, 242, 294, 299, 303
  Clear 13, 25, 142, 241, 353
  Close 8
  Close All 8, 9
  Color 29
  Color-Black Dots 65–66
  Color-White Dots 65–66
  Column Width 149, 152, 196, 201, 216, 232
  Copy 13, 17, 63, 108, 110, 115, 142, 193, 348, 350, 394
  Copy Format 31, 39, 93
  Copy Totals 240, 241, 242, 245, 300, 313, 315
  Correct Spelling 34, 93, 124, 175
  Cut 13, 17, 25, 46, 63, 109, 142, 240
  Delete 9
  Delete Field 242, 250
  Dial 320, 329, 333
  Dictionary 35
  Draw Chart 156–57, 222, 351
  Draw Off 52
  Draw On 25, 51, 52, 71, 72, 143
  Duplicate Chart 157
  Duplicate Report 245
  Echo Off 320, 334
  Echo On 320, 333
  Eject Page 13
  End Text Capture 320, 338, 344
  Erase Chart 157
  Erase Report 245
  Fill Down 146, 162, 163, 171, 191, 211, 212
  Fill Right 146, 164, 171
  Find 27, 28, 173, 254

commands *(continued)*

Find Cell 27, 28, 170, 173, 175, 227, 230
Find Field 242, 243, 254, 255, 297
Font 29, 65, 149, 165
Format 41, 234–35
Freeze Titles Horizontal 155, 170
Freeze Titles Vertical 155, 170, 208
Full Window 14
Go To Cell 149, 170, 229
Go To Page # 27, 28, 45
Grid On 67, 78
Grid Setting 67, 74, 78, 88, 115
Group Picture 64, 67, 110
Hang Up 320, 339
Help 14, 242
Hide Ruler 29
Insert 144, 186, 187
Insert Record 241
Italic 31, 85
Justification 31, 65, 369, 391
Last Cell 149, 170, 227, 228, 230
Macros Off 120
Macros On 14, 120, 174, 283
Make Works Desktop 10, 12, 38
Manual Calculation 154
Match Records 243, 255, 256, 258, 259, 278, 296, 358
Move 143, 171
Multiple Labels 27, 135, 389
New 246
New Page After Total 246, 304
New Pie Chart 156–57, 223–24
New Report 241, 245, 288, 298, 312
New Series Chart 156–57, 217
No Fill Pattern 369
Normal 31
Open 8, 175, 356
Open Cell Note 146, 161
Open Macro File 16
Other 30
Outline 31, 199, 214
Page Preview 77
Page Setup 29, 47, 73, 101, 104, 114, 130, 131, 134, 141, 154, 165, 231, 232, 234, 240, 304, 315
Paste 13, 17, 25, 31, 39, 46, 63, 109, 110, 115, 144, 160, 191, 192, 193, 241, 348, 351, 394

commands *(continued)*

Paste Format 31, 39, 93
Paste Function 144, 160, 192, 193–94, 204, 206, 311
Paste With Options 143, 171, 373
Prepare To Merge 25, 26, 126, 387, 389
Print 8, 26, 77, 102, 112, 117, 121, 128, 134, 199, 240
Print Merge 13, 24, 26, 39, 128–33, 134, 240, 392
Print Preview 112, 117, 199, 233, 241, 293, 300
Print Window 12, 255
Protected 153
Quit 8
Receive 320
Receive File 320, 337, 338
Record Selection 243–44, 255, 256, 257, 258, 259, 290, 298, 358, 382
Remove Page Break 32, 153, 154
Replace 27, 28
Right 199
Save 8, 91
Save As 8, 47, 71, 90, 91, 125, 214, 357
Save Macro File 16, 17
Save Macro File As 16, 121, 285
Select All 13, 142, 149, 195, 241, 320
Select Chart Definition 157, 219
Select Definition 222
Select Picture 24, 25
Select Report 245, 294
Send File 320, 335
Send Text 320, 335, 361
Send To Back 67, 68, 86, 87
Set Attributes 244–45
Set Cell Attributes 149, 150, 166, 171, 198, 213, 216
Set Field Attributes 245, 253, 268, 311, 354, 386, 393
Set Page Break 31, 32, 153, 154, 215, 231, 233
Set Page # 32, 41, 42
Set Startup 7
Settings 321, 325
Shadow 31
Show Active Cell 149, 152, 170
Show All Records 244, 256
Show Clipboard 14, 241, 242, 300, 314

commands *(continued)*
  Show Column Boxes 67, 68
  Show Field Data 24, 26, 134
  Show Field Names 24, 26, 132, 134, 135,
      388, 389
  Show Form 239, 244, 274
  Show Formulas 152–53, 160, 212
  Show Grid 152, 175, 195, 215, 244, 278
  Show List 239, 244, 249, 274
  Show Notes Indicator 147, 152, 162
  Show Ruler 29, 93
  Show Values 152
  Size 29, 30, 59, 65, 149, 165
  Small Window 14
  Sort 148, 172, 188, 200, 244, 275, 293, 302,
      312
  Spacing 31
  Spread Text 63, 65, 68
  Start Recording 15, 120, 170, 174, 283
  Stop Recording 15, 120, 174, 285
  Style 29, 31, 65, 118, 149, 369
  Subscript 31
  Sum This Field 245–46, 299, 313
  Take A Sub-Total On Field Change
      245–46, 303, 305
  Take A Sub-Total On 1st Char 313
  Title Page 32, 42, 101
  To Page # 45
  Total This Field 307
  Underline 31
  Undo 13, 24, 25, 88, 105, 240
  Ungroup Picture 65, 67, 112
  Wide Draw Page 114
communications
  application in Works 317
  document 361
  ending a session 339
  icon 317, 325, 332
  keyboard equivalents 322–23
  programs 2, 318
  settings dialog box 325, 328, 332
  specifications 345–46
Communications menu 328–33
CompuServe 325, 401
Connect To option 333
Control Panel 77
Copy command 13, 17, 63, 110, 115, 142, 193,
      198, 348, 350, 394

Copy command *(continued)*
  shortcuts 171
Copy Format command 31, 39, 93
copying data 3
copyright information 5
Copy Totals command 240, 241, 242, 245,
      300, 313, 315
Correct Spelling command 34, 93, 124, 175
creating text objects 57, 58
crosshair cursor 86
Currently Recording dialog box 285
cursor movement keys 44
custom formats 46, 47
Cut command 13, 17, 25, 46, 63, 109, 142, 240

D

database(s)
  changing the layout of 252
  copying data from 353
  creating 246, 267
  data in 125
  file 127
  flat file 258
  menus 239–49
  merging 125
  mouse shortcuts 263
  moving word processor text to 355
  pasting to 354
  printing information from 239
  programs 2, 237, 248
  projects for 267
  relational 258
  searching 277
  sorting 276
  specifications for 265
  using 237–65
data types, alternate 354
Date field 244
Date Short option 216
Default alignment option 270
defaults 221, 244
default sort order 188
default style 63
default value 220
Delete button 10, 35, 95
Delete command 9
Delete dialog box 10

Delete Field command 242, 250
Delete key, 25, 88, 109, 284
Delete Key Means options 25, 88, 109, 284, 326
deleting objects 55, 56
desk accessories 5
desktop file, renaming a 12
detail area, creating a 227
Dial command 320, 329, 333
dictionary 32, 93, 124
    custom 33
    homonym 33, 96
    main 34
    window 35
Dictionary command 35, 94
Display options 198, 203, 206, 214
dividing data 263
document files 4
    chaining 41
    creating 4
    opening existing 4
    reducing the size of 12
    viewing close up 12
Dollar button 198
dollar signs 163, 211
Done button 247
double arrow 253, 275
double-word errors 33
Dow Jones News/Retrieval 326
Down Arrow key 251, 285
Draw Chart command 156–57, 222, 351
Draw Grid entry box 222
drawing
    in a document 22
    programs 50, 51, 72
    Draw layer 99
Draw Off command 52
Draw On command 25, 51, 52, 71, 72, 143
Draw tool 2, 13, 17, 25, 31, 39, 49–82, 83–90,
        103–13, 166, 196, 197, 351, 368, 375,
        376, 385, 391
    grid feature 80
    default font 84
    keyboard commands 80–82
    macros 71
    making the most of 71
    memory limitations of 62

Draw tool (continued)
    menu 65
    specifications 82
Drive button 5, 9, 91, 360
Duplicate Chart command 157
Duplicate Report command 245

E

Echo Off command 320, 334
Echo On command 320, 333
editing
    features 72
    text 112
Edit menu 8, 17, 24–27, 140, 141–48,
        240–42, 320
Eject button 5, 91, 360
Eject Page command 13
ellipsis 8
End Text Capture command 320, 338, 344
enter box 140, 158, 193
entering text 91
Enter key 209, 251
entry bar 140, 190, 192, 284
envelopes
    addressing 128
    merge printing 131
equal sign 159, 192, 209
Erase Chart command 157
Erase Report command 245
erasing objects 56
Ergotron 404
error-correcting routines 319
error messages 61
exchanging files 359, 360
Export As Rich Text Format check box 24,
        357
Export button 357
Export File check box 359, 360
Export Option button 23–24

F

F key 87, 109
fields 126, 127, 238, 247
    adding 241, 249, 280
    changing 241, 244

fields *(continued)*
   deleting 241, 249, 250
   rearranging 279
   removing data from 241
   renaming 249, 364
   selecting all 241
   splitting 281
Field Attributes dialog box 253, 295, 308,
   394
Field Attributes option 253
field data 252
field names 252
Field Name dialog box 242, 249, 282
Field Name window 246–247, 268
field outline 249
50% Reduction option 233
File menu 8, 10, 23–24, 65, 140–41, 240, 319
files
   browsing through 251
   creating database 295
   exporting 18, 347
   importing 18, 347
   printing database 257
   receiving non-text 337, 338
   redisplaying records in 278
   saving 123
   sending 335
   sorting 256
   splitting 260
   viewing wide 286
Fill Down command 146, 162, 163, 171, 191,
   211, 212
Fill Pattern dialog box 53, 68, 69
Fill Pattern menu 66, 68, 69, 86, 97, 99, 110,
   369, 391
Fill Right command 146, 164, 171
Find Cell command 27, 28, 170, 173, 175,
   227, 230
Find command 27, 28, 173, 242, 254
Finder option 7
Finder's Special menu 7
Find Field command 242, 243, 254, 255, 297
Find Next button 28, 242
Find What entry box 27
FirstName field 283
First Name merge field 127
Fixed option 150

floppy disks, high-density 401
Font command 29, 65, 149, 165
Font menu 23, 28, 151
Font sub-menu 91, 107, 120
font(s)
   applying more than one 177
   Boston 29, 84, 119
   Chicago 29
   default 22, 233
   double-sized 30
   Geneva 29, 99, 165
   Helvetica 85, 91, 101, 106, 113, 119
   LaserWriter 85
   Monaco 29
   New Century Schoolbook 372, 383
   Normal 106
   sizes 30
footers 32, 40–42
Format command 41, 234–35
Format menu 28–32, 149–52, 244–45, 253,
   369
formatting 22, 44, 318
form letters, creating 123
form window 248–49, 252, 264
formulas 139
   absolute 164
   copying 162, 171
   displaying 152
   entering 159, 173, 189, 192
   relative 164
   showing values of 152
Freehand tool 53
Freeze Titles Horizontal command 155, 170
Freeze Titles Vertical command 155, 170,
   208
freezing objects 55
From Column entry box 219
From entry box 11, 219
From Row entry box 223
Full Window command 14
function, pasting a 144

G

General buttons 394
Get Info window 7
Go To Cell command 149, 170, 229

Go To Page # command 27, 28, 45
graphics
    pre-drawn 76
    touching up 75
graphics library documents
    adding 76
    creating 76
graphs, including in a document 22
Grid dialog box 115, 116
grid lines 215, 278
Grid On command 67, 78
Grid Setting command 67, 74, 78, 88, 115
Group Picture command 64, 67, 110

H

H key 79, 115
Handset icon 324
Handshake setting 327, 332
hand symbol 252
Hang Up command 320, 339
hard-disk drive 399
hardware products 399
Hayes command set 324
Header command 41– 42, 101
headers 32, 40– 42, 78, 304
    adding 234
    centering 41– 42
    information in 314
    inserting 234
    maximizing information with 40
Help command 14, 242
Hide Ruler command 29
hierarchical-menu commands 28–29
horizontal alignment 74, 79, 112
horizontal line-fill pattern 88
Horizontal Titles In Row entry box 220

I

icons 4, 5, 12
ImageWriter printer 13, 30, 67, 129, 130, 133, 134, 233, 403
Import File check box 356, 359, 360, 362
Import File feature 5
importing AppleWorks files 359
incoming calls, answering 340

information, strings of 40
Insert command 144, 186, 187
insertion point 85, 144, 371, 382
Insert Record command 241
Install Rule button 291, 292
integrated software 2, 3
interface 1–2
inventory items 188
Iomega 401
Italic command 31, 85

J

Justification command 31, 65, 369, 391
justification options 114
Justification sub-menu 85, 107, 196

K

keyboard commands 31, 45– 46, 261, 262
    navigation options with 251
    using 44, 80, 167–69
Keypad menu 321

L

Label Chart entry box 222
labels 159, 177, 186, 187, 247
LaserWriter II 128, 129, 134
LaserWriter IINT printer 67, 83, 369
LaserWriter IISC printer 67
LaserWriter Page Setup dialog box 122
LaserWriter Plus printer 67
LaserWriter printer 13, 22, 84, 113, 122
Last Cell command 149, 170, 227, 228, 230
LastName field 283
Last Name merge field 127
layouts, creating 72
left indent marker 93
Left Margin box 104
Left option 151
Line Delay options 326
Line Pattern box 53, 68, 70
Line Pattern menu 66, 68, 107
line patterns 69
lines, drawing 118
line thickness 53, 107

line tool 53
line-type indicator 53

M

Mac II 400
MacBinary 320, 342
MacDraw 22, 49, 50
Macintosh Utilities User's Guide 77
MacNet 402
MacPaint 22, 50, 320, 336
Mac Plus 94, 369
macro key combinations 16
Macro menu 14–17, 36, 70, 120, 157, 246, 285
macros 70, 120, 173–74, 281, 286
　activating 15, 285
　automating operations with 341
　playing back 14, 170
　saving 16
Macros Off command 120
Macros On command 14, 120, 174, 283
Mac SE 94, 369, 400
MacWrite 356
main dictionary 35
Make Works Desktop command 10, 12, 38
making text objects 57
Manual Calculation command 154
Manual Feed option 128, 130
margins
　changing all 368
　changing left 289
　default settings 231
Match Records command 243, 255, 256, 258,
　259, 278, 296, 358
Maximum boxes 221
MCI Mail 325, 326, 334, 341, 343, 402
Memory Free indicator 397
memory-resident files 36
menu bar 5, 22
menus 1, 5
　Apple 5, 65, 76, 140
　Chart 217, 222, 351
　Color 31, 151
　Communications 328, 329
　Draw Tools 65
　Edit 8, 17, 24–27, 140, 141–48, 240–42,
　320

menus (continued)
　File 8, 10, 23–24, 65, 140–41, 240–42, 319
　Fill Pattern 66, 67, 69, 86, 97, 99, 107, 110,
　369, 391
　Font 23, 44, 151
　Format 28–32, 149–52, 244–45, 253, 369
　Line Pattern 66, 67, 71, 107
　Mac (standard) 28
　Macro 14, 15, 16, 36, 70, 157, 246, 285, 322,
　331
　Organize 254, 382, 274, 276, 290, 296
　Page Setup 32
　Pattern 86
　Report 239, 245, 257, 288, 294
　Search 27
　Select 148–49, 227, 228
　Size 151–65
　Spell 32, 34, 35, 36, 93, 124
　Style 23, 44
　TotalsPage 245, 299
　Windows 8, 14, 17, 38, 65, 108, 125, 140, 225
merge box 26
Merge button 126, 388
merge printing 125
merging data 355
Microsoft Excel 358, 359
Microsoft File 356
Microsoft Multiplan 358, 359
Microsoft Word 356
Minimum entry box 221
minus sign 209
modems 318, 331, 344, 401
　disconnecting 320
　hooking up 323
　transmission speeds of 324
monochrome display 31, 67
mouse
　shortcuts 168
　using 167
Move command 143, 171
　shortcuts 171
moving data 347
　from the Clipboard 241
moving objects 55, 59
MsWorksDict 34, 93
MsWorksHymn 34

MultiFinder 7, 404
  Application Memory Size 73
  on a Mac Plus 7
Multiple Labels command 27, 135, 389
multiplication 190

N

New button 4, 184, 325, 332
New command 246
New Century Schoolbook font 372, 383
New Page After Total command 246, 304
New Pie Chart command 156–57, 223–24
New Report command 241, 245, 288, 298, 312
New Series Chart command 156–57, 217
Next button 11, 102
No button 23
no-fill pattern 69
No Fill Pattern command 369
No Gaps Between Pages option 134
Normal command 31
Normal Option button 23
Number Of Screens option 326–27, 332
numbering pages 42, 101
numbers, specifying a range of 161
Numeric button 394

O

OK button 28
Open button 4
Open Cell Note command 146, 161
Open command 8, 175, 356
Open dialog box 10, 23, 174
opening screen 4
Open Macro File command 16
operators, arithmetic, 311
Option key 14, 63, 378
Option menu 152–56
Orange Micro 403
organizational charts, creating 113
Organize menu 242–44, 254, 274, 276, 290, 296, 382
Other command 30
Outline command 31, 199, 214
Outline option 150

outline type 30
oval tool 53, 88

P

page break(s)
  adjusting 230
  default 231
  indicator 96
  marker 101, 215
  new 233
  setting 153
page numbering 42
Page Preview command 77
Page Setup command 29, 47, 73, 101, 104, 114, 130, 131, 134, 141, 154, 165, 231, 232, 234, 240, 304, 315
Page Setup dialog box 40, 41, 101, 113, 121, 129, 130, 131, 132–33, 141, 199, 215, 232, 234, 289, 304, 315, 368
Page Setup menu 32
painting programs 50, 51
palette of tools 52, 53
Paper Height entry box 130
Paper Width entry box 130
parity 321, 326
passwords 334
Paste command 13, 17, 25, 46, 63, 109, 110, 115, 191, 193–194, 348, 351, 394
Paste Format command 31, 39, 93
Paste Function command 144, 160, 192, 193–94, 204, 206, 311
Paste With Options command 143, 171, 373
patterns
  brick 66
  checkerboard 66
  fill 65
  gray-fill 66
  line 65
  menu 86
  two-color 66
Percent button 203
Peripheral Land 400
Phone Type setting 327, 332
picture changing 25
Pie Chart Definition window 223, 224
pixels 50, 51, 65, 66

Plot It! button 222, 224
plus sign 212
Pmt function 203, 204
pointer 53, 196, 275
polygon tool 53
PostScript-based printer 67
Practical Peripherals 404
precise-alignment keys 74
Prepare To Merge command 25, 26, 126, 387, 389
Prepare To Merge dialog box 126, 127, 131, 135
Previous button 11
print adapters 403
Print button 11, 102, 199
Print Cell Notes option 141
Print command 8, 26, 77, 102, 112, 117, 121, 128, 134, 199, 240
Print dialog box 11, 12, 128, 129, 199, 377
printer buffers 403
Print feature 12, 130, 233
printing mailing labels with Print Merge 101, 128, 132
Print Merge command 13, 24, 26, 39, 128–33, 134, 240, 392
PrintMonitor spooler 404
Print Preview check box 11, 12, 77, 102, 111, 117, 121, 199, 377
Print Preview command 112, 117, 199, 233, 241, 293, 300
Print Preview window 11, 12, 111, 117
Print Row and Column Numbers option 141
Print Window command 12, 255
Protected command 153
protocols 318

Q
Quick button 35
Quit command 8

R
range of cells 192
rate, interest 204
Receive command 320

Receive File command 320, 337, 338
Receive File dialog box 342
Receive Protocol option 339
Record button 15, 120
Record Future Delay check box 15
recording
    cancel 15
    continue 15
    stop 15
Record Previous Delay check box 15
records
    removing data from 241
    selecting 241, 255, 259
    viewing selected 296
Record Selection command 243–44, 255–59, 290, 298, 358, 382
rectangles, aligning 88
rectangle tool 53, 107
Reduce Or Enlarge option 122, 233
reference area 178–79
relative reference 145
Remove Page Break command 32, 153, 154
Replace All button 27
Replace button 27, 28, 35, 95
Replace commmand 27, 28
Replace dialog box 27
Replace, Then Find button 27
Replace With entry box 2, 95
Report menu 239, 245, 257, 288, 294
reports
    creating 298
    deleting 245
    printing 294
resizing objects 56, 59
Resume Works File 10, 38
Return key 11, 158, 209, 222, 251, 388
Returns option 357
Rich Text Format (RTF) 19, 24, 357, 358
Right Align option 166, 216
Right button 198
Right command 199
Right Margin entry box 104
Right option 151
rounded-rectangle tool 53, 88
rows, sorting 178
ruler 101, 115, 391

S

Save As command 8, 47, 71, 90, 91, 125, 214, 357
Save As dialog box 23, 357, 358
Save button 11, 90, 91, 125, 214
Save command 8, 91
Save Macro File As command 16, 121, 285
Save Macro File command 16, 17
Save Selected Records Only check box 358
saving incoming data in
    telecommunications 344
Scrapbook desk accessory 76, 77, 320, 336
screen space, maximizing 263
scroll arrow 369
scroll bars 95, 251
scroll box 42
Search menu 27–28
search-string entry box 27
Select All command 13, 142, 149, 195, 241, 320
Select Chart Definition command 157, 219
Select Definition command 222
selecting
    objects 55
    text within objects 58
selection handles 58, 64, 197
selection pointer 253
selection rectangle 100
selection tool 53, 100, 115, 371, 378, 380
Select menu 148–49, 227, 228
Select Picture command 24, 25
Select Report command 245, 294
Send File command 320, 335
Send File dialog box 342
Send Protocol option 336
Send Text command 320, 335, 361
Send To Back command 67, 68, 86, 87
Set Attributes command 244–45
Set Cell Attributes command 149, 150, 166, 171, 198, 213, 216
Set Cell Attributes dialog box 203, 205, 214
Set Field Attributes command 245, 253, 268, 311, 354, 386, 393
Set Field Attributes dialog box 269, 270
Set Page Break command 31, 32, 153, 154, 215, 231, 233

Set Page # command 32, 41, 42
Set Startup command 7
Set Startup dialog box 7
Settings command 321, 325
Settings dialog box 328
Shadow command 31
Shift key 64, 67, 88, 197, 391
Show Active Cell command 149, 152, 170
Show All Records command 244, 256
Show Clipboard command 14, 241, 242, 245, 300, 314
Show Column Boxes command 67, 68
Show Day box 269, 270, 386
Show Field Data command 24, 26, 134
Show Field Names command 24, 26, 132, 134, 135, 388, 389
Show Form command 239, 244, 274
Show Formulas command 152–53, 160, 212
Show Grid command 152, 175, 195, 215, 244, 278
Show List command 239, 244, 249, 274
Show Notes Indicator command 147, 152, 162
Show Ruler command 29, 93
Show Values command 152
6 Line Per Inch spacing option 134
size box 140, 224
Size command 29, 30, 59, 65, 149, 165
Size menu 151, 165
Size sub-menu 91, 107, 195
sizing data 326
Skip button 35
Small Window command 14
SmartScrap program 76
Sort command 148, 172, 188, 200, 244, 275, 293, 302, 312
Sort dialog box 188, 256, 274
sorting
    in alphabetic order 188
    in ascending order 148
    in descending order 148
    rows 178
Spacebar 25
Spacing command 31
spelling checker 32, 33–35, 75, 92, 93, 96, 123, 124
Spell menu 32, 34, 36, 93, 124

Spellswell program 32
split bars 140, 169
spoolers 403
spreadsheet(s) 2, 3
    adding items to 200
    building 178
    entering items into 184
    exporting 358
    formatting 165, 195
    icon 184, 359
    importing data into 358
    inserting data into 144
    inventory 183–84
    keyboard-equivalent commands 168–69
    number of columns in 139
    number of rows in 139
    pasting to 352
    printing options 141, 151, 214
    saving 199, 214
    using 137–81
    viewing 169–70
spreadsheet projects 183–236
spreadsheet specifications 180
spreadsheet tips 177
Spread Text command 63, 65, 68
standard text 357
Start Recording command 15, 120, 170, 174, 283
Start Recording dialog box 331
Start Software 403
Stationery option button 24, 71, 90, 114, 371
Stop Bits setting 326
Stop button 15
Stop Recording command 15, 120, 174, 285
straight-line tool 53, 120, 369
Style command 29, 31, 65, 118, 149, 369
Style menu 23
Style sub-menu 85, 107, 120, 196
Subscript command 31
Sum function 160
summary area, creating a spreadsheet 226
Sum This Field command 245–46, 299, 313
SuperMac Technology 404
SYLK files 18, 358, 359
Symantec 404
Symbolic Link format 18
System file 30
System Folder 93, 396

T
Tab key 15, 25, 101, 104, 158, 185, 251, 329, 388
Tabs option 357
Take A Sub-Total On Field Change command 245–46, 303, 305
Take A Sub-Total On 1st Char command 313
target column 75–76
template 46
term 204
text
    creating 108
    editing 112, 123
    entering 119
    field sorting 244
    formatting 108
    moving 25
    storing incoming 342
    styling 72
text box 108
text files
    converting 363
    exporting 356
    importing 356
    using 361
text tool 53, 59, 68, 72, 106, 110, 112, 372
Through Row entry box 224
Time field 244
title bar 218
Title field 395
Title Page command 32, 42, 101
To entry box 11
To Column entry box 219
tools palette 52, 54, 59, 64, 68, 70, 75, 79, 80, 86, 88, 89, 97, 99–100, 106–8, 110, 114, 196, 368, 380
Top Margin entry box 104, 215
Top option 151
Total This Field command 307
TotalsPage menu 245, 299
transferring information 3, 39
transparent object 69
TTY terminal 328, 332
Two Or More Spaces option 357

U

Underline command 31
Undo command 13, 24, 25, 88, 105, 240
Ungroup Picture command 65, 67, 112
Unknown entry box 94, 95
Up Arrow key 95
user interface 1
utility program 359

V

V key 79
values 159
  copying 171
  entering new 164–65
  future 204
  present 204
Values Only button 373
vector points 54
vertical alignment 74, 79, 112
virtual memory 36
VisiCalc 137

W

Wide Draw Page command 114
Winchester hard disk 400–401
  external 399
  internal 399
  removable cartridge 400

windows
  dividing 169
  form 238, 242, 244, 286, 350
  list 238, 242, 244, 250, 287, 350
  menu 8, 14, 17, 38, 65, 108, 125, 140, 225, 242, 373, 394
  multiple 43
word-processing projects 83–126
word-processor application 3, 21–48
  copying database data to 350
  importing graphics into 90
  keyboard-equivalent commands 45–46
  icon 356
  merging database data with 355
  moving data to 348
  specifications 48
  using 21
  wordwrap 72
  Works opening screen 184
  Works-Works Transporter 359

X

Xmodem Data protocol 336
Xmodem error-correcting protocol 320–21
Xmodem Text protocol 336

Z

Zoom box 140
Zoom mode 12

CHARLES RUBIN

After growing up in Los Angeles, California, Charles Rubin attended Antioch College, the University of Southern California, and San Francisco State University. He holds both a Bachelor's and a Master's degree in English and has been writing about microcomputers since 1981. Charles is currently a contributing editor for *Personal Computing* magazine. His work has also appeared in other technological and general-interest magazines, including *PC Week*, *A+*, *LOTUS*, *Newsweek Access*, and *InfoWorld*. His book *The Endless Apple* was published in November 1984 by Microsoft Press. He has also written *Thinking Small: The Buyer's Guide to Portable Computers*. Charles lives in Oakland, California, and has been using an Apple IIe since 1983.

OTHER TITLES FROM MICROSOFT PRESS

THE APPLE® MACINTOSH® BOOK, 3rd ed.
Cary Lu

"The one Macintosh book you'd choose if you could have only one. Virtually anything you might want to know at any level is here."

MACazine

The classic book that accompanied the introduction of the Mac in 1984 is back again and thoroughly updated to include information on all Macs through the Macintosh II. THE APPLE MACINTOSH BOOK provides an authoritative and comprehensive look at the Mac's design philosophy, architecture, hardware and software options, and significant user issues. Author Cary Lu covers selecting the right Mac, uses of the Mac, internal hardware expansion, mass-storage options, local area networks, and more. If you currently use a Mac or expect to use one, you need this book.

416 pages, softcover $21.95   Order Code: 86-96213

WORKING WITH WORD, 2nd ed.
The Definitive Guide to Microsoft® Word on the Apple® Macintosh®
Chris Kinata and Gordon McComb

When you are ready to go beyond simple word processing with Microsoft Word for the Macintosh, this is *the* book of choice. Now updated for version 4, it's filled with inside advice, detailed information, and tutorials on every software feature. Included are scores of excellent tips — many not in the documentation — designed to add power and functionality, no matter what kind of printed documents you want to create. Topics cover: desktop publishing with Word; integrating graphics into a Word document and wrapping text around them; customizing menus and retrieving lost files; linking Word with other applications; optimizing memory management; creating spreadsheetlike tables; and working with lists and multiple columns. Also included are blueprints for newsletters, multicolumn brochures, correspondence, and reports. WORKING WITH WORD is the best, most complete, and most up-to-date book on Microsoft Word available.

752 pages, softcover $21.95   Order Code: 86-96957   (available July 1989)

QUICK REFERENCE GUIDE TO MICROSOFT® WORD
FOR THE APPLE® MACINTOSH®
Lisa Ann Jacobs

This great little guide offers you a handy action-oriented reference to Microsoft Word through version 4. You can look up specific tasks — customizing menus, indexing, underlining text — without knowing the specific Word commands. It's a practical, fast way to understand and use Microsoft Word. Also included is an index to commands and a summary of keyboard shortcuts.

144 pages, softcover $5.95   Order Code: 86-97146

EXCEL IN BUSINESS
Number-Crunching Power on the Apple® Macintosh®
Douglas Cobb and The Cobb Group

"The definitive guide to Excel on the Macintosh...an outstanding reference, for its readability and detail."

Computer Book Review

Microsoft Excel, the powerful integrated spreadsheet, database, and graphics package, lets you perform a variety of tasks for business and personal needs. EXCEL IN BUSINESS will help beginner to advanced users access Microsoft Excel's capabilities in the most efficient way. The authors include practical applications for learning how to produce spreadsheets and graphics; how to work with databases; how to master macros; how to link Microsoft Excel to other programs. Packed with scores of tutorials and dozens of tips. Now updated to version 1.5; includes appendix.

816 pages, softcover $24.95   Order Code: 86-95314

DOUG COBB'S TIPS FOR MICROSOFT® EXCEL
The Cobb Group: Douglas Cobb, Judy Mynhier, Gena Berg Cobb

"Highlights the not-so-obvious things the average user ought to know about using Excel."

Computer Book Review

Douglas Cobb and The Cobb Group have assembled a collection of creative, timesaving tips for you that extract optimum performance from Microsoft Excel. The book is designed for quick lookups and reference, and each tip includes a ready-to-implement example and concise explanations. Every aspect of the software is examined, providing you with an important resource for maximizing Microsoft Excel as a business tool.

384 pages, softcover $19.95   Order Code: 86-95660

THE NEW WRITER
Techniques for Writing Well with a Computer
Joan P. Mitchell

"If you have any writing to do in your life—anything (from letters to business reports)—here's the book for you and your computer."

The Tulsa World

THE NEW WRITER, written by an experienced writing instructor, shows you how to master process writing and how to improve your overall writing skills. Mitchell tells you how to use the computer to work successfully through all the basic writing steps. You will learn how to brainstorm and analyze, edit and revise, communicate ideas visually as well as verbally, and use special computer tools like idea processors, outliners, and spell checkers to produce clear expository works.

256 pages, softcover $8.95   Order Code: 86-95900

DESKTOP PUBLISHING BY DESIGN
Blueprints for Page Layout Using Aldus® PageMaker® on IBM® and Apple® Macintosh® Computers
Ronnie Shushan and Don Wright

DESKTOP PUBLISHING BY DESIGN includes a variety of versatile projects that use the full capabilities of PageMaker for the lastest IBM and Macintosh versions. The authors emphasize the effective use of design elements—typeface, page layout, and graphics to help students create professional looking newsletters, brochures, catalogs, manuals, directories, and even magazines. You will learn not only how to manipulate and manage PageMaker, but how to produce exciting, professional pieces with ease. *400 pages, softcover $19.95 Order Code: 86-96460*

Microsoft Press books are available wherever fine books are sold, or credit card orders can be placed by calling 1-800-638-3030 (in Maryland call collect 824-7300).

The manuscript for this book was prepared and submitted to Microsoft Press in electronic form. Text files were processed and formatted using Microsoft Word.

Cover design by Becker Design Associates
Interior text design by Darcie S. Furlan
Illustrations by Becky Geisler-Johnson
Principal typography by Portland Advertising Typography
Color separations by Wescan Color Corporation

Text composition by Microsoft Press in Baskerville with display in Avant Garde Demi, using the Magna composition system and the Linotronic 300 laser imagesetter.